# The Sikh diaspora

# Global diasporas

Series Editor: Robin Cohen

The assumption that minorities and migrants will demonstrate an exclusive loyalty to the nation-state is now questionable. Scholars of nationalism, international migration and ethnic relations need new conceptual maps and fresh case studies to understand the growth of complex transnational identities. The old idea of "diaspora" may provide this framework. Though often conceived in terms of a catastrophic dispersion, widening the notion of diaspora to include trade, imperial, labour and cultural diaporas can provide a more nuanced understanding of the often positive relationships between migrants' homelands and their places of work and settlement.

This book forms part of an ambitious and interlinked series of volumes trying to capture the new relationships between home and abroad. Historians, political scientists, sociologists and anthropologists from a number of countries have collaborated on this forward-looking project. The series includes two books which provide the defining, comparative and synoptic aspects of diasporas. Further titles, of which *The Sikh diaspora* is the first, focus on particular communities, both traditionally recognized diasporas and those newer claimants who define their collective experiences and aspirations in terms of a diasporic identity.

This series is associated with the Transnational Communities Programme at the University of Oxford funded by the UK's Economic and Social Research Council.

Already published:
*Global diasporas: an introduction* Robin Cohen
*New diasporas* Nicholas Van Hear

Forthcoming books include:
*The Italian labour diaspora* Donna Gabaccia
*The Greek diaspora: from Odyssey to EU* George Stubos
*The Japanese diaspora* Michael Weiner, Roger Daniels, Hiroshi Komai

# The Sikh diaspora

## The search for statehood

Darshan Singh Tatla

First published in 1999 by UCL Press

UCL Press Limited
1 Gunpowder Square
London EC4A 3DE
UK

The name of University College London (UCL) is a registered
trade mark used by UCL Press with the consent of the owner.

**British Library Cataloguing-in-Publication Data**
A CIP catalogue record for this book is available from the
British Library.

Library of Congress Cataloging-in-Publication Data
are available

ISBN: 1-85728 300-7 HB
1-85728-301-5 PB

Typeset by Best-set Typesetter Ltd., Hong Kong
Printed by T.J. International, Padstow, UK.

# Contents

Foreword by the Series Editor                                    vii
Preface                                                           ix
List of tables                                                    xi
Maps                                                             xiii
Introduction                                                      1
Theoretical issues                                                2
Scope of the study                                                8

1 **The Sikhs: the search for statehood**                        **11**
A sect, a community or a nation?                                  11
The making of Sikh ethnic consciousness                          13
The colonial encounter                                           16
Under the postcolonial state                                     21
Search for statehood: the dilemma                                30
Indian nationalism: perils of a nation-state                     34

2 **The Sikh diaspora: a history of settlement**                 **41**
The colonial era                                                  43
The postcolonial era                                             55
Post-1984 emigration: Sikh refugees                              58
Conclusion                                                        61

3 **The Sikh diaspora and the Punjab: dialectics of ethnic
  linkages**                                                      **63**
Economic linkage                                                  64
Social exchange                                                   66
Religious tradition                                               73
Diaspora: a creative site?                                        80

CONTENTS

4 **The Sikh diaspora and the Punjab: political linkages**        **85**
  Early links                                                      86
  Post-1947 associations                                           91
  Issues of mobilization                                          100

5 **Demand for homeland: Sikhs in North America**                **113**
  Main organizations                                              116
  Mobilization                                                    122

6 **Demand for homeland: Sikhs in Britain**                      **137**
  Main organizations                                              138
  Mobilization                                                    143

7 **Mediating between states: Sikh diplomacy and interstate**
  **relations**                                                  **155**
  Indian government and the Sikh diaspora                         156
  Indo-British relations and the Sikhs                            158
  Sikh diplomacy and Indo-us relations                            165
  Indo-Canadian relations and the Sikh lobby                      171
  International organizations                                     180
  Conclusion                                                      181

8 **Call of homeland: models and reality of ethnic mobilization** **183**
  Parameters of mobilization                                      184
  Discourse on the Sikh homeland                                  193
  The impact of the critical event                                196

  Conclusion                                                      209
  Appendices                                                      213
  Notes                                                           227
  Glossary and abbreviations                                      281
  Bibliography                                                    285
  Index                                                           309

# Foreword by the Series Editor

There are about 16 million Sikhs worldwide, the great majority of them located in the Indian sub-continent. Those who live abroad, about one million people, are concentrated in just three countries – Britain, Canada and the USA. However, the overseas Sikhs are a distinctive presence in many places. Indeed Sikhs seem to go to a lot of trouble to make themselves visibly different and recognizable. Nearly always, the Sikh surname is "Singh", meaning "lion". The men wrap their uncut beards and heads in turbans, they carry a comb, wear a steel bracelet, and sometimes wear soldier's breeches with a ceremonial sword. Such "social markers" are a deliberate display – indication that many Sikhs do not want to go down the paths of assimilation or unthinking integration.

Such distancing is very much part of the life of Sikhs "at home" and abroad. The expression "at home" refers particularly to the Punjab, where most Sikhs live, among other peoples and without a homeland of their own. Some scholars (for example Dusenbery 1995: 18–19) suggest that their *Punjabi* identity (in terms of culture, language and sense of place) was more important than their specifically *Sikh* identity for much of their history. Certainly like some other population groups (the Jews come to mind) it is often difficult to decide whether the Sikhs are a religious community, an ethnic group, a nation, a people or even a sect. This ambiguity makes any discussion of the Sikhs particularly enriching to those interested in transnational communities. We are, however, particularly fortunate in having the issue of social definition met head-on by Darshan Singh Tatla in this account.

vii

As Tatla makes clear, we need to add history to morphology. While they remained a separate community, only a few of the Sikhs abroad identified themselves with the political project of constructing a national homeland, known as Khalistan. But this was to change dramatically in 1984 when the Indian government sent in troops to the Golden Temple in Amritsar to dislodge some protestors demanding statehood. The temple was the symbolic centre of Sikhdom and the Indian government could hardly have selected a more sensitive target. As Tatla notes, this episode invites comparison with the destruction of the temple of Solomon. Suddenly the idea of a ethno-nationality with a state of its own flared up and redefined the nature of Sikhdom.

Is this new affirmation of a territorial nationalism sufficient cause to consider the Sikhs a diaspora? As Tatla shows, at least one key component of a conventional definition of "diaspora" is missing. Unlike the Hindu community who often emigrated as indentured labourers, the Sikhs were "free" migrants. They often provided the auxiliaries to the British in their colonial expansion – as troops or train drivers, for example. But Sikhs in trade or agriculture soon augmented the early travellers and settlers. Characterizing such a diverse group as a diaspora can always be challenged, yet the expression does seem to evoke many of the precognitions and behavioural patterns of Sikh settlers in foreign climes. They retained a strong sense of community, related to their "homeland" (vague as that concept was for much of their history), reaffirmed their religious beliefs and rallied around when their heartland seemed to be under attack.

Covering the Sikhs in all their principal areas of settlement, this book has been based on a comprehensive interpretation of published accounts, pamphlets and newspapers. The author has also conducted many interviews in pursuit of his interest. Having worked on his subject for many years, Tatla has an unrivalled command over the sources for this study. One can hardly imagine a more thorough account of an important and arresting theme – the Sikhs abroad and their search for statehood. I am delighted to commend this engaging book to the reader.

Robin Cohen
Series Editor

# Preface

This study is part of a growing literature on the role of diaspora communities in the international arena. In working out this narrative of the Sikh diaspora, I have drawn upon many studies and charted some fresh avenues. In doing so, I have drawn upon many sources for data and upon testimonies of many individuals and leaders of various organizations mentioned in the study. Although I have rarely used such testimony without a corroborative written source, such informal talks were extremely useful in gauging the emotional cultural environment of the Sikh diaspora. In Britain, talks were held with Dr Jagjit Singh Chohan, Gurmej Singh Gill, Avtar Johal, Ajit Singh Khera, Dr Jasdev Singh Rai, Ranjit Singh Rana, Balbir Singh, Balwinder Singh, Gurdeep Singh, Gurmail Singh, Joga Singh and Dr Pargat Singh. In the United States, Dr Gurmeet Singh Aulakh, Ajit Singh Bainipal, Didar Singh Bains, Sher Singh Kanwal, Dr Karamjit Singh Rai, Dr Sukhmander Singh were very helpful. In Canada, talks with Pritam Singh Aulakh, Darshan Gill, Ravinder Ravi, Daljeet Singh Sandhu, Kesar Singh, Narinder Singh, Satindarpal Singh and Uday Singh yielded many insights. I am especially indebted to Ranjit Singh Hansra, Kuldip Singh, and Jawala Singh Grewal as my North American hosts.

For extensive consultation of the Punjabi media, I owe thanks to many, but especially to the late Tarsem Singh Purewal, editor of *Des Pardes*, Tara Singh Hayer, editor of the *Indo-Canadian Times*, and M. S. Sidhu at *World Sikh News*. At Berkeley I was able to consult the Gadr collection with Dr Kenneth Logan's help. The Centre for Research in Ethnic Relations at the University of Warwick, where this study began, provided much impetus by exchange of ideas among many research students and teachers. Among them, I thank Harbhajan Brar, Mark Johnson, John Rex, Zig Leyton Henry and Harry Goulbourne, who supervised my research. I owe it to Robin Cohen's crucial intervention, for saving this study from oblivion. Colleagues from the Punjab Research Group would recognize some elements of their concerns; among them, I am grateful to Narinder Basi, Shinder Thandi, Gurharpal Singh and especially Ian Talbot, who read through an earlier version and offered valuable comments. Thanks are due to my colleagues and others who offered a cheerful working environment at the college: Jagdev Boparai, Rosangela Dempsey, Ranjit Dhanda, Sardul Dhesi, Ann Hynes, Talat Javed, Kathleen Jenkins, Jill Manley, Jean Parry, Sujinder S. Sangha, and especially Chris Watts. Thanks to Ram Singh for searching certain passages from the Adi Granth, and Tejwant Singh Gill for some Punjabi folklore. Caroline Wintersgill and Claire Hart at UCL have provided excellent support. Such a long list of acknowledgements does not diminish my exclusive claim for errors and misinterpretations. Hopefully, this preliminary study will encourage scholars to build a more robust picture. To this end, many primary sources are listed. While my academic concerns are somehow related to my sojourn turning into harsh displacement and loss, I hope Harjeet and Rajwant, my son and daughter, will find within these pages an expression of my affection, anxiety and hope as they grow in the diaspora.

Darshan Singh Tatla
Warwick

# List of tables

1.1 Punjab: population and area 24

1.2 Punjab's legislative assembly elections 25

2.1 Diaspora Sikh population: some estimates 42

2.2 Sikh refugees 59

3.1 The Punjabi media: North America 72

3.2 The Punjabi media: United Kingdom 73

3.3 Numbers of gurdwaras 74

3.4 Sikh *sants* visiting the United Kingdom and North America 75

4.1 Sikh and Indian organizations, 1908 to 1947 92

4.2 Sikh organizations, 1947 to 1990 93

4.3 Diaspora Sikh organizations: links with Punjab 94

4.4 Diaspora Sikh organizations: resources 94

4.5 Reaction to events in Punjab and India, 1960 to 1990 94

5.1 North American Sikh organizations post 1984 117

5.2 North American Sikh organizations: media 117

5.3 North American Sikh organizations: Punjabi alliances 117

6.1 UK Sikh organizations post 1984 139

6.2 UK Sikh organizations: media 139

6.3 UK Sikh organizations: Punjabi alliances 139

Map 1

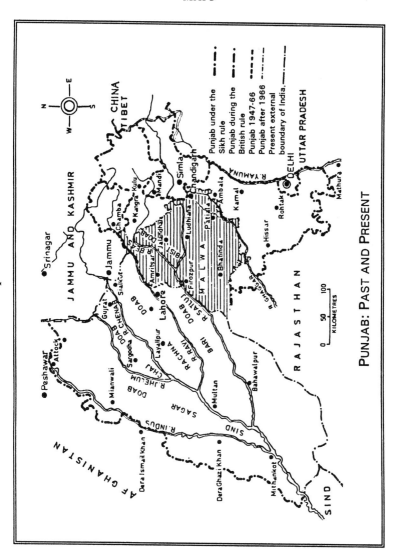

PUNJAB: PAST AND PRESENT

Legend:
- Punjab under the Sikh rule
- Punjab during the British rule
- Punjab 1947-66
- Punjab after 1966
- Present external boundary of India.

Map 2

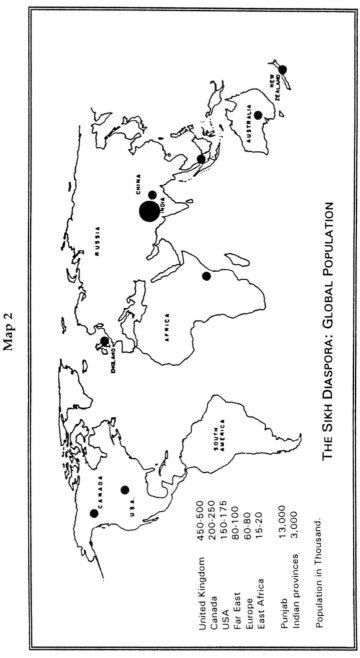

THE SIKH DIASPORA: GLOBAL POPULATION

| | |
|---|---|
| United Kingdom | 450-500 |
| Canada | 200-250 |
| USA | 150-175 |
| Far East | 80-100 |
| Europe | 60-80 |
| East Africa | 15-20 |
| Punjab | 13,000 |
| Indian provinces | 3,000 |

Population in Thousand.

# Introduction

On 3 June 1984, in a meticulously calculated operation code-named "Bluestar", the Indian army stormed the Golden Temple, Amritsar, along with 37 other Sikh shrines in the Punjab, with the specific aim to "remove terrorists, criminals and their weapons from sacred places of worship".[1] After three days of intensive fighting, hundreds lay dead on the sacred *parikarma* (walkabout) surrounding the pool, among them Jarnail Singh Bhindranwale, Shahbeg Singh, Amrik Singh and ordinary Sikh pilgrims including women and children, whose bodies were unceremoniously disposed of in rubbish trucks and cremated; their names perished among the debris.[2] All sacred buildings sustained extensive damage, while the Akal Takhat facing the Harimandir, almost crumbled due to heavy shelling. According to reports, the Sikh Reference Library – with its unique collection of priceless manuscripts of sacred literature, copies of the Adi Granth, letters written by gurus, commands, memorabilia and paintings – was deliberately set on fire. Almost every Sikh household in the Punjab, the rest of India and overseas reacted with anger and shock. The Indian government claimed that the real issue was not certain demands put by the Akali Dal but the maturing of a "secessionist movement" supported primarily by "overseas Sikhs"; nevertheless, a whole community's assumptions, cultural expressions, linguistic meanings and explanations ran in stark contrast to the official statements of the government of India.[3] From a self-confident religious community, the Sikhs rapidly acquired many characteristics of a persecuted minority.

1

This study is devoted to the Sikh diaspora's complex and changing relationship with the Punjab, in particular its involvement and support for an independent "Sikh homeland". It does so by examining the Sikh diaspora's multifaceted relationship with the Punjab, through an exploration of social, economic and political linkages. The study provides a description of overseas Sikhs' close alliances with the Punjab, and furnishes some data on how a cry for an independent homeland has found sympathy and approval from Sikh migrants dispersed in many countries. It surveys overseas Sikhs' changed loyalty as an ethnic community between its homeland, Punjab, and its country, India.

## Theoretical issues

While Sikhs' somewhat spasmodic yearning for an independent Punjab presents major difficulties for a student of Sikh history and political science, migrant Sikh communities' support for a "homeland" raises many complex issues. This phenomenon of intra-ethnic solidarity, of which overseas Sikhs' support for their co-ethnics in the Punjab is just one example among many similar cases across the globe, presents many questions. First, there arises a general question of why members of an ethnic group settled in overseas countries may continue to attach themselves to their country or region of origin or their "homeland". Second, why do some ethnic groups become involved in the issue of "homeland"? Third, how are particular ethnic groups involved in this process? This study focuses in particular on Sikh migrant communities settled in Canada, the United States and the United Kingdom, and is mainly concerned to answer the third question; namely, how overseas Sikhs have maintained a close relationship with the Punjab. However, some brief comments on the first two issues will clarify the basic premises of the analysis.

Taking the historic case of Jewish exile, the phenomenon of ethnic loyalty towards homeland is usually called a diaspora. Diaspora is a term often used by historians to describe the Jewish people's search for a home after their uprooting from the Holy Land; it is identified with memories of Jerusalem, memories of Israel and a belief in the Messiah. It derives from a Greek word meaning dispersion and presumes there exists a "homeland" to which the "diaspora" will eventually return.[4] Through this term, numerous Yiddish-speaking communities have tried to give meaning to their forced pain and tragedy during the long "exile" after the destruction of the second Temple in AD 70. As European thinking turned to the ideas of nationalism as a basis for sharing a particular region by a community, Jewish thinkers linked exile and dispersion with the ideals of self-determination for minorities.

How appropriate is this term for describing modern migrant groups, such as the Sikhs settled in foreign lands? Could Sikhs' attachment to Punjab as an "imagined homeland" be treated as a diaspora? How do we distinguish the experiences of different groups settled away from their land of origin, among whom are refugees, short-term labourers, exiles awaiting their chance to return and migrant groups with varying rights in the host country. In seeking a common theory for the diverse phenomena of human migrations, analysts have suggested "diaspora" to capture the most common experiences of displacement associated with migration: homelessness, painful memories and a wish to return. Some writers are reluctant to extend the term "diaspora" to migrant groups, insisting that a diaspora condition represents a unique and almost mythical experience of the Jewish exile. Chaliand (1989: xiv), for instance, has argued that the term should be reserved for groups forced to disperse, and whose members conscientiously strive to keep past memories, maintain their heritage and are involved in a survival struggle. Maintaining that genocide or ethnocide are part of such groups' experiences, to the classic example of the Jewish, he adds rather reluctantly the Armenians, the Chinese in Southeast Asia, the Indians in the Indian Ocean, South Africa and the West Indies, and the Palestinians.

But minority groups have experienced a wide range of pressures from dominant groups among whom they find themselves (Tabori 1972: 204; Marienstras 1989: 125). Genocide is the extreme form of such policies directed at migrants and minorities in various countries. It refers to a policy of a sovereign state to exterminate an ethnic group. Among lesser forms of control faced by minorities and migrants is ethnocide, a forced cultural integration of a small group into a larger entity. Further down the scale comes acculturation, a less painful route whereby a group gradually loses its identity, consciously or unconsciously, and is acculturated to other values imposed by a strong or majority group. The history of Sikhs, in some measure, attests to a mixture of these elements of compulsion. Moreover, it illustrates rather vividly how a diaspora may develop out of an ethnic group's changing fortunes due to changed circumstances.

In recent studies, a general scheme classifying various minority groups settled away from their countries of origin, or homelands, has been suggested, dividing them into classical, modern and global diasporas. Classical diasporas satisfy some essential conditions: (a) displacement from a centre, (b) a troubled relationship between a diaspora and its host society, (c) a sense of community among the diaspora transcending the national frontiers, (d) promotion of return movement and the reconstitution of the national homeland. But the meaning of the term has widened beyond a victim group to include those migrant groups who have suffered in the process of settlement. The latter have been called modern diasporas. According to Esman (1986: 333), "a minority ethnic group of migrant origin which maintains sentimental or material links with its land of origin" is a diaspora. Sheffer (1986) offers a more inclusive approach:

> Ethnic diaspora are created either by voluntary migration [e.g. Turks to West Germany] or as a result of expulsion from the homeland [e.g. Jews and the Palestinians] and settlement in one or more host countries. In these host countries, the diaspora remain minority groups.

In addition, transnational movements have resulted in migratory groups whose location has led to cosmopolitan and hybridized cultures in host states, which question the narrow nationalist discourses. Such migrant groups, usually professionals, freed from kinship, territory and homeland affections, are called "global diasporas". They are migrant groups who are largely a by-product of globalization, sharing a characteristic of their challenge to host nation-states' hegemonic discourses. Thus, three parallel notions of diasporas are available, each seeking its legitimation: classical, modern and global. In his introductory volume to this series, Cohen (1997: 26) suggests how migrant communities could gain diaspora status by meeting several characteristics:

- Dispersal from an original homeland, often traumatically, to two or more foreign regions.
- Alternatively, the expansion from a homeland in search of work, in pursuit of trade or to further colonial ambitions.
- A collective memory and myth about the homeland, including its location, history and achievements.
- An idealization of the putative ancestral home and a collective commitment to its maintenance, restoration, safety and prosperity, even to its creation.
- The development of a return movement which gains collective approbation.
- A strong ethnic group consciousness sustained over a long time and based on a sense of distinctiveness, a common history and the belief of a common fate.
- A troubled relationship with host societies, suggesting a lack of acceptance at the least or the possibility that another calamity might befall the group.
- A sense of empathy and solidarity with co-ethnic members in other countries of settlement.
- The possibility of a distinctive yet creative and enriching life in host countries with a tolerance for pluralism.

Overseas Sikhs, on a strict criterion of "forced" separation from their homeland, clearly do not qualify as a diaspora. However, the tragic consequences and shock at the destruction of the Akal Takhat in 1984 in Amritsar invite some comparison with the Babylonian tragedy following the destruction of Jerusalem in 586 BC. Applying Cohen's criteria, it seems that overseas Sikh communities fulfil the sufficient conditions of a diaspora, i.e. dispersion, reluctant hosts, contest over homeland and maintenance of an active relationship with their mother country. In the following chapters, this will become more apparent, but for now here is a brief justification.

### Overseas Sikh communities: a diaspora?

For almost a century the Sikhs have been settling in overseas countries. The earliest destinations were the Far Eastern countries. The latest phase of emigration has been engendered by the traumatic events in Punjab, from where hundreds have fled abroad as their lives have been shattered due to persecution. As a religious community scattered away from its centre, Sikhs share a common feeling of displacement, reinforced by several migrations suffered in the twentieth century. The partition of Punjab in 1947 brought havoc to millions of people, who became refugees, crossing the newly formed borders of India and Pakistan under scenes of unprecedented communal violence. Although much of the post-1947 emigration has been "economic" and voluntary, it is plausible to argue, taking a long historical view of the process, that it was effectively part of general dislocation, uncertainty and violence caused by the partition of Punjab. Later political events, such as the Naxalite movement in the late 1960s and the militancy of the 1980s, have contributed to emigration.

Overseas Sikh communities have continued to identify themselves as part of the global Sikh community. This is seen through numerous linkages and networks between the diaspora communities and the Punjab, through memories and myths about holy lands and through pilgrimage. While early migrant communities were small and isolated, and in a sense could be considered as part of an Indian diaspora or more precisely a Punjabi diaspora (Dusenbery 1995), the growing strength of communities abroad coupled with events in the Punjab during the 1980s have reinforced Sikhs' ethnic identity, reinforced social values, religious traditions and linguistic bonds, thus making it a distinct diaspora.

Sikhs, like numerous migrant communities, remain reluctant settlers, sharing uncertainty about their fate in host countries. In Africa and the Far East, where they migrated as empire's auxiliaries, new nationalist governments' policies forced them out. Migration to the West, especially to the Pacific states, was hazardous and they faced racial hostility and exclusion. In Europe, as the destination of the largest overseas community, they have also faced discrimination and nonacceptance.

Sikhs are contesting a homeland. The tragic events in the Punjab during the 1980s have sharpened overseas Sikhs' sense of an endangered homeland. Indeed, a single "critical event" seems to have alerted them to their minority position in a dramatic way, and encouraged their sensibilities in a radical direction – the carving of a territorial state as a homeland. Migrant Sikh communities thus satisfy the psychological and sociological attributes of a diaspora.

There is a further major theoretical issue concerning why and how migrant communities become involved in the "homeland" issue (Tatla 1994b). A proper discussion would require far more space; here are only the barest outlines. Following the French Revolution, as the principle of nationalism triumphed, nation-states emerged, in which states were a reflection of a culturally and geographically homogeneous people. Still, as many studies have pointed out, most of these states are one-nation-group dominant states with fragmented minorities, binational states and multinational states; none has a total congruence of nation-group and state (Anderson 1983; Chaliand 1989, 1993; Connor 1994; Enloe 1973; Smith 1981b, 1983, 1986). In the developing world, the territorial statehood and ethnic cultures differ radically. While almost every nation-state has minority populations, in some there are ethnic groups straddled between two states; the Kurds, the Palestinians and the Kashmiris are prime examples of this. In many African and Asian countries, new nationalist zeal in creating a "national community" from historical boundaries and geographical regions has led to "homeland" struggles. Many minorities have struggled to attain statehood, but equally many have been forced into submission and integrated. As a result of conflict between dominant nation-states and their minorities, wars and insurgencies have created ever more refugees across the globe.[5] Emergence of international relief agencies, including the United Nations (UN), the Unrepresented Nations and Peoples Organization (UNPO) and the NGOs, testify to human upheavals resulting from the new global map (Brett 1995). Arendt (1973: 290) has noted this tragic fallout:

> Since the Peace treaties of 1919 and 1920, the refugees and the stateless persons have attached themselves like a curse to all the newly established states on earth which were created in the image of the nation-state. For these new states, this curse bears the germs of a deadly sickness.

Violation of human rights has increased, primarily due to indigenous nationalists' intolerance of minorities (Stohl & Lopez 1986;

McGarry & Leary 1993; Gurr 1993, 1994). Paradoxically, many imperial regimes were far more tolerant of people with distinct languages, religions or customs. Sharing none of their predecessors' benign tolerance, postcolonial nationalists in the Far East, South Asia and Africa have resorted to various measures from assimilation to genocide. As Kedourie (1970) noted:

> To an imperial government the groups in a mixed area are all equally entitled to some consideration, to a national government they are a foreign body to be either assimilated or rejected. The national state claims to treat all citizens as equal members of the nation, but this fair-sounding principle only serves to disguise the tyranny of one group over another. The nation must be, all its citizens must be, animated by the same spirit. Differences are divisive and therefore treasonable.

Many ethnic communities engaged in the "homeland" struggle have often received crucial help from their co-ethnics settled abroad.[6] The Sikhs provide a particularly illuminating case study of attracting sympathy and support from their co-ethnics settled abroad, support for their struggle towards statehood. The Sikh nationalist movement has embroiled overseas Sikh communities in this debate and mobilization, making them part of a large phenomenon of such ethnic groups in the international arena involved in the "homeland" issue.

## Scope of the study

The dynamics of overseas Sikhs' ties to the Punjab and to Indian polity, the Sikh diaspora's support for a Sikh homeland, and its role in the international arena post 1984, all form the subject of this book. It focuses mainly on the Sikh communities settled in Britain, Canada and the United States, though its scope encompasses the worldwide Sikh diaspora. Chapter 1 reviews the Sikhs' evolution from an ethnic group to its self-definition of "nation in the making". Chapter 2 charts a history of Sikh migration and settlement abroad. Chapter 3 describes the Sikh diaspora's linkages with the

Punjab through social, cultural and religious ties. Chapter 4 chronicles the evolution of diaspora political associations and their impact on Punjab up to the 1980s, including an assessment of the origin and support for the idea of a Sikh homeland before 1984 and the campaign for Punjab's autonomy during 1981–4. The following two chapters describe Sikhs' mobilization as a response to Indian army action on the Golden Temple, Amritsar, and subsequent events in the Punjab. This is followed by a chapter devoted to implications of diaspora Sikh mobilization in terms of intergovernmental relations. The final chapter advances some hypotheses for understanding the nature of mobilization, in terms of the leadership's perception, their understanding of the "critical event", discourse on "Sikh homeland" and utilization of international institutions by the diaspora community leaders. The study advances the understanding of the Sikh diaspora through a synthesis and new data, generating propositions which require further elaboration and validation. Hence any results or assertions are quite tentative and rather modest.

*Sources and terminology*

This study is mainly empirical. It draws on data from several sources: publications of community organizations, pamphlets, manifestos, tracts, and audiovisual material. Extensive use is made of the Punjabi media, many weekly newspapers and magazines. Where a Punjabi source is quoted, translation from the original raises difficulties as certain Punjabi words and phrases have no equivalents in English; a close interpretation is offered instead. As part of the study, interviews and informal talks with leading actors were conducted, but they have been used only on the rare occasions when a written record was unavailable to substantiate a particular argument. Most Punjabi terms are included in the glossary, along with a guide to their pronunciation and orthography; any other Punjabi words are defined on their first occurrence. Social scientists will need little reminder about value-laden concepts, propositions and terms employed in the community discourse. Thus expressions such as "martyrs" and "freedom fighters" in community literature and "extremists" and "terrorists" in governmental literature are quoted with their sources. The glossary also gives variations for those names and places that do not yet have standard spellings. For the sake of consistency, *Punjab* and *Punjabi* are used throughout the book instead of *Panjab* and *Panjabi*; other indigenous terms are indicated in the glossary.

ONE
_____

# The Sikhs: the search for statehood

Fairest of all, o' chums, is this land of Punjab
Like a rose, among flowers all[1]

Bestow upon Sikhs a pilgrimage to Amritsar, a bath in the
sacred pool[2]

As an Indian religious community, Sikhs number about 16 million, forming a majority community of Punjab province, but just 2 per cent of India's total population. Until 1984, Sikhs' loyalty towards India seemed unproblematic at least in its political expression; while maintaining patriotic feelings, they nurtured a strong sense of a separate community, based on a distinct religion, a regional culture and language of the Punjab. This duality posed no heart-searching contradiction for most Sikhs, until June 1984, when as a reaction to the central government's action in the Golden Temple, a wave of strong Sikh nationalism found expression in a militant campaign for a Sikh homeland. Although the movement has been brutally repressed by the security forces, and Sikh politics has been forcibly "restructured" to rejoin the "political process", deep-rooted sentiments remain for a secure Sikh homeland in the Punjab. As the underlying causes remain unaddressed, the issue of Sikh nationalism is unlikely to disappear.

## A sect, a community or a nation?

The emergence of Sikh nationalism in the 1980s, especially in its most virulent form of demand for Khalistan, a Sikh homeland in

11

the Punjab, touches on some complex issues of ethnic conflict in the postcolonial nation-building process in South Asia. It raises issues concerning the nature of Sikh ethnicity, which in a short period of time has moved from group consciousness to political community and staked a claim for a statehood. The form of conflict also calls for an examination of the emerging nature of the Indian state, which despite having evolved a common framework for democratic political bargaining, has faced several regional nationalisms and remains locked in ethnic conflicts.

The Sikh demand for statehood has a number of explanations: economic factors, the crisis of India's federal state relations and the eruption of Sikh ethnonationalism. Economic explanations broadly focus on radical agrarian changes ushered in by the "green revolution", changes that have fuelled many layers of contradictions between the rich peasantry and the unemployed youth. Small farmers have been marginalized by squeezed profits and rich peasantry have railed against central government for better terms of trade. The Akalis have exploited these contradictions by turning it into a communal issue, identifying central government or the Hindu bourgeoisie as the real culprit. The federal state thesis attributes the Punjabi crisis to increasing centralization of power in New Delhi, and manipulation by the Congress Party of a regional elite for its electoral base. Thus the central government of the Congress Party led by Indira Gandhi maximized its poll returns by depicting the Sikh demands as antinational. A third explanation finds Sikh ethnonationalism responsible for the troubled Punjab. By focusing on Sikhs as a nationality, the Akali Dal first fought for a culturally congruent region in the 1960s, extending its claim for statehood in the 1980s. This hypothesis finds much corroboration in Sikhs' own rhetoric and writings, which emphasize their distinctive religious traditions, the Sikh rule over Punjab and a political community destined for independence.

While these perspectives are valuable, the puzzle of Sikh nationalism has thrown up more serious issues. First, in the past decade, several thousand Sikh youths took up arms and died for a "homeland". What moved them? Can rational and economic reasons explain the psychological pull of a nation that "joins a people, in the sub-conscious conviction of its members from all its non-members in a most vital way?" (Connor 1993: 377). Then there is the Akali Dal, a major political party of Sikhs, and how it could mobilize its supporters by invoking certain features of the Khalsa Panth, invariably historic shrines and religious rhetoric, even while pursuing essentially secular pursuits of power sharing. Thirdly, why have even moderate demands by a minority religious community been repeatedly projected by the Indian leaders as antinational? Indeed, what is the nature of the nation-building project undertaken by the postcolonial Indian state which has turned several regional nationalisms into intractable problems? Finally, what is the Sikhs' perception of Punjab as a Sikh homeland, how has it evolved and how widely is this sentiment shared among its constituents, who are divided by economic, social and caste cleavages? How have Sikh leaders articulated regional identity as part of Indian federalism while owing allegiance to political parties, including the Congress Party, the Communists and the Akali Dal? Alternatively, one could follow Brass's (1991) pioneering analysis of a general schema for ethnic communities and ask: how does ethnic consciousness transform into an ethnic community? And how does it express itself as a nationality through changes in its culture, behaviour and boundaries? Finally, under what conditions does an ethnic community claim itself as a nation and demand a homeland; and what are its consequences for ethnic conflict and management?

## The making of Sikh ethnic consciousness

The previous section has obviously posed too many questions to form a viable hypothesis for this short survey. It is suggested that Sikh ethnic conflict should be viewed as a "nationalist project" thrown up by the modernization of a traditional Sikh society in contact and in conflict with certain imperatives of hegemonic features of Indian state nationalism. In order to understand an apparent and dramatic shift in Sikhs' political and social outlook due to the events of 1984, it is necessary to trace the development of Sikh identity and the idea of a Sikh homeland during the recent past. The idea of Punjab as a Sikh homeland goes back to several discrete elements of Sikh history. Punjab, the land of five rivers, is the community's birthplace; it is dotted with historic shrines and it is the cradle of the Punjabi language.

The Sikh identity is rooted in a religious tradition of the Khalsa Panth, which subsumes social, cultural, political and territorial identities. Sikh identity is not based on an abstract creed, but discrete elements of history, myths and memories, intertwined within the region of Punjab. Sikhs, literally the learners, trace their ancestry to ten gurus; the first of them was Nanak (1469–1539), born near Lahore in a Hindu family. Nanak's life is now mixed in myths and memories of the *janamsākhī* (hagiographic) literature. What is certain is that his acquired charisma, superb poetical and musical gifts, simplicity of message, his emphasis on the equality of all men and women before God, rejection of rituals, denunciation of renunciation, and admonition of those in religious and political power became the foundation of a new sect. Nanak's nine successors, through pious preaching in the local vernacular, and the institution of *langar*, a common kitchen to emphasize equality among a highly caste-conscious society, established new centres, including Amritsar, Hargobindpur and Katarpur. By compiling a book of sacred scriptures in 1604, fifth guru Arjan placed it at the centre of the Harimandir, a temple by a pool in Amritsar.

Institutionalization of the faith by the fifth guru attracted the wrath of Punjab's governor, and Mogul Emperor Jahangir ordered him to death. Arjan's successor, Hargobind, added a further building, the Akal Takhat facing the Harimandir; he wore two swords, *miri* and *piri*, signifying temporal and spiritual aspects of faith. By the time of Aurangzeb, a zealot Mogul ruler, keen on conversion, the ninth guru was beheaded in Delhi in 1675. The tenth and last guru, Gobind, was born into this conflict. He built a fort in a hilly area far from Amritsar, at Anandpur. In April 1699, according to Sikh narrative, he founded the Khalsa Panth, a "society of the pure", through an initiation ritual and a dress code; they became the faithful carriers of the new sect. After fighting many battles with Mogul authority, he tried a settlement with the Mogul emperor Bahadur Shah, but was assassinated in 1708. The birth of Khalsa and the Guru Granth, the sacred book, were the two most important events in the sect's history, and they consolidated its followers.

14

In 200 years a sect was transformed into a religious organization; the universality of Nanak's message was constrained and interpreted by the interests of the community and its survival in a hostile environment. The value system of the Khalsa was to be egalitarian, with collective and spiritual authority vested in the Guru Granth, and it was inspired to wage a just struggle against domination. Sikhs were mainly drawn from lower social classes of Punjab's Jat peasantry; the new sect's distinction lay in combining spiritual pursuits with earthly powers by challenging the local rulers. Where other sects, such as the Kabirpanthis and Gorakhnathis failed, Nanak's followers organized themselves into the Khalsa Panth, with a distinct dress code, the slogan *wāhe gurū jī dā Khalsa wāhegurī jī kī fateh*, the greeting *sat srī akāl* and a religious zeal. Cunningham (1849: 34), writing in 1846, was perhaps impressed by the military valour of the Khalsa when he compared the Sikhs' transition with the followers of Kabir, Gorakh and Ramanand; the latter

> perfected forms of dissent, rather than planted the germs of nations, and their sect remain to this day as they left them. It was reserved for Nanak to perceive the true principles of reform, and to lay those broad foundations which enabled his successor Gobind to fire the minds of his countrymen with a new nationality.

The eighteenth century became a period of suffering, martyrdom and resistance against the Mogul tyranny. Banda Singh, a disciple of Gobind, was executed and followed by a vigorous persecution ordered by Lahore's Mogul governors, especially by Zakria Khan, who announced awards for Sikhs' unshaved heads. Ahmad Shah Abdali, the Afghan ruler, pursued them in two major battles, killing 5,000 in 1746 followed by a second battle in 1762 when Sikhs were defeated almost to a man; the two battles are remembered as *ghallugharas* (holocausts). By the 1760s, the Afghan invaders' destruction of Mogul power allowed Sikh chiefs to dominate the central Punjab through 12 *Misls* (confederacies). During the century some new traditions were invented, and an annual gathering at Amritsar by Sikh chiefs became the *Sarbat Khalsa*, the supreme body, where through *gurmatas* and *hukamanamas* differences were resolved and collective tasks set. From these *Misls*, emerged the one-eyed "lion of Punjab", Ranjit Singh (1779–1839), who established the Sikh empire (Chopra 1928; Cunningham 1849; Khushwant Singh 1962). His liberal monarchy patronized many Hindu, Muslim and Sikh historic shrines; the latter were controlled by Udasis, descendants of the first guru[3] (Banga 1978). As befitted a Sikh sovereign, he granted lavish expenditure for the Harimandir. Its buildings were greatly expanded with royal princes' *bungas* and *serais*, while the maharajah's skilled technicians fixed gilded gold and copper plates on to the roof of its central shrine; various European visitors popularized a new name for it, the Golden Temple (Madanjit Kaur 1983). With the death of Ranjit Singh, this "majestic fabric" collapsed but memories of a sovereign Punjab became part of Sikh folklore. The Punjab was annexed to British India in 1849 following two Anglo-Sikh wars.[4]

## The colonial encounter

Colonial rule introduced widespread changes into the continent. Three major ingredients of imperial policy affected the Punjab's "village republics". First, a mutiny by Purbia sepoys in 1857 prompted retired Sikh chiefs and soldiers to join the British in quelling the rebellion. In the newly drawn imperial security map, among the newly classified "martial races", Punjabis became favourite recruits. By the First World War, Sikhs constituted a third of the armed forces and Punjab provided three-fifths of army recruits. Second, Punjab's peasantry, the Muslims and Sikhs, also benefited through the development of Canal Colonies; a network of canals spread through the unpopulated lands in western Punjab (Ali 1988). The British administrators developed a special concern for Punjab's rural peasants, a client–patron relationship whose interests were jealously protected through the Land Alienation Act of 1900, shielding them from the powerful urban moneylenders, mostly Hindus. Whatever the reality of imperial "divide and rule" policy in the subcontinent, in Punjab it amounted to little more than a conscious policy in favour of the rural classes.

*Intra-elite competition and community boundaries*
The European-style education and "print revolution" effected profound changes. It introduced issues of language and scripts, social identity issues for social groups and castes, and for the newly educated Punjabi elite, a discovery of its past, translating its cultural ethos into the modern idioms. As each community established schools and colleges, the common language Punjabi was abandoned. Sanskrit and Hindi were adopted as the medium of instruction by Hindus, Muslims adopted Urdu, and Punjabi became the exclusive language of Sikhs.[5] Another challenge came from Christian missionaries, who converted some Punjabi lower classes. This set up a competing spirit of religious revivalism among the urban elite, producing sharp ethnic boundaries, and the embittered atmosphere often led to communal conflict and violence. The comparatively rich urban Hindus were infused with the aggressively proselytizing social movement of the Arya Samaj preached by Dayanand, a Hindu reformist from Gujarat. Although Sikhs joined hands with Hindus in launching this reformist movement, differences arose on Aryas' *shudhi* methods aimed at reconverting lower classes to Hinduism. Arya Hindus dubbed Sikhism as a mere "sect" and its gurus "pretenders". Through various Singh Sabhas, the first of which was established in 1873, the Sikh reformists took up the challenge. From 1887–8 onwards there was a war of pamphlets, when Muslims and Sikhs tried to rebut Aryas' charges. To Aryas' assertion, "Sikhs are Hindus," Sikh reformers retorted, "Sikhs are not Hindus," the title of a famous tract by Kahn Singh in 1899 (Jones 1976). The new print media at Lahore and Amritsar sharpened group consciousness, creating ethnic boundaries, shaping their sense of religious identity, language and appropriate script.

The Sikh reformers reacted by attempting to weed out all remnants of Hindu practices from the Sikh faith, inventing new rituals and ceremonies for various uses. The ceremonies of the Golden Temple naturally attracted their first fury in 1905 (Oberoi 1994, 1988). The reformers, many from lower social classes, challenged the Udasi managers, popularly known as *mahants* (custodians), who would not allow untouchables to worship at the Golden Temple, contrary to Sikh principles. The Akalis, a new zealot reform group, arose from 1914 to challenge the *mahants'* control of historic shrines. A violent confrontation took place in 1921 at Nankana, the birthplace of Guru Nanak, where 130 Akalis were murdered by the *mahants'* mercenaries. This led to a Sikh Gurdwaras and Shrines Act of 1925, which handed over historic shrines to an elected body of Sikhs, the Shiromani Gurdwara Parbandhak Committee (SGPC). Ever since, the SGPC has played an important role in Sikh affairs and politics. Its elections are keenly contested through its prestige and control of missionaries, managers, priests and servants, and the SGPC has acquired the status of a "Sikh parliament" and "a state within a state".

*Minority politics: painful options*
During colonial rule, Sikhs' political options were constrained mainly by demography. Sikhs formed only 14 per cent of Punjab's population; Muslims made up the majority and the rest were Hindus. As soldiers and peasants, the community's loyalist tradition was grounded in material advantages; pensions, wages, colonists' incomes and land preferential policies cemented a special Anglo-Sikh relationship. The Chief Khalsa Diwan, a major organization at the turn of the century, sought patronage through its loyalist stance.[6] After the First World War, this amicable relationship underwent major change due to several events: the Gadr movement, the Jallianwala massacre at Amritsar in 1919 and a new political body, the Akalis.

From the 1920s, imperial polity was opening up its governance for greater representation of its subjects. While the Chief Khalsa Diwan sought increased Sikh representation in the government, "in view of the admitted political, historical and economic importance of the Sikhs in the province", the Akalis sought accommodation with the Congress, sharing a vision of independent India, and gave qualified support to Congress after seeking assurances on many issues of Sikh symbolic and material representation.[7] However, the nationalist fervour never predominated in the Punjab, despite the presence of some revolutionary groups. This was mainly due to the British administrators' careful policy towards the Punjabi peasantry. Encompassing a coalition of Muslims, Sikhs and Hindu rural leaders, the Unionist Party formed a government, a unique consociational experiment involving three religious communities. Its leaders were committed to strong Punjabi nationality. However, this ministry and a unique phase of Punjabi nationalism was undermined by Muhammad Ali Jinnah's dream of a separate state (Jalal 1985). The 1946 Punjabi elections, held in the shadow of imperial withdrawal, gave the Muslim League an overwhelming mandate, paving the way towards partition (Talbot 1988).

Sandwiched between the Muslims' vision of an Islamic state, and the Congress's India dominated by Hindus, the Sikh leaders were in a quandary. As the Congress leaders acceded to partition in 1943, the events moved too swiftly to let Sikh leaders formulate any serious plan for the community's future (Tinker 1977; Oren 1974). First, the Akalis countered the Muslim League's demand for Pakistan by demanding an *azad* (independent) Punjab, proposing its boundaries to be redrawn by detaching Muslim majority areas. Then, reacting to the "Rajagopalachari formula" in July 1944, they asserted, "Sikhs are also a nation". Tara Singh, the Akali leader, declared Sikhs would not become "slaves of Pakistan or Hindustan". To the Cabinet Mission in 1946, the Akali Dal presented a memorandum arguing Sikhs' claim on the Punjab:

> Whereas the Sikhs being attached to the Punjab by intimate bonds of holy shrines, property, language, traditions, and history claim it as their homeland and holy land which the British took over as a 'trust' from the last Sikh ruler during his minority and whereas the entity of the Sikhs is being threatened on account of the persistent demand of [sic] Pakistan by the Muslims on the one hand and of the danger of absorption by the Hindus on the other, the Executive Committee of the Shiromani Akali Dal demands for the preservation and protection of the religious, cultural and economic and political rights of the Sikh nation, the creation of a Sikh state which would include a substantial majority of the Sikh population and their scared shrines and historical gurdwara with provision for the transfer and exchange of population and property.[8]

A few Sikhs also proposed a rationale for a Sikh state (Swarup Singh 1946; Hamdard 1943). Although the British were sympathetic to the Sikhs' "special case", the community's demography made any proposal impractical. Indeed, some British officers, Major Billy Short and Penderel Moon, felt the Sikhs' best option lay in the new Muslim state; Sikhs could hold the balance of power and save Punjab's partition. When talks with the Muslim League proved fruitless, the Sikh leaders put their trust in the Congress leadership of Gandhi and Nehru, appealing for fairness. Thus, the partitioned Punjab was "Sikhs' gift to India". The search for a Sikh homeland proved to be a cry in the wilderness except for its endorsement from an unexpected quarter of "principled communists" (Gurharpal Singh 1984).

### The partition

On 15 August 1947 two new countries, India and Pakistan, came into being. The boundary line cut through the heartland of the Sikh population,[9] accompanied by ethnic cleansing of horrific proportions; communal riots claimed the lives of half a million people (Randhawa 1954). A total of 12 million people crossed over the new border; Sikhs and Hindus moved out of west Punjab, while almost all of the Muslim community of east Punjab migrated to Pakistan.

Far from suffering disintegration, as some English observers had predicted a century earlier, the Sikhs emerged from imperial rule as a community whose population had substantially increased through natural increase and conversion from Punjab's lower classes. Through interethnic elite competition, they had clearly demarcated themselves as a separate community, with historic shrines controlled by a representative body, and rituals and ceremonies sharply distinguished from their parent society of Hindus. Colonial rule also witnessed a vigorous creativity by Sikh writers in the Punjabi language. The partition of Punjab was an immediate blow, with the loss of fertile lands and 140 sacred shrines, but the tragedy also brought Sikhs into a compact geographical unit, where they could perhaps protect their language, culture and religious traditions. The distinguishing feature of imperial power was that it neither needed nor visualized a unified centralized state, a vision which the new nationalist leaders adopted, typified by the Nehruvian approach to state building. The British recognized India's diversity by incorporating many layers of state structure, from princely states to tribal regions, and hesitated to encroach upon indigenous customs of social and cultural life, emphasizing "recognition" and incorporation into the state's legal and administrative apparatus. Imperial authority was much concerned with representation of various religious and cultural communities; its administrators harboured a somewhat natural sympathy for minorities and indigenous peoples and tribes. Alien rulers tried to balance different communities' claims that the imperial polity's policies led to partition of the subcontinent and not to its Balkanization; this was an incredible legacy of imperialism that few Indian nationalists could acknowledge.

## Under the postcolonial state

Even with partition into India and Pakistan, the British left behind an empire consisting of semiautonomous regions, especially in India. The regions were princely states with a variety of political systems and they included two Sikh states. Within loose borders they contained many tribes, religious minorities with distinct cultures and languages, and they were joined only by railways, roads and rudimentary communications. In independent India, the Congress leaders, as inheritors of power, had set themselves a daunting task of moulding an empire into a modern state. The immediate question of obtaining accession of princely states was resolved through a judicious dose of coercion and persuasion; however, in Kashmir and some northeastern states this policy led to violent confrontation. And another major question remained unaddressed – the place of Hindu nationalism *vis-à-vis* many regional nationalities. While the Congress leaders' secular rhetoric and well-formulated distance from Hindu nationalism could not secure Muslims' consent, could "Hindu-dominated secular polity" ensure equality of India's various nationalities?

India adopted a unitary constitutional structure with a universal franchise, scrapping the colonial system of weighting representation for minorities and reservation of seats, except for scheduled tribes and castes.[10] Three major principles of nation building and governance were laid: (a) secularism with freedom of worship and state noninterference, (b) economic welfare providing substantive citizenship rights, and (c) democratic centralism providing a structure of power sharing between subnational regions and the union state (Austin 1966; Jalal 1995). Haunted by the spectre of India's dissolution, the constitution ruled out the principle of self-determination for regions and nationalities. Instead, it provided for the reorganization of linguistic regions and recognized 14 languages as state languages. Hindi was adopted as the official language of India along with English. However, as the Telgu speakers forced a demand to reorganize their state, a States Reorganization Commission was established in 1953. By the 1980s, the Indian union consisted of 22 states, with 15 official languages.

*Punjab as a homeland*

Although Sikhs had staked a claim on the Punjab as their homeland and holy land in the 1940s, by emphasizing their "bonds of holy shrines, property, language, traditions, and history", it was the partition of Punjab which effectively turned this imaginative vision into a realistic project. In the Indian Punjab, Sikhs constituted a majority in six districts, in another five they formed a large minority.[11] Apprehensive of Congress's intentions, especially its secular credentials (which many Sikh leaders interpreted as Hindu domination by another name), the main Sikh political party since the 1920s, the Akali Dal, set out a case for a culturally congruent Punjabi-speaking region during the first general elections in 1952:

> The test of democracy, in the opinion of the Shiromani Akali Dal, is that the minorities should feel that they are really free and equal partners in the destiny of their country ... to bring home this sense of freedom to the Sikhs it is vital that there should be a [province of] Punjabi-speaking language and culture ... it is a question of life and death for the Sikhs for a new Punjab to be created immediately.[12]

The States Reorganization Commission rejected the Akali memorandum, as it did not possess a "minimum measure of agreement" but it recommended the merging of the princely Sikh states of the Punjab and East Punjab States Union (PEPSU) into the Punjab.[13]

22

Citing this as a blatant discrimination, the Akali Dal launched the first movement for the Punjabi-speaking state in 1955. After a series of compromises, the Akali Dal launched a second campaign for the Punjabi state in 1960–61.[14] The demand was opposed by Punjabi-speaking Hindus, who portrayed it as a demand for independence, declared their language of Hindi in the 1951 and 1961 censuses as part of their strategy and argued for the merging of the neighbouring Hindu dominant states to neutralize Sikh ambitions.

The 1960–61 movement failed and Tara Singh was replaced by Fateh Singh, a rural leader who reformulated the demand, assuring the central government of a purely linguistic motive rather than a religious demand. The movement gained strength in 1965 when the Akali Dal also adopted a resolution distinguishing Punjab as its homeland while calling India its motherland:

> This conference recalls that the Sikh people agreed to merge in a common Indian nationality on the explicit understanding of being accorded a constitutional status of co-sharers in the Indian sovereignty along with the majority community, which solemn understanding now stands cynically repudiated by the present rulers of India. Further the Sikh people have been systematically reduced to a sub-political status in their homeland, the Punjab, and to an insignificant position in their motherland, India. The Sikhs are in a position to establish before an impartial international tribunal, uninfluenced by the present Indian rulers that the law, the judicial process, and the executive action of the State of India is constitutionally and heavily weighted against the Sikhs and is administered with un-bandaged eyes against Sikh citizens. This conference therefore, resolves, after careful thought, that there is left no alternative for the Sikhs in the interest of self-preservation but to frame their political demand for securing a self-determined political status within the Republic of Union of India.[15]

The movement was suspended as Indo-Pakistani hostilities broke in September 1965. Impressed by Sikhs' contribution to the Indian war efforts, the government agreed to the reorganization of Punjab in 1966.

The Akali leaders' ambition to achieve a culturally congruent region was achieved. For the first time in history, Sikhs formed a majority in the new Punjab.[16] However, its borders, the capital, the share of river waters, the management of the Bhakra Dam Project and the neighbouring states' anti-Punjabi policies became the subjects of Sikh resentment against the central government. In the new Punjab, the Akali Dal formed a coalition government in 1967. However, its electoral base was narrow, as Sikh voters were divided into the Congress, the Akalis and small communist parties. The Akalis' experience in this short-lived coalition government alerted them to the central government's increasing interference. Between 1967 and 1980 three Akali coalition governments were dismissed by the central government.[17] The Congress at the centre had changed decisively from the Nehruvian policy of accommodation to an active manipulation of provincial governments, partly necessitated by its loss of support with the rise of regional parties (Map 1, Tables 1.1 and 1.2).

*Towards Punjabi nationalism*

Having achieved the congruence of cultural boundaries, the Akali Dal sought further concessions for provincial powers. Akali leaders' changing perception, from religious nationalism to "Punjab nationalism", was as much to do with changes of leadership from

Table 1.1   Punjab: population and area.

| Year | Area (sq. km) | Population (millions) | Muslims (%) | Hindus (%) | Sikhs (%) | Others (%) |
|------|---------------|------------------------|-------------|------------|-----------|------------|
| 1941 | 256,000 | 28.4 | 53 | 31 | 15 | 1 |
| After partition of Punjab, 1947 | | | | | | |
| 1951 | 122,500 | 16.1 | 2 | 62 | 35 | 1 |
| 1961 | 122,500 | 20.3 | 2 | 64 | 33 | 1 |
| After reorganization of Punjab, 1966 | | | | | | |
| 1971 | 50,260 | 13.2 | 1 | 38 | 60 | 1 |
| 1981 | 50,260 | 16.7 | 1 | 38 | 60 | 1 |
| 1991 | 50,260 | 20.1 | 1 | 37 | 61 | 1 |

urbanite Sikhs as with socioeconomic changes in the Punjab. The "green revolution" brought economic issues to the fore, and Sikh peasants had two major concerns: reduced margins on wheat and rice production, along with increased demand for cheap agricultural inputs, electricity, fertilizers and river water. Moreover, Punjab's uneven development – a highly developed agrarian sector but no corresponding industrial base – led to high unemployment and environmental disorders, further exacerbated by migration of cheap labour from other provinces. A second incentive towards Punjabi nationalism came from the class composition of the community. Incorporation of various lower classes and sects demanded a more liberal vision than a traditional religious nationalism, which had served the Akalis' purposes in the 1960s. This vision was further reinforced by political considerations. Even in the Sikh majority province of Punjab, electoral politics

Table 1.2    Percentage of votes polled by political parties in Punjab's legislative assembly elections.

| | 1967 | 1969 | 1972 | 1977 | 1980 | 1985 | 1992 | 1997 |
|---|---|---|---|---|---|---|---|---|
| Congress (I) | 37.7 | 39.2 | 42.8 | 33.6 | 45.2 | 37.9 | 43.8 | 26.4 |
| Akali Dal | 20.5 | 29.4 | 27.6 | 31.4 | 26.9 | 38.0 | [a] | 37.2 |
| BJP | 9.8 | 9.0 | 5.0 | 15.0 | 6.5 | 5.0 | 16.6 | 10.8 |
| CPI | 5.3 | 4.8 | 6.5 | 6.6 | 6.5 | 4.3 | 3.4 | 2.9 |
| CPM | 3.2 | 3.1 | 3.3 | 3.5 | 4.1 | 1.9 | 2.7 | [c] |
| Other Parties | 7.7 | 5.6 | 2.5 | 0.4 | 4.4 | 1.1 | 23.5[b] | 23.2[b] |
| Independents | 15.8 | 8.9 | 12.3 | 9.6 | 6.5 | 11.9 | 9.6 | [c] |
| Total | 100.0 | 100.0 | 100.0 | 100.1 | 100.1 | 100.1 | 100.6 | 100.0 |

CPI = Punjab branch of Communist Party of India (Right)
CPM = Punjab branch of Communist Party of India (Marxist)
BJP = Bhartiya Janata Party
[a] During the 1992 election, the Akali Dal boycotted the elections. The turnout of voters was 24.3%; in 1997 it was 69.9%.
[b] For 1992 other parties with their respective shares are Bahujan Samaj Party 16.2%, Janata Dal 2.1% and Akali Dal (Kabul) 5.2%. For 1997 other parties with their respective shares are Bahujan Samaj Party 7.5%, Akali Dal (Mann) 2.9%, CPM, Janata Dal and Samajvadi Party.
[c] Included in other parties.
*Sources*: For 1965–85 election, V. B. Singh and S. Bose, *State Elections in India: Data Handbook on Vidhan Sabha Elections, 1952–1985*, vol. 1, *The North*, Part 1, 1987; for 1992 and 1997 elections, Gurharpal Singh (1992, 1997).

could not vote the Akali Dal into power without political alliances. Between 1967 and 1980 they formed three coalition governments. The Akalis' solution was to form an alliance with non-Congress parties for elections and coalition governments. As Indira Gandhi returned to power at the centre in 1980, the Akali coalition government was toppled.

Modernization, encompassing rising prosperity, urbanization and commercialization of the rural society, threw up issues of religious authority and orthodoxy. The Akalis had always projected themselves as champions of the Khalsa, but their pragmatic alliances with the Hindu political parties, once their archenemies, alarmed several puritan groups. These orthodox groups alleged that the Akali Dal and the sGPC had exploited the Sikh shrines for political purposes while paying lip service to the community's spiritual needs and Khalsa traditions. The seminaries of Damdami Taksal and Akhand Kirtani Jatha proposed a strict code of religious behaviour and a programme of moral economy (Oberoi 1993). The Akalis had to compete with such movements from within. This contradiction blew up into a major crisis in 1978 when a confrontation between Akhand Kirtani Jatha and the Nirankaris led to 13 deaths in Amritsar. The Congress Party also exploited the religious divisions and alliances. Zail Singh, Punjab's chief minister 1972–7, constructed a historic route linking Sikh shrines and exposed the Akalis' hypocrisy of lax faith and their apparent fondness for scotch. In 1980, at an annual educational conference organized by the Chief Khalsa Diwan, many arguments were heard for the Sikhs' rights as a nation. A new organization, the Dal Khalsa, demanded a Sikh state. The Congress leaders patronized such dissident groups to discredit the Akalis.

Responding to these developments, the Akalis and the sGPC reclaimed their traditional domain; the sGPC adopted "Sikhs are a nation" in September 1981. However, the notion of Sikhs as a nation had been part of Sikh vocabulary for too long, so its formal adoption had only symbolic value.[18] In 1980, deprived of provincial power by the more scheming central government led by Indira Gandhi, the Akalis mobilized Sikh peasantry in a major campaign for Punjab's autonomy, with a set of economic, cultural, constitutional and religious demands. They revived an old charter for these demands, the Anandpur Sahib Resolution. The resolution was couched in the Sikh idiom, seeking to preserve the "distinct identity of the Sikhs"; it went as follows:

> The Shiromani Akali Dal shall strive to achieve the main objective to preserve and keep alive the concept of distinct and independent identity of the Panth and to create an environment in which national sentiments and aspirations of the Sikh Panth will find full expression, satisfaction and growth.[19]

However, its major concern was a radical renegotiation of powers for the centre and the states, and an explicit recognition of India as a multinational state. The Akali Dal presented a charter of demands to New Delhi based on the Anandpur resolution mainly on four themes: (a) devolution of powers to states and a new federal structure for centre–state relations; (b) transfer of Chandigarh to Punjab, and Punjabi-speaking areas to Punjab; (c) allocation of river waters, farm product prices, central and provincial taxation as well as other financial powers, a quota for Sikh recruitment into the armies[20]; (d) India's gurdwaras to be managed by an elected body of Sikhs, sacred city status for Amritsar, broadcast of scriptures from the Golden Temple. To back up these demands, the Akalis launched their *Dharam Yudh Morcha* (righteous struggle) in 1981. During the next three years, numerous volunteers courted arrest in support of these demands. Apart from minor concessions on religious demands, the central government gave no ground to the Akalis. The central government ran an orchestrated campaign of manipulation, including the induction into Akali politics of Sant Bhindranwale, a puritan leader of a sect.[21] Indira Gandhi, prime minister of India, used the Akali movement to recover her Congress Party's electoral base, especially among the Hindu belt of north India. By ordering the armed forces into the Golden Temple, she promoted herself as a saviour of India, crushing its enemies bent upon the country's breakup.[22]

### Critical event

On 1 June 1984 some 70,000 armed service personnel cut off the Punjab from the outside world. As tanks rolled into the Golden

Temple, the entire Sikh community rose in protest at this "deliberate humiliation", while the rest of the country felt "relief". Thousands of Sikhs tried to march to the Golden Temple, a number of Sikh regiments mutinied, Sikh MPs resigned, honours were returned and a Sikh diplomat resigned.

The Indian Army's assault on the Harimandir, the holiest shrine in Sikh perception, constituted a "sacrilege", a slur on a nation's dignity and integrity, an act of genocide. The Harimandir, literally the House of God, represents a unique entity. Its buildings were built and dwelt in by several gurus, its sacred pool washed away a devotee's sins; at its centre the Guru Granth was an embodiment of their gurus (Madanjit Kaur 1983). To sit in the inner sancto sanctum, listening to continuous hymn singing from early dawn to dusk is a magical moment and mystical experience for the faithful. Through the daily community prayer, Sikhs seek a pilgrimage to the Harimandir. The Akal Takhat and the Harimandir represent respectively the temporal and spiritual authority of the Khalsa, endowed with divine powers. The Akal Takhat, in traditional Sikh discourse, symbolizes the ideal of political sovereignty and a traditional account cites Ranjit Singh, the Sikh sovereign bowing to its authority. The Indian Army's invasion of the Golden Temple was seen as a third *ghallughara*, a historical term pregnant with the community's resistance to its tyrants.

### State terror and cry for independence

Given the unprecedented army action, the loss of life and destruction caused to the Akal Takhat and the surrounding buildings, this traumatic event dramatically affected the community's duality: attachment towards the Indian state on the one hand and membership of an ethnopolitical community on the other (Smith 1981a). The community's loyalty towards its centre as a religious community clashed with its notional citizenship of a polity. This crucial event shifted many Sikhs' loyalty towards Punjab and sharpened their sense of "collective fate and group boundary" (Smith 1981a). Having declared them *tankhayias* (guilty), the Jathedar of the Akal Takhat excommunicated two Sikhs for bringing dishonour: Zail Singh, the president of India, and Buta Singh, a central government minister. The government hurriedly rebuilt the Akal Takhat but this was pulled down by irate Sikh leaders.

As protests and anger spread, Prime Minister Indira Gandhi was shot dead by her Sikh bodyguards. This led to a Hindu backlash against Sikhs in Delhi and other northern Indian cities, in which 4,000 Sikhs were killed by angry mobs. Having secured the Congress victory by presenting Sikhs as villains of India during the December 1984 elections, new prime minister Rajiv Gandhi tried to salvage the Punjabi crisis by signing a "Punjab Accord" with the Akali leader, Sant Harchand Singh Longowal. As part of the accord signed in July 1985, the union government offered elections to Punjab's state assembly in September 1985, and an Akali Dal government was voted into power, headed by Surjit Singh Barnala. While Sant Longowal paid his life for signing the accord, when he was shot dead by militants on 20 August 1985, the Akali government was undermined by the reluctance of the central government to implement key elements of the accord.[23] As the government slipped on its initiative, space was filled by militants, who converted the community's anger and humiliation into a movement for Khalistan by taking up arms. The government thus defined a limited demand for regional autonomy as "secessionist", and dismantled the means to pacify an ethnic community's "public humiliation" by dismissing a popularly elected Akali government in May 1987.

From 1987 onwards the central government unleashed unprecedented terror on the Punjab. After another attack on the Golden Temple in 1988, Punjab was virtually handed over to the security forces with extraordinary discretionary powers, effectively dismantling the legal framework, resulting in anonymous arrests, secret detention, disappearances, extrajudicial killings and systematic practices of torture (Amnesty International reports, Noorani 1984; Jaijee 1995; PHRO). These measures included the National Security Act 1980, the Armed Forces (Punjab and Chandigarh) Special Powers Act 1983, the Terrorist Affected Areas (Special Courts) Act 1984, the Terrorist and Disruptive Activities (Prevention) Act 1985 (TADA), and the Armed Forces Special Powers Act 1990. As the war raged between the security forces and militants, the civilian population was squeezed into two warring forces; for years terror reigned in the countryside.[24] The militants ran a parallel government, and the state finally gained the upper hand in 1992.[25] As outcry against human rights violations became intolerable, primarily due to the efforts of the Sikh diaspora, the Indian government appointed a National Human Rights Commission in September 1993.[26] Besides internationalizing the homeland issue, the state terror also forced Akali leaders to appeal to the world for justice.[27] By 1995 the Supreme Court took up cases of human rights violations, punishing some police officers, taking a dim view of official explanations.[28]

With over 15,000 Sikhs dead in the battle between militants and the security forces, the central government brought back "democracy" after holding a farcical election in February 1992 boycotted by all main parties (Gurharpal Singh 1992). A Congress ministry took charge headed by Beant Singh, who was later killed in a bomb blast. Meanwhile the security forces continued to hunt Sikh militants, pocketing many awards by "successfully" killing them.[29] By the summer of 1995, with the calm of a graveyard, Punjab assumed its "normality" and the central government allowed Akalis back into the political field. In the February 1997 elections, a coalition of the Akali Dal and the Bhartiya Janata Party was voted to power, and a ministry headed by Parkash Singh Badal took charge from the Congress. The realpolitik of resources bargaining and distribution has returned, the Indian state has "managed" another ethnic conflict and the aggrieved group has returned to normal politics by sharing power for the state government.

## Search for statehood: the dilemma

From a religious sect, the Sikhs have made a long journey towards an ethnonational community. Having existed as an ethnic community under colonial rule, they evolved into a nationality within postcolonial India; and they did this through a complex interaction with the state and through community building by their own elite. In 1947 the state played a role in transforming Sikh fortunes by enforcing mass migration into a compact area, then in the 1980s state terror breached Sikh traditions, institutions and legitimacy, leading to a cry for independence.

The characteristic form of nation building among the Sikh community has been undertaken by the Akali Dal since the 1920s.

Projecting themselves as sole spokespeople for the Khalsa Panth, Akalis have argued that the membership of the Panth "transcends distance, territory, caste, social barriers and even race". They have argued that the religious and political interests of the Sikhs are inseparable, and Sikhs joining the Congress Party and other parties compromise Sikh interests.[30] It was argued that "the state must deal with [the Sikhs] as one people, and not by atomising them into individual citizens" and the Sikhs' loyalty to the secular state was contingent upon the state's recognition of the Sikhs as a collective group with a historic "theopolitical status" (Gurnam Singh 1960). The Akalis' control of the SGPC has allowed them to define Sikh identity through control over intermediate institutions, historic shrines, schools and missions. Since the 1980s there has been a vigorous debate about Sikhs' "national" status.[31] Thus, a vigorous dispute has raged regarding the community's unique origins and the distinct identity of the Khalsa Panth[32] versus those arguing that the Sikh identity is largely a product of nineteenth-century social engineering under a benevolent regime. Moreover, it is said that such "nationalistic" rhetoric sits oddly with the original message of Sikh scriptures.[33] The nativist assertion of "Sikhs are a nation" is opposed by others who point the reality of class, sect and caste cleavages and the vexing goals of Sikh leaders, which have ranged from "accommodation" to "separatism". While a majority have been content with provincial power, others believe in sovereign power (Dhami 1977, 1985; Tara Singh 1945).

> We want more powers only for Punjab – it has nothing to do with other states. We are a nation, Hindus are dominant both at the centre and states, while we have no say at the centre. What I demand is a separate constitution for Punjab – right to issue passports, currency and a separate flag as during the reign of Maharajah Ranjit Singh, centre to have only foreign affairs, defence and communications.

For students of nationalism, it is hardly surprising the community's past traditions and history are being manipulated by the Sikh elite as they seek hegemony in politics and other spheres of social life. The Sikh elite has persistently contested the Indian govern-

31

ment's powers to define its agenda by questioning state control over radio and television, the promotion of Hindi at the expense of Punjabi,[34] official conventions such as "Shri", "Shrimati", instead of community conventions such as "Sardar" and "Sardarni", the subsuming of the Sikh marriage custom under the Hindu Marriage Act of 1955, and the community's inheritance customs under the provision of the Hindu Code Bill. The community's alternative conventions compete with official innovations of a "national anthem", "greeting", honours and patronage of arts and literature.[35] This is seen even more firmly in the sphere of "national memories". Despite daily indoctrination through the media and through holidays, monuments and museums, all intended to create new "national heroes" to forge an Indian identity among various nationalities, the Sikh peasantry seems to have stubbornly refused to exchange its "Punjab heroes" (Gillis 1994: 8). Thus, portraits of Punjabi heroes at the Sikh museum in Amritsar contrast sharply with "Indian nationalist" heroes commemorated in state museums. Numerous gurdwaras in the memory of Sikh martyrs act as "arresting emblems of the modern cultural nationalism" (Anderson 1983: 17), while statues of Gandhi and other Indian leaders, officially patronized, pale against the immensely popular heroes such as Ranjit Singh, Kartar Singh Sarabha, Bhagat Singh and others. That the minority narratives are likely to become mere footnotes in "national narratives" is a powerful reminder for gaining "national status".[36] Above all, the Akal Takhat, destroyed and rebuilt, stands both as the rival centre of cultural power and a testimony to the state's callous disregard for Sikh sentiments. The community's psychology and social condition in the periods before and after 1984 are best summed up by two poets. Before 1984 the mood was relaxed and the nation was "half asleep at her guru's feet" (Mahboob 1990). But the events of 1984 seared the trust that had been built for centuries:[37]

Slowly, and surely, the wounds will heal
broken hearts reconciled
new agreements reached, and differences minimized
But the unsaid trust that existed before
has gone, and gone forever.

After 1984 a yearning for Punjab's independence, like other nationalist projects, became both imagined and contentious. While the powerful memory of the Punjab as a sovereign state under Ranjit Singh has fuelled Sikhs' drive for freedom, past myths and memories of Sikh resistance to the Mogul state are being employed to boost this self-image. In addition, Punjab commands a mysterious bond; its many songs narrate the region's beauty and its many tragedies. To quote Harbhajan Singh again:

Of this land terribly torn apart
Among people hacked and hewn
Were I born again
Let Punjab be my homeland again

This inspired imagination of an independent Punjab has, in some way, been legitimized by the reality of violence in anti-Sikh riots following the murder of the Indian prime minister on 31 October 1984. Some 26,000 Sikh refugee families arrived from other parts of India, and over 1,000 Hindu families moved out from Punjab between 1983 and 1986.[38] Migratory flows probably increased from 1986 onwards, but no reliable data is available.[39] Punjab became not only a safe haven, but also a territory and a symbolic area which was seen to be the Sikhs' own.

Above all, there is material interest in capturing the state per se. The state is seen as a powerful resource by the Sikh elite, who have been part of its coercive apparatus in disproportionate numbers. Far from neutral, the state is seen as a very potent force of coercion and persuasion, and state power is advocated for building a national community out of an ethnic community.[40] The elite is aware that political power determines the difference between culture and folklore, law and custom, religion and sect, faith and superstition. The enduring appeal of Sikh ethnonationalism seems to be because its elite perceives a Sikh heritage that needs state protection. This feeling is widely shared by ordinary Sikhs, who were first mobilized for the formation of a more compact Punjab and then for Punjab's autonomy.

Thus, in seeking security for the community's culture, language and religious traditions, the Sikh elite faces a classic dilemma. Having successfully defined itself as a nation, its logical objective is to create a sovereign state for effective political, economic and social power in determining its own destiny. But this conflicts with the Indian state's project of moulding its nationalities into a nation-state. The search for "territorial sovereignty" is as much a product of historical circumstances as a deliberate project by its elite; the events of 1947 and the feeling of humiliation that developed during and after 1984 have found expression in militancy. As the modern "imaginaire" of a homeland has subsumed the Hindu communities, it should not be surprising that an independent Punjab has become "naturalized" with the Sikh psyche (Appadurai 1990; Oberoi 1987).

However, while there is an underlying thrust towards this view, to use Gellner's words that "the political and the national unit must be congruent", this is compromised by pragmatic and electoral considerations. No leading Sikh leader, not even fiery Sant Bhindranwale, demanded outright independence; even the short paragraph of the Anandpur resolution which hinted at the Sikh sovereignty was diluted when presented to the government. The struggle for a Sikh state arose as a direct result of the Indian state's action at the Golden Temple. The dominant strand of the Akali Dal, on the other hand, has been to share power at the provincial level while promoting a notion of Punjabi nationalism, by offering a coalition with Punjab's Hindus. Given the Sikhs' religious tradition of tolerance and the Akali Dal's experience of coalition politics, a yearning for statehood could find accommodation in a federalized Indian polity. A stable coalition at the provincial level, with devolution of some federal powers, could perhaps strengthen Punjabi nationalist vision within a federalist India.

## Indian nationalism: perils of a nation-state

The rise (and fall) of Sikh ethnic nationalism must be situated within the context of postcolonial Indian state formation, which has engendered and confronted it. The Sikh demand for a linguistic region, and then for a renegotiation of centre–state relations were indistinguishable from similar demands by other regions. In response to the Akalis' demand for acknowledging India as a multinational state, the government asserted:

The Indian people do not accept the proposition that India is a multi-national society. The Indian people constitute one nation. India has expressed through her civilization over the ages, her strong underlying unity in the midst of diversity of language, religion etc. The affirmation of India's nationhood after a long and historic confrontation with imperialism does not brook any challenge. (White Paper 1984: 17)

A cursory examination of the Indian state's policies towards Punjab, Kashmir and some peripheral provinces suggests a rethinking about the nature of India's state-building process. Why, for example, have minority Kashmiris, Punjabis and peoples of the northeastern states been subject to hegemonic and violent control, using terror as a weapon? How can Hindu nationalism pass for Indian nationalism? Wars or aggressive postures have been used as tools in building an official nationalism[41]; and Christians, Muslims and more recently Sikhs have been treated as "others". The project of Indian nation building needs to be examined from three vantage points: its historical context, its ideology and consequent differential impact upon various communities, and the rise of Hindu nationalism.

Historically, the integrating of diverse cultures into a national culture started with colonial rule. By 1900, along with provincial sentiments, say of Bengal and Maharashtra, a general culture of caste, *varana*, and a host of Hindu myths and symbols was articulated into Hindu consciousness, being the citadel of Indian culture:

The work of integrating as a collection of myths, beliefs, rituals and laws into a coherent religion and shaping an amorphous heritage into a rational faith known now as "Hinduism" were endeavours initiated by Orientalists (Knopf 1980, quoted in Thapar 1989).

This Oriental construction of "Hinduism" inspired new nationalists, through revivalist movements in various provinces, but especially in Bengal, Gujarat and Punjab. It became the basis of an overarching "Hindu tradition". While the Indian National

35

Congress widened its framework by adopting cultural nationalism, parallel Hindu organizations left no doubt among minorities
about its constituents and *ethnie*.[42] Despite some Congress
leaders' secular credentials, the essential spirit and mobilization
appeal of the Congress was firmly entrenched in a reformed
liberal Hinduism. According to a member of its constituent
assembly, the secular India was "the maximum of generosity of a
Hindu dominated territory for its non-Hindu population", but on
closer examination, it emerges that the state has been far more
generous to Hindus.[43] Instead of openly aggressive identification
of India as a Hindu nation, the secular version allows the existence
of other traditions, but insists on their subordination to an
overarching Hindu framework (Embree 1972, 1990; Mahmood
1989).

Arguably, the Indian state, as it has evolved over 50 years, can
be characterized as an ethnocracy[44] that has privileged the dominant Hindu communities in three characteristic ways. (a) By dis-
proportionately recruiting civil, military and government elites
from the majority ethnic group.[45] (b) By employing cultural attributes and values of the dominant ethnic community for defining its national ideology, its history, language, religion and moral
values; thus the Indian national identity is neither ethnically neutral nor multiethnic, but derived from a Hindu world serving the
language of universalism. (c) The state's institutions, its constitution, its laws and monopolization of power have had different
effects on different communities, empowering the dominant ethnic community, a common feature of postcolonial states in Africa
and Asia. Myron Weiner has observed:

> In country after country a single ethnic group has taken
> control over the state and used its powers to exercise con-
> trol over others . . . in retrospect there has been far less
> 'nation-building' than many analysts had expected or
> hoped, for the process of state building has rendered many
> ethnic groups devoid of power or influence. (1987: 36–7)

The state has dismantled rules and safeguards devised by the
imperial rulers for fair representation of minorities and for re-

straining majority's tyranny. The adoption of universal franchise has put minorities at a disadvantage, especially in ethnically divided provinces such as Punjab and the northeastern provinces. Its constitutional centralism has led to manipulation and repression of regional nationalisms. Even the second chamber of parliament has no provision for articulating and safeguarding provincial interests, a common practice in many federal polities. Thus, the democratic franchise is effectively for majorities, while minorities are subject to "hegemonic control", including spells of "violent control". In such a context the main ethnic group can effectively "dominate another through its political, economic, and ideological resources and can extract what it requires from the subordinated".[46]

From the 1950s, India's state-building process has affected various non-Hindu communities in a differential way. While adoption of Hindi as official language has put regional languages on the defensive, the drive towards integration and unification of personal laws has aroused suspicion of the Hindu hegemony.[47] In the resources-bargaining process, the central government's enormous powers have reduced provinces into mere municipalities.[48] In the cultural field, central control over education, radio and television, arts and literature, has seen the propagation of Hindu epics and Hindu traditions (Pollock 1993). The mechanics of control have varied from denying access to resources to downright repression with a systematic assault on regional identities.[49] The state-building apparatus has disarticulated non-Hindu identities by defining such ceremonies through a universalistic Hindu order, thus the national anthem, the flag, forms of address, the honours system and state ceremonies are encoded in Hindu mythology.[50]

The rise of Hindu nationalist parties, especially the Bhartiya Janata Party from 1980 to its demolition of Babri Mosque, Ayodhya, in December 1992 have added anxiety for religious minorities.[51] These parties are forging a new Hindu identity out of the mosaics of Hindu communities, so that "each element in this sometimes awkward BJP-VHP-RSS axis (political party, missionary agency, training institute) has had its own part to play in a concerted bid to take control of the country in the name of

Hindutva".[52] Hindu nationalists have a long journey ahead in their aim to create a unified Hindu community, especially as the southern Hindus do not share their enthusiasm for Hindi. However, as rapid modernization levels any caste differences and lessens sociocultural heterogeneity, and as the state provides resources for integrationist projects, the northern Ram may well be adopted by southern Hindus (Rudolph & Rudolph 1988; Manor 1993).

Thus, India's governability crisis, arising from the disintegration of the Congress Party in the late 1970s, has seen extensive manipulation of regional elites and appeal to dominant Hindu voters, due to the central government's electoral compulsions. Slogans such as "nation in danger" and "foreign hand" have become common with the paramilitaries and ultimately the army employed to "fix agitators and extremists".[53] The Indian polity faces enormous tasks in moulding its many nations into a "nation-state" through homogenizing ideologies and repression inherent in forging such a nation-state. Or it could revert back to its early and more realistic project of governing a multinational state, by encouraging regional diversities and building them into the formal structure of a multinational state with substantive citizenship. Whether the dominant Hindu elite could be persuaded from its militantly nationalist ideology towards a vision of pluralist federalism, would determine the fate of Sikhs and other minorities. Forcing unity by further strengthening of the central government could transform "regional forces into secessionist elements" and may disintegrate the country (Brass 1990: 132). Various models of federalism provide judicious division of central and state powers, with adequate safeguards for minorities.[54] Ethnic diversity needs representation through multiple loyalties, with state political structures providing material and symbolic recognition for regional national communities through institutions, ceremonies, flags, and conventions – all the trappings of a state.

While accommodation is the art of politics, as the "restructured" Sikh leadership demonstrates in the 1990s, India's increasingly Hinduized identity and centralization are likely to alienate the Sikh community, both symbolically and materially. The Sikh dilemma and its search for statehood will continue to feed periods of accommodation and rebellion until the Indian state incorporates or subjugates it. The Sikh diaspora is also engaged in this debate and mobilization. The following chapters discuss how overseas Sikhs have contributed to the Punjab and to Indian polity.

# TWO

# The Sikh diaspora: a history of settlement

*Khatan gya – gone away for fortune?*[1]

Of about a million Sikhs abroad, over three-quarters live in just three countries; namely, Britain, Canada and the United States. For a community of 16 million, the proportion of overseas Sikhs is strikingly high, far above that of any other group, except Gujaratis and Mirpuris. No other province has exported so many of its people abroad, especially during the past three decades. The fact this emigration has taken place from a small tract of central districts in the contemporary Punjab lends support to the thesis of a drainage of human resources at an astonishing rate, given that the region itself was on the threshold of massive economic transformation due to the "green revolution" and started importing labour from neighbouring provinces.

Situated on the grand route from Kabul to Delhi, Punjab has seen a mixing of many races and cultural traditions. Waves of invaders have arrived over the centuries, from Aryans to Afghans and also the Moguls. Traders of different races, Afghans, Parsis, Persians, and others operated in Punjabi towns, facilitating trade between the Indus Valley, Persia and the Middle East. However, the history of Sikh emigration is a comparatively modern phenomenon, starting with the establishment of British rule in the Punjab. It can be conveniently divided into two major phases: the colonial emigration and the postcolonial emigration. However, the period after 1984 needs special attention as it consisted of Sikh refugees fleeing from the violent conditions in the Punjab. There are considerable difficulties in charting a comprehensive emigration map of the Sikh diaspora; there are serious gaps in our knowledge of Sikh settlers in Europe and the Far East, especially in Australia, Thailand and Indonesia, but the situation is somewhat better for Malaysia, New Zealand and North America.[2] Not enough is known about crucial factors of emigration from Punjab; for example, how important was the so-called military migration nexus? Given these gaps, a preliminary picture may be gathered from the extant literature (Map 2 and Table 2.1).

**Table 2.1**  Diaspora Sikh population: some estimates.

| Country | Period | Population | Main location |
|---|---|---|---|
| | Colonial period, 1860–1947 | | |
| Americas | | | |
| Argentina | 1950s | 500–1,000 | Major cities |
| Mexico | 1930– | 1,000–1,500 | Major cities |
| Canada | 1905–1913 | 7,500–10,000 | British Columbia |
| USA | 1905–1913 | 7,500–10,000 | Imperial Valley, |
| | 1920–1947 | 3,000 | Sacramento |
| East Africa | | | |
| Kenya/Uganda | 1885–1950 | 5,000– | Nairobi/Mombasa |
| Tanzania | 1880–1920 | 750– | Dar-es-Salaam |
| Europe | | | |
| UK | 1930–1947 | 1,500 | Midlands, Scotland |
| Far East | | | |
| Australia | 1890–1910 | 1,500–2,500 | Sydney, Woolgoogla |
| Fiji | 1890–1910 | 200–500 | Suva |
| Hong Kong | 1900–1940 | 10,000–5,000 | Hong Kong |
| Malaya States | 1865–1940 | 30,000–35,000 | Kuala Lumpur, Perak, Selangor |
| New Zealand | 1890–1910 | 200–382 | Farmlands |
| Philippines | 1910–1930 | 4,000–2,500 | Manila, Quezen City |
| Thailand | 1920–1940 | 2,500–5,000 | Bangkok |
| Indonesia | 1880–1940 | 3,000–6,000 | Sumatra, Jakarta |
| Middle East | | | |
| Afghanistan | 1900–1930 | 2,000–2,500 | Kabul |

**Table 2.1** *Continued.*

| Country | Period | Population | Main location |
|---|---|---|---|
| | Postcolonial period, 1947–90 | | |
| Americas | | | |
| Canada | 1960–1990 | 147,440 | Vancouver and Toronto metros |
| USA | 1960–1990 | 125,000 | California, New England |
| Europe | | | |
| United Kingdom | 1960–1990 | 400,000–500,000[a] | London, Midlands, North |
| Germany | 1960–1980 | 2,500 | Cologne |
| Far East | | | |
| Australia | 1950–1970 | 2,500 | Woolgoogla, Sydney |
| New Zealand | 1950–1980 | 2,500 | Farmlands |
| Singapore | 1940–1950 | 32,000 | North of the city |
| Middle East | | | |
| Abu Dubai | 1970–1980 | 7,500–10,000 | Transient labour |
| Iraq | 1970–1980 | 5,000–7,500 | Transient labour |

[a] Population for several countries is indicated by bands for want of a precise figure.
*Sources*
East Africa: Mangat (1969), Sidhu (n.d.)
Far East: Sandhu (1969), Sidhu (1983)
Americas: for Canada the number indicated is from the 1991 census; for the colonial period see Chadney (1984), Johnston (1988b, 1988c); for the USA see La Brack (1988b)
UK: Knott & Toon (1982), Directory of Religions (1997)
Rest of Europe: estimates

## The colonial era

The imposition of British rule in the Punjab in 1849 on a predominantly rural society generated some profound changes and set in motion a process of gradual integration of its economy into the colonial economic system. Punjab's communication expanded rapidly; between 1873 and 1903 its rail system expanded from 400 miles to over 3,000 miles, and the network of its canals saw an astonishing expansion from 2,744 to 16,893 miles (Calvert 1936: 107). Due to canal irrigation, Punjab became a major wheat-producing region; its export market included Great Britain. Two major colonial initiatives produced a conducive environment: (1) several irrigation projects were developed by diverting river waters leading to the development of Canal Colonies in the western districts; (2) the emergence of Punjab as a favourite region of recruitment for imperial armies (Brief 1984). These two developments in combination encouraged Punjabis to venture out, first within the province from central districts to newly irrigated wastelands of the western areas, and abroad. The Canal Colonies established in wasteland areas, called "bars", led to interdistrict migration, enabling thousands of Jat Sikh peasants of Amritsar, Jullundur, Gurdaspur, Hoshiarpur and Ludhiana to reach the Canal Colony districts of Lahore, Lyallpur, Multan, Montgomery, Jhang and Shahpur. Two new cities of Lyallpur and Montgomery were established and soon grew up into busy trading centres.

By the turn of the century, many peasant families felt able to send one of their men abroad as they could pay for the fare to the Far East and then onwards to the Pacific states. The fare of 200 rupees from Calcutta to Hong Kong and then to Vancouver represented the price of two acres of land by the turn of the century. The responsiveness of Punjabi villagers to opportunities in the far-lying countries, *Telīa* (Australia), *Mirkin* (America) and later *Vilayat* (Britain) was facilitated by the Punjabi economy's integration into the international economy. While agrarian changes encouraged internal migration, the army recruitment policy led to overseas emigration. Of the "martial races" of the Punjab, Jat Sikhs became favourites for army recruitment. From 1858 to the First World War, the share of Sikh regiments increased sharply, and they were deployed in many British colonies: Malaya in the Far East, the Mediterranean, British African colonies and protectorates and in Europe.

Sikh soldiers who saw distant lands were inspired to settle away from the sedentary rural life. Since army service was usually short-term, many of them sought their fortunes abroad when they retired. Army recruitment offered the only outlet for young men tied to the traditional occupation of farming. By enlisting in the armies, many Punjabis could see the outside world either as part of regimental locations or by emigrating after army experiences. In many Punjabi villages, retired army personnel would narrate their adventures to the young, while their brick-built houses with army wages lent authority to their tales. Besides receiving pensions, army men also enjoyed high status and other perks; they could buy land in the Canal Colonies on preferential terms. Thus, thousands of young Sikhs of central Punjab aspired to enlist into the exclusive Sikh regiments and dreamed of the new world. Gradually, the migration experience of Punjabi peasants found many expressions through songs and folklore (Nahar Singh 1987–9). At Punjabi fairs, singers gently mocked the emigrants' dreams:

> For twelve years you roamed abroad,
> for what fortune?
> What did you bring in return?

As the army became a major career for numerous rural Sikhs and Muslims, many songs became popular among Punjabi women, lamenting their men's absence abroad or in the regiments:

> A crow on my roof,
> might not the foreigner return today?
>
> O' crow, I offer you sweets,
> go and bring a message from my beloved abroad.
>
> That delicacy you be served
> Prattle o dusky crow
> on my love's advent from afar

Similarly, many war songs have become part of Punjabi folklore:

> The wedded and newly wedded brides gather around
> Curse the English Lord, who has taken their men to wars
>   abroad
> O'Sahib, if brides wait for too long, you will lose the war.
>
> What a beautiful day it was, when my beloved returned
> sitting under the mango tree, I heard his tales
> of enemy's strength, noisy aeroplanes and fierce
>   combats.[3]

*Between coolies and independent labour*

While the development of the Canal Colonies and army recruitment acted as a catalyst for migration, the beginning of Punjabi
emigration needs to be located in the context of Indian emigration
to colonies, which started much earlier in the eighteenth century.
Two factors meant that Punjab entered this emigration cycle quite
late: Punjab became part of the Indian Empire a century late; and
the shipping agencies, following the flag, did not establish their
posts until the 1880s. By then over two million Indians had been
exported to distant colonies of White settlers in Fiji, Malaya, the
West Indies and the African continent for the exploitation of raw
materials and plantations.

With the abolition of slavery throughout the British Empire in
1807, the system of recruitment from India as a chief source of
labour export was also overhauled. After many reports of ruthless
exploitation of Indian labour in the colonies, coupled with a high
mortality rate during transportation, the East India Company introduced a system of indenture in the 1830s.[4] Although new legal
procedures for the shipping agents were issued, the indentured
system, with all its legal safeguards, according to an eminent
scholar, became a "new system of slavery" (Tinker 1974, 1976,
1977). By the end of the nineteenth century, Indian labourers were
spread across both self-governing dominions and colonies as a
truly imperial phenomenon.[5]

Escaping the worst features of the indentured system, Punjab
entered the orbit of colonial labour migration in the 1860s, when
some Punjabis were enlisted by colonial agents. As agency houses
spread towards Punjab, a few colonies had stopped importing
labour, whereas the Far East and other colonies were still demanding labour for their newly opened regions. By the 1880s
emigration regions had expanded from the southern and eastern
provinces to the northwestern provinces. Fiji's labour was initially
supplied by the southern provinces, but by the 1880s over two-
thirds of its new recruits were enlisted from the northwestern
provinces, and a few came from Punjab. However, Punjab's entry
into the indentured system in the 1870s was a "disappointment".
The first few hundred Punjabis so recruited were found "unsuit-
able" by the planters in the West Indies, who protested that these
Punjabi migrants

are very objectionable as field labour. Many absconded to the Spanish main, refused to work in the fields, and nearly all have been unruly and troublesome.[6]

On the other side of the globe, Punjabis and Pathans who arrived in Fiji also caused trouble by objecting to their conditions. Sir Everard Thurn, the colony's governor, observed their previous occupation as "soldiers or something of that sort" and unused to labour. Tinker (1976: 29) noted that Punjab's migrants were unlike other Indian labourers:

> Sikhs were an unusual group in the India emigration: they were prepared to fight for their rights. The mass of poor labourers mainly from Madras, and the traders and shopkeepers from Gujarat, who formed the bulk of the emigrants were not prepared or organised for struggle.

Those Punjabis recruited by an agent in 1914 complained bitterly of their broken dreams in Fiji, where Indian labour came mainly from the hinterlands of Barodas. These Punjabis sent a petition complaining:

> We, the Punjabis, now residing in Fiji Islands left our country on the inducement and representation of Wali Mohamed and Atta Mohamed; castes Syed, residents of Karnana, Tahsil Nawanshahar, District Jullundur, Punjab. They have been sending our people during the last five years and on each steamer 45 or 46 men are being emigrated while they take 35 Rupees as their commission for each individual and 5 Rupees from the Shipping Company.[7]

The colonial planters' preferences and regulations affecting agency houses were in conflict as an experienced agent for Trinidad at Calcutta told the Colonial Office in 1913:

> It does not appear to be generally understood that we are confined in our recruiting to a class of people who are not the most robust of the natives of India. The enlistment of

47

Punjabis, Sikhs and Nepalis is forbid, as well as those men who have formerly worked as soldiers and policemen. ... The result is that we are confined to drawing our recruits from people who are exposed to famine, drought and flood ... and who at times are forced to undergo long periods of semi-starvation.[8]

Many independent Punjabi migrants sought to take advantage of free passage legislation to many colonies of the empire. Indians could enter the British colonies with a minimum of difficulty, but their entry to most of the dominions was closed after the First World War. The government of India acknowledged such political facts but asked that the White dominions' policies should be so framed "as to avoid wanton injury to the self-respect on non-European British subjects with emphasis put upon exclusion on educational grounds not on grounds of race". Sikhs later contested the "spirit of the free passage" within the empire in a dramatic way in Canada. Sikh emigrants' destinations, in general, were determined by a mixture of factors: indentured labourers went to a prefixed destination; the free labourers could try various colonies and dominions while those emigrating through army connections landed with their British officers in new colonies.

### The Far East

Early Sikh migrants to the Far East were those employed in the police, security forces and railways. These services were in high demand in the Far Eastern colonies. The crucial catalyst was usually the personal influence of British officers who had old Punjabi connections. Thus, when British officer C. V. Creagh, deputy superintendent of police, was transferred from Sind to Hong Kong in 1865–6, he recommended his trusty Sikh policemen from Punjab for the Colony's new police. This resulted in 100 Sikh migrants going to Hong Kong in June 1867, perhaps the first Sikh emigrants to go abroad. Officials were so impressed, they recommended further recruitment.[9] In the 1890s there were three Singh Sabhas in Singapore, Penang and Taiping, and in later years they established close connections with the Chief Khalsa Diwan in

Amritsar. By 1939 Hong Kong's police force comprised 774 Indians, almost all Sikhs, along with 272 Europeans and 1,140 Chinese. In 1952 the police force was Hong Kongized and the Sikh personnel were expelled; many migrated to the United Kingdom.

Sikhs also entered Malaya via army connections; they were recruited by Captain Speedy in 1873 to combat Chinese insurgency among Perak's tin mines. These Sikh recruits were subsequently drafted into other government services and formed the nucleus of state security forces, following the Malay states' passage into British control (Sandhu 1969, 1970). As the security forces expanded, the government started recruiting directly from the Punjab. When news of opportunities in Malaya spread, many independent Sikh migrants arrived and obtained employment in Perak's mines. However, the Malay States Guides and the Straits Settlements Sikh Contingent, two of the principal government bodies employing Sikhs, were disbanded in 1911 and 1926 respectively. Malaya's Sikh population was estimated at 8,295 in 1921; it increased to 15,145 in 1931 and remained at that figure until independence in 1965. In 1980 it was estimated at 32,685 with Punjabi Hindus comprising 5,148. As for geographical location, a quarter of Sikhs live in the capital, the rest of them are in Perak (9,483), Selangor (5,949) and Penang (2,397) with a few in other provinces.[10] The occupational structure has also changed; while moneylending became an important activity from the 1930s, the majority continued to work as policemen, watchmen, dairy farmers and bullock cart drivers till the end of the Second World War.[11]

From Malaya many Sikhs drifted to neighbouring Thailand or Sumatra, while more ambitious individuals set out for Australia and New Zealand. Australia attracted some Sikhs in the 1890s from Hong Kong and the Malay states, which had completed ten-year contracts with the police and security services. Similarly, a few retired policemen from Hong Kong entered New Zealand (McLeod 1984a; Lepervanche 1984). After landing in New Zealand, some left for Fiji, lured perhaps by stories of sugar-cane fortunes. Sikh policemen were also recruited for Fiji from Shanghai and Hong Kong under contract. Some probably stayed after their contract expired.

*East Africa*

African protectorates attracted both indentured and free labour. Indentured labourers were recruited mainly for the Ugandan Railways project in the 1890s. The railway line was constructed by migrant labourers from Punjab; most of them were Muslims and the rest were Sikhs and Hindus. The Sikhs were mostly artisans of the Ramgarhia class. As the railway line progressed, imported labour rose sharply, from 3,948 in 1896 to 6,086 in 1897; another 13,000 men arrived in 1898.[12] A scheme of land plots for Indians employed on the railways was devised as an inducement for permanent settlement, but this was not carried out. Nevertheless, many labourers stayed on. Uganda's Indian community rapidly expanded, and from 1903 it started competing with the Arabs and Swahilis as traders.

Another route for Sikhs to East Africa was through the army. After assuming the company's responsibilities in 1895, the British government decided to establish the East African Rifles with headquarters in Mombasa. At the outset, it comprised 300 Sikh soldiers, 300 Swahilis and 100 Sudanese. During the next few years, the East African Rifles participated in campaigns against Arab rebels and other insurgents. Sikh troops were also employed to quell the mutiny by Sudanese troops in October 1897. However, the contingent was not replaced at the expiration of its contract in 1900. In 1898 the Uganda Rifles and the East African Rifles were merged into the newly founded King's African Rifles for regular service in Nyasaland and Somaliland as well as Uganda and the East African Protectorate.

In Kenya the total number of Sikhs employed in the railways and security services during 1895–1901 was nearly 3,000 (Mangat 1969; Gregory 1972; Hill 1949: 168). They built the first gurdwara at Kilindini in 1892 (Kaur 1977: 66). After the railway line was completed, many Sikhs returned to Punjab. By the 1911 census there were just 324 Sikhs among 2,216 Indian migrants, increasing to 1,619 out of 45,633 Indians in 1921. A second phase, between 1920 and 1929, saw skilled workers migrate to Kenya. By 1948 the Sikh population of Kenya was 10,663, and by the time Kenya gained freedom in 1960 it had increased to 21,169. Kenyan Sikhs participated vigorously in trade unions, sports and various community associations. They were mainly concentrated in Nairobi and in Mombasa, capital of Coast Province, and their occupational structure was highly skewed towards skilled jobs: carpenters, fitters, turners, builders, electricians, clerks, teachers, contractors and shopkeepers.[13] After Kenyan independence, Asians were compelled to leave. Many Sikhs migrated to the United Kingdom and other countries.[14] A few wealthy businessmen stayed on, confident enough to exploit the new nationalist government's economic priorities.

### North America

The beginning of Sikh migration to North America is again attributed to army connections. After parading in London for Queen Victoria's Golden Jubilee in 1887, a Sikh regiment travelled to British Columbia before returning home. In the following years, some of these former servicemen turned up at the Pacific Coast ports of San Francisco and Victoria. They were joined by Sikhs from the Far East, who sailed towards America after serving their terms in the police or the army. Sir Harry Johnson, who had met some of these Sikhs, observed:

> Reserve soldiers of the Indian army who have served with the Malay police or the Hong Kong police . . . in the spirit of adventure they drifted across to the Philippines Islands and engaged themselves in the services of Americans. . . . From there they found their way to Hawaii and then to the States, and some of them stayed in California and others came on.[15]

In March 1903 there were about 300 Sikhs in British Columbia. However, wages were rising from $1.5 to $2 a day and the industry was expanding, so it required more labour. From March onwards, ships arriving from Calcutta brought many Sikhs along with a few Punjabi Hindus and Muslims. In addition, some Sikhs arrived from the Far East. Between 1904 and 1908 over 5,000 Sikhs had settled in British Columbia. However, racial tensions rose sharply. In 1907 some 500 White workers attacked South Asians at a lumber mill in Bellingham, Washington. In August an Anti-Asian League was formed, and the mayor of Vancouver wrote to Governor-General Lord Grey: "the situation with regard to

Hindoos is far more serious, and to speak frankly I see no solution for it, except quietly checking the exodus from India".[16] Sikhs were referred to as Hindus during this period. Teja Singh, a Sikh missionary who was studying at Columbia University, was summoned for help. Shuttling between California and British Columbia's Sikh community, he played a major part in forming the Khalsa Diwan Society in 1907 and proposed the building of a gurdwara. Taraknath Das, an educated Bengali, also offered help; he had set up the Hindustani Association and was inspired by an altogether different idea of Indian independence. However, the government took several measures to stem the "tide of turbans". First a bill disenfranchized all natives of India who were not of "Anglo-Saxon parents". This was followed by an Order in Council in 1908, a "continuous journey" clause for new immigrants. Anti-oriental feelings rose high, and racism broke into song (Ferguson 1975; Hess 1969):

> To orient grasp and greed
> We'll surrender, no ever.
> Our watchword the 'God save the King'
> White Canada for ever.

Sikhs responded with petitions. As a continuous journey from India to Canada simply could not be made, it hit the Sikhs most, as was intended. In February 1908, when the *Monteagle* brought 186 South Asians, nearly all of them were deported under various pretexts. These measures specifically aimed at Sikhs from the Far East produced rapid results; between 1909 and 1913 just 27 passengers were accepted. Even wives and children of those in Canada were covered by the provision. Angry and frustrated, Sikhs held protest meetings, filed cases in courts and sent many petitions to John Morley, secretary of state for India. As a court declared the "continuous journey" provision invalid, the government issued another Order in Council. The government also announced a scheme to settle South Asians in Honduras.

The Khalsa Diwan Society led a delegation to Ottawa, pleading fair treatment for the Sikhs by dropping the "continuous journey clause". The government of India also protested against the Canadian government measures, arguing these restrictions violated the spirit of "free movement of peoples within the British Empire". Badly hit by the immigration restrictions of Pacific states, many Sikhs felt stranded in the Far East. In May 1914 Gurdit Singh, a Sikh businessman, chartered the Japanese ship *Komagata Maru* and collected 376 passengers from Hong Kong and Shanghai, fulfilling just about all the requirements of Canadian immigration laws. The ship anchored at Victoria harbour on 23 May 1914. However, after protracted negotiations, the *Komagata Maru* was forcibly returned. On landing at the port of Calcutta, anger exploded into a bloody clash between the awaiting policemen, resulting in many casualties. The unsuccessful voyage of the *Komagata Maru* dented many Sikh soldiers' loyalty to the empire, and opened their minds to Congress's nationalist propaganda.

Meanwhile many Sikhs, almost one in three, slipped out of British Columbia to the neighbouring states of Washington, Oregon and California, where conditions were slightly better. In Washington and Oregon they moved into well-paid jobs in the lumber industries; others gained employment on the Pacific Railways; and the unskilled formed roaming bands of farm labourers from the rice-growing areas of Marysville and Yuba City to the fruit areas of the Sacramento Valley. In 1910, parallel to Vancouver, a Pacific Khalsa Diwan Society was established with the help of rich landowner Jawala Singh under the inspiration of Teja Singh. Jawala Singh supported many Punjabi workers on his ranch and also arranged scholarships for students at Berkeley. A gurdwara was established in Stockton in 1915.

Sikhs' presence in the Pacific states was as irksome as in Canada, and their work pattern was resented by White workers.[17] Due to strict immigration controls and racial hostility promulgated by the Asiatic Exclusion League, the situation grew worse. Immigration controls meant they could not bring their families, but a novel solution appeared. Lala Hardayal, a Hindu intellectual, was experimenting with his revolutionary ideas, and sought freedom for India as part of his philosophy. Sikh workers responded to his ideas with unusual enthusiasm. As Hardayal gave a call to return to India, over 3,000 Sikhs left the Pacific states, reducing the Sikh population there to a few hundred. Just 700 Sikhs remained in Canada; they worked in lumber mills and logging camps, and some of them were illegal immigrants. Only in 1947 did they gain voting rights, and in 1950 a new quota for Indian immigration opened the way for fresh Sikh migration.

Between 1904 and 1923 over 10,000 Sikhs had settled in California but due to strict immigration rules, introduced in the 1920s, their strength was reduced to just 3,000 in 1947. Between 1923 and the 1930s there were probably about 3,000 illegal migrants who entered from the Mexico border. They lived in small isolated communities from 1920 to 1947. They could not own land, as in May 1913 the California Alien Land Act restricted the right to register land to American citizens only. In 1917 further restrictions barred Asian immigration, and the right of Asians to become American citizens was lost in 1923, when the US Supreme Court delivered its verdict in the Thind case on a Sikh farmer's right to buy land. The court ruled that Asian Indians could not be classified as "free White persons", so they were not entitled to citizenship. They had no voting rights. These Sikh men eventually married into Mexican families in the Imperial Valley. In a survey of Mexican-Sikh families in the late 1960s, Littlejohn (1964) warned of the imminent dissolution of the Punjabi community:

> The first generation are beginning to die out and the second and third generation are rapidly losing their ethnic and religious identifications as Punjabis. Complete assimilation to American culture whether of the Mexican-American or Anglo variety appears inevitable within a generation or two unless a substantial number of new Sikh and Moslem immigrants both male and female appear on the scene. Given present US immigration policies, the likelihood of this occurring, although theoretically possible, seems rather remote.

Sikh cultural life was gradually replaced by a younger generation who were baptized as Catholics, spoke English and Spanish at home, and married among Americans or Mexicans (Leonard 1992). However, this process was completely reversed as during the 1950s American immigration policies opened the gates to Asian migration.

# The postcolonial era

With the British departure from India in August 1947, the partition of the Punjab led not only to a vast process of internal migration, it also encouraged emigration to overseas countries. By the 1950s many British colonies had gained independence while the Far Eastern countries had stopped Punjabi immigration as soon as they gained freedom. However, new avenues for migration opened up. Britain itself started importing labour and became a major destination for Sikh emigrants. More surprisingly, North America reopened its gates to South Asians, reversing its earlier policies. The opening of the West coincided with the partition of Punjab. Many Sikh refugees uprooted from Pakistani Punjab and facing uncertainty, especially in the congested districts of Doaba, took the gamble to settle abroad. The Malwa region joined in this exodus some years later. From the 1950s, thousands of Sikh peasants sailed for Britain and Canada, while America attracted a mixture of peasants and professionals.

*United Kingdom*

In the nineteenth century a lonely Sikh prince, Dalip Singh, lived among the royal aristocracy. With the British annexation of the Punjab in 1849, Dalip Singh was exiled to Britain in 1856. The last heir to the sovereign Punjab, he lived much of his life on a Suffolk estate and died in 1893. At the turn of the century, a few Sikh artisans, princes and Punjabi students passed through Britain and returned home after their brief sojourns. It was in the 1930s that a small community of Punjabi Muslims and Bhatra Sikhs grew up in the Midlands and in the North, most of whom worked as pedlars. The Bhatra Sikhs emigrated from a cluster of villages in Sialkot district, while the Muslims came from Jalandhar district.

From the 1950s, as Britain started importing labour from its colonies, many Sikh ex-servicemen were persuaded to migrate by the voucher system. Others mortgaged their land to pay for the passage. Although their intention was to make a quick fortune and return, a succession of restrictive immigration laws coupled with a taste for new life meant the return was postponed, and families joined for permanent settlement. Migration from Punjab peaked in the late 1960s, gradually decreasing almost to a halt in the 1980s.[18] Britain's Punjabi Sikhs were augmented by East African Sikhs from Kenya and Uganda in the 1970s, and a further addition comprised Far Eastern Sikhs, especially from Hong Kong, who used their connection with the "mother country". These "twice migrants" tended to settle in London's suburbs, while Punjabi Sikhs bought their first houses near their factories. Estimates of Sikh population in the United Kingdom vary from 300,000 in 1981 to over 500,000 in the 1990s,[19] with a concentration in the Midlands industrial towns and in the North. The first-generation Sikhs worked mainly as industrial workers, only a few were employed in clerical and professional jobs. However, Sikhs from the Far East and East Africa brought capital and professional skills, and they have also moved to a better class of housing. However, irrespective of their background, Sikhs have shared middle-class ambitions of good education for their children and put a high premium on house ownership. As the second generation is now passing through schools and colleges, the occupational and social structure of the community is undergoing radical changes, from predominantly manual industrial labour to skilled occupations.

### United States

Both Canada and the United States reversed their earlier policies on Asian immigration in the 1940s. In the United States, the Luce-Cellar Bill (Public Law 483) removed Asian Indians from its "Barred Zone" in 1946 and allocated a quota of 100 immigrants per year. This quota was gradually increased. Old Sikh migrants sent for their relatives and fresh migrants rushed in thousands. Between 1950 and 1966 a majority of Asian Indians arriving in the United States were Sikhs. After 1966 the ratio of Sikh emigrants among Indians dropped progressively; in the 1980s it was probably less than 5 per cent. In rural areas of California the Sikh population has increased swiftly; Yuba City, a peach-growing area, had 400 Sikhs in 1948 and 6,000 in 1981. They had built three gurdwaras, the first of which was opened in 1967. The Sikh population of America was estimated at 60,000 in 1980, increasing to 180,000 in the 1990s.[20] Thus fresh migration has completely reversed the process of a disappearing minority group to "one of the fastest growing immigrant population" (La Brack 1988b). With fresh arrivals, the occupational structure has also undergone a radical shift from a predominantly rural farming community of the California valleys to a significant number of professionals. The geographical distribution has also changed form early migrants' concentration in the Imperial, Jan Quin and Sacramento Valleys of California; new arrivals have settled evenly in New England and the southern states, though the Sacramento Valley contains the highest density. In rural areas they are mainly engaged in farming orchard crops, peaches, prunes, almonds and walnuts; while among professionals the majority are doctors and engineers.

### Canada

Canada, like America, liberalized its immigration policies in the 1960s, leading to a sharp rise in Sikh immigration. In addition to a quota for Indian emigrants, regulations regarding the entry of relatives have allowed old Sikh migrants, only a few hundred in the 1940s, to call their kin to join them. This has created a process of chain migration. As a result, the share of independent professionals from India has fallen sharply; from over 40 per cent in the period 1968–72 to less than 2 per cent in 1983–4; in 1984, 94 per cent of Indian immigrants were sponsored relatives (Johnston 1988b). Twenty years of chain migration have meant the number of South Asians has increased from a total of 7,000 in 1961 to 67,710 Sikhs and 69,500 Hindus in 1981. Of these, 22,392 Sikhs and 6,865 Hindus had settled in Vancouver. According to the 1991 census, Canada's Sikh population was 195,000; and with a primary migration of nearly 5,000, the Canadian Sikh population is rising more sharply than any other Western country and is likely to overtake the British Sikh population in the next decade. The major destinations of Sikh migrants are British Columbia and Ontario. The increase in numbers has been reflected through associations and the number of gurdwaras. Starting with three gurdwaras in the regions of Vancouver and Victoria, four more were established in the 1980s. In Toronto four gurdwaras were established during the same period.

From the 1970s, Sikh migrants have also worked in the Middle East, usually on fixed-term contracts. With oil price rises in 1974, many Arab countries launched major construction projects in

Dubai, Oman, Saudi Arabia, Bahrain, Iraq and other countries. Thousands of Sikh peasants and artisans emigrated as contractual labour. However, their numbers have fluctuated sharply due to demand factors and also due to hostilities in the region.[21]

## Post-1984 emigration: Sikh refugees

Post-1984 Sikh emigration deserves careful study. From the 1980s, Punjab witnessed unprecedented political mobilization and increasing incidents of violence. As a reaction to the army action in the Golden Temple, several militant groups sprang up and campaigned for Sikh independence. The bloody clashes between militants and the security forces led to many civilian casualties, and from 1987 as the security forces adopted a "bullet for bullet" policy, virtual suspension of the judicial system closed almost all avenues for seeking justice. Sweeping powers assumed by the security forces resulted in indiscriminate killing, including hundreds of civilians suspected of abetting terrorism, a term interpreted quite liberally. Insecurity was also created by the anti-Sikh riots following the murder of the Indian prime minister on 31 October 1984, when many Sikhs became a target of violence in New Delhi and northern Indian cities, creating an exodus of Sikh families to the Punjab. Some families tried to escape abroad (Table 2.2).

No reliable data are available on overseas Sikh refugees. However, certain characteristics are suggestive of their probable numbers and settlement in various countries. All emigrants are young males who have fled their homes due to fear for their own safety or that of their families. Their destination is usually decided by a particular person's acceptance in a country or by encouragement from friends living abroad. Thus Thailand, the Philippines, Malaysia and Singapore in the Far East have each become home to perhaps several hundred refugees. Similarly, Belgium, Germany and the Netherlands are European countries with sizable populations of Sikh refugees, ranging from perhaps a few hundred to several thousand. Starting in 1984, 1,083 Indian citizens sought asylum in Germany, in 1986 the number increased to 6,554, and in 1996 it was 4,130; presumably the majority of these applicants

**Table 2.2**   Sikh refugees.

| Country | Year | Population | Main location |
|---|---|---|---|
| Europe | | | |
| Austria | 1990– | 500–600 | |
| Belgium | 1981– | 4,500–6,000 | Brussels |
| Denmark | 1981– | 1,250–1,500 | Copenhagen |
| France | 1982– | 3,000–4,000 | Paris |
| Germany | 1981– | 11,000–13,000 | Cologne, Hamburg, Stuttgart, Frankfurt |
| Netherlands | 1984– | 2,500–3,500 | Amsterdam, Rotterdam |
| Norway | 1984– | 750–900 | Oslo |
| Switzerland | 1983– | 3,000–4,500 | Zurich, Geneva |
| UK | 1984– | 5,000–7,500 | London, Midlands |
| Far East | | | |
| Australia | 1984– | 700–1,000 | Sydney |
| Thailand | 1984– | 1,500–2,500 | Bangkok |
| Hong Kong | 1984– | 500–600 | |
| Malaysia | 1984– | 500–750 | |
| North America | | | |
| Canada | 1981– | 4,500–7,500 | British Columbia and Ontario |
| USA | 1984– | 7,500–9,000 | California, New York |

*Sources*: All estimated figures have been deduced from reports assuming Sikhs are about half the total Indian asylum seekers. The following sources were used to calculate the above estimates: for United States, INS figures; for Canada, Immigration and Refugee Board reports; for UK, Immigration and Nationality reports; for all other countries, UNHCR figures for Indian asylum seekers. For Far Eastern countries, the UNHCR could not provide any figures, hence these are approximate numbers. Many other countries, such as Italy, Portugal, Russia, Spain, Sweden and New Zealand, each had less than 500 Sikh refugees.

were Sikhs. None was accepted as a refugee, but a majority have been granted a temporary stay. The United Kingdom has also granted temporary stay for asylum seekers, although the numbers are uncertain. Between 1979 and 1985 out of 67 Sikhs that applied for asylum, 4 were accepted. From January 1984 to September 1992 some 5,900 Indian citizens, excluding dependants, had applied for asylum; the majority of these applicants were Sikhs. Since 1984 no applicants have been found to be "genuine refugees", but nearly 800 of those refused asylum have been granted exceptional leave to stay.[22] In the 1990s, the asylum seekers from

India increased gradually from 126 in 1987 to 3,255 in 1995.[23] In several cases, medical reports confirmed they were tortured by the Indian security forces.[24]

Canada, although most liberal of all the Western countries, has taken a tough attitude towards Sikh applicants. Between 1981 and 1984, 2,800 Sikhs had applied for asylum, but they were ordered for deportation by the Conservative government. Sikhs pleaded that, in ending the moratorium, Canada was condemning many Sikhs to interrogation by the Indian police, sending them to jail, torture and even death. But most were unable to prove they would be subjected to persecution if they returned to India. Sikh leaders have made repeated unsuccessful representations to the Canadian authorities to have this decision rescinded. In 1987 a shipload of Sikh refugees who arrived from Europe were given a hostile reception.[25] Arriving from Rotterdam in July 1987, on the cargo ship *Amelie*, 173 men and one woman landed at Charlesville, on the southwest coast of Nova Scotia. The immigration minister took a hard line, and Sikhs were further surprised by the public outrage and lack of sympathy. Community leaders offered bonds and hired legal firms for assistance. However, the government was remarkably indifferent to their pleas and its attitude contrasted sharply with the sympathetic hearing accorded other groups of refugees.[26] Still, because of the large Sikh community already settled in Canada, the number of Sikh refugees seeking asylum has been large – about 500 applicants annually since the 1980s.[27] The United States also has several hundred Sikh refugees, of which only a few have been granted asylum. From 34 Indian asylum seekers in 1990, numbers increased to 4,623 in 1994 then 8,010 in 1996. The Immigration and Naturalization Service assumes that Sikhs form a majority of Indian applicants. Sensational stories have appeared in newspapers, highlighting "economic migrants" in the guise of refugees, while the number of cases granted asylum has been small.[28] Several cases are being contested through the courts as India has demanded extradition of certain Sikh applicants.[29]

Overall, although many countries have provided protection under refugee laws to fleeing Sikhs, only a few Sikhs have been granted refugee status in any country. Partly because of strict refugee policies in European countries, and the perception of Sikh applicants, almost all such applicants are treated as economic migrants. The dividing line between illegal economic migrants and legal refugees has become blurred, and this was dramatically displayed by the case of a Sikh illegal migrant; deported from Germany in May 1994, he was tortured to death within days of his arrival in India.[30] Some countries have sent independent observers to India to assess Sikh applicants. Faced with many Sikh applicants in 1991, Switzerland sent a mission to India; according to its report, "the brutal methods used by the police and paramilitary forces are driving an increasing section of common people to express their sympathy and support for the militants". Although the team did not approve of "the manner in which the militants carry on their struggle", it confirmed the existence of a warlike situation in the Punjab.[31] Others have sought expert counsel or drawn on other countries' assessments, thus the Canadian Immigration and Refuge Board and the United States Department of Justice have prepared substantial reports on the changing situation in the Punjab. The presence of Sikh refugees, with their experience of an embittered Punjab and their uncertain status, has affected the general atmosphere of the Sikh diaspora.

## Conclusion

Almost a million Sikhs currently live abroad; a majority emigrated voluntarily, a small minority were "pushed" by political events and most recently several thousands fled to escape state violence. Although many countries have Sikh communities, Britain, Canada and the United States account for three-quarters of Sikh emigrants. During the colonial period, single men ventured abroad to seek their fortune, but the postcolonial migrants came as settlers. Decolonization has also seen remigration of Sikhs from East Africa and the Far East to countries of the West. The overseas Sikhs share a common experience of discrimination, as an easily identifiable group of "outsiders" and a culture-bearing group. Variously labelled as East Indians in Canada, Asian Americans in the United States and Blacks or Asians in the United Kingdom, most Sikhs have acquired citizenship. However, becoming citizens in a legal sense has not eased their integration into the host society's social and political structure. As an easily identifiable group, they seem to share a sense of collective fate. This is often revealed through racial incidents, by latent or explicit hostility towards their cultural or religious demands and the general insensitivity of their hosts. Although having different social backgrounds and diverse migration experiences, a majority of them can still trace their roots to the greater Punjab, even as the land they left behind has undergone partition and further reorganization.

If the diaspora grows out of painful propulsion or separation of people from their homeland, Sikh migrant communities obviously fail to meet this essential criterion. But this needs to be qualified for the post-1984 migrants, who were forced to abandon their homes due to the political situation in the Punjab. However, on an alternative definition, which emphasizes migrants' relationships with their homeland, overseas Sikhs constitute a diaspora. And as will be seen later, in many ways the Sikh diaspora is a microcosm of the Punjab's Sikh society. How the overseas Sikh communities have interacted and maintained an active relationship with the homeland, and the kind of exchanges built with the Punjab are considered in the following chapters.

THREE

# The Sikh diaspora and the Punjab: dialectics of ethnic linkages

Under oath you are, my love, in lands afar to return again to your
native land

Lo, my brother has from far off lands sent a hand-fan with tuning
bells bedecked[1]

Overseas Sikh communities have a complex web of exchanges
with the Punjab in an ongoing process of mutual dependence.
Sikhs have sought to reproduce many of their social norms, culture and religious values in their new homes and social networks
in various cities of Britain and North America. This process has
been facilitated by a strong attachment to the Punjab, cheaper
travel, and the increasing availability of media and communication channels, resulting in many kinds of contacts and flows of
information to and from the Punjab. The net result is a collective
identity that, despite the local and national influences of each
country, has strong Sikh and Punjabi elements embedded in it.
The Sikh diaspora's interrelationship with the Punjab can be conveniently understood in terms of economic, social, religious and
political linkages. There is an urgent need for further research on
much scattered material about the linkages of the early Sikh migrants. However, the emphasis here is on contemporary developments within the diaspora's multifarious connections with the
Punjab (Barrier 1989).

## Economic linkage

Early Sikh migrants remitted a high proportion of their earnings to support their families left behind. Most had intended to return to Punjab and dreamt of a comfortable family life. As many shared a peasant background, owning land in their ancestral villages was considered "real wealth". Reflecting this, considerable amounts of overseas remittances went to augment family farms by buying more land in the home village, sometimes in nearby villages or even in other districts and states. From the 1960s, farm prices in Doaba villages rose sharply due to this factor. Sikhs with nonfarming backgrounds invested in new houses and urban properties besides maintaining considerable savings in the banks. Many village and town banks had large savings accounts deposited by overseas Sikhs. These remittances have enriched the rural economy of the Punjab, resulting in the establishment of factories, warehouses, machine workshops and transport companies in Jalandhar, Ludhiana, Chandigarh and other towns. The impact of Sikh visitors, increasing in volume after a lull due to violent conditions has benefited the Punjabi economy in general.[2] While a few Sikhs have built houses for retirement, many others have invested in various businesses.

Schemes for "help-back-home" have taken many forms, from individual remittances to "Welfare Societies" for particular villages. Thus, for example, two large villages in Jalandhar and Hoshiarpur district have received considerable aid from their ex-villagers in the West.[3] In Canada another village society has highlighted its pioneer migrants by publishing a book.[4] Various Punjabi charities have been beneficiaries of diaspora benevolence. A collection box at the Khalsa Diwan Society, Vancouver, and the Sikh Missionary Society in Southall on behalf of Pingalwara, a major charity institution for the destitute in Amritsar, suggests such practices are well established. Many educational institutions, hospitals and charities have benefited from overseas remittances. In 1900–10 the Sikhs' premier institutions, Khalsa College, Amritsar, and Kanya Mahavidiala School, Ferozepore, received substantial overseas help. Funds are usually channelled through dedicated missionaries, *granthis* or *sants*.

Several projects were funded from Malaya, such as Bhai Ditt

Singh Kanya Pathshala and Takhat Singh Girls High School at Ferozepore. From East Africa, Sikh migrants sent large donations for Diwan's Educational Conferences, schools and other charities.[5] Thus, Sant Domeliwale, based in the Midlands, undertook several projects involving four schools, a college in east Punjab and repairs to historic Sikh shrines in west Punjab and Pakistan.[6] Appeals and donations for religious causes and charities appear regularly in the Punjabi media. A hospital of 80 beds in a rural setting was undertaken wholly from British and North American donations.[7] A similar hospital has been built in the memory of Kartar Singh at Sarabha.[8] Another village, Sang Dhesian, has established a college for women, which offers an innovative curriculum of computer training, nursing and textile technology along with liberal arts.[9] A further college in rural Jalandhar has been built by a British businessman in memory of his son, who died young while studying at the London School of Economics.[10] Among many other projects, Batala Kar Seva Project and Guru Gobind Singh College at Jandiala are further examples of overseas aid. The Batala Project consists of a sacred pool, a museum and a college.[11]

In aggregate terms, the contribution of overseas Sikhs to the Punjab's educational, social and economic projects must be substantial. Though little documented, the "green revolution" strategy in the Punjab was partly financed by emigrants' remittances. The financial clout provided by relatives abroad helped many Punjabi peasants to take risks with the newly introduced hybrid varieties of wheat in the 1960s. In parts of Jalandhar and especially Hoshiarpur, where waterlogging formed a major hindrance to farm productivity, overseas funds provided for many preventive measures. Similarly, investments in new agricultural machinery, seeds, harvesters and tube wells were undertaken from overseas funds. From Britain, under a scheme set up by the Punjabi government, many Sikhs helped their relatives by sending tractors. Finance Minister Dr Jagjit Singh Chohan, who later played another role, visited Britain in 1968 and appealed to Sikhs:

> The Punjab government appreciates the contribution of overseas Sikhs in the development of the Punjab. To facilitate this valuable assistance, the Punjab government has

through liaison with central and foreign governments formulated a scheme under which you can now send a tractor or other agricultural machinery to your relatives without paying excise tax. This would mean your relatives will get a valuable component of machinery to increase productivity on the land. You would be helping them in a most effective way.[12]

It is estimated that about 3,000 tractors, mostly Massey Ferguson, were sent to Punjab. Total remittances from overseas Sikhs formed a substantial sum, a quarter of the total remittances to India from abroad, estimated to be half a billion American dollars ($500 million) per year (La Brack 1989; Helweg 1983). However, estimates of these annual flows are beset by many difficulties, and there is no serious study on how they have been used either at a village level or as a whole; there seem to have been multiple uses.[13]

## Social exchange

Overseas Sikh families continue to draw on the Punjab to bring husbands or wives for their offspring. An extended family is the norm for many Sikhs, especially in Canada, and it has expanded their economic power and prestige. Each country's immigration laws have to some extent modified this matrilineal behaviour. British Sikhs due to stringent laws, as a rule, do not look for a Punjabi bride or bridegroom. In Canada, the liberal immigration laws have encouraged them to choose brides and bridegrooms from the Punjab. A Canadian Sikh marriage alliance has often meant that a family emigrates, rather than just a bridegroom or bride. Marriage partners are now increasingly chosen across the continents.[14] In choosing partners, social castes and groups continue their significant roles. Endogamy and adherence to social classes in terms of marriage partners apply; thus Jat Sikhs tend to marry into Jat Sikh families, Bhatras with Bhatras, while Ramgarhias marry into their own groups. Outmarriages into the host society are almost insignificant, while interreligious marriages with Hindus or Muslims almost rare. A Sikh marriage is invariably conducted in a gurdwara, through the *anand karj* ceremony. A legal ceremony is also concluded in many gurdwaras; both the legal and religious ceremonies are completed simultaneously. The marriage rituals, such as *milni*, and the "bride dowry" continue to play their part in the marriage alliances. For many families, marriage remains an important occasion to display their solidarity and wealth among their kin. The practice of the "dowry" has assumed considerable proportions and has been exercising the minds of community leaders in all three countries.[15] Older parents have served as important functionaries in the continuation of rituals and ceremonies.

In all countries, Sikhs have consciously tried to maintain cultural and social norms of their origins. In a sense, the Punjabi diaspora seems to have accepted little influence from the host societies' cultural and social milieu as far as family norms are concerned; indeed, the direction of change suggests consolidation rather than fragmentation. This contrasts sharply with the earlier period of Sikh migrants in North America, who were cut off from their families due to stringent immigration controls. As a result, a small Punjabi-Mexican community had grown up in the Imperial Valley through interracial marriages (Leonard 1992). Outmarriages which were quite common among earlier Sikh males, especially in the Imperial Valley of California, have proved an exception. The governing principle for family relations retains elements of Punjabi patriarchal society. The emphasis on family *izzat* (honour) is central to interfamilial relationships, with stipulated duties of sons and daughters, and rather firm ideas about the place of a woman within a household.

While marriages are invariably arranged, rules and rituals associated with ceremonies such as birth, marriage, death and kinship relationships derive many conventions from Punjabi society. All existing research suggests that second- and third-generation Sikhs also adhere, by and large, to Punjabi cultural norms (Thompson 1974; Chadney 1984; La Brack 1988b). The reproduction of Punjabi cultural life, through the popularity of video films, Bhangra groups, *balti* or *karhahi* restaurants, and *salwar kameej* showrooms of Southall and Vancouver, attests to the existence of a vibrant ethnic market. Indeed, concern has been expressed about excesses of patriarchal values, such as unethical marriage alliances, especially in Canada, and the abuse of sex determination techniques.[16]

## Language and culture

Punjab's predominantly rural society is an heir to a varied heritage of traditional dances, folktales and many festivals. Some of them are reproduced in the diaspora. Thus, traditional dances such as *bhangra* and *giddha* are quite common at various social occasions. At political rallies, revolutionary poetry is equally common; while a *bhangra* band plays at most weddings and *dhadis* narrate ballads of bravery against the Mogul rulers, the glory of Sikh rule, the Anglo-Sikh wars and other martyrs' songs in the gurdwaras. Romances of *Hir, Mirza*, or folktales of *Dulla* and *Puran* still attract a considerable audience. The rise of the video culture and the decline of cinemas has led to many videos produced especially for diaspora tastes. The Punjabi dance *bhangra* has become a byword for Asian music, especially in Britain. Although it had a humble beginning in the 1960s, several bhangra groups became quite prominent by the 1980s.[17] Among these bands, Malkit Singh, with his melodies of nostalgia, has become very popular.[18] While maintaining their regional roots in Punjabi lyrics, the bhangra bands are trying to "cross over" into Western music. British bhangra groups perform in places as far apart as Los Angeles, Frankfurt and Singapore, whereas Punjab's pop singers make regular appearances in the diaspora. Punjabi and Asian films, videos and magazines marketed through Asian shops have added to the family entertainment and cultural environment of Sikh families and have contributed to a metropolitan Punjabi identity.

Of the Punjabi sports, *Kabaddi* still remains popular. Matches have been organized in Britain every summer; in North America there are matches in Vancouver and Yuba City. Teams from Punjab, England, Canada and Pakistan have taken part in tournaments in Southall, Vancouver and Yuba City during the past decade. These international events require considerable cooperation, as shown by this letter from across the Atlantic:

You will be glad to note that the Khalsa Diwan Society, Vancouver is holding its annual sports tournament on 16–

18 May 1992. Reputed players from Canada, usa, uk and India are taking part. On behalf of the Society I request you to bring your Kabaddi team with 12 players to take part in this tournament. . . . The society will provide for your group free boarding, lodging and medical facilities during your stay in Canada. . . . Your participation in the last year's tournament was a great success.[19]

Punjab's ministers or officials have accompanied these teams, and business people have provided shirts, overalls and cash. Some players, such as Fiddu, have become household names and *Kabaddi* players have even formed a society to negotiate better rewards.[20] Players from home have been honoured by various gurdwaras; this happened when a women's hockey team from Punjab made a tour of Britain, Canada and California. A number of Sikh athletes have also been sponsored by the gurdwaras.

Punjabi, the language of Sikh scriptures, has gradually become a fundamental part of Sikh identity. This attachment to language has resulted in the establishment of many weekend schools managed by gurdwaras. As the spoken language of Sikh homes is invariably Punjabi, second- and third-generation youngsters are growing up in a bilingual environment. Many are encouraged to gain literacy through weekend schools. In the United States, residential camps for young pupils during school holidays provide an intensive course in music, language and religious studies. The number of young British Sikhs who can read and write Punjabi has shown a slow but steady increase.[21] Their problems in learning Punjabi have seen much discussion through regular conferences of Sikh teachers and through the Punjabi media. The poor quality of teaching is mainly attributed to the lack of relevant teaching materials. In recent years, bilingual Punjabi learners are getting some recognition from enterprising publishers, who have published dual-language books for infant and junior pupils. For high schools, Sikh teachers have published a variety of teaching materials.[22]

Almost all gurdwaras maintain a library of religious literature, fiction, history and general books. Where there is a comparatively large Sikh population, such as Southall in London or Surrey in

South Vancouver, local libraries have also responded by stocking Punjabi titles and newspapers. Moves to run community schools with Sikh religion and Punjabi language as major parts of the curriculum are in their experimental stages in Vancouver and Southall.[23] In Vancouver two Khalsa schools have established Punjabi and Sikh studies as an integral part of the school curriculum.[24] In British Columbia, despite many efforts by some teachers and community leaders, Punjabi has found no recognition in mainstream schools. It is mainly through summer camps and voluntary gurdwara schools that young Sikhs learn their mother tongue. In America, summer camps are organized regularly and an intensive course in Punjabi is usually available. Learning Punjabi at university level is available at the University of British Columbia, and in America at the Universities of Columbia and Berkeley. Graduate students with an interest in South Asian studies join these classes and pass various modules.

Community leaders have often canvassed for Punjabi language provision on radio and television across the three countries. In Britain the BBC's Asian language provision has been questioned by Sikhs' assertion that Punjabi, as the main spoken language of South Asians, is being discriminated against by a forceful minority of Hindi and Urdu protagonists.[25] Similarly, Canadian and American business people have sponsored some programmes on television. In Canada, Punjabi programmes are well established; on a typical Saturday, a variety of programmes are relayed on a multicultural channel, among them *Rangila Punjab*, *Sanjha Punjab* and *Ankhila Punjab* seem quite popular. Efforts to launch a worldwide Punjabi channel have not yet succeeded, but such rumblings suggest strong sentiments towards the community's linguistic heritage.

This linguistic inheritance is also seen through a considerable corpus of diaspora literature spanning creative fiction, travel writing and poetry. Diaspora Punjabi literature unfolds a world of Punjabi sensibilities and its relation with the host societies. Major themes revolve around nostalgia, alienation and narratives of familial crises. Poetry, the largest component of this literature, consists of heroic ballads and religious songs alongside revolutionary chants. Such Punjabi publications by diaspora writers have attracted critical acclaim from literary critics and prizes from the Punjab. There are literary societies in all major cities with a Sikh population. Britain's first Progressive Writers Association was formed in Southall in 1964. Alongside its literary societies, which date from the 1970s, Canada also boasts a drama group. Canada and Britain hold regular poetry sessions and literary events.

Diaspora writers have organized three international conferences: a World Punjabi Writers conference was held in London in 1980, this was followed by a second in Vancouver and a third in Hong Kong in 1991. In June 1997 a major international gathering of Punjabi writers took place at the Milwaukee campus of the University of Wisconsin; it received generous funding by a local Sikh businessman, Darshan Singh Dhaliwal, and coincided with the establishment of a chair in Punjab studies. Darshan Singh Dhaliwal has also patronized a major literary academy of the Punjab, and a Canadian award is offered to Punjab-based authors.[26] Such literary and social events in the diaspora find regular coverage in the news media of Punjab.[27]

Another vital link between Punjab and its diaspora is the press. The Punjabi media in each country consists of weekly newspapers and monthly and quarterly magazines. They have been established by enterprising businesspeople and writers (Tables 3.1 and 3.2). From the first Punjabi monthly, established in 1907 in Vancouver, to the contemporary *Des Pardes*, a Southall weekly, the Punjabi media has played a vital role by informing overseas Sikhs about their homeland. Of the defunct weeklies, the *Gadr* launched from San Francisco, was the most prominent; it circulated in the Punjabi diaspora of Canada, the Philippines, Hong Kong, China, the Malay states, Siam, Singapore, Trinidad and Honduras.[28]

Of the contemporary media, *Des Pardes* has the largest circulation among the diaspora. It started as a four-page sheet in April 1965; its rival, the *Punjab Times*, was launched in the same year (Tatla and Singh 1989). In North America, Vancouver has been the centre of the Punjabi media for almost a century (Tatla 1994a). For the past two decades, the *Indo-Canadian Times* has held the lead among weekly papers. Proprietors balance their risks by considering political alliances and patronage. This process is well illustrated by an ex-financier of the *Punjab Times*:

71

Table 3.1   The Punjabi media: North America.

| Year | Title | Editor/proprietor | Place | Language |
|------|-------|-------------------|-------|----------|
| | | Newspapers | | |
| 1984 | Sangharsh | Sukhdev S. Dardi | Vancouver | Punjabi |
| 1985 | Awaz-e-Quam | ISYF | Toronto | Punjabi |
| 1985 | Fulwari | Surjit Sangra | Vancouver | Punjabi |
| 1985 | World Sikh News | WSO | Stockton | Punjabi |
| 1986 | Chardhi Kala | ISYF | Vancouver | Punjabi |
| 1986 | Itihas | Jagdev S. Nijjar | Toronto | Punjabi |
| 1988 | Express News | T. S. Hayer | Vancouver | English |
| 1992 | Hamdard | | Toronto | Punjabi |
| | | Periodicals | | |
| 1981 | The Farmworker | CFU | Vancouver | English/Punjabi |
| 1984 | The Truth | Dr R. M. Singh | Quebec City | English |
| 1985 | Sahitak Kirnan | Mohinder S. Ghah | Yuba City | Punjabi |
| 1986 | Jago | S. S. Kanwal | San Jose | Punjabi |
| 1986 | Sikh News and Views | Collective | Willowdale | English/Punjabi |
| 1987 | Surti | R. S. Rania | Toronto | English/Punjabi |
| 1987 | The Sikh Herald | Raghbir S. Samagh | Toronto | English |
| 1987 | Tasveer | T. S. Hayer | Vancouver | English/Punjabi |
| 1987 | Kalm | Darshan Gill | Vancouver | Punjabi |
| 1987 | Nawin Awaz | Hardial Bains | Vancouver | English/Punjabi |
| 1988 | Sikh Times | T. S. Hayer | Vancouver | English |
| 1988 | Sanwaad | Sukhinder | London (Ont.) | Punjabi |
| 1989 | Watan | Sadhu/Hundal | Vancouver | Punjabi |

ISYF = International Sikh Youth Federation
WSO = World Sikh Organization
CFU = Canadian Farmworkers Union

Taking the latest issue of our new Punjabi paper . . . I went to India. I landed in Delhi on 1st December 1965. Through our newly appointed resident correspondents in Delhi, Iqbal Singh Sachdeva and Daljit Singh, who were also our relatives, we made contacts with Gurmukh Nihal Singh, an ex-governor of Rajasthan. The latter immediately arranged our meeting with the Indian Prime Minister.[29]

While the weekly newspapers have some respect for market forces, literary magazines express the personal idiosyncrasies of their "writers" – high goals in a society that attaches much pres-

**Table 3.2**  The Punjabi media: United Kingdom.

| Year | Title | Editor/proprietor | Place | Language |
|------|-------|-------------------|-------|----------|
| | | Newspapers | | |
| 1965 | Des Pardes | Tarsem S. Purewal | Southall | Punjabi |
| 1965 | Punjab Times | Surjit Singh Minhas | Southall | Punjabi |
| 1985 | Awaz-e-Quam | ISYF | Birmingham | Punjabi |
| 1987 | Punjabi Guardian | Inderjit S. Sangha | Birmingham | Punjabi/English |
| | | Periodicals | | |
| 1960 | Sikh Courier | P. M. Wylam | London | English |
| 1987 | Sikh Pariwar | R. S. Rana | Birmingham | Punjabi |
| 1967 | Lalkar | H. Brar | Southall | English/Punjabi |
| 1985 | Pardesan | H. Bedi | Southall | Punjabi |
| 1984 | Khalistan News | KC | London | English/Punjabi |
| 1983 | Sikh Messenger | Inderjit Singh | London | English |
| 1990 | Sikh Reformer | S. Thandi/A. Singh | Coventry | English |
| 1989 | Sewadar | Collective | London | English/Punjabi |

ISYF = International Sikh Youth Federation
KC = Khalistan Council

tige to its writers and the written word. These magazines have been launched by individuals with political, religious or literary missions. Many titles have appeared since 1961, when *Basera* was first published, Britain's earliest literary monthly. For political associations, these magazines are an essential means of communication and mobilization. Apart from the diaspora press, magazines and newspapers from Punjab and New Delhi are available through retail shops. Religious monthlies, such as the *Sikh Review* from Calcutta, and the *Sikh Courier* and the *Sikh Messenger* from Britain, have attracted subscribers across the diaspora. Through diaspora funds, some periodicals from Punjab were supported, including the *Daily Akali* of Lahore, *Akali te Pardesi* of Amritsar, *Desh Sewak* and *Kirti*[30] (Isemonger & Slattery 1919). Many leftist periodicals survive due to overseas patronage.

## Religious tradition

A distinctive mark of the Sikh diaspora is the dedication with which gurdwaras have been built. The location and history of gurdwaras are intimately connected with the settlement pattern of

Table 3.3   Numbers of gurdwaras.

| Period | USA | Canada | UK |
|---|---|---|---|
| 1908 | – | 1 | – |
| 1915 | 1 | 5 | 1 |
| 1955 | 2 | 6 | 2 |
| 1960 | 3 | 7 | 4 |
| 1990s | 60[a] | 75[a] | 202[b] |

[a] Estimates from Shergill (1986).
[b] Weller (1997).

Sikhs (Table 3.3). Gurdwaras have served many functions, providing social, educational and political activities as well as being religious centres. The political and religious concerns of the Sikh community have usually been associated with a gurdwara; its management committees have provided a base for aspiring community leaders, and a place to honour and receive dignitaries from both the host society and the Punjab. For early Sikh settlers, gurdwaras provided crucial support till they could find accommodation.[31] Until 1957 a single gurdwara in London served the entire British community, then numbering a few hundred. This was purchased through the patronage of the maharajah of Patiala in 1911. Canadian Sikhs built a gurdwara in 1907 under the leadership of Teja Singh, who further inspired Californian Sikhs to open a gurdwara in Stockton in 1912. The number of gurdwaras has kept pace with the growing Sikh population. By the 1990s there were about 160 gurdwaras in Britain; Canada had 75 and the United States about 80.

Alongside gurdwaras, religious societies exist to further various causes, ranging from strictly religious activities to educational and other charitable works. Thus, Guru Amar Das Mission from Oxford has financed eye operations for partially sighted people in rural Punjab and helped some rural health centres since 1979. The Sikh Missionary Society, Southall, was established in 1969 on Guru Nanak's fifth quincentenary. It has provided basic information by publishing many pamphlets on Sikh ceremonies. Besides helping various charities, it has arranged classes for Punjabi learning, Sikh studies and an annual camp for pupils.[32] A British mission led by Kuldip Singh has toured many European and Far Eastern countries, offering educational camps for youngsters.

**Table 3.4**  Sikh *sants* in the United Kingdom and North America: visiting years.

| Sant | Punjab Centre | Years[a] |
|---|---|---|
| Teja Singh | Mastuana (Faridkot) | 1908–11 |
| Jagjit Singh (Namdhari) | Bhaini Sahib (Ludhiana) | 1967– |
| Gurbachan Singh (Nirankari) | Delhi | 1967–78 |
| Darbari Das | Lopon (Faridkot) | 1968–74 |
| Amar Singh Burundi | Nanaksar (Ludhiana) | 1969– |
| Harbans Singh Domeliwale | Domeli (Jalandhar) | 1970–90 |
| Ishar Singh Rarewala | Rara Sahib (Ludhiana) | 1970–75 |
| Sadhu Singh | Nanaksar (Ludhiana) | 1970– |
| Gurmel Singh Baghapurana | Baghapurana (Ferozepore) | 1971 |
| Mihan Singh Siarhwale | Siarh (Ludhiana) | 1972–94 |
| Gurdev Singh | Nanaksar (Ludhiana) | 1975?– |
| Puran Singh Karichowale | Karicho, Kenya | 1977–83 |
| Gian Singh | Kutya Johlan (Jalandhar) | 1974– |
| Kirpal Singh Radhasoami | Beas (Jalandhar) | 1979 |
| Gurbachan Singh Kambliwale | Jalandhar | 1980– |
| Nihal Singh Harian Velan | Hakampur (Jalandhar) | 1985– |
| Jagjit Singh | Harkhowal (Hoshiarpur) | 1987– |
| Nahar Singh | Nanaksar (Ludhiana) | 1989– |

[a] Years refer to the period during which visits took place, the early data indicating the first visit made either to Canada, Britain or the United States. In most cases all three countries would be covered within a single visit.

Societies in Canada have similar aims. In Vancouver, summer camps for pupils are held annually. The Sikh Educational and Cultural Society of Ontario has arranged some seminars. Sikhism is not a proselytizing religion, it maintains no organized missions and conversions are not encouraged. However, Harbhajan Singh Yogi, based in Los Angeles, has among his followers some 3,000 American Whites who follow the Sikh faith. Accompanied by his American followers, Yogi has often visited Britain and other countries.[33] However, the kind of conversion started by Harbhajan Singh Yogi was the subject of long queries both in US Sikh circles and in the Punjab.

Sikh community leaders have also been brought together by various anniversaries of Sikh gurus (Table 3.4). Guru Nanak's quincentenary in 1969 was a grand occasion for an international gathering in London, and later in 1973 Guru Teg Bahadur's anniversary was celebrated again at the Royal Albert Hall. As the centre of faith, Amritsar has attracted generous overseas donations. In 1995 the Nishkam Sewak Jatha of Britain took the responsibility of repairing the golden domes of the Harimandir, the central shrine. By early 1996, £120,000 had been spent on the project with donations from Britain, North America and other countries.[34] Individuals have financed many local projects, usually in their villages of origin.[35] Many village gurdwaras have a room built by a foreign son or daughter. Historic shrines and other projects have received numerous donations from abroad.[36] A major memorial to Gadr heroes in Jalandhar attracted substantial funding from the diaspora, while the *Desh Bhagat Parvarik Sahayta Kmeti* received funds from North America in the 1940s and 1950s.[37]

### Rituals and practices

From Southall to Stockton, religious ceremonies and rituals within gurdwaras are remarkably uniform. At the centre of the worship is the Guru Granth, the sacred book. The early morning starts with *asa di var* and is followed by the standard community prayer. The day ends with *rehras* and *kirtan sohila* in the evening. On weekends, at large gurdwaras, *ragis* (hymn singers) are followed by *dhadis* (traditional bards), who narrate heroic tales from Sikh history. As the number of gurdwaras has increased, so have their incomes.

Pioneer Sikh settlers prudently accepted compromises within the gurdwaras, such as the use of chairs in the congregation hall of a Stockton gurdwara, but compromise is no longer needed and orthodoxy has returned. Early Sikhs in Vancouver and Stockton attended the gurdwara with bare heads until the 1960s, when the compromise was rejected in favour of orthodoxy. Such changes have come partly through the sheer willingness of Sikh males to wear a turban and partly through orthodox Sikhs' determination to favour traditional practices. While the Stockton transition was smooth, aided by a saint, the Canadian compromise led to a fierce controversy. The Khalsa Diwan Society of Vancouver was embroiled in a lengthy battle between the bareheaded and orthodox Sikhs. The two sides fought elections on this issue and took the case to court.[38] Changes were in place by the mid 1970s and gurdwaras are now managed by baptized Sikhs. Still, a majority of Sikh males are clean-shaven; paradoxically, pioneer Sikh settlers were orthodox in dress. However, the number of *amritdharis* in the last two decades has gone up, especially as older male Sikhs are retiring into the familiar turbans.

During this transition to orthodox practices, debate on rituals has also taken place, especially on the election of gurdwara managers. A partial incorporation of *panj piyaras* (five beloved ones) as managers has taken place, and proposals to form a national body of gurdwaras have been under consideration without any resolution.[39] Management committees for gurdwaras are normally elected every two years from adult Sikh males and females of the area. Invariably, two factions emerge to fight for the management of a gurdwara. The prestige and income of major gurdwaras has meant that such elections are keenly contested with political alliances among the Akalis, Congress and Communist Sikhs. Elections at the Ross Street gurdwara, Vancouver, the Richmond gurdwara, New York, and the Singh Sabha Gurdwara, Southall, led to major mobilization as they are prestigious institutions. Ad hoc amendments to election procedures have created many disputes involving lengthy and costly court litigation. Questions regarding "proper" procedures for managing gurdwaras, slight variations in baptismal practices, role and renumeration of *granthis*, fees charged for Akhand Path and other religious services, all continue to generate much debate.

These somewhat old issues are competing with new ones regarding "correct Sikh practices" on funerals, abortion, divorce and amnesia. Guidelines have been sought from Amritsar and contested among competing parties as a dispute has grown. Thus, a gurdwara in Surrey, British Columbia, saw a violent clash when chairs were removed from its *langar* hall. A year later, in September 1997, the management committee of a Southall gurdwara sought to amend its constitution to enable Sikh shopkeepers who sell tobacco or own beer shops to become members of the gurdwara committee. This led to furious debate and resignation by the majority of committee members. In both cases, competing parties sought the authority of Akal Takhat *jathedar* from Amritsar.[40] Similarly, laws of host societies have seen contests and deliberations about taking an oath on the Guru Granth in court, as well as keeping a copy of the holy book on court premises.[41]

In general, these disputes arise as rival factions try to legitimize their own positions by exposing each other for disregarding certain rituals. In the absence of a central organization in any of these countries, local disputes have led to bitter infighting with appeals to religious authority in Amritsar. While the Akal Takht *jathedar* has intervened in numerous disputes, competing interpretations of an event usually mean that such cases cause controversies. In September 1995, after a World Sikh Convention in Amritsar organized by the Shiromani Gurdwara Parbandhak Committee, a World Sikh Council was floated, presumably to tackle these issues. However, this council is yet to nominate its diaspora members. Apart from prominent community leaders, religious authority has usually been vested in the traditional saints, who have exerted considerable impact on the diaspora.

### Saints and pilgrimage

Since the 1970s, *sants* (saints) have become part of the diaspora and have contributed to the consolidation of religious tradition. They are traditional preachers from the Punjab who have sustained the faith of older Sikhs and inspired the young (La Brack 1988a; Tatla 1992). They have an abiding influence on the public life both of the Punjab and among the diaspora Sikhs. The earliest *sant* was Teja Singh, who led a deputation to Ottawa in 1911 on behalf of British Columbian Sikhs. In the 1980s, Puran Singh presented a petition to Downing Street for a student's right to wear a turban. Particular followers of a *sant* usually arrange such tours. Some *sants* have built their own gurdwaras, especially those relating to the Nanaksar tradition. Thus a magnificent gurdwara in Vancouver was built by Mihan Singh, while Gurdev Singh manages a gurdwara in the English Midlands and Toronto, and Amar Singh has established gurdwaras in Britain, Singapore and Canada.

In some ways, these gurdwaras have also become models of religious worship with a strict routine. Their popularity has led to orthodox practices in the mainstream gurdwaras. What is more, such standards are gravitating towards those of Punjabi society. Such *sants* have influenced the lives of many families in the diaspora. By insisting on strict adherence to religious orthodoxy, *sants* have helped in bringing the standards of social and religious norms of the diaspora closer to Punjabi society. After 1984 the roles of some *sants* and these gurdwaras have become contentious, linked with the issue of religious authority and the legitimation of Sikh political aspirations.

Pilgrimage has also played its part in the diaspora. Historic places associated with gurus, especially Nankana, the birthplace of Guru Nanak, and the palaces of Ranjit Singh, the Sikh ruler in Lahore, inspire hundreds of Sikhs to visit them.[42] An annual pilgrimage from each country leaves for Nankana in Pakistan every November, in time for the birthday celebrations.[43] These tours are organized by commercial agents, who also conduct tours to other sacred places in the Punjab and India. In recent years, a summer tour to Hemkunt in the Himalayas has become quite popular. In Britain, Sikhs pay homage to Maharajah Dalip Singh's Elveden estate in Suffolk. Schemes to buy the Elveden estate and preserve relics of Sikh heritage have exercised many minds.[44] In North America the preservation of the Gadr inheritance has taken place in Berkeley and San Francisco.

Religious exchange is not restricted to mainstream Sikhism. Its various sects, Namdharis, Nirankaris and Radhasoamis, have also established themselves in the diaspora, asserting their distinction through various institutions and lifestyles. Thus, for example, the Namdhari chief, Jagjit Singh, has visited his followers in Britain and elsewhere, celebrating with them the *Baisakhi*, organizing classical music competitions, marrying many couples and giving counsel on administrative matters. The Nirankaris, though small, have created several centres in Canada and Britain. They were often visited by their chief, Gurbachan Singh, though the growing antagonism between Nirankaris and Sikhs has led to mutual suspicion and acrimony in some areas.[45]

Another social group deserves special mention in this respect. The Chamars, with opportunities offered in the diaspora, are in the process of chalking out a radical path for themselves (Juergensmeyer 1982). Using the past hostility between the Jats and Chamars in the rural life of the Punjab, the Chamars have built their separate places of worship. They have debated vigorously about the appropriate faith they should adopt, Sikhism, Hinduism or Buddhism, and about Ad-dharm identity, an indigenous religious tradition of Punjab's Chamars. They have also deliberated on the issue of the "sacred book". Exchanges through the Punjabi press captured the process of boundary construction. Thus, Mohinder Badhan, a convert to Buddhism, who argued for the Buddhist option, got a sharp retort from Mihar:

> Dr Ambedkar was if anything a Hindu, for he married a Hindu woman at a ripe old age. He embraced Buddhism only in the last six months of his life. Your claim that Buddhism believes in equal respect to all saints is nonsense, there is no god or saint in that religion. Are not Buddhist Chinese fighting their Vietnamese and Tibetan brothers? We can only find salvation in Ravidas.[46]

The debate continued for several years. While a few have converted to Buddhism, making a clean break from Hinduism as well as Sikhism, the majority have asserted a distinctive role on the border of the Sikh Panth.[47] The search for a new identity drew alliances and support from Punjabi and Indian leaders, including Prithvi Singh Azad and Jagjivan Ram, a government minister. The Guru Ravidas Foundation was established in India with a general aim of linking the diaspora Ravidasis. The majority have been content to keep within the orbit of Punjabi religious life, by emphasizing "Ravidas" as a guru who has been accorded an equal place in the Sikh scriptures. They have eventually settled to keep some distance from the Sikh faith, while retaining common gurdwara rituals and Punjabi identity.[48] Thus, the present situation in the Ravidasi temples is quite similar to the gurdwaras; with the Guru Granth at the centre of worship, emphasis is shifted to the recitation of Ravidas *bani* and an improvised version of prayer. Thus overseas opportunities have allowed Chamar communities to reassess their past and assert their vision through religious institutions, from a position of economic power and equality that they had lacked in the Punjabi villages.

## Diaspora: a creative site?

Indeed, the diaspora has become a creative site for individuals and groups who have contested their positions within the society and reinterpreted it to suit their new locations. Social groups such as Ramgarhias and Mazhabi Sikhs have used their new economic wealth and opportunities to consolidate links with their peers in the Punjab and to redefine their group identity.[49] Such discoveries and reinterpretations range from mystical religious experiences to academic explorations; two British-born Sikhs discovered their heritage by going on a pilgrimage to Pakistan. A Sikh from Britain led a team of artists to discover the popular arts of rural Punjab.[50] From Britain, Gurcharan Singh Lote undertook to spend several years in producing a handwritten copy of the Adi Granth, while a Canadian Sikh has translated the Adi Granth into English, another has devoted many years to translating it into French.[51] The diaspora creative works have become part of Punjabi literature.[52] For some members, the discovery of family lineage or tradition has been a satisfactory occupation. Thus a Saini Sikh has compiled a directory while another has compiled a guide to Chana families, linking them to their ancestors in the Punjab (Directory 1988). In Britain, Sikh army veterans have kept up the memory of Anglo-Sikh bonds through regular meetings (Tatla 1993).[53]

In America a Sikh Foundation was established by scientist Narinder Singh Kapany; it has undertaken many projects for the dissemination of Sikh religion, literature and arts.[54] Besides organizing the first Sikh Studies conference at Berkeley, it has published a number of tracts and books. Another society, the Sikh Missionary Center, Detroit, sought to correct the Sikh coverage in various encyclopedias.[55] An association of Sikh professionals has funded the Sikh Heritage Award for an American, while the Sikh Welfare Foundation of North America at Durate, California, offers free tapes and religious literature. However, a major initiative came in the 1980s when Sikh societies in Canadian cities formed the Federation of Sikh Societies with the singular aim of establishing a chair of Sikh studies at a university. By 1984 it had raised $250,000 and negotiations started with the University of British Columbia for the chair. The federal government cleared this project in 1988, but it was with considerable reluctance. A Sikh scholar was appointed to this pioneering and prestigious post in an overseas country. Following Canadian success, the Michigan Sikh Society raised enough funds for a Sikh studies programme at the University of Michigan. Parallel to this development, funds from local gurdwara committees and donations from some influential Sikhs enabled a similar programme at Columbia University.[56] In 1996 a Sikh businessman from Illinois, Darshan Singh Dhaliwal, endowed a chair of Punjab studies at the University of Wisconsin.[57] A further chair in Sikh studies at the University of California, Santa Barbara, has been funded by Narinder Singh Kapany in memory of his mother. Both chairs will be filled by September 1998.

With the endowment of Sikh studies positions at these prestigious universities, the diaspora is likely to become a creative site for academic studies. Research generated by such scholars in the diaspora has already established high standards of analysis; it has also generated heated controversies. In particular, the contribution of Sikh scholars at the Universities of British Columbia and Michigan have become contentious. Dr Pashaura Singh's doctoral study at the University of Toronto on the editing of the Adi Granth was questioned for its methodology as well as the "real intentions" of the scholar. A group of scholars from Chandigarh were considerably helped by similar-minded Sikhs in Los Angeles, who charged the Toronto scholar with blasphemy. They extended their offensive against other foreign scholars' meddling into Sikh studies. During 1992–4 several individuals cooperated across Britain, Canada and America to organize four conferences at Berkeley, Toronto, London and Los Angeles to counter such "misinformation" regarding Sikhism.[58]

Another scholar's research on the Singh Sabha movement's role in the formation of Sikh identity also led to a bitter debate. In a major reinterpretation, Harjot Oberoi (1994) at the University of British Columbia argued that the rituals associated with the Sikh orthodoxy were only a century old, and were at best a reinvention, derived as a variant of the Sanatan Hindu tradition. His conclusion that Sikh identity was thus an "imagined and constructed" tradition created a fierce opposition from the same group of scholars and led to a number of further publications.[59] They sought an end to such research and the removal of Harjot Oberoi from the Sikh studies chair. In their views, Oberoi had undermined the faith from a privileged position. In both cases, appeals were made to the SGPC, Amritsar, and to the moral sanction of the Akal Takhat. That they almost succeeded in isolating the first scholar and in embarrassing the second and his university, show both the persuasive powers of diaspora Sikh professionals and the vulnerability of the central religious authority to ideas that required a far more sophisticated approach for a balanced evaluation.[60] In the meantime, bitterness created by this controversy has divided the community and disappointed many sympathetic academics; the chair's future remains uncertain, a cumulative loss for the community.

Despite short-term upsets at two universities, the concern and patronage of diaspora Sikhs has enabled Sikh studies to become part of Western scholarly debate and discourse. Dr Gurinder Singh Mann at the University of Columbia has devised a comprehensive course on Sikh studies, setting an agenda for research (Hawley & Mann 1993), and several students engaged in scholarly monographs at various universities have shown some progress (Tatla 1996). Another scholar Nikki Gunninder Kaur Singh, with her reinterpretation of the Sikh theology and scriptures, has floated an interesting thesis. After examining the feminine principle underlying the Sikh scriptures, she has argued that *sati*, pollution and purdah have no sanction in the Sikh tradition. She also questioned many Sikh parents' misuse of modern technology to determine the sex of a child and consequent cases of abortion for female foetuses. In a further study, she concluded that "overwhelmingly Hindu and Islamic pressures have over the centuries reinforced and even today continue to reinforce the patriarchal values that are difficult to breach".[61] Surely, diaspora contributions in the field of Sikh studies have come of an age and will continue to generate discussions both in the diaspora and the Punjab. One can also point out much innovative work undertaken by the diaspora's skilled engineers and other specialists, who have created software programs for the Punjabi language and developed religious projects on CD-ROMS. Several informational packages on the Internet have become available; Sikh encyclopedias and the Guru Granth are now available on CD-ROM, a major feat given their size.[62]

To conclude, Sikh communities have actively produced cultural and religious traditions that bond them to their former homes. Through many exchanges with the Punjab, transfer of resources, contacts and networks, overseas Sikhs have influenced the Punjab's economic and social life, and its rural economy; the Sikh diaspora has revitalized its social and religious norms. But this exchange remains subtle, symbolic and unquantifiable, involving values, ideology and norms. What is certain is that Punjabi society continues to exert a varied and significant influence upon the emerging new Sikh identities in the diaspora.

# FOUR

# The Sikh diaspora and the Punjab: political linkages

Coolie, a coolie, they call us, what a shame!
how we are insulted in foreign lands
Why don't we control our own country?[1]

Alongside social, economic and religious ties, the Sikh diaspora possesses a long history of political links with the Punjab. These linkages have provided mutual support and exchange between the diaspora political groups and their patrons in the Punjab. The diaspora has provided funds, support and mobilization for various issues emanating from the homeland. Over the past 30 years, political groups formed in Britain and North America have forged direct links with the main political parties of the Punjab. Although individuals have joined the mainstream political parties of their host states, the activities of political groups directly linked to Punjabi politics have generated far more passion and mobilization. Indeed, for many activists, these exclusively Sikh or Punjabi organizations have been a stepping-stone for joining the mainstream parties.

In the pre-1947 period, the Chief Khalsa Diwan had established direct links with several Sikh societies in overseas countries. The formation of the Khalsa Diwan Society in British Columbia and California was inspired by the Chief Khalsa Diwan, Amritsar. Small communities of Sikhs in East Africa and the Far Eastern countries in the early years of this century forged close links with the Khalsa Diwan members, who in turn informed them of various Punjabi issues. A number of Singh Sabhas were gradually set up throughout the Far East; they provided funding for numerous Punjabi causes, particularly in establishing schools and colleges, and often rallied political support. The newly established Sikh media, such as *Khalsa Advocate* and *Khalsa Samachar*, carried news of such diaspora connections. There were many symbolic gestures of support for the Gurdwara Reforms Movement launched by Akalis, including the participation in the Jaito Morcha by a Canadian Sikh delegation.

## Early links

*The Gadr movement*
Of the early links, a major episode took place in the Pacific states. Starting as a minor issue of Sikhs' perceived right to settle in any part of the British Empire, it soon gathered momentum, leading to an exodus of Punjabis back to India. It arose when a few hundred Sikh ex-army men from the Far East tried to settle in the Pacific states. From 1902–3 this movement out of the Far East gained considerable strength, as each ship from the East brought more migrants to San Francisco and Victoria. The arrival of Sikhs both in California and British Columbia added to the already charged atmosphere of hostility towards Japanese and Chinese, the "yellow menace", as White workers called them. The Sikhs' presence irked indigenous residents, and it was not only their numbers but also their lifestyles and their appearance (Doreen 1979). Conspicuous in their colourful turbans, they huddled together in colonies, worked as gangs and "washed in the open". Vancouver's city council asked the assistance of the federal government to stem this tide.

The brewing hostility erupted into an open conflict as a small community of Sikhs faced racial hostility and immigration barriers. In 1908 even men that had already been admitted could not call on their families to join them. From 1903 to 1907, as more migrants arrived, the immigration authorities took further steps to deport them on health grounds and other hastily enacted rules. By 1908 several respectable Sikhs were publicly humiliated, a few physically dragged back on to the ships, others through a ban on their re-entry and general racism. Subject to greater hardships and racial slurs, they formed the Khalsa Diwan Society (KDS) in 1907 and sought the advice of Teja Singh, an educated and saintly figure. Under Teja Singh's guidance, they built the first gurdwara, where they deliberated their fate, besides providing refuge and accommodation to newcomers. The Khalsa Diwan Society took cases of those refused permission to land, through legal battles, petitions and memorandums. Teja Singh led three deputations; the first went to Ottawa with a petition calling for the lifting of the Orders in Council which had effectively barred further Indian immigration into Canada,[2] arguing:

> We would ask you to consider, is there any process of law or regulation that can be directly used to justly strip a loyal British subject of his intent to travel or reside in any part of the empire; if not, then why this restriction?[3]

Another delegation went to the India Office, London. They faced hostility all around them; the only support came from a church society who pleaded with the government for better treatment:

> Does imperialism mean Canada for the Empire, Australia for the Empire, India for the Empire, or can there be two definitions for subjects of one and the same Empire? If there is but one recognised definition under the flag over which the sun is supposed never to set, then it is for us to see that no injustice shall minimise the rights or privileges of that citizenship, whether the holder is black or white.[4]

As most arrivals were ex-soldiers, they imagined it was their right to settle anywhere in the empire. Consequently, they blamed Britain for letting them down.[5] As the atmosphere became bitter, by 1911 only 2,342 of the 6,000 Canadian Sikhs stayed behind; the rest crossed over into the neighbouring American states, although the difference in racial hostility was only a matter of degree. Balwant Singh and Bhag Singh, who had served in the army with distinction, were publicly humiliated when their wives and children were refused admission; they were allowed to enter in 1912, but only after a lengthy legal tussle. Weekly meetings held in the gurdwara saw many angry members, which found expression in many ways. They stopped wearing army badges at public functions, and the gurdwara turned down a request by the mayor of Vancouver to honour the visiting Duke of Edinburgh in 1913.

A dramatic showdown between Sikhs and the Canadian immigration authorities took place with the arrival of the ship *Komagata Maru*, which arrived in Vancouver on 21 May 1914. Its passengers were refused permission to disembark, and the ship was ordered back on 23 July after protracted negotiations. As the ship anchored in Calcutta, the passengers became embroiled in a bloody confrontation, and 26 people were killed, among them 20 passengers and 4 policemen. Gurdit Singh, their leader, had disappeared in the fracas while 172 passengers were arrested and escorted to the Punjab (Johnston 1979).

Henceforth the mood was of militancy and the fire was supplied by two intellectuals, Taraknath Das and Lala Hardayal, who called for India's liberation. While Hardayal preached to California's Indian students, Taraknath Das was a familiar sight among Vancouver's Sikhs. This situation exercised some Punjabi officials, who were also aware of its adverse impact on Sikh regiments, claiming that it

> specially affects the Sikhs from whom many of our best soldiers are drawn and on whom, from the mutiny onwards, we have been accustomed to rely with confidence for whole-hearted support of the British Raj. For the first time in their history there has now been serious discontent among them and this has been largely due to, or at least made possible by, the exploitation of their grievances in this matter.[6]

In a further note, Punjab's special status in British India was noted:

> The seriousness of the question, as regards the British empire in India, is that the people of Punjab, the chief recruiting ground for the Indian army, are the class of Indians

practically affected, and the grievances of the Sikhs regards Canada have been very skilfully utilised by agitators to excite discontent in the Punjab. . . . The classes of Indians who go to South Africa are of no military importance; but the Sikhs, ever since the mutiny, have been a most important element, and the attempts of agitators to tamper with them have been closely connected with immigration grievances.[7]

From 1912 a revolutionary movement started to form in the Pacific states. The government obtained the services of Mr Hopkinson, a Eurasian, who spied on Indian activists hinting at a conspiracy to overthrow British power in India. And in March 1913 the KDS and the United India League sent a further delegation to London, through Balwant Singh, Narain Singh and Nand Singh Sihra, who then travelled to India for a meeting with the viceroy about immigration problems, especially how they affected their families. Meanwhile, Hardayal's revolutionary vision was shared by many Sikh workers, who formed the Hindi Sabha in 1913 (Puri 1993; Josh 1978; Johnston 1988a; Buchignani et al. 1985). From its San Francisco base, it soon launched *Gadr*, a weekly newspaper which promulgated revolution against British rule in India; it yelled:

Time for prayer is gone,
take the sword in hand.
Time is now to plunge in a battle,
mere talk serves no purpose,
Those who long for martyrdom,
will live forever as shining guideposts.[8]

When Hardayal gave a call for return to India at meetings held at Fresno and Sacramento on 9 and 11 August 1914, over 3,200 Indians, most of them Sikhs, left the Pacific states. Rather innocent of the Punjabi peasantry's steadfast loyalty towards the raj, they faced stiff opposition in their declared aim of Indian liberation. Moving into Gadr headquarters, the police apprehended many revolutionaries and the movement crashed on 21 February 1915,

when its leaders had expected a revolt at some military canton-
ments along with a general uprising. The dream of armed revolution was over. Revolutionaries were tried in 12 special tribunals
and given exemplary sentences.[9]

In California the remaining revolutionaries were tried under
the San Francisco Conspiracy Case.[10] Although short-lived, the
Gadr Movement had a major impact; it fractured the amicable
Anglo-Sikh relations and gave credence to some administrators'
suspicions of a further conspiracy, creating an outlook which
culminated in the Jallianwala massacre in 1919.[11] The Gadr activists inspired a spirit of freedom, secular and socialist ideology,
and helped in the establishment of the Communist Party and the
rise of leftist thought among the Punjabi peasantry. Its leaders'
sacrifices, especially those of Kartar Singh Sarabha (1896–1915) at
the young age of 19, became part of Punjab's heroic tradition,
inspiring the Babbar Akalis and Socialist Party activists such as
Bhagat Singh (d. 1931), who became another martyr.

*Other political associations*
It is worth noting a few pre-1947 developments in other countries
of the Sikh diaspora. In Britain the Indian community was quite
small with a few Sikhs. Some random incidents created a few
ripples in Anglo-Indian relations. The first Sikh in Britain was
Prince Dalip Singh, heir to the Punjabi throne. Exiled to Britain in
1856, he spent a largely contented life on a Suffolk estate, hunting
and socializing with other royals and the aristocracy. Later he
became a rebel and undertook frantic visits to European capitals;
he also went to Russia with proposals to invade India and claim
his sovereignty over the Punjab. As the India Office and Punjab's
officials assessed him capable of arousing the Sikh masses for the
Sikh raj, his activities were severely curtailed. Frustrated and
dejected, he died in Paris in 1893, his wish to return to his native
land buried with him in Elveden (Alexander & Anand 1979;
Ganda Singh 1980).

Some Sikh students arrived in Britain for education; among
them Teja Singh and his friends formed a Khalsa Jatha of the
British Isles in 1907. They also raised funds for a London
gurdwara, for which the Maharajah of Patiala, a frequent visitor to
London, contributed substantial funds. Besides the election of a

few Indians to the parliament,[12] Britain also saw political activities by Indian students. Shyamji Krishnavarma, who had fled to Paris in 1887 and launched the *Indian Sociologist* in 1905, moved to London; his house in Highgate, India House, became a hostel for student revolutionaries (Popplewell 1988; Silverman 1989). There, Vinayek Sarvarkar, a law student, became a fiery nationalist and inspired a Punjabi student, Madan Lal Dhingra, to shoot Sir William Curzon Wyllie on 1 July 1909. As a result, India House was put under surveillance, ending its revolutionary activities. In 1914 Annie Besant floated the Home Rule for India League, later renamed the India League. Krishna Menon, another student, served as its secretary in 1928. In another random incident, Udham Singh, a vagrant Sikh, killed an ex-governor of Punjab at a public meeting in London during 1939. He was promptly hanged for the crime but became a martyr (Grewal & Puri 1974). In the 1930s, when a few hundred Punjabi migrants had settled in Britain, they formed a social club, the Indian Workers Association in Coventry.

In the Far East many developments took place within the police and military garrisons of Sikhs. Most notably, during the Second World War, when the Japanese armies overran these countries, Sikh migrants and some sepoys of Sikh regiments joined a newly formed Indian National Army. For a brief period, this force of 20,000 soldiers of the Indian National Army, almost one-third of whom were Sikhs, posed a serious threat to the security of British rule in India. They were finally defeated in 1944.[13] The pre-1947 community associations are summarized in Table 4.1.

## Post-1947 associations

As the Sikh communities in North America and Britain grew in numbers and became well established in the 1960s, a number of political groups sprang up in the Sikh diaspora, forging direct links with Punjab's political parties. Among them the Akali Dal, several leftist groups and the overseas Congress were formed. Although a detailed history of each association would require far more research, a broad picture can be suggested (Tables 4.2 to 4.5).

Table 4.1   Sikh and Indian organizations, 1908 to 1947.

| Period | Association | Centre | Causes |
|--------|-------------|--------|--------|
| | North America | | |
| 1908–1947 | Khalsa Diwan Society, BC | Vancouver | Sikhism, racism |
| 1911–1912 | Hindi Sabha | Oregon | Indian independence |
| 1913–1919 | Gadr Party | San Francisco | Indian independence |
| 1908–1911 | United Indian League | Vancouver | Indian independence |
| 1912–1914 | Hindustan League | Vancouver | Social welfare |
| 1918–1919 | United India League | New York | Indian independence |
| 1918–1920 | Hindustan Students Association | New York | Indian politics |
| 1918–1920 | Hindu Workers Union of America | New York | Indian politics |
| | United Kingdom | | |
| 1922–1947? | India League | London | Indian independence |
| 1938–1947 | Indian Workers Association | Coventry | Social |

Note: Apart from the Khalsa Diwan Society, all other organizations had mixed membership with Hindu, Muslim and Sikh members.

## Communist and leftist groups

The Communist Party of Punjab emerged from the Gadr leadership of the 1920s (Gurharpal Singh 1984). It has passed through several phases from the Kirti Party and the Lal Group to the three communist parties of contemporary Punjab. Although the electoral base for leftist groups remains quite limited, the leftist ideas, idealism and ideology have inspired many Punjabis beyond its immediate membership. Migrants from the Doaba region, where leftist parties had some success, helped to establish leftist groups in Britain and Canada, though America's skilled migrants were relatively free from communist influence.

In Britain, Vishnu Dutt Sharma, Jagmohan Joshi, Avtar Johal and other communists played a major role in organizing the first Indian Workers Association (IWA) in 1957.[14] During its early years the IWA assisted many Punjabi migrants with form-filling services and in "regularizing" their documents; quite a few had travelled on "dubious" passports. Gradually the IWA extended its role to "representing" Indian workers' issues at local and national level. Branches were established in many cities of Sikh population, and eventually the IWA became the largest organization with 16,000

**Table 4.2** Sikh Organizations, 1947 to 1990.

| Period | Association | Centre | Causes |
|--------|-------------|--------|--------|
| | Canada | | |
| 1947–2000 | Khalsa Diwan Society | Vancouver | Sikhs, immigration |
| 1952–1970 | ªEast Indian Welfare Committee | Vancouver | Racism, immigration |
| 1973–2000 | ªNACOI | Canada | Representation |
| 1977–1990 | ªEast Indian Workers Association | Vancouver | Racism, workers |
| 1975–1977 | ªIPANA | Vancouver | Racism, workers, emergency |
| 1975–1980 | ªBC Organization for Fighting Racism | Vancouver | Racism, immigration |
| 1976–2000 | Akali Dal of North America | Canada/USA | Sikh issues |
| 1980–1983 | ªCanadian Farmworkers Union | British Columbia | Farmworkers |
| 1981– | Federation of Sikh Societies | Canada | BC Sikh studies chair |
| 1978– | Babbar Khalsa International | Vancouver | Orthodoxy |
| 1970– | Akhand Kirtani Jatha | Vancouver | Religious issues |
| | United States | | |
| 1970– | Sikh Study Circle | New York | Sikhism |
| 1972– | Nankana Sahib Foundation | New Jersey | Pilgrimage |
| 1976– | Sikh Council of North America | California | Religious |
| 1976– | Sikh Association of America | California | Punjab, religious issues |
| 1981– | Sikh Cultural Society of America | New York | Religious |
| 1983– | North American Akali Dal | Los Angeles | Punjab, religious issues |
| | United Kingdom | | |
| 1957–2000 | ªIndian Workers Associations | Southall | Immigration, racism |
| 1971–1973 | ªAssociation of Asian Communists | London | Race, workers |
| 1976–1977 | ªSouthall Youth Movement | Southall | Racism, youth issues |
| 1967–2000 | Akali Dal | London | Sikh issues |
| 1971–1977 | Sikh Homeland Front | London | Sikh homeland |
| 1976–2000 | ªIndian Overseas Congress | Midlands | Indian issues |
| 1960– | Akhand Kirtani Jatha | Birmingham | Religious issues |
| 1970– | ªFederation of Indian Societies | London | Indian issues, racism |

ª These are interreligious organizations with Hindu and Sikh members; although in virtually all of them, the Sikh members constituted a majority.

NACOI = National Association of Canadians of Indian Origin

IPANA = Indian Peoples Association of North America

Table 4.3  Diaspora Sikh organizations: links with Punjab.

| Punjab | North America | UK |
|---|---|---|
| Congress Party | Indian Overseas Congress | Indian Overseas Congress |
| Akali Dal | Akali Dal | Akali Dal |
| Communists | EIWCC/IWA/IPANA | IWA |
| Bahujan Samaj Party | Ambedkar/Ravidas Groups | Ravidas/Ambedkar Groups |

IWA = Indian Workers Association
IPANA = Indian Peoples Association of North America

Table 4.4  Diaspora Sikh organizations: resources.

| Factors | IOC | Akali Dal | Communists |
|---|---|---|---|
| Authority | INC, Punjab | Religious | Ideology |
| Patronage | IHC's Patronage | Akali Dal | CPI (R), CPI (M), CPI (ML) |
| Institution | Gurdwara | Gurdwara | Gurdwara |
| Class/caste | Chamars/Jat Sikhs | Jat/non-Jat Sikhs | Jat/non-Jat Sikhs |

CPI (R) = Punjab branch of Communist Party of India (Right)
CPI (M) = Punjab branch of Communist Party of India (Marxist)
CPI (ML) = Punjab branch of Communist Party of India (Marxist–Leninist) Naxalite groups
IWA = Indian Workers Association
IHC = Indian High Commission
INC = Indian National Congress
IOC = Indian Overseas Congress

Table 4.5  Reaction to events in Punjab and India, 1960 to 1990.

| Years | Event | Groups mobilized | Reaction |
|---|---|---|---|
| 1962 | Indo-China Hostilities | All groups/IWA | Support, protest |
| 1965 | Indo-Pakistan War | All groups | Support, funds |
| 1953–66 | Punjabi Suba Movement | KDS | Volunteers and funds |
| 1968–69 | Naxalite Movement | Leftist/IWA | Support, IWA split |
| 1970–71 | Chandigarh Issue | Akali Dal | Support |
| 1972 | Indo-Pakistan War | All groups | Support |
| 1975–77 | Emergency Rule | IWA/IPANA | Protest, support |
| 1977–78 | Janata Government | Ravidasis | Protest |
| 1978 | Akali-Nirankari Clash | Babbar Khalsa | Support |
| 1981–83 | *Dharam Yudh Morcha* | Akali Dal/KDS | Support, volunteers, funds |

KDS = Khalsa Diwan Society, Vancouver
IWA = Indian Workers Association
IPANA = Indian Peoples Association of North America

members. Moreover, its leaders proclaimed, the IWA undertook only "all-Indian issues, irrespective of sects, parties and religious affiliation and used only democratic methods". Its working was affected by major events in India, especially those affecting the Communist Party. In 1962, due to Indo-Chinese hostilities, the Communist Party of India (CPI) was split in two, the CPI Right and the CPI Left. It led to a split in IWA ranks; the Southall branch, which dominated the organization, switched support to the CPI (R) while most branches in the Midlands and the North allied themselves with the CPI (M). A further split came as the Naxalite movement sprang up in the Punjab during 1968–9, when some Midland leaders allied with the new revolutionary party, the CP (ML) and a new IWA (ML) was formed (Dewitt 1969; Josephides 1991).

During the early 1970s, leftist organizations mobilized mainly on issues of immigration, racism and workers' rights. During their heyday, these organizations provided vital support to Punjab's communist parties, through funds, publicity and mobilization. Several communist leaders from Punjab such as Jagjit Singh Anand, Harkishan Singh Surjeet and others have been regular visitors to Britain and North America. However, by the 1980s, many factors had eroded their influence. As the IWA celebrated its fiftieth anniversary in 1988, its branches were almost extinct; the Southall branch had become an advisory agency, and its old cinema building, once a lively centre, was converted into a civic centre. Piara Singh Khabra, one of its many activists, became a Labour MP in 1992 and was re-elected in 1997. Although splinter groups were united in 1989, most of their members had gone over to new Sikh organizations.[15]

A slightly different picture emerges in Canada, where students affected by the Punjab Naxalite movement became politically active in Toronto, Vancouver and Edmonton. In the early 1970s they challenged the existing moderate associations, such as the East Indians Welfare Association (EIWA). In 1973 the East Indian Defence Committee (EIDC) was formed by such radical student leaders in response to growing racial tension. Paradoxically, it allied itself with the orthodox group in the Khalsa Diwan Society, during its dispute over the issue of *mona* Sikhs. The EIDC gradually became a Maoist group (affiliated to the Albanian-leaning Communist Party), involved in vigilant actions against racial harassment of East Indians in Vancouver. Another broadly leftist organization, the East Indian Canadian Citizens Welfare Association (EICCWA) was an early attempt to form an organization independent of any gurdwara. Like others, this "Welfare Association", as it was popularly known, took on some political functions, such as an increased immigration quota for Indians. In British Columbia there were some exclusive Punjabi causes too. A major issue was that of Punjabi farm workers who comprised almost three-quarters of the 16,000 seasonal workers of the Fraser Valley. They had difficulty in forming a union amid the cases of exploitation, especially of female workers. This led to a prolonged struggle for the formation of the Canadian Farmworkers Union in 1980 (Gill 1983).

Punjabi politics has seen much mobilization among the leftist groups. The Indian Emergency (1975–7) was opposed by some communist groups jointly with the Akalis, while moderate leftists provided support. In Britain, Vishnu Dutt Sharma, an IWA leader from Southall, endorsed the emergency, branding its opponents as CIA stooges.[16] Passions ran high as the IWA in Southall was accused of hobnobbing with the Congress Party. In those two years the IWA leaders fought organizational elections on this issue.[17] They protested against the Indian prime minister when she visited the Dominion Cinema, Southall, accompanied by Punjab's chief minister, Darbara Singh.[18] During the emergency period, there were several clashes between Congress supporters and communist groups in London and Vancouver. From 1970 to 1972 the Punjab Naxalite movement was greatly supported by its Canadian and British comrades.[19] Moderate comrades were on the defensive and faced admonishment, leading to many revolutionary pamphlets and denunciations.[20] Since almost every political development from the homeland has caused a frisson in the diaspora, an activist in Toronto's Indian community who tried to bring together various groups on a common platform to fight against racism, was exasperated:

> The dominating conflicts within the East Indian community are still the conflicts of the first generation immigrants and in this, the politics of India is playing a significant role

in shaping the attitude of the community. Every political crisis in India leads to renewed interest in Indian politics among the East Indian migrants and as a result new conflicts in Toronto emerge. As it is impossible to pacify the interests of first generation immigrants in the Indian politics, it is impossible to eliminate the conflicts within the East Indian community on that issue. . . . The negative impact of this conflict in regard to the Indian politics on the development of a broad front around the issue of racism, can only be minimised with the development of a clear and non-sectarian approach towards the issue of racism which affects the majority of East Indian immigrants regardless of their stand on Indian politics. (Bharti 1978)

Like Britain, Canada's leftist organizations tackled issues of racism and immigration policies, usually by forging alliances with other Asian or Black groups. These leaders have debated issues of cooperation with other Black groups, acceptance of official patronage and various strategies to tackle racism and immigration controls.[21] It is only with the rise of second- and third-generation Sikhs that the first generation's passions about distant homes would be replaced by local issues.

Although leftist associations have encouraged open membership, in practice they are dominated by Sikhs, attracting little support from other Indians, thus they have a few Punjabi Hindus and even fewer other Indians. They try to project their image as "Indian", as host societies' require "national" representation. In Canada the Department of Multiculturalism has encouraged umbrella organizations for its grant criterion and other "representational" aspects. Given the diversity of South Asian communities, the Gujaratis, the Punjabi Hindus and the Sikhs, such umbrella bodies become rather unwieldy, their membership elitist and their mass support slight; their survival remains crucially dependent on a continuous dose of official patronage.

In Britain such national organizations are more of the "grand alliances of leaders" without ordinary membership, such as the Federation of Indian Organizations. In Canada the NACOI perhaps fulfils this role, set up in 1975–6 by a grant from the Department of Multiculturalism. The Indian Peoples' Association of North

America (IPANA), another pan-East Indian organization, was active during the emergency period, but it lacked popular support; indeed, it was almost wound up except for a temporary lease of life during the Farmworkers Union struggle. Thus, pan-East Indian organizations in Canada reflect the official imperative of "seeking one ethnic voice per ethnic group" glossing over "real communities".[22]

### Congress and other associations

An Indian Overseas Congress (IOC) was organized in Britain and Canada in the 1970s and it attracted many Sikh members. The IOC's fortunes remain tied with the Congress governments in the Punjab and New Delhi. In both India and the Punjab, Sikhs have held major positions in the Congress group, and at some gurdwaras, especially in Vancouver and in the Midlands, Congressites and Akalis have competed over the control of local gurdwaras. Besides these, there are Ambedkar and Ravidasi Associations, representing the interests of particular sects or social groups. During the 1980s, the Ravidasis, who are traditionally Congress allies, switched their support to a new national party, the Bahujan Samaj Party. All these parties and associations have organized rallies on various occasions. Thus, in 1975, with the first non-Congress ministry in New Delhi, the Ravidasi Associations protested against this "Brahmin-dominated" government of the Janata Party.[23]

### The Khalsa Diwan Society and the Akali Dal

The Khalsa Diwan Society (KDS) is the oldest Sikh organization; functioning since 1908, it was affiliated to the Chief Khalsa Diwan, Amritsar, until the 1920s. Its history is intertwined with East Indians' struggle to make a respectable home in Canada. By 1914 it had several branches in British Columbia and it operated a cohesive network of membership and gurdwaras. After the Gadr exodus, it served the East Indians and spoke for the whole of the South Asian community in Canada until the 1960s. However, the fresh arrival of Sikhs and other South Asians in Canada fractured the organization. In the early 1950s a dispute arose within the KDS executive committee, with the traditionalists arguing unsuccessfully for the exclusion of clean-shaven Sikhs. In 1952 a group of "traditionalists" broke with the KDS to found a second Vancouver gurdwara and the Akali Singh Sikh Society. The affiliated KDS gurdwaras gradually became independent of the KDS Vancouver. These developments together with an increase in the non-Sikh, South Asian population effectively undermined the KDS's earlier role as a representative for the entire South Asian community. Some competing organizations were formed in the 1970s. Chief among them was the Akali Dal. In Britain Sant Fateh Singh, the Akali Dal leader from Punjab, encouraged British Sikhs to form such an association during his visit in 1966. It was formally launched in June 1968.[24] The Akali Dal of North America emerged much later in the 1970s, after some local community associations had sprung up: the India Society of Yuba-Sutter, the Hindustani Welfare and Reform Association of the Imperial Valley and the Sikh Cultural Society of New York. From these came the "national" organization, in the form of the Sikh Council of North America. In 1976 the Council held a conference in Berkeley, presided over by Lily Carter, mother of the American president.[25] A year later this became the Akali Dal of North America, duly inaugurated at Vancouver with representatives from the two countries.

The Akali Dal took up turban cases and also argued that "Canadian Sikhs" is a proper category for Sikh enumeration instead of "East Indians" or "Canadians of origins in India", often used for official purposes. It also called upon the government to recognize gurdwaras and community organizations as consulting bodies instead of the "spurious" pan-Indian organizations that claimed to represent the Sikhs. In Canada the Akali Dal faced tough competition from the oldest and prestigious Khalsa Diwan Society of Vancouver. By the late 1970s many leaders within these organizations cooperated and competed on various local issues. As the campaign for Punjab's autonomy started in 1981, they all came together.

*Into mainstream politics*
Given the community leaders' orientation towards Punjabi political associations, the Sikhs' participation in national political parties is just beginning. An early exception to this rule was Dalip

Singh Saund (1899–1973) who was elected a congressman in 1956 and served for three terms as a Democrat representative. He had migrated in 1919 and became a successful rancher in the Imperial Valley. In Britain a Sikh MP was elected to parliament in 1992 and in 1997 two Sikh MPS were elected. In 1993 two Sikhs were elected to the Canadian parliament. In British Columbia two Sikhs became provincial ministers, Ujjal Dosanjh and Moe Sihota. It was mainly through the effort of Sikh MPS Gurbax Malhi and Harbance Dhaliwal that Canada agreed to open a liaison office in the Punjab. In 1994 Malhi visited Punjab as part of a Canadian trade team to New Delhi led by the Canadian premier, and the Punjab office was opened in January 1997. In the June 1997 elections a third Sikh MP was elected, one of the Reform Party candidates.

## Issues of mobilization

The leftist groups have mobilized on a broad range of issues. The Akali Dal, the KDS and other Sikh organizations have concerned themselves with issues of Sikh identity, taking up turban and kirpan cases, the teaching of Punjabi and other "representational" aspects. In all three countries, indeed in many other countries with a Sikh population, the Sikh dress and some religious practices have led to sustained campaigns; the male turban has created much hassle. Although an ordinary part of dress in the Punjab (where many Hindus also wear it), the turban in the overseas situation has meant a contest of an individual's will and a symbol of group solidarity. Sikh women's dress has also needed justification. Another article of dress, the kirpan worn by baptized Sikhs, is normally characterized as an offensive weapon in Western countries; it has also led to several contests in various schools and other public places. Similarly, taking an oath on Sikh scriptures was a new question requiring clarification; the list of practices which seem potentially odd in a Western context is quite long.

### Turbans and kirpans

These cases of identity marks have been contested in almost similar situations in each country. In Britain three cases are well known. The first case arose when Manchester Sikh G. S. Sagar, a bus garage worker, applied for the post of conductor in 1959. He was turned down as his turban violated the service rules. Sagar's offer to wear a blue turban with a badge was considered by the Transport Committee, which after "considerable research and discussion" disallowed exceptions to the rules.[26] Sagar's campaign, involving the local gurdwara and Manchester Sikhs, took seven years to reverse this decision. But it did not help T. S. Sandhu, a Sikh bus driver in nearby Wolverhampton. He started wearing a turban on returning from sick-leave in July 1965, but he was sacked for violating the dress code. After two protest marches,[27] 65-year-old Sohan Singh Jolly declared he would immolate himself on 13 April if the Transport Committee did not alter its policy.[28] Charan Singh Panchi, an Akali leader, bowed out as he could hardly match Jolly's dedication.[29] This threat embroiled the Indian ambassador, Shanti Sarup Dhawan, who met the Transport Committee on 29 January 1968 and appealed to the Department of Transport, warning it of the serious effects of a suicide.

A Punjabi Akali leader, Gurnam Singh, met the Indian prime minister, Mrs Indira Gandhi, in New Delhi over the issue.[30] The mayor of Wolverhampton described the Sikh threat as blackmail and finally the Public Transport Authority agreed to change the rule (Beetham 1970; Reeves 1989). The chairman explained how they had been "forced to have regard to wider implications". Then came the issue of crash helmets, leading to several years' struggle when Sikhs were given an exemption from wearing the safety helmet when riding a motorcycle. The turban issue arose again when a Sikh student's application was turned down by a headteacher, who knew that the student would be wearing a turban. This case turned into a major legal battle up to the House of Lords, which resolved the case in Sikhs' favour. In the 1990s a European directive on the use of personal protective equipment at work is being resisted by turban-wearing Sikhs. Paradoxically, the British government is unwilling to support the exemption it has given under its own laws.[31]

In North America there has been a similar number of cases involving the turban and other items of dress. A Canadian Sikh, Gian Singh Aujala, won a case against Pincurtan Security when he was sacked for changing his appearance, similar to T. S. Sandhu in

Wolverhampton. In 1986 an Edmonton boy, Suneel Singh Tuli, was allowed to wear a kirpan in his school after a contest at the Human Rights Commission. Another pupil, Parmvir Singh at Peel School, was also involved in the kirpan tangle; his case dragged on for two years before he was allowed to wear it.[32] Ranjit Singh was discharged from Canada's armed forces over a helmet issue.[33]

However, it was the uniform of the Royal Canadian Mounted Police (RCMP) which generated a major controversy. In 1987 Baltej Singh Dhillon applied for enlistment in the RCMP and qualified in 1991, but his turban broke a long tradition of RCMP headgear. It led to a national debate, at times highly emotional, with petitions and several court rulings.[34] In October 1989 Calgary MP Barbara Sparrow presented the Canadian parliament with a petition signed by 68,582 people; it demanded the RCMP to remain a "Canadian institution" by retaining its uniform.[35] As soon as the Canadian solicitor-general decided that Sikhs could serve in the RCMP with turbans in March 1990, the popular press turned the affair into an emotional "Canadian versus Sikh" issue with headlines such as, Who rules here? Sikhs were further snubbed by the Royal Canadian Legion (RCL), which barred Liberal member Ram Raghbir Singh unless he removed his turban.[36] Further humiliation came as the RCL denied veteran Sikhs from participating in the remembrance parade.[37] The issue went to the Human Rights Commission and ex-Mounties challenged its ruling in court.[38] From January to June 1994 the controversy raged, members of the British Columbia assembly and some Jewish organizations rallied round the isolated Sikhs.[39] Sikh MP G. S. Malhi raised the issue in parliament in June 1994, calling Sikhs' exclusion "a sad day for Canada".[40] Sikh veterans' feelings were assuaged by the Queen, who invited them to her "tea party".[41] After almost five years of struggle, in July 1994 the court ruled that Sikh Mounties' had the right to wear a turban, and Kuldip Singh, another Sikh, won the right to wear a turban in the Winnipeg Legion.[42]

The tiny town of Livingston, California, has about 100 Sikh children in its schools. About 10 were baptized and started wearing the kirpan. The Chima family's children, Rajinder Singh, Sukhjinder Kaur and Jaspreet Singh, were excluded from their school in January 1994 for wearing kirpans. The case led the

California Senate to amend the law so that Sikh students could wear a kirpan of appropriate size. However, the state governor vetoed the bill. The Livingston Union School District Trustees have sought advice to reconsider the ban, in line with other school districts in the Bay Area and parts of California, which allow kirpans with blunted blades and worn underneath clothing.[43]

### The issue of Sikh homeland

Before 1984 the idea of Sikh separatism in Britain and Canada appealed to few Sikhs. In Britain some leaders involved in the "save the turbans" campaign were the first to raise the issue of a Sikh homeland. The attitude of the Wolverhampton Transport Authority alerted them to their helplessness, and according to Charan Singh Panchi, despite repeated appeals to the Indian High Commission in Britain, they gained little sympathy. Whatever the reasons for the Indian high commissioner's reluctance to intervene in this "delicate matter", it led to bitter heart-searching among Akalis, some of whom questioned the Indian government's attitude towards the Sikhs. Davinder Singh Parmar thought a Sikh high commissioner would have been more sympathetic to the Sikh causes, while Panchi blamed the Indian High Commission squarely and joined the Sikh Homeland Front, when it was set up as a breakaway group from the Akali Dal.

The arrival in Britain of Dr Jagjit Singh Chohan in 1971 channelled these ideas into a small group of like-minded Sikhs, including Devinder Singh Parmar. Dr Chohan, an ex-minister in a short-lived government of Akali dissidents, raised the Sikh Homeland slogans at a demonstration in Hyde Park in September 1971. He also placed a half-page advertisement in the *New York Times*, making several claims about a Sikh homeland:

> At the time of partition of the Indian subcontinent in 1947 it was agreed that the Sikhs shall have an area in which they will have complete freedom to shape their lives according to their beliefs. On the basis of the assurances received, the Sikhs agreed to throw their lot with India, hoping for the fulfilment of their dream of an independent, sovereign Sikh homeland, the Punjab.[44]

In another tactic, Dr Chohan unfurled a Khalistani flag in Birmingham, witnessed by several hundred Sikhs. His activities were termed anti-Indian by many Sikhs, who felt deep affection for India.[45] In December 1971 the KDS Vancouver and a Leeds gurdwara in Britain were first to pass strictures against Dr Chohan. He also faced insults at a Wolverhampton gurdwara. Using a full-page advertisement in the Punjabi media, Dr A. K. S. Aujala, leader of the Akali Dal, warned against "traitors", clearly implying Dr Chohan and his associates. Most gurdwaras objected to Dr Chohan's campaign and restricted his entry. To show its displeasure with the ideas of Sikh separatism and perhaps to strengthen the hand of moderate Akalis in Britain, the Indian authorities arrested Chohan's supporter, Giani Bakhshish Singh, during his visit to Punjab on 15 November 1972. Detained for a year without trial, he was released only after intervention by the British government. Frustrated by strong opposition, the Sikh Homeland proponents took to the Punjabi media. In a letter published in *Des Pardes*, Charan Singh Panchi warned:

> Sikhs have to realise that there is no future in India domi-nated by Hindus. The honour and prestige of the commu-nity cannot be maintained without state power. Sooner we realise this challenge better it will be for us to set our objective of establishing a sovereign Sikh state in the Pun-jab. We cannot keep ourselves in bondage for ever. Our leaders act like beggars in New Delhi.[46]

Several letters followed to counter his arguments, some by Akalis, leftist groups and ordinary Sikhs. The debate, however, continued for several years. Denounced by community leaders and denied entry into major gurdwaras, Dr Chohan continued his singular campaign through various tactics. For a short while his campaign received some publicity by the unexpected election of Zorawar Singh Rai, an activist of the Sikh Homeland Front, as president of the Akali Dal in June 1972.[47] Rai proclaimed that the Indian high commissioner could not enter any gurdwara. Although this was far from true, it underlined the fact that Akalis were now split into two competing factions: the main group was led by Joginder

Singh Sandhu, who launched the Punjabi weekly *Shere Punjab* and sought the Indian High Commission's patronage; there was also a small dissident group advocating "Sikh Homeland".[48] Dissidents embarrassed the Indian High Commission through protests, the first on 15 August 1973, Indian independence day. In 1975 the Sikh Homeland Front was split due to differences between the mobile Dr Chohan and the modest Charan Singh Panchi. Dr Chohan kept the issue in the news through protests and visits to Punjab; in August 1977 he proposed Punjab should be renamed Sikh Homeland. Two years later, in November 1979, he took up the issue of radio transmission from the Golden Temple.[49] In this cause he was joined by some religious-minded people; they set up an International Golden Temple Corporation and held meetings at the Shepherds Bush gurdwara during 1979–82.[50] Besides extending an invitation to Sant Jarnail Singh Bhindranwale to visit Britain (which did not take place), the corporation arranged a World Sikh Festival in July 1982 with a seminar entitled "Sikhs are a nation". This coincided with Ganga Singh Dhillon's campaign in America, which addressed the Sikh Educational Conference in Chandigarh, emphasizing "Sikhs as a nation".[51] This again rekindled the debate in the Punjabi media on the issue of homeland and whether Sikhs constituted a nation.[52]

Parallel to Britain, but starting later, Surjan Singh led a small group based in Vancouver who propagated the idea of Sikh independence.[53] The group advertised its application to the United Nations for an "Observer Status" in October 1981; the idea was promptly rejected. They set up a "Republic of Khalistan" office on 26 January 1982 with a "Consul-General" who issued "Khalistani passports" and "Khalsa currency notes".[54] Dr Chohan offered support to bolster their campaign, but Canadian Sikhs had little sympathy with it. During the Baisakhi festival procession in April 1982, the Khalistani activists were beaten up and allowed to join only after they took down their placards.

However, events in the Punjab were fast moving towards "normalizing" the question of a "Sikh homeland". In 1978 there were 13 deaths as a result of a violent clash in Amritsar between the Akhand Kirtani Jatha, a group of orthodox Sikhs, and the Nirankaris, a heretical sect. This incident provoked much anger among several Sikh associations, who expressed sympathy and criticized the Indian government's role in encouraging this sect. A committee of British Columbian Sikhs condemned "atrocities committed against the devout Sikhs by the Nirankari Mandal in collaboration with the police in Amritsar, Kanpur and Delhi in which dozens of Sikhs have been mercilessly murdered and hundreds seriously injured".[55] This led to a partial rapport between Sikh Homeland protagonists and other community leaders. However, although Sant Bhindranwale wrote a letter to Dr Chohan "appreciating his services to the Panth",[56] even this commendation did not enable him to reach Sikh audiences within any gurdwara.

*The Punjab autonomy campaign*
In September 1981 the Akali Dal launched its campaign for Punjab's autonomy, popularly called *Dharam Yudh Morcha*. Although it attracted some qualified support from leftist groups, this campaign drew vigorous sympathy from diaspora Sikh associations. Aware of the Sikh diaspora's considerable resources, Harchand Singh Longowal, president of the Akali Dal, wrote a general letter to diaspora Sikhs:

> I am sending this special letter to all of you because you should know what is happening to the Panth. It is now 144 days into the *Dharam Yudh Morcha*. Some 17,557 Sikhs have courted arrest. You should take a deputation to the Indian High Commission office on 17 October, with a letter stating how Sikhs are being repressed in India. You should make the world aware how India is treating the Sikh Panth and to show that all Sikhs, wherever they are, share the anguish of Panth. I am stating with firm conviction that the *Dharam Yudh* will continue until the cruel Indian government agrees to our just demands.[57]

The Akali leader's appeal received endorsement from many organizations, and the Khalsa Diwan Society, Vancouver, took the lead by passing a comprehensive resolution on 18 October 1981:

The KDS Vancouver, BC demands from the government of India to stop discriminatory policies against the Sikhs. Like other nations, justice should be done to the Sikhs by accepting reasonable demands. The families of the martyrs and those of injured on account of the recent movement and those suffered in Nirankari clashes be awarded suitable compensations. The KDS Vancouver, fully supports the Special Resolution "The Sikhs ARE A NATION" [emphasis in original] passed during March 1981 by the general body of Shiromani Gurdwara Parbandhak Committee, Amritsar, Punjab, India. The KDS Vancouver further declares its full support to Shiromani Gurdwara Parbandhak Committee to represent the Sikhs' case at the UN.[58]

Major gurdwaras also passed resolutions of support. The Akali Singh Sikh Society, Vancouver, wrote a stringent letter to Indian and Canadian authorities, asking them to accept the status of "Sikhs as a nation".[59] A gurdwara in Winnipeg submitted a memorandum to Lloyd Axworthy, minister of immigration and manpower, stating:

We feel that the Canadian government should direct its officials not to give impetus and support to the Indian government's interference in Sikh religious organisations. We, the Sikh citizen of Canada, request the Canadian government, as a member of the United Nations, to protest against the atrocities being committed by the government of India on the Sikhs. Their legitimate demands are contained in the Anandpur Sahib resolution dated April 1973 as their rights and privileges as members of the SIKH NATION [emphasis in original].[60]

Several marches were organized in support of the Punjab autonomy campaign. During such a protest in Toronto, some unknown persons fired at the procession when it passed near the Indian Consulate Office on 14 November 1982, injuring three Sikhs and a policeman. Leading Sikhs blamed the Indian consulate for orchestrating violence to malign the Sikh solidarity.[61] To coordinate the growing campaign, a *Dharam Yudh Morcha Action Committee* was formed from 21 societies across Canadian cities on 23 July 1983. Besides assuring that the Sikh congregation of Canada was fully behind the leadership of Sant Longowal, the committee asked all gurdwaras

> to offer prayers to the successful conclusion of *Dharam Yudh Morcha*; gurdwaras should publicise the Punjab issue and relay accurate news; each gurdwara should contribute generously to *Shahidi* [martyrs] fund.[62]

The level of diaspora support was warmly welcomed by Punjabi leaders, who thanked them, especially the Khalsa Diwan Society, Vancouver:

> For those of you from Canada who not only have sent us money but also the *Jatha* to participate in the struggle, the Akali Dal is grateful to all the Sikhs of Canada. We do hope you would continue to give the same kind of support to the common cause of the *Panth*.[63]

The Punjab autonomy campaign also allowed space for community leaders to assert their position with their followers. The Khalsa Diwan Society, Vancouver, normally a battleground for Canadian Sikh leadership, assumed even greater importance. In the 1982 elections to the society, the Sandhu Group proposed a manifesto of orthodox measures, "no one will be allowed to address the Sikh congregation without covering their head first", although this issue had been settled by then. At the next elections in 1983, both groups promised a better Punjabi school, a major library and new facilities for the *langar*, but it was their commitment to the Punjab autonomy campaign with which they garnered most of their 11,500 voters. The stakes were so high that an Akali leader from Punjab made this appeal:

> At the critical times when we are engaged in the Panthic struggle, the control of Ross Street Gurdwara must be in the hands of those sympathetic to the Sikh-Panth. The Khalsa Diwan Society has already contributed very signifi-

cantly to the cause of Sikhs in the Punjab, those elected in the past year have proved worthy of their offices. I was very impressed by their dedicated work when I was on a tour of Canada. I appeal to voters to elect only those persons who are clearly committed to the cause of the Panth and disown those whose activities will weaken religious and other progressive tasks undertaken by the Society.[64]

The Nanar Group, backed by the Akali Dal, accused its opposition for collaborating with the Congress, who would sabotage the Punjab cause, printing the Congress Party of Canada's constitution that "promotes the policies and philosophies of the Indian National Congress". As the Punjab campaign progressed, the diaspora exchange became more extensive. On a request by Punjab's Akalis, a memorandum was presented to the Indian High Commission in each country. Despite heavy rain, some 2,000 Sikhs marched to the Indian Consulate Office in Vancouver.[65] In a symbolic and much publicized gesture, five Sikhs (the second group from Canada) departed for Punjab on 4 November 1982.[66] Support for the Punjab campaign became a matter of competition between various leading Sikh leaders and the gurdwaras.[67] Solidarity with the Punjab campaign not only provided legitimacy for particular community leaders, it also enhanced their general standing within the community.

The British Sikhs' support for the Punjab autonomy campaign ran parallel to Canada. A rallying march attracted some 5,000 people on 7 February 1982 in London. When the Indian prime minister, Indira Gandhi, arrived at the Royal Festival Hall to inaugurate the Festival of India in March 1982, she faced an Akali protest joined by the IWA and the Hind Mazdoor Lahir. At her reception in the Grosevenor Hotel, a few Sikh representatives were carefully chosen from the loyalist Namdharis and Ramgarhias. During the autonomy campaign, Dr J. S. Chohan gave another call for independence:

The Shiromani Akali Dal has struggled for the interests of the Sikh Panth since 1920s. . . . By passing the Anandpur Sahib resolution on 4 August 1982, and by presenting 45 demands to the Union Government, the Akali Dal has effectively crystallised the Sikh struggle in the right direction. . . . However, Akali leaders are still not categorical about their political goals. Why are you going around begging a measure of autonomy or a larger share of economic rights? . . . You must decide and openly declare once for all the rightful demand for a sovereign Sikh state.[68]

However, the Akalis were in no mood to change the objectives of this movement into a campaign for sovereignty. During the Punjab autonomy campaign, and especially from 1983, there were weekly collections in all prominent gurdwaras; the monies were sent to Amritsar and the amounts were displayed on noticeboards. A few gurdwara managers visited the Akali leaders in Amritsar, conveying their support and solidarity.[69] Starting in 1983, Puran Singh Karichowale led several rallies of Sikhs in support of the Punjab campaign. Thus on 10 May 1984 over 8,000 Sikhs paraded in the streets of London and presented a memorandum to Indian and British authorities. While the Indian prime minister warned that "donations to extremists" could be harmful, funds flowed both from Britain and North America to support the campaign.[70] On instructions from Amritsar, the Akalis also burnt copies of the Indian Constitution. They began a process of reorganizing various branches to coordinate the increasing momentum of support. However, these plans were shelved as the June 1984 tragedy effectively ended the Punjab autonomy campaign and sealed their credibility.

To conclude, ideas, ideology and politicians from the Punjab have affected the formation of associations in the diaspora. Such interrelationships have found consolidation through visits, exchange of resources and ideological support. All major political events in Punjab such as the Naxalite movement, the Indian emergency, and the autonomy campaign found vigorous mobilization among various segments of the Sikh diaspora. Three wars in which India was involved with its neighbours saw much patriotic fervour. While issues of wages, racism and immigration have involved leftist groups, the issues of ethnic identity, language and Punjab's autonomy have impinged upon traditional community leaders. Common to all organizations has been the role of gurdwaras as pivotal centres of mobilization. However, as the Indian security forces invaded the Golden Temple, reaction among the Sikh diaspora was extremely volatile and demand for an independent homeland became a rallying point for a large section of the community.

# FIVE

# Demand for homeland: Sikhs in North America

Whose evil eye has cursed my dear Punjab
Whose tyrannical feet have trampled on this beautiful rose
O' politicians, O' players of vile games
Return the unsheathed sword to its scabbard
Let smiles return to my mother land[1]

Just as the Punjab autonomy campaign launched by the Akali Dal
had received considerable support from North American Sikhs,
the Indian government's army action in the Golden Temple drew
a vigorous reaction, leading to a cry for a Sikh homeland. As news
spread on the evening of 3 June 1984, many Sikhs converged on
their neighbourhood gurdwaras and extraordinary gatherings
took place. The army had taken control of the Golden Temple; as
news bulletins flashed pictures of the devastated Akal Takhat
building, many Sikhs were angry, some cried openly, others had
difficulty in believing the reality of the news.[2] The assault was
interpreted as an act of sacrilege, a premeditated brutality, a gesture of contempt, the beginning of a process to destroy Sikh traditions; indeed, many considered it genocide.

Various gurdwaras said prayers for those who fought for the
sanctity of the Golden Temple; at a major gurdwara in Vancouver,
an emotional appeal for funds saw many women taking off their
golden bangles while barely concealing their tears. A call for
protest saw many thousands turned out on Sunday 10 June, when

processions were held in Vancouver, New York, Edmonton, Calgary, Toronto, San Francisco and Los Angeles. In Vancouver the procession started from Ross Street gurdwara towards the Indian consulate building; on the way the crowd shouted *"Khalistan zindabad"*, and cries denouncing India could be heard hundreds of yards away with many protesters yelling for revenge.[3] Angry Sikhs were involved in several incidents over the next fortnight, and an officer from the Indian embassy was beaten up.[4] Copious debate flowed through the columns of various Punjabi weeklies. One letter is typical of the emotionally charged atmosphere:

We should be ashamed of ourselves. We are dishonoured, . . . worthless, just like dead. Undoubtedly, we will build more religious places, become rich, but how will we ever regain our dignity? Where shall we find those priceless manuscripts of Guru Granth burnt by the Indian armies? Our leaders are quarrelling among themselves even now. What for? Is this humiliation not enough? Our youth in custody, many women dishonoured, children lodged in jails; for Guru's sake, let us unite now and forgo small differences. It is time for a calculated and suitable revenge; it is right time for sacrifices.[5]

Pamphlets and printed sheets were circulated, and news cuttings from English papers were pasted on gurdwara noticeboards. While the Punjabi media testified to the anger among ordinary Sikhs, sober analysis also began. An editorial in the *Sikh News*, a newly launched weekly, compared the Sikhs' tragedy with other diasporas:

Without debating the merits, magnitude or the quality of injustices done, there could be general agreement that history has not always dealt kindly with either the Jews and Palestinians. Both groups had aspirations for a homeland, but the Jews have transformed their dreams into a reality. The Palestinians' cause, though equally just, has been poorly served. Neither the Jews nor the Palestinians lacked money, nor did they lack committed people. Why then the

114

difference? It may well be that the Jews had two thousand years to have their strategy. Nevertheless, the fact remains that when Jews walked into Israel, world opinion escorted them. They had prepared the world carefully. . . . The Palestinians on the other hand, present entirely the other side of the coin. The world is entirely ignorant and blind to the justice of their cause. . . .

Now the question arises – how do the Sikhs appear to the world? The Indian government would like nothing better that the international community should brand us "terrorists". Proof is not necessary. When a lie is repeated often enough, people begin to believe. From the point of view of the Indian government, such a policy makes perfect sense. The dilemma is how do we respond? When a Sikh leader publicly proclaims a reward for the head of Indira Gandhi, how do we seem to the world? . . . The Sikh nation's cause has to be fought simultaneously on three fronts each requiring a different strategy, tactics and weapons. The three fronts are (a) the hearts and minds of our own people; (b) the international community; (c) the Indian government. We cannot neglect any front, or we may win the battles but lose the war. How does the Sikh community appear to the world? Are we like the Jews struggling to right a momentous wrong or like the Palestinians with little sense of the past, a chaotic present and little hope for the future? If the shoe fits, wear it.[6]

While many Sikhs cried for an independent Sikh state, Khalistan, as the only solution, a few dissented. The broadcaster CBS found a representative from Yogi Harbhajan Singh's centre in Los Angeles who denounced the idea of a separate Sikh state. The Federation of Sikh Societies of Canada along with the Sikh Society of Calgary placed three half-page advertisements in the *Calgary Herald*, starting on 14 August 1984, quoting Mahatma Gandhi's pledge that in case of betrayal, "the Sikhs could take their swords in hand with perfect justification before God and man". Narrating the Sikhs' contribution to the Indian independence movement, it contrasted the atrocities committed by the Indian army during the Golden Temple siege.[7] When on 31 October there came news of the assassination of India's prime minister, Mrs Indira Gandhi, it brought a sense of relief, overtly demonstrated in some places by the distribution of sweets. However, any jubiliation was soon dimmed by reports of the Sikh massacre in Delhi. Frantic efforts were then made within gurdwaras to collect money and clothes for the Sikh victims.[8]

## Main organizations

Intense political activity followed the events of 3 June 1984. Akali leaders were questioned within gurdwaras and through the press; they were asked to resign for they had "betrayed the Panth". It was paralyzed as its members deserted by denouncing their leaders as Indian state "collaborators". New Sikh leaders, mostly clean-shaven men hitherto unbothered with community affairs, came forward to form new organizations. Three major organizations were formed while smaller groups sprang up locally, including the Panth Khalsa, the International Sikh Organization, the Sikh Association of America and the California Sikh Youth. Other organizations with Sikh membership suffered, including the Indian Overseas Congress and leftist organizations such as the East Indian Workers Association and communist groups. Only the "Republic of Khalistan", until then a fringe group led by Surjan Singh, gained credibility. All were drawn into heated debate about who was responsible for the Amritsar tragedy. A summary of new organizations formed in 1984 is provided in Tables 5.1 to 5.3.

### The World Sikh Organization

The World Sikh Organization (wso) was formed in New York during a tumultuous meeting at Madison Square Gardens on 28 July 1984 from several thousand Sikhs of America and Canada, including some from Britain and the Far East. Didar Singh Bains, a millionaire from Yuba City, became its chief patron, and Jaswant Singh Bhullar, a retired major-general who had arrived from Punjab, became its secretary-general. The wso announced its international council, representing major states of America and Canada; it had two separate wings, wso-Canada and wso-America, with

**Table 5.1**   North American Sikh organizations post 1984.

| Organization | Year | Centre |
|---|---|---|
| Canada | | |
| International Sikh Youth Federation | 1984– | Vancouver, Toronto |
| World Sikh Organization | 1984– | Edmonton, Vancouver |
| National Council of Khalistan | 1986– | Vancouver |
| Babbar Khalsa International | 1981– | Vancouver, Toronto |
| USA | | |
| California Sikh Youth | 1984–86 | New York |
| Sikh Youth of America | 1986– | New York, Freemont CA |
| World Sikh Organization | 1984– | New York |
| International Sikh Organization | 1986–87 | New York |
| Anti-47 Front | 1985–86 | Bakersfield |
| Babbar Khalsa International | 1985– | San Jose CA |

**Table 5.2**   North American Sikh organizations: media.

| Media | Organization | City | Years | Language |
|---|---|---|---|---|
| World Sikh News | WSO | Stockton | 1985–96 | English/Punjabi |
| The Sword | WSO | Edmonton | 1985 | English/Punjabi |
| Awaz-e-Quam | ISYF | Toronto | 1985–86 | Punjabi |
| Chardhi Kala | ISYF | Vancouver | 1986– | Punjabi |
| The Sikh Herald | ISO | Edmonton | 1985–89 | English |
| The Khalsa | CK | Toronto | 1990–92 | English |
| Shamsheer-Dast | ISYF | Vancouver | 1985–86 | English/Punjabi |

WSO = World Sikh Organization
ISYF = International Sikh Youth Federation
CK = Council of Khalistan
ISO = International Sikh Organization

**Table 5.3**   North American Sikh organizations: Punjabi alliances.

| Organization | Punjab | Period |
|---|---|---|
| International Sikh Organization | United Akali Dal | 1985–86 |
| Council of Khalistan | First Panthic Committee | April 1986 |
| ISYF (Rode) | Damdami Taksal | 1984– |
| ISYF (Satinderpal Singh) | Second Panthic Committee | November 1988 |
| Babbar Khalsa | Babbar Khalsa | 1980– |
| Dal Khalsa | Dal Khalsa | 1992– |

ISYF = International Sikh Youth Federation

space for other countries, especially the United Kingdom.⁹ Ganga Singh Dhillon, well known for his work through the Nankana Sahib Foundation and a strong protagonist of Sikh nationalism, was elected president of wso-America.

A charter and constitution of the wso were approved. According to its constitution, the wso "will strive for an independent Sikh homeland by peaceful means". The wso has projected its image as an umbrella organization working for the Sikh right to self-determination in the Punjab, stressing its use of peaceful means. From Stockton, California, it launched *World Sikh News* in January 1985. This bilingual weekly aims to "project the voice of Sikhs across the world", giving news of the "independence struggle" and highlighting Sikh participation in America's "social and cultural life". The wso opened its offices in New York and Ottawa. While the new administrators had little knowledge and experience in dealing with the community matters, they soon learned to offer advice and organize rallies and to promote the Sikh cause at various governmental, legal and educational institutions.

The wso has drawn wide support among American and Canadian Sikhs; its membership in 1987 was estimated at 16,000, with a high share of Sikh professionals who contributed substantial funds for the cause of "Sikh freedom". It has often stressed that "the fundamental beliefs of Sikhs are enshrined in the United States constitution". Starting on a single issue of the Sikh homeland, the wso has gradually become involved in various community matters, the turban issues, the wearing of the kirpan by Sikh pupils and the management of gurdwaras. Its officials have been chosen through a mixture of elections and nominations.¹⁰ Its meetings are usually held in gurdwaras. While it competes for funds and community support with other organizations, it has sometimes led to bitter feuds with other leaders at the local level, especially in Canada, where the wso faced the powerful International Sikh Youth Federation and the Babbar Khalsa. However, according to wso officials, it has undertaken projects "in the face of utmost opposition", not only from outsiders but also from within the community.¹¹ Plagued by a serious rift at a very early stage, the wso avoided complete paralysis by dismissing its first secretary-general, whose work had aroused suspicion.[12] Ganga Singh Dhillon was also implicated in this episode and dismissed.[13]

### The International Sikh Youth Federation

The International Sikh Youth Federation (ISYF) was established in August 1984 by Harpal Singh, who had also fled from the Punjab. During his brief stay in Britain, he had helped Jasbir Singh in launching the International Sikh Youth Federation in Britain. In Canada he launched the new organization through two large meetings held in Vancouver and Toronto. Lakhbir Singh, who had family links with Sant Bhindranwale, became its convener, and a much revered leader. The ISYF soon emerged as the largest Canadian organization, with a stated membership of over 20,000; its most active centres were in Vancouver and Toronto with branches operating in many cities. In America it tried to establish a base in California, with branches in San Jose, Fresno and Los Angeles. In its first meeting, held in Vancouver on 10 November 1985, a resolution for an independent Sikh state was passed by several thousand supporters.[14]

The ISYF has functioned mainly through gurdwaras; its members have taken over the management of various gurdwaras, giving it a platform and funds for mobilization. This was not easy in Toronto and Vancouver, where the main gurdwaras were already in the hands of equally vociferous Khalistani managers. The ISYF has bargained with local leaders to gain a foothold. In Vancouver its main effort was directed at Delta Surrey Gurdwara, controlled by Congress Sikhs before 1984. After two years it took effective control of this major gurdwara. At Ross Street, the most prestigious Canadian gurdwara, it could not displace the WSO's control.

The ISYF's constitution incorporates an active struggle for an independent Sikh state.[15] It launched a Punjabi weekly, *Awaz-e-Quam*, through close cooperation with its sister organization in Britain. Its annual meeting has been attended by delegates from many other countries. However, the ISYF was beset with factions and suffered a major split in 1988. First, Harpal Singh, its chief organizer, fell from favour because he was alleged to have links with "Indian intelligence". Secondly, division followed on from

Jasbir Singh Rode's release from jail in 1988, when he abandoned the idea of Sikh independence and agreed to "freedom for the Sikhs within India". This compromise was interpreted as a betrayal; as a result, a rival ISYF was established under Satinder Pal Singh, who took most of the members with him. This development led to bitter disputes within the organization and control of some gurdwaras. At Delta Surrey, the Rode faction was dislodged by the new group. The new ISYF also took over a weekly, *Chardhi Kala*. Of the two ISYFs, the Rode faction declined rapidly, especially after its convener, Lakhbir Singh, left for Pakistan as his application for asylum was rejected. Due to various leadership disputes and factional fighting within the two organizations, the ISYF as a whole has lost many members and its credibility.

*The Babbar Khalsa*
The Babbar Khalsa is mainly based in Vancouver and its members have been drawn from the *Akhand Kirtani Jatha*, an orthodox group of baptized Sikhs. The Babbar Khalsa came to prominence after the Sikh–Nirankari clash in 1978. It became a staunch defender of Sikh orthodoxy. Its constitution clearly commits its members to an independent state:

> To work for the establishment of Khalsa rule where there would be no distinction on the basis of caste, colour, race, religion, origins or regional differences.[16]

Based on close-knit membership, the Babbar Khalsa's activities were mainly confined to the preaching of orthodoxy. However, in the post-1984 period it took an unequivocal stand on Sikh independence. Although the core membership of Babbar Khalsa has remained fairly small, its adamant fundamentalist posture and activities have attracted much publicity in the press.[17] Thus in 1985 an Indian weekly alleged that the Babbar Khalsa was providing armed training for the liberation of Khalistan; the story was concocted.[18] Among its most charismatic members, Talwinder Singh Parmar emerged as a controversial leader; his close associates distanced themselves, suspecting he was an "Indian intelligence man", while ordinary Sikhs were impressed by his bravado pronouncements and apparent commitment.[19] He came to Canada in the 1970s, then returned to take part in the Punjab autonomy movement in 1982, and fled from Punjab as police implicated him in criminal acts. He spent a year in a German jail from June 1983 to July 1984, and India requested his repatriation. He was released from jail during the Amritsar tragedy and he soon emerged as a major figure among British Columbian Sikhs. The police arrested him as a prime suspect for plotting a bomb on the Air India plane that blew up over the Irish Sea on 27 June 1985, and they questioned him several times during the next two years.[20]

Sometime in 1988 he left Canada and joined the Punjab militant movement via Pakistan. He was expelled for his anti-party activities shortly before his death, on 15 October 1992, in an alleged "police encounter"; his charred body was disposed of unceremoniously by the police. His "martyrdom" became an occasion for celebration among his followers while confirming the suspicions of Air India flight victims.[21] As a consequence, the organization was split into two groups. The Babbar Khalsa (Talwinder group) is led by Ajaib Singh Bagri supported by Chatar Singh, Massa Singh and Jassa Singh, while the main group's leaders are Gurdev Singh in Vancouver and Rampal Singh in Toronto. With the death of Babbar Khalsa chief Sukhdev Singh in July 1992, the overseas organizations have suffered decline; the controversy surrounding his death also damaged the strict orthodox image of the organization.[22]

## The Council of Khalistan

The Council of Khalistan emerged from the dissenting voice of Dr Gurmeet Singh Aulakh and his associates, who had earlier worked in the wso. Earlier in 1984 he abandoned his professional career in Massachusetts to devote himself full-time to the "cause of freedom". However, due to differences within the wso, especially over the role of J. S. Bhullar, he organized the International Sikh Organization in 1986, then on his nomination by the Panthic Committee from Punjab to represent Sikhs in North America, the Council of Khalistan was established. It set up an office in Washington DC, where Dr Aulakh became an effective lobbyist and won considerable sympathy from many American gurdwaras for funding his campaign. His efforts have resulted in the censuring of India's human rights record in the Congress, as will be discussed in the next chapter. He has established links across Britain and Europe to mobilize financial and moral support. Among smaller organizations, the Dal Khalsa was established rather late in 1993 with Jasbir Singh Bajwa as its president and branches in Toronto and Vancouver. An American branch has Pritpal Singh as its chief and is based in New Jersey.[23]

## Mobilization

These organizations have shared a common objective: an independent Sikh state. However, their methods of mobilization and resources differ significantly and their activities can be discussed under three headings: (a) resources and media, (b) rallies and linkages, and (c) dissension and Canadian–Sikh relations. Lobbying of the government is discussed separately but some of their other activities are outlined below.

### Resources and media

Both the wso and isyf started with considerable funds donated by ordinary Sikhs. The gurdwaras have been the most important sources for funds and mobilization. Therefore, the struggle over the control of gurdwaras started immediately after the launching of new organizations. Besides the substantial incomes of various gurdwaras, the prestige and central place of main gurdwaras in the whole community attracted the new leaders into their management.[24] Major gurdwaras, such as the prestigious gurdwara at Ross Street, Vancouver, and Richmond gurdwara in New York became centres of contention. At Ross Street gurdwara the new committee in 1985 was chosen from the wso activists by its several thousand members. Since then a coalition of the Akali Dal and the wso have managed it, while the isyf made a concerted challenge in 1990. Its ex-president, Bikar Singh Johal, survived an assassination attempt and this led to some fights between the wso and isyf supporters. In the 1992 elections, the isyf established its control. The second major gurdwara at Delta Surrey also fell into the hands of the isyf in 1986. However, in 1990 the isyf (Rode) backed by the Babbars won the elections. Thus, a combination of the wso and the isyf has controlled major gurdwaras. Broadly, the wso is considered moderate and has received support from many Akalis, whereas the ISYF has been considered uncompromising. As the ISYF is divided into two factions, its power to dictate has shrunk. At Toronto, Lakhbir Singh's presence had ensured easy control, but from 1988 these alliances have been unpredictable. Only the Council of Khalistan has enjoyed the support of several American gurdwaras, without involving itself in the local rivalries or elections.

The gurdwara routines have seen considerable changes due to the events of 1984. Although religious services remain the same, Sikh devotees now listen to *dhadis* narrating the atrocities of the Indian government, heroic resistance by the Sikhs, and glory of the sovereign Sikh state under Ranjit Singh. Anniversaries and festivals such as *Baisakhi* are occasions to confirm Sikhs' commitment for liberation. On important occasions, prayers and hymn singing are followed by appeals for funds for Khalistan. Some gurdwaras controlled by Sikh saints have also come under strong scrutiny by the new political leaders. Though no *sant* was required to take up a public declaration, those suspected of hobnobbing with the Indian government were denounced.

For some, there was also fear of intimidation and violence. Sant Mihan Singh's followers faced some angry questions both in Coventry and Vancouver as the *sant* was thought to be a close ally of the Indian home minister, Buta Singh. Many politically active followers deserted him but his quietist attitude also brought some followers, who found weekly routines at other gurdwaras too politicized.[25] Arguments and political differences within the community have become the subject of intense discussion, leading occasionally to violence and a charged atmosphere. The Sikh Cultural Society of New York, for example, had to suspend four of its members who participated in the Indian independence parade in 1985.[26]

The second major source for each organization is the media. While large organizations such as the WSO and ISYF have established their own media mouthpieces, smaller ones have relied on the local media, pamphlets and personal appeals through gurdwaras. Of the newspapers, the WSO's *World Sikh News* became a leading bilingual weekly, with shrewd comments and a lively letters page. Though, in recent years, both its size and editorial control seem to have slipped. *World Sikh News* editorials have underlined the need for Khalistan, with a critical line on India's policies towards minorities. It has often underlined its belief in the inevitable collapse of Indian polity:

> What is being forgotten is the historical inevitability of the collapse of India and the creation of more than 20 nation-states in the subcontinent. This will release tremendous energy of the people now bottled up by the reactionary colonial Indian system. . . . It is quite clear that India's existence is a permanent threat to peace in South Asia where nations are engaged in defensive spending rather than ameliorating the lot of the people. The US administration must look at India in this long term angle rather than a partner in development of trade and commerce. . . . What is important is to build up international public opinion to force India to grant right of self-determination to its people to opt for freedom.[27]

The ISYF newspaper *Awaz-e-Quam* did not survive when a rival faction of the ISYF took over *Chardhi Kala*, another Punjabi weekly. *Chardhi Kala* has now been positioned to compete with the more popular *Indo-Canadian Times*. A monthly, *Shamsheer Dust*, was also launched for several issues. The Council of Khalistan has issued a broadsheet, while Dr Aulakh's associates brought out several papers in the last decade, including the *Truth* and *Sikh Herald*.[28] These papers have reported the news and events from the Punjab, providing comments and rallying supporters for funds. Besides using their own media, leaders have also responded with replies and letters in the mainstream English newspapers. The English media's coverage of Sikh issues has also been noticed by the WSO and other organizations. After a campaign by some local Sikhs, in Stockton and in San Diego, routine terms such as "Sikh terrorists" were replaced by "suspected Sikh extremists" and "according to police sources".[29] Dr Aulakh has often appealed to world leaders through letters in the American media; here is an example[30]:

> The international community must understand that a plebiscite would give the Sikh nation an opportunity to

determine its fate through peaceful, democratic means. Khalistan will eventually be free. India is not viable politically, morally or economically. It will eventually break up into its natural parts as the former Soviet Union has. However, we can end the bloodshed and free Khalistan through the democratic mechanism of the plebiscite. I urge the international community to choose the peaceful option.[31]

Other activists have edited papers promulgating their views on the Sikh situation. Sher Singh Kanwal published *Jago*, a monthly carrying news and analysis of the Punjabi situation. Besides sending Amarjit Singh as its own representative on Capitol Hill, the ISYF has kept up its propaganda with its weekly paper, *Chardhi Kala*. Many pamphlets have been published by these organizations. Thus, on the tenth anniversary of June 1984, the ISYF and Dal Khalsa jointly issued a pamphlet asking Sikhs to remember the Amritsar massacre. They argued that India's disintegration will not only liberate Sikhs but many other nationalities: the Muslims, Tamils, Nagas, Jharkhandis, Mizos, Kashmiris, Christians and others.[32] With India becoming a minor power, its neighbouring countries could then devote resources to economic programmes for the poor instead of spending them on defence. It also alleged that India's secularism and democratic system is a mere camouflage for Hindu domination over minorities.

The mainstream Punjabi media have also undergone changes, mainly moving from pro-India towards pro-Punjab. The circulation for Punjabi papers and journals, as a whole, has increased. Divisions within the community were sharpened and reflected in the media; angry letters to various editors have been followed occasionally by physical threats. While the *Indo-Canadian Times* took a sympathetic stand on the "Khalistan issue", it was duly denounced by leftist organizations, as pandering to "sectarianism, separatism and violence" and its editor was seriously wounded in a shooting incident.[33] He published a biography of Sant Bhindranwale widely distributed in Western countries. Effusion of emotional poetry by amatuer writers matched those of established writers; established writers were mostly leftist and they were largely critical of Sikh separatism. Gurdev Singh Mann, a noted Punjabi writer, was inspired to recount the destruction of the Akal Takhat in a long poem; many writers on the left offered a view of India as a multinational country that could or should accommodate Sikh demands.[34] Others have advocated a solution by emphasizing the broad Punjabi nationality, while a few have simply condemned Sikh nationalism as mere fanaticism. *Canada Darpan*, a leftist weekly from Vancouver, carried a vigorous attack on Sikh separatists, blaming almost equally the Akalis and Congress for the tragedy.

### Rallies and linkages

The WSO and the ISYF have organized regular rallies and meetings in local gurdwaras up and down the country. At such rallies, resolutions are passed affirming Sikh resolve for independence. Thus, in Sacramento on 28 July 1991, the WSO passed a resolution alleging that "since 2 June 1984, Khalistan has been occupied by the immoral and corrupt forces of the evil Indian regime"; it went on:

> Amnesty International, Punjab Human Rights Organisation, and several other human rights organizations have repeatedly reported these brutal incidents in their reports. In spite of these, the Indian government continues its inhuman and brutal acts against the innocent Sikhs. On this day we appeal to all freedom loving nations to boycott India economically until the Indian government stops its inhuman treatment and allows the international human rights organisations to observe and investigate independently.[35]

Sikh festivals, such as Nanak's anniversary in November, have taken on a political hue. Every November in Yuba City a procession celebrates the Sikh founder's day. For many years the chants of *Khalistan zindabad* have formed part of this gathering.[36] Meetings have been held to "pay homage to martyrs", and Punjab has produced quite a crop from 1987 onwards, often through encounters between militants and security forces.[37] Of the many such meetings held, the following is typical:

> The Sikh Youth of New Jersey are performing *Kirtan* in the memory of Sikh martyrs of Khalistan Commando Force,

Bhai Sahib Labh Singh, Lt Gen. Surjit Singh Panta, Gurjit Singh Kaka, Sukhvinder Singh Sandhu, Gurcharan Singh Khalsa [Dal Khalsa] and many unknown Sikhs who have laid down their lives for the liberation of Khalistan in recent months. Also to honour all those Singhs now in jail for the honour of the Sikh nation, including Simranjit Singh Mann, Gajinder Singh [Lahore] Satnam Singh [Lahore] Gurpartap Singh and his friends [New Orleans jail] and several others who are sacrificing their precious lives for the cause of *Panth*. . . . A prayer will be said for them.[38]

On important days in the Sikh calendar, leaders have expressed their resolve and solidarity, thus the wso president, Dr M. S. Grewal, sent greetings to the "Sikhs of the world":

On the auspicious occasion of the birth of the Khalsa nation, the [wso] rededicates itself to the liberation of Khalistan. Let us all unite to face the challenge posed to the Sikh identity.[39]

As part of the campaign, various seminars have seen participation from Sikh leaders.[40] In Chicago, Sikh and Kashmiri leaders attended the Parliament of World Religions in September 1993; both leaders were opposed by Indian religious delegates. Dr Aulakh has visited many universities to address Sikh students, putting the case for Khalistan. At Berkeley he joined in a debate in December 1991, where a majority supported him, while a few dissidents called his campaign a suicidal package.[41] Credit was sought by the wso, whose leaders participated in the un International Ethnic Parade in July 1987. The wso has also questioned other organizations' rights to represent Sikh interests, especially exposing the nacoi in Canada for its "lack of interest" in representing the true Sikh viewpoint.[42]

From 1984 onwards, visiting Indian leaders have faced protests. Thus the Indian prime minister, Rajiv Gandhi, faced a strong Sikh rally at the Commonwealth meeting in Vancouver, later in Washington,[43] then again in New York during his address on nuclear proliferation at the United Nations on 9 June 1988.[44] In May 1994 the Indian prime minister, Mr Rao, faced a joint protest by

Kashmiris and Khalistanis of 3,000 people.[45] Sikhs were again joined by Kashmiris in San Francisco, where a Hindu community fundraiser for Congressman Stephen Solarz was disrupted.[46] The Indian independence day on 26 January has seen regular Sikhs and Kashmiri protests.[47] On the fiftieth anniversary of Indian independence, in August 1997, which saw much enthusiasm among overseas Indians, the Sikh participation was confined to Congress, and other patronized Sikhs, while many organizations either boycotted these functions or held protests.

Each organization has built its links with particular Punjabi leaders. Because of these links, considerable funds have gone to the Punjab. While the Babbar Khalsa has supported its parent organization in the Punjab, the wso has made no alliance with any militant group. It has provided general support and funding for Sikh victims of state repression. Aid has been sent by all organizations for Delhi and other victims of state repression. Like the wso, the Council of Khalistan has not aligned with any militant group, and its financial support to the Punjab has been negligible; its strategy was to lobby the government representatives. The ISYF (Rode) has firmly aligned with the Bhindranwale family, first supporting the United Akali Dal in 1985–7, then on the release of Jasbir Singh Rode, providing him substantial finance for *Aj di Awaz*, a Punjabi daily launched by him from Jalandhar.

The rival ISYF (Bitu) has provided considerable support to particular militant leaders in Punjab and Pakistan through finance and moral support. In a confrontation, Indian consulate officials in Lahore were beaten by Canadian Sikhs.[48] Smaller groups such as the Sikh Youth of California and others have sent support to their respective contacts in the Punjab. In turn, they have sought support from the Punjabi leaders. Thus, Dr Aulakh publicized the fact that the Panthic Committee had nominated him as its representative.[49] Again in 1995, Dr Aulakh was applauded for his services in highlighting Punjab issues at international organizations.[50] However, these alliances saw many changes as particular militant leaders were killed or groups merged to form new alliances.

Support for particular leaders often led to passionate arguments among members of a particular organization. Sikh leaders visiting North America with records of sacrifices have received enthusiastic welcome,[51] while others who are considered to have betrayed the Panth are spurned.[52] Many Sikhs who have lost their relatives in the Punjab have been honoured at local gurdwaras. As part of the exchange with Punjabi leaders, appeals have been made to take a particular course of action. Thus at the prompting of Dr Aulakh, a resolution passed by Houston Sikhs in August 1994 was presented to Manjit Singh, acting head of the Akal Takhat, asking him to lead a "Quit Khalistan Movement". Dr Aulakh also offered his opinion on the SGPC's Global Sikh Meeting at Amritsar in September 1995. Although no organization ever gave a call to overseas Sikhs to return and join the struggle, individuals were inspired nevertheless. Five Canadian Sikhs left for Punjab and were eventually killed.[53]

Besides keeping contacts with Punjabi leaders, North American leaders have made extensive contacts with European Sikhs. The Babbar Khalsa has fostered close links with its sister organization in Britain and expanded its influence, especially in Europe.[54] It has also tried to cultivate friendship with other diaspora communities. A meeting with the Fresno chapter of the Muslim Friendship Society led them "to identify the mutual areas of interest and [to] develop [an] effective strategy to voice the plight of the minorities as well as explore the avenues for relief to the victims".[55]

Since 1984 many disputes within groups have resulted in violence, usually over the control of a gurdwara, or cases involving assaults on various officials of the Indian High Commission. In a major incident, Malkit Singh Sidhu, one of Punjab's junior ministers, was attacked during a private visit to attend a marriage ceremony in Vancouver. The minister had tried to speak in West Mount Gurdwara, where Khalistanis forced him out. He was later ambushed and hurt slightly. In another incident, Dr Gurpartap Singh Birk, Sukhvinder Singh, Gurinder Singh and Jasbir Singh Sandhu were arrested in May 1985 in New Orleans for an alleged plot to kill Bhajan Lal during his visit to America[56]; Bhajan Lal was the chief minister of the Indian province of Haraana. A number of Canadian Sikhs were concerned about their Punjabi relatives or were arrested while on a visit there, leading to governmental intervention. Tejinder Singh Raipur, a Hamilton Sikh, was acquitted of the June 1986 charges of conspiracy to commit sabotage in India. On 2 July his brother Balbir Singh was shot dead by the police in the Punjab. The case involved the issue of human rights, as defence lawyer Michael Code explained:

> The postmortem showed that he died of a contact wound at the back of the head . . . in which the gunshot was travelling downwards through the body and it had left blackening and charring around the edges of the wound indicating that the gun had either been in contact with the back of the neck or else within inches of the back of the neck. This obviously was consistent with an execution and was inconsistent with the sworn affidavit filed by the Indian police in Hamilton. (Kashmeri & McAndrew, 1989: 148)

Code alleged that "the Indian police were producing perjured affidavits in Canadian courts".[57] Another Canadian Sikh, Daljit Singh Sekhon, was interrogated by security forces and charged under the TADA.[58] Balkar Singh, an ISYF activist from Canada, was arrested in Amritsar in 1987 while on a visit to his relatives.[59] Although his lawyer filed a writ of *habeas corpus*, he was still tortured: hamstrung from the ceiling, electric shocks to his sexual organs, armpits and head, while his legs were forced into a straight line, rather like the splits. He was released only after the intervention of the Canadian authorities on 26 October 1988. His torture led to the Canadian government making a strong protest to the Indian high commissioner. However, he was arrested again in April 1992 in Toronto and charged this time for supporting terrorism.[60] Maninder Singh, a Toronto Sikh, was arrested by the Delhi police when he was returning to Canada.[61]

From 1984 onwards, spiralling violence in Punjab forced the Sikh youth to flee abroad. Many cases were supported by Sikh organizations in North America. Jasbir Singh Bajwa, who had applied for refugee status, was ordered for deportation on 11 May 1988. The WSO supported him, including his right to wear a turban in custody.[62] Similarly, Ranjit Singh Gill and Sukhminder Singh Sandhu, arrested in May 1987 in New Jersey, fought their case against extradition demanded by the Indian authorities; they were supported by the WSO and their case was heard at Manhattan's Metropolitan Correction Center. The Punjab Human Rights

Organization sent an affidavit by scientists, barristers and social workers attesting India's low regard for human rights and how the charges had been framed.[63] Only a few Sikhs were granted asylum as a result of this campaign.[64] Petitions have been sent to members of parliament on behalf of leading Sikh activists arrested by the Punjab police. Thus, in December 1992, Ajit Singh Bains's arrest was voiced in the parliament by Derek Lee and David Kilgour, the local MPs, after prompting by local Sikhs.[65]

### Dissension and Canadian-Sikh relations

The case for a Sikh state has not found unanimous support within the community; opposition has come from many quarters, as well as from outside. Sikh communists have argued for a broad class war rather than a narrow nationalist struggle. During 1984–5 meetings organized by leftist groups were regularly disrupted by the ISYF supporters, leading to occasional scuffles. Writer Gurcharan Rampuri was beaten up at a public meeting while Vancouver lawyer Ujjal Dosanjh, later to become a minister in the British Columbian government, was attacked by a gang.[66] The leftist groups have proposed an alternative solution to the Punjab problem. The East Indian Defence Committee, an organization with many Sikh members, advised the government in September 1984:

> The army should be taken out of Harimandir Sahib and the reconstruction should be given to Baba Kharak Singh and his associates. Chandigarh and other Punjabi speaking areas should be given to the Punjab. A village should be taken as a unit of measure. Water and electricity issues should be referred through the Supreme court. The government should not interfere into Sikh religious matters and it should look carefully into the complaints of the Sikh community. Gurdwaras should be used only for religious purposes, no arms should be taken into them except the *kirpan*. Separatist and imperialist powers should be given a crucial beating and defeated. The solution to the Punjab problem and the Sikhs is not to play into the hands of imperial powers or advocate separatism but to maintain the unity of India and solve the issue amicably.[67]

And Ujjal Dosanjh argued:

> I have invited you here simply to state, once and for all, to
> the world that an overwhelming but silent majority of the
> Sikhs residing abroad in Canada, United States of America
> and Great Britain, although aggrieved, are Indians to the
> core, and want their just place in one India and want very
> sincerely and strongly to reject the attempts of a handful of
> individuals to give a separatist tinge to the injured feelings
> of a community. Khalistan is not our demand, all religious
> and political grievances are soluble within the context of
> one united India. The attempts to promote a division of
> India or violence associated with those attempts are not
> condoned by the overwhelming but silent majority of the
> people residing abroad. I ask those of us who have raised
> separatist slogans to reconsider their position and come
> and join hands with all of us.... We have not only the
> integrity, communal harmony and unity of India at stake
> but also the credibility and respect of our community in
> Canada and other parts of the world.[68]

Dosanjh's stand was rebutted by many other readers, including
the Khalsa Diwan Society.[69] "[If] Ghadar leaders could wage a
war from San Francisco seventy years ago", argued one Sikh,
"why aren't we justified in demanding Sikh independence?"[70]
Another Sikh, Gurdev Singh Chohan, responded to Dosanjh's
letter:

> Ujjal Dosanjh [*Vancouver Sun*, 3 April] seems all wet behind
> the ears to say that ethnic minorities must 'integrate'.
> Canada highlights multiculturalism. The Sikh commu-
> nity's wide support for Khalistan in no way detracts from
> Canadianism. Just let him look at what American Hebrews
> have done for Israel. Dosanjh obviously continues to
> exaggerate since he conveniently charges the 'proponents
> of Khalistan' with violence, terror etc. [which is] non-
> existent in fact. As the elusive 'silent majority' he is
> neither silent nor majority, spotlighting himself in a false
> controversy.[71]

Another communist group led by Hardial Bains denounced the idea of Sikh separatism, calling instead for a socialist state. In a major publication of its kind, Bains (1985) blamed Indian leaders for fanning Hindu fundamentalism. In 1992 he called for the release of his brother Ajit Singh Bains, a retired judge and human rights activist, by posing many searching questions to the Indian state's law officers.[72] In Bay Area another leftist organization, Anti-47 Front, issued a pamphlet against Sikh separatism.[73]

However, a more serious threat and opposition came from the Canadian government. With the Air India plane crash in June 1985, the federal government took an increasingly hostile attitude towards Sikh leaders.[74] Under obvious pressure from India, the government almost conceded Sikh complicity in the disaster. A British Sikh was extradited to Canada and convicted of the Narita Airport bombing.[75] Canada's foreign secretary declared that some Sikh groups constituted the "most serious internal security threat", and asked intelligence agencies, the Royal Canadian Mounted Police (RCMP) and the Canadian Security Intelligence Service (CSIS) to pursue Sikh activists. In addition, he called for a boycott of the WSO, the ISYF and the Babbar Khalsa. The government also took a harsh view of the Sikh refugee claimants. The issue of Sikhs' civil rights was raised in the parliament by Mrs Copps:

> We have a responsibility to ensure that the RCMP or CSIS is not aiding or abetting the persecution of the families of Canadian nationals back home in their homeland as a result of the exchange of erroneous information.[76]

Undeterred, the Foreign Affairs Ministry duly endorsed the Indian government's claim that Sikh community temples were being run by "extremists". In an interview with the *Vancouver Sun*, the foregin minister promised help to "moderate Sikhs" to enable them to wrest control of their community organizations from a handful of "extremists". After the Department of Multiculturalism grant to the Macauliffe Institute of Toronto for a feasibility study, the National Alliance of Canadian Sikhs was launched in 1992; its initial funding was $130,000 and many of its members were drawn from the ISYF and other organizations.[77] The wso opposed the launching of a government-sponsored organization, and protested to the minister concerned, Mr Gerry Weiner.[78] Mr Gian Singh Sandhu, the president of wso-Canada reminded the minster: "The wso has represented Sikhs without any grant or subsidies from the government, yet the Minister has the nerve to proclaim the alliance as a principal organisation representing Sikhs. Would the government stop interfering in the internal matters of ethno-cultural communities and the Sikh community specifically?"[79]

The Canadian government's meddling in Sikh affairs was applauded by the media. Taking an increasingly hostile attitude towards Sikhs' involvement in Punjabi affairs, some papers dubbed it as a terror campaign. The events in Punjab have created "a bitter echo, poisoning relations between the Federal Government and the Sikh community with mistrust between Sikhs and other Canadians".[80] The role of Babar Khalsa leaders, in particular, attracted the media's venom. A Reform MP, Vale Meredith, discovered its charity status and sought its reversal.[81] Sikh leaders face an uphill task of convincing the Canadians that the result of this stereotyping has created problems for ordinary Sikhs. According to a Canadian-based scholar, Joseph O'Connell, the post-1984 situation has led to circumstances where

> criminal cases affecting Sikhs in Canada in which investigating or prosecuting officials have been found to have compromised their integrity and credibility of their work. . . . This repeated violation of the normal legal guidelines in the case of Sikh defendants has alienated many Sikhs and undermined public confidence in Canadian investigative and judicial agencies that deal with minorities. (O'Connell et al. 1988: 444)

In his annual report, Gian Singh Sandhu summed up the community leaders' predicament under increasing surveillance by government agencies. He advised Sikhs to offer no cooperation:

> increased harassment, misinformation, distortions and invasion of privacy, intimidation and violation of our fundamental rights of civil liberties. The amateurish cloak and

dagger behaviour of various investigators, . . . lack of significant convictions, convinces us that further cooperation is a waste of time. It feeds a fiction about the Sikh community which never had any foundation or basis except in the paranoid perceptions of Indian officials. . . . The Sikh community and its friends are now part of a ping-pong game of exchanged misreporting, fabrications, garble, mumble and slurs in which csis appears to play a central role. . . . In future, in those rare cases where information requested is specific, limited, and important to assist national security, . . . in all such cases, Sikhs are advised to hold meetings only in the presence of a lawyer, newspaper reporter or an opposition Member of Parliament.[82]

The image of Canadian Sikhs as a "troublesome and violent community" has affected organizations' campaigns and strategies, both alienating support from ordinary Sikhs and causing a distrust of the Canadian police and justice departments.

Responding to the tragedy in Punjab, Sikhs formed a number of associations. After the initial outcry against the Indian government, these associations have tried to establish themselves by controlling some gurdwaras and setting up the media. Through protests, rallies and the media, they have highlighted the plight of Sikhs and argued for an independent Sikh homeland. Despite opposition from within the community and from other agencies, the issue of an independent homeland has continued to generate a heated debate. While the massive support for such a cause has subsided, various organizations have continued to draw support from the community.

# SIX

# Demand for homeland: Sikhs in Britain

Arise, O' my brothers and sisters, arise
Share the responsibility
When the nation is in peril
Don't turn your back now[1]

British Sikhs, like the North American community, reacted with extreme anger and sadness to the Indian army's action in the Golden Temple. They turned out for a mammoth protest on 10 June 1984, against the "desecration of the holiest shrine" of their faith. Over 25,000 Sikhs from all walks of life joined in a march from Hyde Park to the office of the Indian High Commission in Aldwych, denouncing the Indian government and shouting *Khalistan zindabad* (must have an independent Sikh state, Khalistan).[2] In the march were leaders of the Kashmiri Liberation Front and Nagas. Except for some slight damage to the Indian High Commission in the late hours of that night, the protest passed off peacefully. Several gurdwaras organized local demonstrations in Birmingham, Bristol, Coventry and other cities.

The anger of ordinary Sikhs over the army action in the Golden Temple found expression in many others ways.[3] Responding to a call in the Punjabi media for the "liberation of the Golden Temple", several volunteers offered themselves, but the idea was soon dropped as the Indian government introduced new and strict visa regulations. Punjabi newspapers carried angry letters from Sikhs, and the English media also saw some correspondence

137

and editorials.[4] Between 3 June and 31 October 1984, when the news came of the Indian prime minister's assassination by her two Sikh bodyguards, many developments had taken place within the community. Two new organizations were formed, the Khalistan Council and the International Sikh Youth Federation, both committed to nothing less than an independent Sikh state. The press reported celebrations among Sikh circles in Britain following the news of the Indian prime minister's death.[5] Later they were attributed to a few irresponsible community members. Celebrations were dimmed by the news of anti-Sikh riots when many gurdwaras organized financial help and materials.[6]

While the Indian authorities defended the army action in the Golden Temple in terms of India's unity, Sikhs in Britain were outraged over what they thought was the deliberate desecration of their most sacred historic shrine. Explanations offered by the community, its different set of assumptions and its language ran in stark contrast to Indian official statements. Videotapes and books explaining why the action had become necessary by the Indian High Commission to gurdwaras and many Sikh homes were brought together and publicly burnt in the gurdwara premises. A call given to boycott Indian banks and other official organizations was taken up; a gurdwara in Wolverhampton shifted its account to a British bank. A Sikh journalist wrote to the Indian High Commission to condemn the Indian army's characterization of *amritdhari* Sikhs.[7] The government of India announced visa requirements in a move to curb "Sikh extremism from abroad".[8] Sikhs who had acquired British citizenship faced bureaucratic controls, besides extra cost. The Punjabi traditional games taking place in various cities were cancelled for the rest of the year.[9] The photos of Sant Bhindranwale, along with Shahbeg Singh, Amrik Singh and other prominent Sikhs killed in the army action in Amritsar, appeared in several British gurdwaras.

## Main organizations

The Akali Dal leaders who had sustained support for the Punjab autonomy campaign were condemned at various gurdwaras as the Indian state's collaborators. Calls were made for the formation of new organizations dedicated to the cause of Sikh freedom. Intense political activities took place across the country for the rest of the year. New organizations formed in this period are summarized in Tables 6.1 to 6.3.

**Table 6.1** UK Sikh Organizations post 1984.

| Organization | Year | Centre |
|---|---|---|
| Khalistan Council | 1984 | London |
| ISYF (Rode) | 1984 | London, Midlands, North |
| ISYF (DT) | 1984 | London, Midlands, North |
| ISYF (Chaherhu) | 1984 | London, Midlands, North |
| Babbar Khalsa | 1978 | Midlands, North |
| Dal Khalsa | 1984 | London, Birmingham |
| Punjab Unity Forum | 1986 | London |

ISYF = International Sikh Youth Federation

**Table 6.2** UK Sikh organizations: media.

| Media | Organization | City | Year | Language |
|---|---|---|---|---|
| Khalistan News | Khalistan Council | London | 1984– | English |
| Awaz-e-Quam | ISYF | Birmingham | 1985– | Punjabi |
| Wangar | Babbar Khalsa | Birmingham | 1985–94 | Punjabi |
| Sikh Pariwar | Dal Khalsa | Birmingham | 1985–92 | Punjabi |

ISYF = International Sikh Youth Federation

**Table 6.3** UK Sikh organizations: Punjabi alliances.

| Organization | Punjab | Period |
|---|---|---|
| United Akali Dal | United Akali Dal | 1985–86 |
| Khalistan Council | First Panthic Committee (Zaffarwal) | 1986– |
| ISYF (Rode) | All-India Sikh Students Federation | 1984– |
| ISYF (DT) | Damdami Taksal | 1984–88 |
| ISYF (Chaherhu) | Second Panthic Committee | 1988– |
| Babbar Khalsa | Babbar Khalsa | 1984– |
| Dal Khalsa | Dal Khalsa | 1982– |

ISYF = International Sikh Youth Federation
DT = Damdami Taksal

139

## The Khalistan Council

The Khalistan Council was elected at a large and stormy meeting of several thousand Sikhs on 23 June 1984 in Southall, west London.[10] And the meeting severely criticized Akali Dal leader Giani Amolak Singh and his associates who had led the Punjab autonomy campaign from 1981; all of them were forced to retire. The Akali Dal was swept aside by the new organization, the Khalistan Council. Dr Jagjit Singh Chohan, long ostracized for his idea of a separate Sikh homeland, was given support and a free hand to lead it. The council announced its other four members: Gurmej Singh of the Babbar Khalsa, Sewa Singh of the Akhand Kirtani Jatha, Karamjit Singh representing the youth, and Harmander Singh from the reorganized Akali Dal. A businessman offered an office in central London, appropriately named Khalistan House, where several volunteers undertook the campaign amid furious meetings and enquiries. The council's appeal for funds was given a generous response, and within two months its funds reached £100,000. The community's turmoil was under close watch by the Indian authorities. As the BBC broadcast a short statement from Dr Chohan, regarding the consequences of sacrilege committed by the Indian prime minister through attacking the Golden Temple, a major diplomatic row erupted. It was the first of many fissures to run through Indo-British relations, which were thought to be progressively worsening due to the Sikh factor.[11]

The Khalistan Council leaders started by arranging meetings at various gurdwaras up and down the country where, amid cries of *Khalistan zindabad*, issues of freedom and news of the Punjab were discussed by anxious Sikhs. The council tried several ventures, including the radio programme Voice of Sikhs, launched in May 1985. This ceased broadcasting after a few months due to pressure from India.[12] The council also made a strong bid to contact various governments; at one time it claimed Ecuador was willing to recognize the "exiled government of Khalistan". An Ecuadorian diplomat spoke at a Birmingham rally, but this gesture proved empty.[13]

After two years the council started showing strains due to differences among its members. In 1986 the Babbar Khalsa representative, Gurmej Singh, effectively parted company by forming a "Government in Exile" in Birmingham. Karamjit Singh resigned while Khaira was already suspended, due to a family feud; they were replaced by other members. After a decade of campaigning, the Khalistan Council has lost its mass appeal, and its active supporters have dwindled to a small number of Dr Chohan's admirers. This has not deterred Chohan's campaign; his speeches, mixed with a wry sense of humour, are eagerly listened to by the audience in various gurdwaras. Of all the organizations, the Khalistan Council has presented a consistent case for sovereignty by emphasizing a secular vision; it abhors violent means to achieve this objective. Dr Chohan has continuously pointed out the existence of India's extensive network of *agents provocateurs* working to malign the legitimate movement among the Sikh diaspora.

### The International Sikh Youth Federation

While the Khalistan Council represented a somewhat older and moderate leadership, a more "youthful" organization was inspired by Jasbir Singh "Rode", a nephew of Sant Bhindranwale. Jasbir Singh Rode had arrived in July 1984 from Libya, where he had worked as a small contractor. At a meeting on 23 September in Walsall, Harpal Singh and Jasbir Singh announced the formation of the International Sikh Youth Federation (ISYF), with a 51-member panel headed by Dr Pargat Singh. Its constitution was issued and panel members were sworn in. According to its constitution, the organization will work for the "establishment of a sovereign Sikh state", and to realize this goal it will make Sikhs aware of their "religion, the past struggle for independence, unique identity, and its status as a separate nation and national flag".[14] Within months of its formation, the ISYF established 21 branches in different cities; its membership was estimated at 16,000 in 1985, with Birmingham and Southall branches having over 1,000 members each. However, its leader, Jasbir Singh, after a short visit to Pakistan, was detained in December 1984 and deported under pressure from the Indian government.[15] The ISYF mounted a strong protest, alleging that Jasbir Singh's emphasis on baptism became a sore point for the Indian government, which sought his extradition.

The ISYF led the campaign for a Sikh state by holding a monthly meeting at a gurdwara, where its leaders rallied supporters and

collected funds. Many foreign delegates attended its annual convention in September. In common with its Canadian sister organization, the ISYF has lent full support to Bhindranwale's family,
first to the United Akali Dal led by Baba Joginder Singh, then to
Jasbir Singh. His stand of "Sikh rights within the Indian national
framework" disappointed many members, and a dissenting
group was formed as the ISYF (DT).[16] Earlier in 1985 Gurmel Singh
had obtained several letters from Damdami Taksal leaders in the
Punjab to legitimize his claim for leadership, but he eventually fell
into disgrace. From 1988, besides the main ISYF (Rode), the ISYF
(Bitu) has supported the Second Panthic Committee,[17] and the ISYF
(Chaherhu) has allied to the Panjwarh group.[18]

### The Babbar Khalsa

Parallel to the Canadian organization, the British organization is
also well known for its members' strict adherence to orthodox
traditions.[19] Before 1984 the majority of its members belonged to
the *Akhand Kirtani Jatha* and were content to recite scriptures
through night-long hymn-singing sessions. A leading member of
Babbar Khalsa, Gurmej Singh, was nominated to the Khalistan
Council; he has also maintained an office in Birmingham and
headed a government in exile. His application for British citizenship evoked a severe diplomatic row between Britain and India,
as the Indian government branded him an "extremist".[20] The
Babbar Khalsa has maintained a close relationship with its parent
organization, highlighting its leaders' aims and activities; in December 1984 an appeal by its Punjabi leader was issued under the
blaring heading "War declared against Hindu imperialism".[21] The
Babbar Khalsa seems to have committed itself to a militant strategy and did not abhor violent means, as many of its posters and
declarations have called for revenge. As the death rate in Punjab
rose, especially during 1990–92, its monthly publication *Wangar*
headlined such news as signs of victory.[22] With an occasional
caution about the ethics of violent strategy, some of its leaders
seemed to be basking in the glory of murderous trails.[23] Gurdeep
Singh, a Babbar leader on a visit to Canada, outlined this strategy:

> The organization has always stood against the killing of
> innocents and fellow travellers and those who are not

guilty. However, we should deal [kill] the police and others who are obstructing our path, but this should only be undertaken without any consideration of personal revenge or enmity.[24]

In July 1992 Gurdeep Singh, who had gone to Punjab to participate in the movement, surrendered in a highly publicized platform; his confession was seen as a betrayal of the militant movement and led to a major setback for the organization.[25] The organization partially controls three gurdwaras, two in the Midlands and one in the North. Differences have also arisen since the nomination of Balbir Singh as its chief in 1994.

### Other organizations

Mention should also be made of Dal Khalsa, a small group consisting of Jaswant Singh Thekedar, Manmohan Singh, Mohinder Singh Rathore, Manjit Singh Rana and a few others. They all came from the Punjab, either as refugees or through other means. The Dal Khalsa rose to prominence after an Indian plane was hijacked to Lahore by Gajinder Singh and four others, all of whom were jailed. Jaswant Singh Thekedar arrived in Britain in 1982; he wrote a short book and produced a map of Khalistan, but his activities were limited among a few friends in Southall.[26] Ranjit Singh Rana has also been prominent in literary activities; he floated a scheme to offer awards for Punjabi writers.[27] The Dal Khalsa leaders have also split under accusations of being "paid agents" of Indian intelligence.[28] They have provided assistance to hijackers jailed in Pakistan. Besides these groups, some gurdwara managers have arranged seminars and publications.[29]

## Mobilization

Despite sharing a common aim of Sikh independence, support for each organization within various sections of the community is far from uniform. Their activities to mobilize supporters can be discussed under four broad headings: (a) resources and media; (b) rallies and linkages; (c) dissension and Anglo-Sikh relations; (d) representation to the government. Representation is discussed separately, but the other activities are considered below.

*Resources and media*

Apart from the Khalistan Council, which had established an independent office in London, the two other organizations have used gurdwaras as their centres. Gurdwaras have provided funds and a ready audience for their campaign. Due to the sheer strength of its members in 1985–96, the ISYF members challenged many gurdwara committees, normally coalitions of Akalis, Congress and IWAS. The IWAS had always played an active part in local gurdwara politics; their members saw no contradiction in being a communist and becoming part of a gurdwara's management. This was especially the case in Derby, Leicester and Nottingham. The ISYF forced elections at the Midlands' major gurdwaras, leading to its control. In London, again due to the strength of the local branch, the ISYF effectively took charge of the Singh Sabha gurdwara. At Smethwick the ISYF persuaded two parties to withdraw the court case and won the elections held in December 1984, dissolving the stronghold of Communist and Congress committee members. At a Luton gurdwara in May 1985, the ISYF fought against the Congress committee members.

A similar situation developed in Huddersfield and Coventry. However, in Coventry it competed with the Babbar Khalsa, leading to police intervention amid many ugly scenes. For a few years its management was taken over by a women's committee.[30] At a Kent gurdwara this erupted into violence as the ISYF supporters fought against other groups.[31] The struggle to control gurdwaras led to lengthy litigation at many places.[32] A few gurdwaras controlled by *sants* also faced difficulties and managers clarified their respective stands.[33] By 1986 the ISYF had established a strong presence in several gurdwaras. The ISYF has probably used some gurdwara funds for its rallies, for advertisements in the media and the printing of its various pamphlets. However, its major source of funding has come from direct appeals to the congregation, through members' donations and collections by its branches, which have raised money from sympathetic supporters.

The differential support for each organization reflected to some extent the differentiation of the community. The Khalistan Council tried to extend the "common struggle" against a "Brahmin-led" Indian state,[34] and sought out groups to join it. It has held conventions among various groups. A Ramgarhia Panthic Convention was held in a Birmingham gurdwara, assuring "full support for the Khalsa Panth of which Ramgarhia is an integral part".[35] However, as time passed, the position of Ramgarhias has become more complex. While condemnation of the army action in the Golden Temple was unequivocal, later events have divided them into two factions, one supporting the independence campaign and another refraining, but still taking strong exception to abuses hurled at Zail Singh, a Ramgarhia and president of India.[36] However, Ramgarhia gurdwaras have contributed to Delhi's Sikh victims.[37] The Bhatras have shown enthusiasm for the homeland cause; their gurdwaras have been the venues of many conferences. Among Sikh sects, Namdharis have shown little interest; indeed, some members are probably opposed to the movement. The Ravidasis have been unambiguous in standing aloof from the Khalistan issue.[38] The Jat Sikhs have dominated the Khalistan movement, though divided by ideology and patronage.

Major organizations have established newspapers and used them for mobilization. Besides a monthly, *Khalistan News*, launched by the Khalsa Council, it has also brought out pamphlets and a major report on Punjab's troubles. Dr J. S. Chohan is a prolific columnist; his contributions frequently appear in the Punjabi media, extolling the independence struggle. He has often offered advice through "open letters".[39] The ISYF launched a Punjabi weekly, *Awaz-e-Quam*, which has consistently advocated the Sikh state and covered news and views from the Punjab.[40] However, the weekly received a major setback when its editor, Raghbir Singh, was arrested in early 1995 and threatened with deportation for "reasons of national security".[41] The ISYF has published pamphlets and produced songs and videos. The Babbar Khalsa ran a monthly, *Wangar*, from 1987 to 1994. Similarly, Ranjit Singh Rana, a Dal Khalsa leader, produced a monthly for several years. The Khalistan Council has also used mainstream Punjabi media for mobilization and funds through a typical appeal:

> The Golden Temple is the spiritual source of the Sikh faith. Whenever the oppressors and powerful have dishonoured it, they have invited ruin upon themselves and their dynasties. The Sikh nation has always come out stronger while

facing such genocides. Almost every Sikh household in India has in some way contributed to the sacrifices for the Sikh nation. . . . We, who are living overseas, it is duty of every Sikh household to . . . pay tributes to the spirit of our martyrs.[42]

Each organization has presented its vision of the Sikh state. While the Babbar Khalsa has published a series of essays on a "charter of Khalistan" through the monthly *Wangar*, the Council of Khalistan has publicized the Panthic Committee's framework for such a state.[43] K. S. Sihra (1985a, 1985b), who had floated the idea of a "Sikh Commonwealth" to sustain "self-awareness", wrote extensively to promulgate Sikhs' rights to independence. Davinder Singh Parmar carried on his one-man crusade through the *Khalistan Times*.[44] Similarly, Swaran Singh, a businessman, has campaigned for the homeland.[45] During this period, gurdwara routines have changed perceptibly. At major gurdwaras, *dhadis* narrate martyrs' tales combining the contemporary heroes with those from the past. Among these groups, Gian Singh Surjeet, Jago Wale and many other *dhadis* have composed songs in memory of contemporary martyrs such as Labh Singh, Avtar Singh Brahma, Anokh Singh, Shahbeg Singh and others (Pettigrew 1992b).

Several Punjabi writers have published creative works on the tragedy. Thus Gurdev Singh Matharu narrated the history of the Akal Takhat, Balhar Randhawa's many poetry books celebrated Sikh "martyrs'" sacrifices and echoed the tragic conditions facing the community.[46] Another poet, Baldev Bawa, wrote a long poem evoking memories of Punjabi life. The emergence of the Khalistan movement has also affected the mainstream Punjabi media; the propaganda war waged through various weeklies and pamphlets became particularly intense during the years 1985–7. *Des Pardes*, a leading weekly, gained further circulation. Due to its "communalist" stand, its editor was boycotted by leftist and Punjabi Hindus led by Vishnu Dutt Sharma.

### Rallies and linkages

Apart from special meetings on important dates in the Sikh calendar, all organizations have held annual conventions during the summer. At such meetings, resolutions have been passed for a

Sikh homeland and leaders declared solidarity with their brethren in the Punjab and appealed for funds.[47] Besides some parliamentarians, these conventions have been regularly attended by foreign delegates from North America and Europe, including leaders of other estranged minorities, the Kashmiris, the Nagas and occasionally the Afghans. In 1990 the Khalistan Council passed the following typical resolution:

> On 26th April 1986, that Panthic committee made public the resolve of the Sikh nation to constitute itself in a sovereign state that shall bear the name Khalistan. This convention, on the fourth anniversary of that historic occasion pledges its full support to the ideal of that sovereign state and urges all individuals, parties and organisations that oppose the said ideal shall be given no recognition nor cooperation of any kind. This convention urges Sikhs all over the world to abide by the law of the country they are settled in and be good citizens wherever they are but be aware of the agents of the Indian government who roam around provoking strife in various gurdwaras for the very specific purpose of discrediting the Sikh settlers in the eyes of the host society.... This Convention urges ... to take new hope from the events of East Europe and other parts of the world which herald the dawn of the era of freedom of peoples.... This convention urges all national governments to link their aid and trade programme with India to its human rights record.[48]

As part of the campaign, protestors have greeted visiting Indian ministers with placards such as "Sikhs are a nation", "Khalistan Zindabad" and "India quit Khalistan". Thus Indian Prime Minister Rajiv Gandhi faced over 2,000 protestors in October 1985.[49] His visit was preceded by the arrest of four ISYF members from Leicester, who were jailed for plotting to kill him.[50] Another protest awaited the next prime minister in 1994, when he concluded the Indo-British agreement on protection of investments and held talks on nonproliferation of nuclear weapons. A more angry band greeted Punjab's police chief, K. P. S. Gill, during his visit to London.[51] Visiting Sikh leaders have also been questioned or honoured. Thus Basant Kaur, wife of the late Beant Singh, was warmly welcomed by several gurdwaras and individuals who offered her financial help.[52] Other leaders, such as Darshan Singh and Manjit Singh, both *jathedars* of the Akal Takhat, have faced many questions.[53] Only with the election of the Akali-Janata government in the Punjab in early 1997 did some gurdwara committees welcome Punjabi leaders. In August 1997 an Akali minister spoke at the Southall gurdwara, although at the same time, two Babbar Khalsa activists were arrested for allegedly plotting to kill a deputy inspector general of Punjab's police, also on a visit to London.[54] During August the celebrations of India's fiftieth anniversary were marred by protests in Leicester, Birmingham and London.

Sikh activists have approached British political parties regarding their stand on the Punjabi question. The Labour Party's concern was limited to "human rights" only, and is presumably due to its old connections with the Congress. Its leaders paid glowing tributes to India's successive Congress leaders in managing India's democracy and dismissed the idea of self-determination for Sikhs.[55] The Green Party, although an insignificant force in British politics, formulated a lengthy solution that supported Sikhs' rights to self-determination.[56] The Scottish National Party also endorsed Sikh self-determination:

All nations of the world have a right to self-determination. In that context, both the Sikhs and Scots are still struggling to seek what is rightfully theirs. We are therefore united in our love for liberty. . . . The SNP, of course, rejects every means other than the democratic one to regain our independence. . . . At the same time, we do acknowledge that in many other parts of the world minorities suffer from oppressive imperialism. Those are obviously different conditions, and require different responses.[57]

Due to Sikh voters' concentration in some inner-city areas, a few MPs have voiced their concern about the Sikhs' plight in parliament. While there is no record of the Tory Party's collective stand on the Sikh homeland, in 1986 a dispute arose within the Anglo-Asian Conservative Association of West London; the branch was eventually dissolved by Conservative Central Office due to "Sikh domination".[58]

As the Punjab became a battleground for a protracted war between militants and security forces, leading to many cases of human rights abuse and a mounting death toll, both the Khalistan Council and the ISYF became involved in the human rights issue. Dr Jasdev Singh Rai, an ex-president of the ISYF, set up the Sikh Human Rights Group in Southall, and the ISYF established the Khalsa Human Rights in 1992 with an office in a Leicester gurdwara. Both groups have held exhibitions to expose "India's ghastly human rights record". They have supported the cases of Karamjit Singh Chahal and Raghbir Singh, two activists under detention. Karamjit Singh Chahal, a Luton Sikh, was detained in August 1990 under the National Security Act.[59]

Cases of Sikhs' relatives in Punjab who have been tortured or killed by the security forces have also been highlighted. Among them, the Khalsa Human Rights brought the case of Tejinder Singh, reported "disappeared" in 1993.[60] And the case of Jaswant Singh Khalra has received wide publicity.[61] Cases of Sikh visitors to Punjab who have also been harassed or arrested, have also been taken up; among them is the case of Mrs Kuldip Kaur, who was released after considerable publicity and intervention by her MP.[62] Besides providing support for Sikh refugees in Europe, they have assisted Amnesty International and other human rights agencies in Europe. Some human rights activists from Punjab have been helped to present their cases at international venues. Thus, Ajit Singh Bains and D. S. Gill of the Punjab Human Rights Organization have briefed British MPs at the House of Commons.[63] In several meetings held at the House of Commons by Sikh lobbyists, cases of human rights abuses and the demand for a Sikh state have been argued.[64] Another group, the Sikh Study Forum, has also contributed to an awareness of the human rights situation in Punjab.[65]

Strict visa regulations between Britain and India were slightly relaxed only in 1990 with the change of Indian government when the Congress government was replaced by the Janata Party headed by V. P. Singh. Kuldip Nayar, the new ambassador, took some credit in scrapping a long list of Sikhs under surveillance by India House (Nayar 1991). He was also able to establish some rapport with the Sikh community and paid a visit to the main gurdwara in Southall, the first time an Indian diplomat was received after June 1984.[66] A feature common to all organizations is their close but shifting alliance with particular groups and leaders in the Punjab. Through such linkages, considerable financial help has gone to the Khalistan movement and to families of "martyrs" killed or tortured by the security forces. Thus the first Sikh Shahidi Sammelan organized by the Damdami Taksal in 1985 received considerable finance to honour families of Sikhs who had died in the Golden Temple.[67] While much affected by developments in Punjab, the diaspora leaders have also sought to influence these events. Thus, as a reaction to the Punjab Accord of 1985, leaders and major gurdwaras rejected it as a betrayal of the community's interests. In the early 1990s they called for a boycott of the 1992 elections. While the ISYF has followed the fortunes of Jasbir Singh and the Bhindranwale family, the Khalistan Council has allied itself with the Panthic Committee formed in 1986.

After its declaration of Khalistan on 29 April 1986, the Panthic Committee nominated Dr G. S. Aulakh, an American Sikh, as its chief representative; Dr J. S. Chohan sought nomination from the second Panthic Committee nominated by Jaffarwal. The formation of a third Panthic Committee under Dr Sohan Singh split the ISYF members. Such fluid alliances in the Punjab militant groups from 1987 onwards led to bitter controversies between the diaspora organizations and their leaders. But they were intended to give credibility to particular leaders, when certain Punjabi leaders had clarified "true representatives" abroad. The relationship between the Khalistan Council and the ISYF became acrimonious with the murder of Harmander Singh Sandhu, a Punjabi leader, in January 1989. Dr Chohan condemned this murder while the Babbars and the ISYF felt "satisfied" with the explanation offered by the Panthic Committee members.[68] For a few years, militant leaders published their versions of major events in the British Punjabi media.

Besides fostering links with the Punjab, leaders have extended associations across the diaspora, especially in Europe and North America. The ISYF (Rode) and the ISYF (Chaherhu) have established branches in Europe; Rode's close allies are based in Co-

150

logne and Frankfurt with another branch in Switzerland. The Babbar Khalsa, besides supporting many refugees, has established branches in France, Germany, Norway and Switzerland.[69] After the death of Talwinder Singh Parmar, the Canadian Babbar leader, the European branches split up, especially affecting Belgium, where many members switched their support to the late leader's legacy.[70] The Dal Khalsa has established branches in Europe, especially in Norway, Switzerland, and Germany.[71] Exchange between leaders across the diaspora has also led to diplomatic rows, leading to restrictions by the immigration authorities. The issue was raised in the British parliament when an American Sikh was denied entry into Britain:

> Until March of the last year a Mr. Gunga [sic] Singh Dhillon a Sikh with an American passport had been allowed unfettered entry to the United Kingdom. However when he arrived in August of last year he was prevented from entering the United Kingdom and sent back on the next available plane. . . . This gentleman well-respected in America and known to both Republicans and Democrat politicians at Capitol Hill was denied entry . . . at the whim of the corrupt Indian government.[72]

The immigration minister, Mr Waldegrave, also dealt with Harjinder Singh Dilgeer by serving a deportation order.[73] Gurmej Singh, Babbar leader, was denied a visa for Australia,[74] on an earlier occasion; he was deported by the US authorities while crossing over to Canada. In Bucharest an attempt was made on the life of the Indian ambassador to Romania, Mr J. F. Ribeiro, on 20 August 1991. Three Sikhs involved in the Bucharest incident became the subject of negotiation as Romania's consul, Mr Liviu Radu, was abducted by Sikh militants in October 1991; he was later released unconditionally on 25 November after 48 days.[75] Assistance for two Sikhs at their trial was provided by the Punjab Human Rights chapter in Britain.

### Dissension and Anglo-Sikh relations

Opposition to Sikh separatism has come from several quarters. Members of the Indian Overseas Congress were confronted by angry youths at several gurdwaras. They also halted the Indian independence day celebrations in Derby on 14 August 1984. Congress members were thrown off gurdwara committees in due course. In 1985 the Congress President Sohan Singh Lidder was wounded in Luton and an ISYF activist, Sulakhan Singh Rai, was charged with the attempted murder. He was also charged with the plot to murder Tarsem Singh Toor, a businessman and Congress activist of Southall, who was shot dead by unknown assailants.[76] To rejuvenate the Overseas Congress, a prominent Sikh and ex-union minister, Swaran Singh, arrived in 1985 but left after organizing the Punjab Unity Forum, later known as the Sikh Forum, to cultivate "unity among Indians abroad".[77]

The cause of Indian unity and the fight against Sikh separatism also came through an unexpected quarter. *Sandesh International*, the only weekly that had endorsed the Indian government's policy on the Punjab, started a major campaign for the unity of India; it took careful notice of those who had burnt India's national flag at many places.[78] This campaign was undertaken by Darshan Das, a new sect leader of Sachkhand Nanak Dham, preaching Hindu-Sikh reconciliation and opposing separatism. Amid the allegation that he was a "ploy of Indian agencies", Darshan Das, a Punjabi Hindu, established a centre in Handsworth surrounded by many followers. At the height of the tensions in 1984, the newly discovered saint startled many Sikhs by promising to send a gold-wrapped copy of the Guru Granth to the Golden Temple to replace the original destroyed during the fighting. He also announced that Sachkhand Nanak Dham was carrying out repairs to the damaged Akal Takhat and Sikhs should not give donations for this purpose to any other organization.[79]

A subsequent call challenged anyone to burn the Indian flag in the Slough–Gravesend area. When the following weekend some Sikhs duly set fire to the Indian flag, Das's supporters were severely beaten up in the resulting clash. After that, the saint's close followers published a torrent of propaganda for "Indian patriotism" and "world peace" with regular columns "reinterpreting Sikh scriptures". Undeterred by such high ideals, an angry band of Sikhs tried to burn down the sect's headquarters in Birmingham, and the continuing hostility between the sect and the

Khalistanis boiled over when he was killed during a prayer meeting in Southall.[80]

Opposition by Punjabi communists is far more significant, as the IWAs have always been dominated by Sikhs. Although a few Hindus held important positions, Sikh labourers effectively provided the backbone of protest marches against racial discrimination and immigration laws. However, like the Akalis, the IWAs were also ill-prepared for the Punjabi crisis. Some IWA leaders branded the demand for a Sikh state as sectarianism, in line with Punjab's two communist parties, who also alleged it was a foreign conspiracy.[81] They offered the old favourite theory of "imperialist powers conspiring to break up India" and blamed in equal measure the Congress government and the Akalis for the Punjabi crisis. Only a splinter group of Punjabi communists in the IWA(GB), became more critical of the Indian government's role in handling the Punjabi situation, and its solution was a total revolution for India's economic and political problems.

Many Sikhs abandoned the IWA; resignations took place *en masse* in Leicester and Derby, disowning the communists' stand. In Birmingham the IWA workers who tried to distribute a pamphlet in front of a gurdwara received a severe beating. This was the first of a series of fights that continued for several years in the Midlands.[82] As the number of communists murdered in the Punjab increased, the differences were exacerbated.[83] Police had to intervene in many fights between ISYF and IWA supporters. The ISYF president, Dr Pargat Singh, and his successor were also involved in physical attacks by unknown gangs.[84]

Opposition to the Sikh homeland campaign also came from Punjabi Hindus, led by Vishnu Dutt Sharma, who launched *Charcha*, a monthly to woo "the patriotic section of Sikhs and the Punjabi population", and encourage "unity" among Indians. A leading Punjabi Hindu businessman published an appreciation of the Indian prime minister, Indira Gandhi; while Ram Kaushal, a proprietor of Hindi weekly *Amardeep*, launched the weekly *Punjabi Darpan* and there were some discernible differences between Hindus and Sikhs in various cities.[85] The new weekly's coverage replaced the *Sandesh International*, which had ceased publication in 1986 when its editor, Ajit Sat Bhamra, was jailed for heroin smuggling. He was also alleged to have close links with the

Indian High Commission. Another paper, *Shere Punjab*, also made an appearance for a short period. However, if winning the hearts of the Sikh readers was a priority, the means employed were not straightforward,[86] for both *Punjabi Darpan* and *Shere Punjab* were owned by Hindus and their circulation remained small. The leftist papers, such as *Lalkar* or *Lokta*, had even smaller circulations, but they kept up their slogans of internationalism, working-class solidarity and revolutionary changes.

In the general cries of "Sikh terrorism" throughout Britain, the chief constable of the West Midlands Constabulary warned, after a visit to Punjab, that several hundreds were involved in "terrorist activities".[87] This led to a strong reaction and a vigorous denunciation by community leaders. At a meeting arranged between the police chief and Sikh delegates, a petition was presented:

> Our homeland is now being mercilessly trampled on by Indian security forces with the so-called aim of curbing extremism, which in practice, has meant denying justice to thousands of victims of state terrorism. . . . Reports of daily killings of Sikh youth, and secret trials without adequate provision of any decent legal assistance, and a policy of 'shoot to kill' by the police authorities has been reported by the British and international press and these reports have been confirmed by some humanitarian organisations.[88]

To conclude, the Indian government's action in the Golden Temple has helped to create three major organizations that have campaigned for an independent homeland. Indeed, the vigorous support for Dr Chohan, his rapport and rehabilitation among the community during the past decade, all add up to an enormous change in the community's outlook. Perhaps a broad sympathy and a yearning for an independent homeland has become a permanent feature of a section of the British Sikh community.

# SEVEN

# Mediating between states: Sikh diplomacy and interstate relations

Give it a serious thought, my brother, why we have no standing in the world?[1]

During the past decade, leaders of the Sikh diaspora have lobbied various government officials, parliamentarians and international agencies. This has necessarily led the Sikh diaspora into the realm of "international relations". In this meddling role between host states and India, the strategies of Sikh leaders have been defined by their perceptions, by their resources and also by the lobbying system of each country. In the United States, where ethnic diplomacy is well established as part of the congressional proceedings, they have gained considerable influence; whereas in Britain and in Canada, which have parliamentary systems, the Sikh diplomacy had limited scope (Wilson 1990; Shain 1994).

The Sikh interaction with state officials and human rights agencies has been prompted by three factors. First, as supporters of a particular organization became involved in legal or even criminal cases due to various disputes, especially involving members of the ISYF and the Babbar Khalsa, the interference of police and governmental agencies has forced its leaders to respond. Secondly, a sharp escalation in human rights abuses in the Punjab has led them to establish human rights groups, who have lobbied the representatives or parliamentarians and sought the support of international agencies. Thirdly, and perhaps the most significant factor, the Indian government's pressure on host states to control what it termed "Sikh terrorism" has prompted community leaders to rebut "India's disinformation campaign" at international venues.

## Indian government and the Sikh diaspora

The Indian government's assessment of the Sikh diaspora's role in the Punjab is contained in a White Paper (1984).[2] In a report of 58 pages, 9 are devoted to overseas Sikh organisations' and how they fostered separatism in the period up to 1984:

> Several secessionist Sikh organisations are operating abroad. The chief among them which have raised the slogan of 'Khalistan', or a 'separate Sikh state' are the National Council of Khalistan, Dal Khalsa, Babbar Khalsa and Akhand Kirtani Jatha. The 'National Council of Khalistan' headed by Dr Jagjit Singh Chohan is active in the UK, West Germany, Canada and the USA. The Dal Khalsa activities are mainly in UK and West Germany, while the Babbar Khalsa is operating largely from Vancouver in Canada. The Akhand Kirtani Jatha has units in UK and Canada.

It then describes various activities of these organizations, relying rather uncritically on newspaper reports. Members of Dal Khalsa get particular attention; in particular Jaswant Singh Thekedar's role within "various congregations" in Britain. As seen in Chapter 4, before June 1984 the total sum of these leaders' activities was almost negligible. Both Jaswant Singh Thekedar in Britain and Talwinder Singh Parmar in Canada were little-known figures. Dr J. S. Chohan had built up a small network, but he was boycotted by all major gurdwaras and organizations until June 1984. The White Paper also quotes approvingly of the "Johan Vanderhorst Affair", based on the *Vancouver Sun's* report; this was at best an "inspired lie".

However, following the army action in Amritsar, and amid reports of the many protests from overseas Sikhs, the Indian government revised its assessment, reporting a total of "twenty-six organisations working for Khalistan".[3] Accordingly, three steps were taken: first, strict visa regulations for overseas visitors; secondly, stepping up of surveillance of Sikh groups by key embassies like Toronto, Vancouver, London, Washington, New York, Bonn and Paris; thirdly, the bringing of diplomatic pressure on host states to stop the spread of diaspora Sikh nationalism.[4] Besides official channels, India's concern was expressed in parliament, the media and many publications. In a debate prompted by a us congressional hearing on the human rights situation in the Punjab, the Indian government blamed Britain, Canada and the United States as major centres of Sikh "extremism". Not only did these countries allow Sikh activists freedom to campaign, but according to one member, the us proceedings on the Punjab showed its sinister plans:

A platform to spread anti-India feelings with the vociferous participation of extremist Khalistani leaders like Ganga Singh Dhillon and Jagjit Singh Chauhan. The whole country has been outraged at this briefing on a subject which is exclusively India's internal matter that has been sought to be internationalised by vested interests with a pernicious motive.[5]

Another member alleged the CIA was trying to "infiltrate our organisations" through educational and political bodies and took exception to British leniency towards Sikhs,[6] while Mrs Thatcher had made "pleasant noises about her concern about India's unity", but she lets "secessionist and extremist Sikhs" operate from Britain. Canada was helping by "providing them grants".[7] In the reply to the debate, members were assured that India had taken a serious note:

In certain countries like UK, Canada and America, over-indulgence has been shown to these terrorists. It is really very regrettable and we have made it very clear to these countries that India's friendship will depend upon the treatment that these people get.[8]

The Indian government put pressure on host states to curtail the Sikhs' campaign, to ban funds coming to the Punjab which, it alleged, were "used to buy arms for militants", and prohibit the publication of propaganda materials. Many activists have been questioned by police and intelligence agencies as a direct result of India's pressure; most noteworthy among them is the Canadian government's surveillance of Sikh organizations. Many violent incidents have been attributed to foreign Sikhs. In 1995, when Punjab's chief minister was blown up in a bomb blast, three Sikhs from abroad were implicated.[9]

## Indo-British relations and the Sikhs

Although India's importance as a senior member of the Commonwealth has been in decline since the 1960s, due to Britain's changed priorities in the international arena, the presence of a large community of British Sikhs added further tensions in this relationship (Lipton & Firn 1975; Malik & Robb 1994).[10] Britain had already earned the ire of Indian diplomats, with a BBC broadcast of Dr Chohan's statement about the consequences of sacrilege at the Golden Temple and a "tough interview" with the Indian prime minister.[11] The British assurances that anyone breaking the laws of the land will be punished appropriately, fell far short of Indian expectations, seeking exemplary action beyond a legalistic position. The Indian High Commission alleged, "Sikh extremists here are not only being allowed to break the laws of this land", they were also "inciting communal passions". Calling it "an internal matter" for the British authorities, the spokesman pleaded:

> Our very simple proposition to Her majesty's Government is that since we are friendly countries, British citizens should not wage war against India from here. The British government has given us protection but we are very unhappy about these extremists. We know who the extremists are and we have pointed them out. There are no more than a few dozens and most of them have British passports.[12]

The Indian embassies were given police guard, but Indo-British relations were believed to have reached an all-time low due to Britain's "soft approach towards Sikh militants". When Indian Prime Minister Rajiv Gandhi visited Britain in September 1985, several Sikh activists were rounded up and the police foiled a "conspiracy" to murder him.[13] India's displeasure over Britain's lax attitude was conveyed through the cancellation of a British Aerospace Exhibition planned in New Delhi and the visit of Mr Heseltine, secretary of state for defence, in December 1984.[14] India also cancelled a £65 million order for Westland helicopters; and an order for British Sea Harrier jets and Sea Eagle missiles, worth £175 million, became the subject of lengthy negotiations. During her visit to India in April 1985, Prime Minister Thatcher tried unsuccessfully to salvage Britain's export of aircraft missiles to India.[15] Even the threat of reduction in foreign aid, if the helicopter deal did not materialize, was reported to be ineffective.

Turning "Sikh extremists" into a major agenda, the Indian government demanded several measures, including an extradition treaty and a ban on funds. In April 1986 a formal request was submitted to the British foreign secretary, Sir Geoffrey Howe, who offered to amend certain sections of the Fugitive Offenders Act governing the extradition rules between the United Kingdom and Commonwealth countries.[16] In an obvious reference to India's increasing pressure, the minister of state for foreign and Commonwealth affairs, Mr William Waldegrave, outlined the government's position in November 1988:

> We have been closely in touch with the Indian government during the past few days to find ways of strengthening our cooperation to combat the activities of extremists within the framework of our laws. That cooperation is something to which the Indian government understandably attaches great importance, and it has assumed a central place in the political relations between the two countries.... The extremists number perhaps a few hundred at most.... But organisations are active in the Sikh community whose main purpose is to offer help and support to the extremists in India. Those organisations have been able to draw on the moral and financial support of many Sikhs in Britain who

do not share that objective. I call on all decent Sikhs in Britain to ensure, before they give their support to an organisation, that they are clear about its intention.[17]

After years of pressure, Britain agreed to a bilateral treaty in January 1992. An extradition treaty was signed in September 1992, covering the tracing, freezing and confiscation of terrorist funds and the proceeds of serious crime, including drug trafficking, and presented to the British parliament in July 1993.[18] During the debate, opposition members questioned its need, and particular safeguards for Sikh and Kashmiri citizens. Many MPs expressed reservations, while Terry Dicks and Max Madden raised strong objections. Roger Godsiff, with many Kashmiri constituents, argued:

> How can the government argue that there are sufficient safeguards to ensure that, under the treaty, the person being extradited, 'would not be prejudiced . . . or be punished, detained or restricted on grounds of political opinion' when the Indian army is daily carrying out a war against the people of Indian-held Kashmir and when under the Indian constitution, it is an act of treason for any Indian national to advocate secession by any part of the union from the state of India?[19]

Many members thought the treaty was made necessary due to the arms trade at the expense of human rights, as one-third of British exports to India related to arms. The treaty was approved by 123 MPs and opposed by 38; significantly, it was supported by Labour MP Piara Singh Khabra, a Sikh himself representing a constituency with many Sikh voters. Its passage was hailed by the Indian ambassador, L. M. Singhvi, as "probably the most significant" event between Indian and Britain.[20] As a concession, India allowed Amnesty International a guided visit. The Indian home minister also thanked Britain for understanding India's position, and asserted, "India is not a multinational entity like some of the states around us which are splitting up; it is a multicultural civilisational reality whose existence or permanence cannot be questioned".[21]

During the last decade, prompted by Sikh lobbyists, members of parliament have expressed concern at India's excesses in the Punjab. Terry Dicks, a Conservative MP from Hayes and Harlington with a large number of Sikh voters in his constituency, emerged as a consistent campaigner, often attending annual meetings of the Khalistan Council. On several occasions, he has spoken on the Sikh situation in the Punjab. In November 1988 he underlined the historic Anglo-Sikh connections and the "contribution that Sikhs have made in two world wars", and gave a list of decorations won by Sikh soldiers as proof of their "loyalty and devotion to our country".[22] He also alleged that "Indian security services" are operating within the Indian community. Mr William Waldegrave responded by narrating cases of Sikh violence in Britain:

> The activities of the terrorists are not confined to India. In October 1985 a plot was uncovered to assassinate Prime Minister Rajiv Gandhi during his visit to the United Kingdom. A moderate Sikh leader Tarsem Singh Toor was murdered in January 1986. Another Darshan Das Vasdev was shot dead in November 1987 and three other attempts were made on the lives of leading Sikh moderates. In all those cases, those responsible have been tried and convicted.[23]

Max Madden, Labour MP for Bradford West, also has many Muslim and Sikh voters. Having visited Punjab as part of a joint team of British and European parliamentarians,[24] he reported his findings to parliament and recalled some disturbing abuses of human rights:

> I shall never forget the Sikh farmer whose 14 years old daughter was raped and drowned by a police officer. The father was brutally beaten by police three times over two days. He was seeking the return of his daughter's body for cremation. He was warned that if he did not stop complaining, what had happened to his 14 years old daughter would happen to his seven years old daughter. The father is refusing to wear shoes until he gets justice.[25]

He has also tabled many questions, including some on the Indian government's response to human rights violations.[26] The Indian government has often repeated the charge of Sikh terrorism, so seeking clarification, he questioned the home secretary:

> How many British and non-British nationals in each of the last five years have been (a) arrested, (b) charged (c) convicted (d) acquitted over offences relating to the funding of terrorism in India?

To which the home secretary replied, none.[27] Madden also put a written question about gurdwara funds being used for militants in the Punjab, to which John Patten replied that charity commissioners

> have used their power of enquiry in some 17 cases involving allegations of misuse or misappropriation of funds, during the last three years, by charities connected with the Sikh community living in the United Kingdom.[28]

Parliament has heard the issue of human rights in Kashmir and Punjab on several occasions. In a major debate on Sikh human rights in the Punjab in November 1991, Terry Dicks remarked:

> I want to mention yet again in the House the persecution of Sikhs in the Punjab. Members of the Sikh community living in my constituency and Sikhs throughout the world have been concerned for the safety of family and friends living in the Punjab. The rape of young women, the beating of old men and the murder of young boys, to say nothing of the imprisonment without trial of many thousands of innocent people, has been going on since 1984 and continues unabated. Indian security forces are killing hundreds of innocent Sikhs in encounters and there is evidence that those forces have swept through villages in the Punjab intent on nothing less than widespread slaughter.[29]

He also reminded MPS how the Sikh homeland issue forms the British empire's legacy in India:

In 1947, when India obtained its independence it was the British who accepted a guarantee by the Hindus who make up 84 per cent of the population that the self-determination of the Sikhs in the Punjab will be recognised. On that basis the British government granted India its independence. Unfortunately for the Sikhs, the British government has done nothing to enforce the guarantee and successive Congress party dominated Indian governments have been able to ignore the pledge ... The refusal of the Indian government aided and abetted by Britain to keep their word has led to Sikh people to call for their own independent state.

Replying to the debate, Mr Tristan Garel-Jones, minister of state at the Foreign and Commonwealth Office, advised the British Sikhs:

We urge all decent, law-abiding Sikhs in this country to deny moral and financial support to those organisations that contribute to the misery and suffering brought to the Punjab and India by extremist violence. .... The Sikhs have the right and will receive a sympathetic hearing from my Hon Friends and me, but the Sikhs must also recognise that the cause they seek to serve will not be helped unless their condemnation of violence and extremism is wholehearted. ... That is how they can best contribute to the cause in which they believe.[30]

Over the years, many members have sought to link British aid to India's record on human rights.[31] Jeff Rooker, an MP from Birmingham, enquired of the Indian High Commission regarding the use of British aid for projects in Kashmir and Punjab.[32] John Spellar (Warley West) raised the human rights question in 1994, especially India's TADA law, which takes away "the basic right of free speech and political opinion"; a "worrying section" states:

Any action taken, whether by act or by speech or through any other media ... which questions, disrupts or is intended to disrupt, whether directly or indirectly, the sovereignty and territorial integrity of India; or which is intended to bring about or supports any claim ... for the cession of any part of India or the secession of any part of India.[33]

The persecution of Sikhs by Indian security forces again figured in 1995, when the issue of "unclaimed bodies" in Amritsar was highlighted; Terry Dicks broadened the issue:

Recognition of the rights of Sikhs who are living in the Punjab is all that Sikhs elsewhere want. That means the right of self-determination and to strengthen the call for an independent Khalistan. ... There should be no aid programme to India because aid is tied to human goods practices. I believe that our government should break off all diplomatic ties with India. ... For Sikhs in the Punjab, we should read Muslims in Kashmir.[34]

Another member, Jacques Arnold (Gravesham), observed the British responsibility in the matter, commenting on the haste with which "we left India and of the lack of care at the time to ensure that the legitimate rights of the Sikhs were sustained". The Sikh factor was also responsible for an apparent discord over the Queen's visit to the Indian subcontinent on the fiftieth anniversary of the transfer of power. Just before the visit, Indian Prime Minister Inder Kumar Gujral advised the Queen not to visit Amritsar for fears it might fan Sikh militancy.[35] Foreign Secretary Cook's suggestion of mediation over Kashmir also annoyed India. However, it prompted many British Sikh leaders to lead a campaign to welcome the royal tour.

While the ISYF president, Amrik Singh, wrote a supporting letter, a delegation headed by Bachittar Singh left for Amritsar to welcome the Queen "on behalf of British Sikhs".[36] The Queen laid a wreath at the Jallianwala Bagh and visited the Golden Temple where, it was reported, the Sikhs provided an enthusiastic welcome.[37] To the Indian demand for an apology over the Amritsar massacre of 1919, some Sikh leaders contended that the imperial crime paled into insignificance compared to the Indian government's oppression in Amritsar.[38] At the Commonwealth meeting in Edinburgh a fortnight later, Sikhs and Kashmiris joined to protest against the visiting Indian premier, Mr Gujral. The Indian government has viewed the Sikh lobby and its campaign on human rights in the Punjab as a major factor in the strained relations between the two countries.

## Sikh diplomacy and Indo-US relations

The Sikh lobby in the United States has made more extensive contacts with members of Congress, projecting the issue of Sikhs' human rights and also seeking endorsement for Sikhs' rights to self-determination in the Punjab. The Council of Khalistan has established an office in Washington DC. Earlier support came from California members with Sikh voters, Norman Shumway (Stockton), Wally Herger (Yuba City) and Vic Fazio, who have heard Sikhs' pleas with sympathy. In the past decade, as part of this exchange between Congress members and Sikhs, many members have been honoured and given fundraising dinners, and a few have sought conversion.[39] The poor history of Indo-US relations has also provided the Sikh lobby with a space for argument. With Pakistan as a stable ally since 1959, India has been peripheral to US strategic and political interests in the region. Moreover, India's policy of nonalignment and support for the Russian block and its habit of "moral pontification" at the United Nations has annoyed American diplomats (McMahon 1994; Kux 1992; Chary 1995; Gould & Ganguly 1992). Bilateral trade has also played its part; while the United States is important for India as its largest trading partner, India's trade is insignificant for America.[40] Although Indo-US relations have considerably changed in recent years, Congress members remain open to persuasion by interest groups, especially over human rights abuses.

These factors have facilitated the Sikh lobbyists on Capitol Hill. When the Indian prime minister, Rajiv Gandhi, visited the United States in June 1985, he was not only met by a strong Sikh protest, he was also angered by the Press Council's invitation to Ganga Singh Dhillon, a Sikh nationalist. During the visit, the Indian premier was assured of American interest in "India's unity". Reagan and Gandhi talked about American arms supplies to Paki-

stan, the militarization of the Indian Ocean and the nuclear proliferation in South Asia. India's worries about Sikh extremism found
no official response, although the FBI charged some Sikhs when
they discovered a plot to assassinate the visiting premier and an
Indian minister. During Gandhi's second visit in 1987, the Sikh
lobby had persuaded several Congress members to ask President
Reagan to raise the question of suppression of human rights in the
Punjab.[41]

Among the prominent Congress members, Dan Burton, a Republican from Illinois, gradually emerged as a consistent supporter of the Sikh cause. He has sponsored many resolutions in
the Congress and castigated India for its "profound lack of respect
for Sikh life and culture".[42] In 1986 he urged India to give Sikhs
"full access" to the Golden Temple by removing all military presence from the shrine; Congress supported the "territorial integrity
of India" while condemning terrorism, but urged the prime minister and responsible Sikh leaders to achieve a "political solution".[43] In 1987 Shumway led a special order debate when
members familiarized themselves with the Sikh demands and
Punjab's geopolitical situation.[44]

Vic Fazio thought "the disparate people of India cannot be
united by India's undemocratic treatment of the Sikh community,
who should be provided with the opportunity to negotiate
autonomy from the central government of India". Lipinski observed that information from the government-controlled Press
Trust of India is unreliable, while India disallows foreign journalists, diplomats and human rights organizations into the Punjab. A
member underlined Punjab's importance, "though not as important as Soviet Union or the apartheid in South Africa", but located
on the Indian border with Pakistan, "just 150 miles from the Soviet
Union", it could have profound implications for the "future of the
Indian subcontinent".[45] In October 1987, on a request by Vic Fazio,
the Congressional Research Service summarized how the Punjab;
crisis affected US interests:

> a. Because the crisis has exacerbated India-Pakistan rela-
> tions, it has made it all the more difficult for the US to
> pursue its policy of supporting Pakistan militarily in its
> stance against the Soviet occupation of Afghanistan. b. The

crisis affects the lives of thousand of immigrant Sikhs in the US, who are troubled and fearful for the fate of their relatives and friends, and it appears to be stimulating a greater flow of Sikh immigration, both legal and illegal. c. The conflict also appears to have brought another terrorist movement to the US, and possibly given scope for counter intelligence operations by Indian intelligence agencies here.

Sikh lobbyists have persuaded Congress members to link US aid to India's record of human rights abuses on Punjab's population. From 1988, as international agencies reported widespread abuses, several Congress members were convinced of the need to send a warning to India.

*American foreign aid to India*

From 1988 an annual Congress debate has taken place on India's violation of Sikh human rights; members take a bipartisan approach. After a visit to India, Shumway introduced a congressional resolution (HC Res. 343) concerning "human rights of the Sikhs in the Punjab of India" in August 1988.[46] The debate is usually initiated as an amendment to the House Foreign Aid Bill. In 1989 an amendment proposed by Herger attracted vigorous debate and was defeated by eight votes only, with 204 members voting for the amendment and 212 against.[47] In 1991 Dan Burton sponsored a more stringent resolution to stop the US development assistance programmes for India unless international agencies were allowed to monitor human rights.[48] In 1992 a similar resolution was passed which led to a small reduction in developmental assistance to India.[49] Burton reintroduced a bill to the Committee on Foreign Affairs in the House of Representatives in 1993, seeking to link US development assistance with the repealing of five special detention laws.[50] Supported by 28 members, Burton introduced the amendment:

> The atrocities that the world has seen in Bosnia are equally as bad in a place called Kashmir and Punjab in Northwestern India. The problem is the world does not know these atrocities because they will not allow human rights groups

such as Amnesty International into the area. They will not allow television and the media in there. . . . These are some of the things that are taking place in India today: 16,740 innocent people killed in Kashmir alone, burned alive, 558; 2,800 women and children raped; 110,000 Sikhs killed since 1984; 38,000 imprisoned without charge.

Gary Ackerman, a pro-India Democrat, opposed the bill, observing that it would punish the "poor people". Another representative, Abercrombie, argued that the issue was not about Democrat versus Republican:

> No one is a better friend of India than I am. . . . The Indian people are being sold short on their conviction and commitment to democracy by the action of the army in Kashmir and Punjab. I have been there. There are no more decent people than the Sikhs.

Robert Torricelli (New Jersey) felt outraged that India could deny "access to human rights organisations". If Congress could discuss Bosnia and Cambodia, he wondered "why the mounting death toll in the Punjab is met with only silence?". According to another member, "this amendment will only hinder India's efforts to arrive at a solution to this difficult and complex domestic problem" and reminded the house of India's "most promising markets for US products". Another member commented on "Pakistani aid to the militants". Although the amendment was defeated by 233 votes to 201, the resolution showed the strength of the Sikh lobbyists against the combined forces of the Indian embassy and some American Hindu leaders.[51] However, on 17 June 1993 the House of Representatives unanimously adopted a measure to cut $345,000 allocated for the International Military Education and Training (IMET) programme. This small but symbolic cut invited widespread comment from the Indian media.[52]

Alongside these events, the House Foreign Committee's Subcommittee on Asia and the Pacific held a hearing to discuss the foreign aid to South Asia on 28 April 1993.[53] John Malott of the State Department emphasized: "Human rights have become an important issue in our dialogue with the Indian government". He insisted that India's antiterrorist act, TADA, was inappropriate: "We are concerned about [its] overuse". But Malott did not favour linking aid to India with its human rights performance, as proposed by the Burton amendment, on the grounds that most of the aid was humanitarian. However, other members called attention to India's poor record on human rights. Holly Bukhalter pointed out: "Many of the police responsible for torture, disappearances and executions of detainees in Punjab have been promoted to senior positions. Given the appalling level of state-sanctioned abuse in the Punjab, the achievement of 'normalcy' in the state cannot be a model of any kind for the resolution of Kashmir conflict".

India's record of voting against the United States at the United Nations also became an issue, when on 24 May 1995 the us Congress passed the Burton amendment, effectively cutting $364,000 from the International Military and Education Training (IMET) programme due to India's voting record.[54] Dan Burton, chairman of the Western Hemisphere Subcommittee led the amendment.[55] This action upset the Indian caucus, forcing a full debate when the Burton amendment was defeated by 210 votes to 191. While Mr Bereuter, chair of the House Subcommittee on Asia-Pacific Affairs, cautioned its impact on Indo-us relations, stakes for this amendment were so high that the Indian embassy called up the chairman of the Indian Human Rights Commission, Justice Ranganath Mishra, who briefed Congress members on India's efforts in improving its human rights record.[56]

Besides raising the issue of Punjab in the Congress, several members have written to the us administration to change its policies towards India. Some Congress members sought clarification regarding India's conduct in the Sikh homeland from the Indian prime minister during his visit to the United States in May 1994.[57] Similarly, Peter King wrote to Secretary of State Warren Christopher on 4 August 1993 regarding India's violation of Sikhs' human rights in its homeland.

*Support for self-determination*

Sikh lobbyists have also sought support for Sikhs' rights to self-determination. This received a considerable boost when Pete Geren introduced such a resolution stating:

The Sikhs of Khalistan, like all peoples of all nations, have the right to self-determination and should be allowed to exercise this right by pursuing the independence of their homeland, Punjab, Khalistan. The UN should hold a plebiscite in the Sikh homeland so that Sikhs can determine for themselves under fair and peaceful conditions their political future.[58]

In a separate move, Gary Condit wrote a letter to the president, supported by 15 senators, seeking a UN-sponsored plebiscite for a peaceful resolution of the Sikh homeland.[59] The president responded: "I am aware of the chronic tensions between the Indian government and the Sikh militants, and share your desire for a peaceful solution that protects Sikh rights. . . . Human rights is an important issue in US-Indian relations".[60] This brief reply created a furore in India.[61] While a Sikh leader thanked the American president, the Congress Party warned of destabilization plots by outsiders.[62] The Indian ambassador, S. S. Ray, met the assistant secretary of state, Robin Raphael, expressing India's strong objection, particularly to the president's wording of "Sikh rights".[63] The US officials clarified that the president did not support the demand for Khalistan and merely referred to minority rights as "Sikh rights".

More letters followed to the US administration. The State Department's Annual Reports to Congress on human rights in the Indian subcontinent have been keenly contested by governments and ethnic lobbyists.[64] In February 1994, 29 Congress members wrote seeking a stoppage of US aid to India.[65] In another letter in October 1995, 35 Congress members asked the president to recognize Sikhs' rights to "self-determination" and to "allow a plebiscite in Punjab and Kashmir under the auspices of the UN so that Sikhs can peacefully decide their political future".[66]

Congress members have also expressed concern at the proposed extradition treaty with India.[67] They suggested an amendment similar to that contained in a US–UK treaty concluded in 1986, whereby Irish nationals in the United States should form part of the statement of the treaty.

Following the establishment of the Sikh lobby on Capitol Hill, American Hindus have also become embroiled.[68] The Sikh lobby has tried to win over prominent pro-India Congress members.[69] In the 1992 Congress elections, Stephen Solarz, a pro-Indian lobbyist from New York, was supported by many Hindus, while Sikh lobbyists opposed him; he lost the election. Prompted by the American Hindu lobby, 15 Congress members formed a caucus to counter the hostile propaganda against India in the 102nd Congress.[70] Earlier in 1989, Raj Dutt of the Indian American Political Action Committee lobbied against the Shumway and Burton amendment. In New Jersey a Hindu lobby persuaded the state senate to pass a resolution commending Chief Minister Beant Singh's role in bringing peace to Punjab; the resolution was rescinded after a strong Sikh objection. In California, India was condemned for its human rights abuses in Punjab and Kashmir.[71]

Among American Sikhs, Dr Aulakh has emerged as an effective lobbyist who has convinced several influential figures, including Dante Fascel, chairman of the Foreign Committee, and Gus Yatron, head of the Human Rights Subcommittee, both formerly known for their staunch pro-India views and now on record as criticizing India for failing to come up to their expectations.[72]

## Indo-Canadian relations and the Sikh lobby

If Congress proceedings seem like a morality play, the Canadian–Sikh interaction unfolds as a tragic drama, with an image of Sikhs as a "violent and troublesome" community firmly entrenched in its official and public sphere. This has largely come about due to a spate of violent incidents within the community and especially with the Air India plane disaster, when the entire community was maligned.[73] In this scenario, bravado speeches and high-profile appearances of some Babbar Khalsa leaders have lent credence to the public's suspicion of terrorism. According to one spokesman, the alleged bombing of the Air India plane, which the media attributed to Sikh activists, had above all led to the premise that "rightly or wrongly, . . . we [Sikhs] are bombers of Air India and killers of 329 people".[74] The incident was strongly condemned by the ISYF and the WSO.

An important factor in this maligning has been the Indian government's contention that Canadian Sikhs are fuelling the Punjab troubles. As Sikh protests gathered pace in the aftermath of army action in the Golden Temple, Indian Prime Minister Indira Gandhi urged Canada "not to help Sikh separatists".[75] Indo-Canadian relations were thought to be under strain, especially as both countries valued each other as the leading nonaligned leaders of the Commonwealth.[76] After the Air India disaster, this diplomatic pressure hardly needed further proof, although investigations were by no means pointing towards Sikh activists. The Canadian foreign secretary, Mr Joe Clark, almost agreed with the Indian government in 1986 by assuring that "Canada and Canadians will not tolerate . . . those who advocate or practice violence". In a clear reference to Sikh extremism, he added, "The line must be firmly drawn when peaceful dissent becomes violent confrontation", and he immediately offered to sign an extradition treaty.[77] Although the wso lobbyists presented a memorandum to the parliamentary committee on 31 May 1986, stressing Canada should resist India's undue pressure, its pleas were of no use.

### The extradition treaty

An Indo-Canadian extradition treaty was hastily concluded on 6 February 1987,[78] where Canada's foreign secretary pledged co-operation from Canadian intelligence services to counter Sikh extremism.[79] Unlike Britain, the Canadian parliament did not debate the treaty. To a question by John Nunziata (York South-Weston) regarding "assurances . . . to the Canadian Sikh community that the extradition treaty will not be abused", the foreign secretary replied that the treaty included the language of the Canadian Charter of Rights.[80]

### Directing the ethnic group's agenda

Increasingly the Canadian government viewed Sikhs' support for an independent homeland as illegitimate and treated it differently from claims by other ethnic groups. The government's attitude hardened, and in December 1987 the foreign secretary asked seven provincial premiers to boycott three Sikh organizations, the wso, the isyf and the Babbar Khalsa, saying:

The activities of these organisations have been a significant irritant in our relations with India. The government of India has taken particular exception when elected officials attend functions sponsored by these organisations.[81]

The issue was serious enough to warrant a major debate in the parliament.[82] The Liberal Party caucus led by Sergio Marchi (York West), sought the withdrawal of the letter, and raised the matter "with a certain degree of sadness" in the House of Commons:

> That this House, while condemning violence, and terror- ism as political instruments affirms that all Canadians, re- gardless of origin must not be subjected to any coercion, intimidation or other action by the Government designed to prevent their free and peaceful expression of their opin- ions and concerns about events and issues in Canada or in other lands, and, that this House therefore demands that the Government provide Parliament with all relevant in- formation that led to its aforementioned communication with the Provinces and provide the Canadian Sikh commu- nity with a full, public opportunity to defend its honour and integrity and . . . issue a full apology to all Canadians, and to the Canadian Sikh community in particular.

The issue at stake was how government could force changes on an ethnic community's agenda. Were Sikhs different from Canada's other ethnic groups, such as Lithuanians, Latvians, Ukrainians and others who were lobbying independence from the Soviet Union? Mr Rils thought the letter echoed a double standard:

> While I listened to the Hon Member's remarks I could not help but think that years ago Jews living in Canada urged and worked for the creation of Israel. Today Palestinians as well as Canadian citizens are urging the creation of a homeland for Palestinians. On Parliament Hill, we have seen demonstrations of people of Croatian origin urging the creation of a Croatian state. We have seen Ukrainians,

173

Slovaks and a long list of people appear on Parliament Hill, in all their own way, and I might add in their own peaceful way with an emphasis on the word 'peaceful' indicating their concern for the creation of a homeland or a state for their people. . . . Is there something different here? Again, people of Sikh faith are urging the creation of a homeland for their people. I do not see much difference between that and the Jews some years back urging the creation of the State Israel.

Members with significant Sikh voters strongly objected to the letter's intent. Ms Copps (Hamilton East) asked whether "to advocate the creation of an independent Sikh state, Khalistan was to be boycotted, we would not be allowed to attend functions of 'Ukrainian' and many of eastern bloc countries including Lithuania". She pointed out: "Many nations around the world are fighting for an independent cultural and political identity. . . . [Are] Canadians then to say that we will attend no functions organised by the Tamil community?" On violence, she countered as a Catholic, "If another Roman Catholic is caught robbing a bank or in some way breaking the law of the land, somehow all members of the Roman Catholic Church are now persona non grata?" She criticized Clark for appealing "to a sense of racism which says that this organisation will be blackballed by all Canadians because the Minister claims some members are involved in so-called violent activities".

Mr Stevnd J. Robinson (Burnaby, BC) asked: "Who is running the foreign affairs policy of Canada? Is it the secretary of state for Foreign Affairs or is it the Government of India?" He thought it reprehensible "to dictate to elected officials at the provincial level and presumably to officials at the local level and even officials in his caucus which organisations they could meet with in Canada". Mr Jim Manly (Cowichan–Malahat–Islands) wondered how to draw a line: "Members attend meetings of Ukrainians, Estonians, Latvians and Lithuanian organisations. The Eritrean have long been involved in long term struggle against Ethiopia for independence". He drew a parallel with early Sikh settlers in his constituency and a recent raid on a Duncan Sikh temple. Mr Manly also observed how the Department of External Affairs "dragged its feet all the way and put up roadblocks against the creation of a chair of Sikh studies at UBC".[83] The secretary of state for external affairs, Joe Clark, defended his letter, saying:

> Activities of a small, militant minority in the Sikh community represent the most serious internal security threat Canada faces today. Undeniably this minority seeks to dismember a friendly country, either through peaceful means or violent means. My friend the Hon Member for Edmonton-Strathcona [Mr Kilgour] asked the other day whether there was not a difference between the World Sikh Organisation and the other two. Indeed, Sir, there is a difference, but the constitution of the World Sikh Organisation clearly states that one of its objectives is 'to strive through peaceful means for the establishment of a Sikh nation, Khalistan'.

He ruled without further elaboration that the WSO constitution was "incompatible with Canadian policy". He then told members about the Babbar Khalsa: "an Indian-based international organisation comprising Sikhs whose objectives are the eradication of Sikh apostasy and the establishment of Khalistan.... The Canadian branch is relatively small, but its total devotion to Sikh independence and its willingness to undertake acts of violence makes it a serious source of concern". He catalogued a series of incidents, in which its members and the ISYF were involved:

> In May 1986, members of the Montreal area of Canadian Babbar Khalsa were involved in a plot to place a bomb on an Air India flight to New York. Two were convicted and given life sentences. On 25 May 1986, four members of the ISYF attempted to assassinate a visiting Punjab state Minister in British Columbia. They were each sentenced to twenty years for this offence. As a government, Sir we cannot ignore these facts, nor can we ignore other cases of terrorism that we have encountered.

Then he added something which seemed trivial, but obviously significant to the government of India:

Moreover these two organisations have occasionally attempted to dupe Members of Parliament or public figures in Canada into supporting their cause . . . , for example, by having them photographed under the Khalistan flag or wearing buttons indicating support for Khalistan.[84]

However, when the House of Commons' Multicultural Committee asked Clark specific questions about his allegations of Sikh terrorism, the foreign secretary refused to appear before it. Instead, he told the Justice Committee that wso should, "stop advocating the dismemberment of a friendly country [India]". The wso leaders assured the parliamentary committee that the organization abhors violence in pursuit of its objectives. But their arguments obviously carried far less weight than India's deputy high commissioner, Mr M. L. Tripathi, who in a letter had pressed action against these organizations. He had also cited in evidence a joint Sikh demonstration on 12 October against the Indian prime minister, Rajiv Gandhi, during his visit to Vancouver for the Commonwealth meeting. He produced a sheet of paper from a spokesman of Punjab's Panthic Committee, saying that the wso, the isyf of Britain and Babbar Khalsa of Canada have helped it.[85] Gian Singh Sandhu wrote an angry letter to the external affairs minister, challenging him to prove "unsubstantiated charges of Sikh terrorism":

> As president of the wso, I am prepared to put my office and reputation on the line. If he [Clark] or his ministry can provide the documentary evidence beyond a reasonable doubt that would stand in a Canadian court. . . . I am prepared to resign as president immediately. . . . In fairness, I ask Mr Clark to do the same. If he cannot fully prove the accusations, I believe he owes it to Sikh community which he has maligned, to seven premiers whom he has misled and to the numerous elected officials whom he has misinformed, to resign as Minister of External Affairs. (Kashmeri & McAndrew 1989)

At Toronto in April 1988, local Sikh leaders met Barbara McDougall, the deputy foreign minister; they sought an equation of Sikhs with Ukrainians, Poles and others involved in homeland campaigns.[86] However, the Sikh campaign for a separate state became "as nothing more than a terrorist campaign", largely due to the role of Indian intelligence.[87]

## Human rights and refugees

Although Canada annually accepts over 10,000 refugees, the largest of any country, its treatment of Sikh claimants underlined the poor image of the community. This was seen in the reception given to 174 Sikh claimants from Europe brought by a Dutch ship and dumped in a small village of Nova Scotia. They were, by several accounts, treated more harshly than other asylum seekers.[88] While allegations flew about their criminal records,[89] the wso and the Khalsa Diwan Society, Vancouver, offered bonds and provided services of a law firm to defend them.[90] They were released after sponsorship was received, while the wso advised them to "observe the laws of Canada regardless of your view of the Punjab situation".[91] The government called an emergency session of parliament on 11 August 1987, speeding the passage of a bill to "contain the widespread abuses in the refugee system".[92] Mr Cassidy (Ottawa Central) compared this dramatic gesture with a past episode in Canadian-Sikh relations:

> It is reminiscent of the rules in place before World War I which said anyone who wished to emigrate to Canada from the Indian subcontinent could do so provided they came here directly. A group of Sikhs did so in 1914 and they were turned back away. . . . Let us not be panicked by the fact that 174 Sikhs entered Canada a month ago. Let us not be panicked into saying that proves that there are security questions which require that the House be called back at this time.

Some Sikh claimants for refugee status were subject to a lengthy review process. Thus a Sikh who was cleared through rcmp and csis, and recommended for asylum by the Refugee Status Advisory Committee,[93] was held up by the minister as Indian authorities applied for his extradition. Another Sikh, Amrik Dhinsa, was deported almost by a public trial. Several Sikhs who are awaiting asylum decisions are said to be under consideration for extradition by India.[94] Of the several thousand Sikh applicants, a few have been granted asylum, as this may affect "commercial or other relationships with the government of India".[95]

In this atmosphere, Sikh lobbyists' pleas to link Canadian foreign aid to India's record of abuses in Punjab was dismissed by the government. However, pressure came from other sources. A parliamentary mission to Punjab was presented with evidence of abuses by security forces; as a result several MPs raised the issue of aid and India's poor record of human rights.[96] Some members also questioned whether unwarranted surveillance by the CSIS violated the rights of ethnic Canadians to engage in political dissent. Mrs Suzanne Duplessis, parliamentary secretary for external affairs, replied, "Canada has sought to incorporate human rights considerations in its aid programme, and India is trying to improve the situation in the Punjab".

With the new Liberal government in 1993, two Sikh MPs were returned to parliament, Gurbax Singh Malhi (Toronto, Malton) and Harbance Singh Dhaliwal (Vancouver South). Ujjal Dosanjh and Moe Sihota were elected to the British Columbia assembly, and both became ministers in the provincial government. The two Sikh MPs have often raised the issue of Punjab in the Canadian parliament. In March 1994 Malhi noted, "Reports of atrocities in Bosnia, Punjab, the Sudan, South Africa and elsewhere should shock every citizen around the world". In June 1995 Dhaliwal reminded the house of "two of the darkest incidents in recent times . . . Operation Bluestar the attack on the Golden Temple, one of the Sikhs' holiest shrines itself, and the Tinanmen Square massacre". In 1996 on the twelfth anniversary of June 1984, Malhi reminded members how "innocent worshippers were killed by the brutal attack of the Indian army on Sikhs' holiest shrine".[97] Malhi also raised the question of the illegal detention of Canadian Sikhs in India. Christine Stewart, secretary of state, assured him of the government's concern and "our high commissioner has assisted in every such case". Mr Dhaliwal reminded MPs about the disappearance of Mr Khalra, a Sikh human rights activist who had visited Parliament Hill in 1995.[98] Raymond Chan, secretary of state for Asia Pacific, assured members that the government had made repeated representations to India regarding Khalra's case, including high-level talks during the Team Canada mission to India in January 1996.

The Air India tragedy has continued to cast a shadow on Indo-Canadian relations, with Sikhs portrayed as the villains. In May 1995 the Canadian parliament again discussed the tragedy, prompted by John Nunziata (York South-Weston) with a private member's bill, seeking "a royal commission of enquiry into the Air India disaster of June 23 1985 which claimed the lives of 329 people". He alleged that the Mulroney administration tried to cover up for some government agencies. Malhi tried to exonerate Sikhs: "For too long, the Sikh community has lived under a great shadow of suspicion created by the media reports that someone from the Canadian Sikh community may have been responsible". And according to Mr Beaumeir, another member, after $20 million and ten years,

> we have not solved this horrible crime . . . this only in-creases misunderstanding of the community . . . we must have a royal commission to remove this scar that has formed on this nation's history.

But Ted White (North Vancouver, Referendum) implicated the Sikhs, saying that "one of the major suspects is already dead". Quoting the *Ottawa Citizen* (14 April 1994), he said, "Another suspect, Mr Manjit Singh, also known as Lal Singh, is in prison in India"; a third person was arrested. Dhaliwal, who had become parliamentary secretary to the minister of fisheries and oceans, supported the motion. However, after a lengthy debate, the motion was dropped. In the June 1997 elections, the Liberals again formed the federal government and Dhaliwal joined the federal government as a revenue minister. As community leaders pre-pared for the centenary of Sikh presence in Canada in October 1997, Dhaliwal's inclusion in the federal government provided comforting news from this "irksome minority" whose behaviour has bedevilled Indo-Canadian relations for much of the twentieth century.

## International organizations

Besides representation to governments in the three countries, international organizations have also been approached. At the United Nations, Sikh leaders have lobbied various subcommittees, including a request for NGO status (non-governmental organization status).[99] In many memorandums submitted to the United Nations, Dr Manohar Singh Grewal, WSO president, has pleaded:

> Sikh nation is in agony. . . . Your excellency, as Secretary General of the World Organisation, you represent the conscience of humanity and the UN inspires hope for freedom and justice. . . . Thousands of innocent Sikh orphans, widows and older parents whose loved ones have been lynched, for them freedom of religion and expression have been reduced to the 'right to cry in the wilderness'. . . . Their voices, though inaudible amidst the media blitz of misinformation and deception, are appealing to the world community and the UN to urge the ruling regime of India to stop the genocide of the Sikhs.[100]

Sikh activists presented their case at the UN World Conference on Human Rights in Vienna in 1993, opposing the Indian delegation.[101] Many presentations have been made at other international venues.[102,103] Punjabi leaders have been helped to send memorandums to the United Nations to seek moral injunctions against "atrocities" committed by the Indian regime.[104] In 1993 the Council of Khalistan gained membership of the Unrepresented Nations and Peoples Organization (UNPO). However, it was revoked, as the chairman explained:

> The steering committee considered a number of serious complaints concerning the Council of Khalistan's admission as a member of UNPO. The issue does not concern the admissibility of the Sikh people to UNPO but is limited to the question of the representative character of the Council of Khalistan as representing the Sikh nation.[105]

Sikh leaders have participated in international conferences and seminars. After a seminar on Sikh freedom and the Indian state in September 1991, Norway linked its foreign aid to India's human rights record.[106] As a Sikh participant in the seminar was arrested on his return, the Indian government received a stern admonishment.[107]

## Conclusion

The diaspora Sikh leaders have gained considerable knowledge of international agencies, and have progressively learned diplomatic techniques and the language of human rights. In the United States, they have joined the well-established ethnic diplomacy of such groups as African Americans, Cubans, Haitians, Koreans, Filipinos, Chinese, Vietnamese, Dominicans, and Mexicans, all trying to influence us policy. The Sikh homeland issue, in a limited sense, has thus entered the international arena. The Indian government has used sanctions of trade, travel restrictions and surveillance, but the legal framework of host states has allowed Sikh activists a space for promulgating their political views. The Indian state's objective to control, limit and manipulate the Sikh diaspora's influence, through various measures on host states, had a varying impact.

Britain has largely adopted a policy of noninterference, but Canada has succumbed to Indian pressure by severely restricting Sikh organizations' activities and rights to promote freedom for its homeland, leading to considerable tension in Sikh-Canadian relations. In America they have discovered that by focusing on the homeland and human rights issues, considerable goodwill and support of Congress and the us administration can be won. Given their limited resources, Sikh organizations and their leaders have exploited host states' legislatures and legal frameworks to attract world attention to the plight of their brethren in the Punjab, despite India's concerted effort to muzzle their voices.

# EIGHT

# Call of homeland: models and reality of ethnic mobilization

Hackled abroad, with nothing to sustain in the native land
Aliens we are, without a country to own[1]

The land of Punjab is in agony
Calling all its well-wishers
Tangled in many woes
Come and share my grief[2]

The Sikh diaspora's attachment to the Punjab, as seen in previous chapters, has resulted in a complex social, cultural and political interaction. These transactions took a radical course when a section of the Sikh diaspora began articulating the demand for a Sikh homeland. This was mainly an emotional reaction to the Indian army action in the Golden Temple. However, subsequent events in the Punjab have institutionalized this protest through the formation of new organizations who have sought the support of international agencies and government representatives. The diaspora movement for a Sikh homeland raises several complex issues of which just three are touched on here: first, the parameters within which a diaspora mobilizes; secondly, the characteristic nature of discourse on the Sikh homeland; and thirdly, the impact of a "traumatic event" upon ethnic consciousness and collective loyalty.

## Parameters of mobilization

It is possible, indeed reasonable, to dismiss Sikh mobilization as a shifting reaction to a Punjabi event, as the event recedes, so the diaspora mobilization dwindles away. Many such mobilizations in the past suggest this pattern; the Indo-Pakistani and Sino-Indian hostilities saw Sikhs and other Indians rallying behind the Indian government, the Punjabi Naxalite movement drew considerable support from Sikh leftist groups, while the years of the Indian emergency divided the diaspora. Much earlier, the Gadr movement was a special kind of mobilization triggered by peculiar conditions in the Pacific states. How different is the contemporary mobilization? There is a prima facie case for treating it somewhat differently for the intensity of passions involved but also due to its impact on collective ethnic loyalty and identity. The Indian army's action in the Golden Temple, sudden and unexpected as it was, is one of those "crucial events", whose impact is likely to last far longer. It has already punctured Sikhs' patriotic fervour towards India, leaving a permanent scar on their minds. In finding the parameters of diaspora mobilization, two factors need to be considered; the internal environment of the community and its external relationship with the host society. Within the community, the role of leadership and internal differentiation of the community helps to understand the level of mobilization.

*Role of leadership*

How did the new community leaders cope with the tragedy? Did they just ride on the popular wave of anger and swim in it? What were their efforts in channelling the community's anger into an effective movement? In short, what was the role of the leadership, and how did it perceive the crisis and the tasks? Obviously, new leaders started in a sudden rush of emotional outburst and anger – all were united on the need for an independent Sikh state. The tragedy called for nothing less. Initially, this position evoked massive support from ordinary Sikhs. The organizational skills of leaders and their outlook then played a decisive part in building their respective organizations. In trying to establish themselves, leaders had to compete for resources. Although sharing a common aim, their mutual suspicion and distrust, and operation within a close-knit community in all three countries dissipated the initial enthusiasm. Competition and personal rivalry have played a major part in each organization's evolution. New leaders not only competed among themselves, but within each organization, they also faced ambitious local leaders and activists, leading to local disputes and poor organization.

Since community resources were concentrated in the gurd-waras, this led to bitter struggles to control major gurdwaras. This process led to an eventual loss of credibility, especially for the ISYF, whose tactics seemed manipulative and unethical to the ordinary Sikhs. The tension and the violent incidents it caused between the ISYF and other groups at some gurdwaras, and the infighting among the ISYF factions, aroused ordinary Sikhs' suspicions regarding the leaders' motives. In these takeover bids, many activists created a bitter atmosphere in some gurdwaras. Moreover, as the gurdwara managers changed every two years, new alliances had to be built, creating unprincipled groupings at particular gurdwaras.[3] The only groups to fare any better were the Khalistan Council in Britain and the Council of Khalistan in America, operating independently of gurdwaras. The ISYF in Britain and Canada and the WSO in Canada lost much of their momentum due to this factor.

The Khalistan Council, the ISYF, the Babbar Khalsa and others have adopted a competitive approach, leading to squabbles on the venue and the form of a protest march, petitions regarding human rights abuses and lobbying of the government. Thus, in Washington DC, besides Aulakh's office, Dr Amarjit Singh from the ISYF has competed with him, while the WSO acquired an office in the city, a prime site but little used. In Britain three Sikh human rights groups competed with each other. This internal bickering and competition is also evident in their alliance and help for particular groups in the Punjab, in aid sent to distressed families or in cases such as hijackers in Lahore.[4]

Another characteristic that affected organizational structure and its effectiveness revolved around the style of leadership. Loyalty was owed to a particular leader rather than to collective responsibility and public accountability. In this the Sikh diaspora leaders' perception reflected the Punjabi pattern, "pre-modern norms and mentality" and derived essentially from the world of Jat social culture of individual domination and "unable to carry 'Sikh values' of cooperation" (Pettigrew 1995: 189). None of the organizations evolved an amicable solution to incorporate local leaders within the hierarchy nor a smooth system to ensure a change in leadership. Excessive secrecy led to a breakage in the vertical linkages (Uday Singh 1987). The removal of a particular leader, such as Harpal Singh, Ganga Singh Dhillon or Jaswant Singh Bhullar, illustrated the failure of these procedures. Nonincorporation of local leaders created local disputes and bitterness. The ISYF simply announced its new leadership at an annual meeting by deference to Lakhbir Singh, ignoring local leaders' dedication or alliances. As Lakhbir Singh lost his grip over the organization, much of its legitimacy was lost. Since many leaders had built no place in the community before 1984, none rose to command a high level of popular support. Except for Dr J. S. Chohan in Britain, Dr G. S. Aulakh in America and Gian Singh Sandhu in Canada, no credible leader emerged to command widespread respect within the community.

Leaders' problems were also confounded by a divided community; its three social groups, the Jats, the Ramgarhias and the Mazhabis, offered different levels of support. The Mazhabis, or Ravidasi as they are increasingly known, have played no role in the engulfing crisis, as their elite were involved in chartering a new identity which, in effect, was a position of countering the "Jat domination of Sikh identity". Among the Sikh sects, the Namdharis found themselves in a similar situation to the Ravidasis; they blamed the Jats for politicizing a universal faith by arousing religious sentiments and deliberately provoking the latest confrontation with the state. The Ramgarhias offered support but this became increasingly qualified. The Jats, the overwhelming majority, remain politically divided into the Akalis, the communists and the Congress. Having alienated the Akalis, new community leaders eagerly fought against Congress and communist Sikhs, leading to an embittered and divided community. Many Sikhs who abandoned other organizations had considerable organizational skills, but they found little favour from the new leaders. A few urbanite Sikhs were soon tired of action-oriented leadership, and could ill-afford the displeasure of the Indian High Commission for too long.

A major factor affecting their credibility was related to the organizations shifting alliances with the Punjabi leaders. The formation of many militant groups in the Punjab led to confusion and bitter controversies for overseas organizations. While the Babbar Khalsa kept a stable alliance with its parent organization and steadily acquired esteem for dedication and discipline, it was compromised in a spectacular way in 1992. The ISYF had to suffer a major setback due to its leader's radical shift in 1988, which broke the organization into two major factions, leading to internecine fighting over resources and members. The World Sikh Organization, which kept a more balanced liaison with Punjabi leaders, has suffered less on this account. However, differences between Dr G. S. Aulakh and Dr J. S. Chohan were mainly due to recognition by different Panthic Committees in the Punjab.

Each organization's rhetoric for mobilization requires further analysis. The Khalistan Council, the wso and the Council of Khalistan have explicitly emphasized commitment to the Sikh homeland through peaceful means. The Babbar Khalsa leaders seem to have identified the struggle as a religious war with violence as a necessary part of their strategy. Alliances between the ISYF and various militant groups, plus its involvement in some violent incidents, suggest that ISYF leaders have adopted high-handed techniques. In much of the published literature by various organizations, there is a consistent pattern of invoking particular couplets from the Sikh scriptures, couplets which emphasize resistance and "martyrdom" as means to an end.[5] There are repeated references to Sikh "sacrifices" for the Hindus and for India's liberation; other passages describe how the community was "betrayed". The numerical figures of Sikhs killed in the independence struggle are regularly relayed, and India's "tyranny" is compared with Mogul persecution in the eighteenth century, rolling out names of Zakaria Khan, Mir Mannu and other tyrants. The presentation of the Sikhs' case to the host societies through the English media suggests crude and assertive proclamations rather than persuasive and effective communication.

Many Sikh activists have also expressed reservations regarding the level of violence in the "freedom campaign". Canadian Sikhs felt that the community's image was being undermined by the strategy of its militant leaders, whose violent campaign in the Punjab had derailed its legitimate demands:

> The culture of violence has wrapped us all. We are being sucked into a 'black hole' from which there is no escape. The root cause of Punjab insurgency is forgotten. Both the law enforcer and the insurgent are engaged in a dance of death. They are playing a macabre game of attack and counter-attack, making mockery of life itself. Each party blames the other for being the instigator, while venting their rage in an orgy of vengefulness.[6]

In many ways, leaders' actions, perception and foresight have reflected the social milieu of the Sikh diaspora. In Britain and Canada, new leaders arose from the first-generation settlers, whose peasantry background and utilitarian outlook did not encourage an ideologically committed movement. These two communities can be easily classified as a "proletarian" diaspora of limited resources, especially in terms of articulating its demands as a collective group (Armstrong 1976: 407). By contrast, American Sikh leaders with professional backgrounds have created an ideological movement. The establishment of a bilingual weekly and a network of contacts by the Council of Khalistan and the wso leaders reflected a far more sophisticated approach. This contrasted sharply with the crude exchange employed by the ISYF and the Babbar Khalsa, with various government and public agencies sowing seeds of misapprehension over their means and ends. Such suspicions were sharpened by community leaders' lack of communication skills as they interacted with the host society's institutions and the media. Only the Council of Khalistan was somewhat effective in highlighting issues of Sikh human rights by concentrating its limited resources on Capitol Hill.

*India, host states and the international arena*
Another major factor in assessing the mobilization potential is the host environment for ethnic politics. Due to their sheer location,

the diasporas have generally helped to internationalize major issues emanating from their homeland. In America, where ethnic
diplomacy is part of the foreign policy making process, the
Indian government's efforts to portray the Sikhs' campaign as no
more than terrorism won only a limited success. In Canada the
Indian government's pressure, in the wake of some violent incidents, especially the Air India plane disaster, led to a hurriedly
agreed extradition treaty followed by a boycott of Sikh organizations; as a result, Sikh activists have been dealt with punitively.
The Canadian policy partly evolved in response to public opinion,
which saw Sikhs as a troublesome minority. An Indian diplomat
compared Britain with Canada; in Britain "a small number of
Punjab extremists succeeded in embittering Indo-British relations
throughout the 1980s". But compared to Canada, Britain was unwilling to undertake tough action, and the diplomat warned that
"partisan, politically motivated agitation about India's problems
in British parliamentary, political and media circles can only lead
to estrangement and bitterness between the two countries"
(Rasgotra 1994: 110–11, in Malik & Robb 1994). In Britain the
government resisted much of New Delhi's pressure, but kept a
measured distance from the Sikh campaign; a few activists were
picked up at strategic times to appease the Indian government,
and an extradition treaty aimed at Sikhs and Kashmiri Muslims
was ratified only after considerable resistance.

Community leaders have, however, gained some empathy from
other diaspora communities facing similar predicaments. Sikh
leaders have cultivated bonds with fellow communities, such as
Nagas, Kashmiri Muslims and Tamils, as part of their campaign,
while their relationship with the Hindu diaspora has become
detached and occasionally hostile. Thus the demolition of
Ayodhya mosque in December 1992, when some Muslims in
Britain retaliated by damaging some Hindu temples, did not attract Sikh sympathy as it would have done in the past (Kundu
1994; Burlet & Reid 1995). In all three countries there was also
some local sympathy from other ethnic communities, notably by
some Muslim and Jewish organizations in Canada.

The Indian government's direct interference into the Sikh
diaspora's activities can only be gauged through secondary evidence. Its official statements viewed the Sikh diaspora as poten-

tially subversive. The White Paper (1984) asserted that "the ideological underpinning for the demand for a separate Sikh state was provided by certain members of the Sikh community in foreign countries" and "the essence of the problem in Punjab was not the demands put forward by the Akali Dal in 1981 but the maturing of a secessionist and anti-national movement with the active support of a small number of groups operating from abroad". Besides concluding extradition treaties with Canada and Britain, the Indian government has put pressure on these states, demanding the repatriation of Sikh activists and restrictions to be placed on their international contacts.

Measures such as surveillance, freezing of funds for Punjab and pressure on the Punjabi media were put into operation, reflecting New Delhi's sensitivity towards the Sikh diaspora's role and its attempts to circumvent its influence through the full force of existing or new laws. It is difficult to assess how far these policies succeeded in denting diaspora Sikh campaigns; certainly the new extradition treaties could not put any "terrorists" on trial, and no unlawful use of gurdwara funds was revealed under scrutiny. So perhaps these measures were part of creating a public warning to influence the general atmosphere within the diaspora Sikh communities. This was possibly in line with the White Paper (1984) insight into why overseas Sikhs are involved in the homeland campaign:

> Some are misinformed or misled by interested parties, some others may be vulnerable to pressures in those countries. It is not always easy for the affluent abroad to identify themselves with the basic socio-economic interests of the working Sikh masses in India. For some of them the troubles in Punjab were a good opportunity to project themselves as leaders of the Sikh community.[7]

To this end, the Indian official discourse tried to articulate the idea of India as the Sikh community's homeland, against the community's natural orientation towards Punjab.[8] In such a statist approach, the understanding of diaspora Sikhs' anguish seemed rather a low priority, as was the respect for their civil rights in host states. In a letter to an MP who had written on behalf of her Sikh voters, the Indian embassy in London replied:

> It is not true to say that the safety of the friends and relatives of your constituents is under threat: in fact the threat to their safety has been removed by the army action.

Unmindful of the Sikhs' wounded sentiments over the destruction of the Akal Takhat, an Indian official almost assumed a threatening tone:

> Not enough credit has been given for maintaining intact the central shrine of the Golden Temple, the Harmandir Saheb [sic]. Had the security forces been given a free hand 'Operation Bluestar' would have been over in less than 30 minutes without the loss of life of a single soldier. . . . It is doubtful if any European forces would have accepted such iron discipline and supreme sacrifice . . . no humanist seems to have bothered when hundreds of innocent men, women and children were murdered by Bhindranwale's hit squads.[9]

The Indian media correspondents sent frequent reports of diaspora Sikhs' "emotional outbursts"[10] describing them as "romantics, fools or knaves", and living in the "make-believe world of their own"[11] along with evidence of foreign conspiracies.[12] The role of the community media has been the subject of criticism in the Indian press.[13] Sikh leaders could hardly match the resources of the Indian diplomatic service and its patronizing of the media with frequent news briefings, videos, and press statements. An American Sikh leader, seemed overwhelmed by the Indian campaign, when he observed:

> Indian intelligence seeks to damage our movement for Khalistan in at least two ways. a. by trying to shape the issue in the international arena as one of human rights, not of freedom and b. by falsely characterising our struggle as a terrorist movement. Our main issue is freedom. Indeed, it

is our lack of freedom which leaves us victims of the violation of human rights by the India government.[14]

A Canadian Sikh took strong exception to disinformation techniques by the Indian media, and he noted a suite of five glossy
pamphlets under the title "Facets of a Proxy War". Each pamphlet
addressed a specific facet of terrorism: connections, activities,
revelations, links and human rights violations. Each pamphlet
accused Sikhs of terrorism. He observed the clever ploy[15]:

> The mention of downing of Air India plane on 23 June
> 1985 under the heading 'terrorism in the skies' is a
> Machiavellian ploy, unbecoming of the Indian govern-
> ment. The proxy war has wrongfully concluded sabotage
> [not yet proven]. By innuendo the report accused Manjit
> Singh alias Lal Singh for the crime [as yet no trial or
> conviction].

It is only in the field of human rights that the Sikh diaspora scored
some sympathy from the human rights agencies. Here also they
had to challenge the well-entrenched notion of Indian democracy
by highlighting the conditions of the Punjabi population; no elections had been held for a decade. As a widely publicized report
complained, it was

> an eye-opener to those who view India as a democratic,
> civilised and tolerant society. . . . Baselessness of this pre-
> mise is evident for the failure of the Indian state to hold any
> credible enquiry into the glaring cases of human rights
> violations much less punish the guilty.[16]

Indian propaganda also won an easy victory; the international
media portrayed the Sikh community as "terrorists".[17] This led to
objections from many non-political Sikhs, who saw it as wholesale
slander. The National Sikh Centre (formerly known as the Guru
Gobind Singh Foundation) tried to rebut "false propaganda about
Sikhs as terrorists" and encouraged them to "become aware of
themselves as a community".[18] However, it seemed a losing battle
as the Indian state exerted its influence on host states, and a

variety of policy options such as patronage, awards, recognition and visa restrictions were used to affect the Sikh separatist campaign and the community's attitudes. Nor was its interference limited to political matters. The setting up of a "Sikh Studies" chair at the University of British Columbia was subjected to Indo-Canadian diplomacy, saved only as prominent academics rallied around the issue. Even a detached scholarly work on Sikh nationalism in Sweden was not immune from the ire of the Indian authorities.[19]

## Discourse on the Sikh homeland

A cursory examination of the Sikh diaspora's literature since 1984 provides ample proof of how the "crucial event" in the Golden Temple has turned a secure ethnic group's outlook towards a search for a homeland. The anguish was translated into a cry for "Sikh homeland" and a need for independence was elaborated; thus Ganga Singh Dhillon pleaded:

> We are not looking just for a piece of land. We are looking for a territory where Sikhs can protect their women and children. Where a Sikh can become a master of his own destiny – where our religious shrines are not allowed to be run over by army tanks. You can call it an independent Punjab, a sovereign state or Khalistan. What we are asking for is a homeland for the Sikh nation. (Dhillon 1985)

A mythological case was advocated by K. S. Sihra, a British Sikh:

> God gave the Sikhs their land, a rich and fertile land blessed with much sun and irrigation, the land of five rivers, the Punjab ... Maharajah Ranjit Singh gave the Sikhs their state, later handed in trust, first to the British then to the Hindu raj – but the Sikhs never surrendered their ultimate sovereignty to any power other than their own. Today after forty years abuse of their trust, the Sikhs are ready to create again their independent, sovereign state. (Sihra 1985: 55)

In another book, he set out a charter for the new Sikh state, and his analysis of contemporary India ran like this:

> It is abundantly clear for all to realize that the India of today is a superficial state imposed from above by the transfer of power from the British Raj and in a sense is a continuation of that Raj by trickery and perversion in many ways and is an un-natural outcome. . . . Several nationalities of India in their territorial units, which like Khalistan, should be able to form their own sovereign states of Mahrashtra, Tamil Nadu, Assam, Sikkim, Nagaland, Mizoland, Kerala, Jammu and Kashmir and come together in a new economic union as the European Economic Community with full freedom for self-development in unity and mutual regard for each other. The reorganization of India on the basis of regional ethnic nationalities with distinct ethnic language and cultural background has become imperative as the only satisfactory primary answer to end the perpetual conflicts with the underground movements that have constantly engaged the police and the army in the several nationalist states since 1947 at great economic cost and loss of life. (Sihra 1985: 10)

Elaborating on the community's predicament, a Canadian Sikh S. S. Dharam visualized three alternatives:[20] (a) to accept the status quo, "which will ensure a certain death for the community"; (b) to campaign for the Anandpur Sahib Resolution, which would only lead to being "entrapped by the government's false promises"; (c) to campaign for an independent homeland. This last alternative, he suggested, was the "most realistic option". He also noted how the 1984 events have contributed to the idea of a homeland:

> The concept of Sikh homeland which appeared to exist only in imagination has now taken a turn for reality, which will certainly be attained in due course of time. Khalistan, a dream of some, and fanciful wish of many, has now become the demand of all Sikhs. The voice of the people is the voice of God. (Dharam 1986: 90)

194

The international platform has also made Sikh leaders aware of how self-determination for national minorities is an acceptable dialogue. The WSO and the Council of Khalistan leaders have advocated self-determination for Sikhs in many resolutions:

> The UN Charter recognises every nation's right of self-determination. On the basis of this recognition of the fundamental human rights of liberty and freedom by the world body, Sikhs living in occupied Khalistan have the right of self-determination in their homeland. We the American Sikhs support their just and legitimate demand for self-determination and renew our solemn pledge to continue to support their just and legitimate demand by all legal means so that our brothers and sisters living in occupied Khalistan can also enjoy the same glow of freedom as we enjoy in our great nation of the United States of America.[21]

While a Sikh homeland is meant to create an environment to safeguard the religious traditions, paradoxically, this theological argument has also been used to oppose this demand. Gurutej Singh Khalsa (1985: 84), an American convert to the Sikh faith, asked fellow Sikhs to reconsider their commitment, as the creation of a Sikh homeland will only restrict the Sikh faith's universal appeal:

> This cannot just stop with putting on an orange turban and calling for a homeland. True spiritual education is needed. We must develop public relations tools and skills so as to correct this damaged view of what a Sikh is. Next, we must seriously bridge this gap between Indian origin Sikhs and other Western Sikhs. This religion belongs to no one nationality. It is not to be confined to a homeland, for the nature of the Khalsa is a sovereign, spiritual nation which knows no physical boundaries. Then this religion will be viewed as a lifestyle that the rest of world not only wants but has a right to . . .

This theological vision would also appeal to some Sikh sects such as Namdharis, and perhaps to a section of Ramgarhias.

Maluk Singh Chuhan, a British Sikh, was surprised at the mild tone of the "controversial" Anandpur resolution:

> It describes Sikhs as a religious minority and protection of religious rights is demanded for the sake of national unity. The fact is that Sikhs are not a religious minority of the Indian nation. Sikhs in India are one of the nations of India, India is a multinational country. . . . The question that Sikhs constitute one of its nations is not negotiable. . . . It is an internationally known principle that all nations have a right of self-determination, be they Palestinians, Basques, Jews, Kurds, Welsh or others.[22]

A liberal vision of Sikh nationalism has come from student intellectuals. Thus the Khalistan Society at the London School of Economics called upon all Punjabis, not just Sikhs, to struggle for "freedom, prosperity, justice, equality, liberty and human rights". The struggle is for an "independent Punjab" and for equality for all religious minorities within its "secular and democratic political system".[23]

## The impact of the critical event

The sacrilege committed by the Indian armed forces' massive action in the sacred precinct in Amritsar in June 1984 touched a raw chord in the Sikh psyche. Irrespective of their background, all Sikhs were affronted by this wanton injury by the Indian government; it seemed a deliberate and blasphemous act. Until 1984 the Sikh loyalty towards India on the one hand and an ethnic community on the other, had achieved a harmonious balance, but the events in the Golden Temple put it to a severe test. The constraints it imposed on Sikh sensitivities can only be gauged by statements like this:

> Let us burn our Indian passports, we no longer belong to India. . . . We are Americans and Sikhs and proud to be so. We are not just American Sikhs.[24]

A similar sentiment was expressed by a British Sikh:

> I always said I was first Indian, second Sikh. For all these years, I've kept my Indian passport, but now I feel like burning it.[25]

The dishonour and hurt felt by Sikhs led to a spontaneous response in the diaspora, with protest marches and various other developments that generated anger against Indian officials and an outcry for independence – part of the Sikh collective consciousness, but an idea that needed no expression before June 1984. Individual expressions of this consciousness can be read through angry letters to the media, personal narratives and creative writing. Poems probably best convey this anger and the enfolding tragedy:

> Take care of the turban, o'Sikh
> oppression has surpassed all past limits
> Burning all you cared,
> beautiful flowers, indeed the whole yard
> Charred is your beautiful Punjab.[26]

Ravinder Ravi, a Canadian Punjabi poet, wrote of the tragedy:[27]

> From Palestine to Irish struggles
> the pens that rolled copious tears,
> why has the ink suddenly dried?
> The land of Punjab is shackled,
> terror loose and our motherland cries
> where are my red-faced sons? where are them?
> The angry and rebellious ones to restore my honour?

Apart from poetry, many popular songs were recorded in the immediate aftermath of June 1984. They narrated the Sikhs' fierce resistance to Indian army action during the siege, eulogizing the new martyrs.[28] Several individuals risked their careers to fight against this sacrilege.[29] This critical event brushed away traditional political associations and replaced them with new organizations and leaders, rehabilitating a few much ostracized Khalistanis of the 1970s in the process.

In the immediate aftermath of 1984, the profound sense of humiliation produced an unprecedented mobilization. New leaders summoned shared sentiments to restore the "community's honour"; they got an enthusiastic response.[30] Thus, the ISYF's call stated commonly shared emotions:

> As every member of the Sikh fraternity knows already, the Khalsa Panth is passing through a very difficult and dangerous period of its history. In the so-called Indian democratic republic, the proud and respected Sikh nation's culture, religious traditions, identity and integrity are being crushed. The Indian government is using all its power including the army, the police commandos, armoury and tanks to annihilate the Sikh nation. . . . The army invasion of the Golden Temple, the humiliating demolition of the Akal Takhat, the burning down of the Sikh Reference Library, priceless manuscripts of the Gurus, handwritten copies of the Guru Granth Sahib, and sacred letters of our Gurus. Ten thousand Sikhs were killed by the Indian army's butchers. These were atrocities committed by the Indian government and these cannot be overlooked despite lies spread by the government. The black deeds of Indira Gandhi and Rajiv Gandhi's governments are writ large.[31] . . . After Indira's assassination, innocent Sikhs in almost every large city of India were murdered by the Hindu majority at the connivance of the Indian government. Daughters and mothers of the Sikh nation were humiliated, their property burnt. After three decades, Sikhs were, once again, reduced to the status of refugees.

The cry for *raj karega Khalsa* (the Khalsa shall rule), always ambiguous in the past, suddenly caught political overtones and was readily employed. By using a common language derived from Sikh theology, the crucial event was interpreted as a threat to the survival of the community; calling for sacrifices, through such appeals to fellow Sikhs, they were asked to understand the predicament. The use of common Punjabi words and phrases, drawn from a rich vocabulary of Sikh theological and literary tradition, became a rallying cry:

> Our martyrs . . . fought for the community and sacrificed for our nation's sake. Following our martyrs' legacy, the International Sikh Youth Federation is holding its annual conference in British Columbia's capital city, Vancouver with the cooperation of Khalsa Diwan Society. This annual convention would inform you of the Indian government's massive misinformation and propaganda against the Sikh community. How the Indian Consulate are brandishing us extremists and fanatics among Canadians, spreading hatred. How the Indian state is using the media, radio, TV and other communication channels to denigrate our just and gallant movement for independence and survival.[32]

The community's tradition of martyrdom was invoked in speeches and written appeals. After many years its potential for mobilization still existed:

> The Indian fascist regime has suppressed our rights and initiated a wanton destruction of our will and economy. They have been dissuading us from seeking the fulfilment of those contractual pledges – to respect Sikhs' right for sovereignty – ever since independence. When all such efforts failed, they launched a regime of oppression and barbarity in June 1984. This was an attempt to wipe our national identity off the face of earth. . . . Yet thanks to the courage and sacrifices of our brave martyrs, the Sikh nation stands upright and firm in the face of Indian tyranny. In spite of the genocide of June and November 1984 and the international terrorism that has been unleashed, our war of independence goes unabated.[33]

The tragedy was interpreted in many ways; while a few called for a re-examination of Sikhs' basic beliefs, others emphasized a decisive battle for freedom, and still others adopted a "quietist" position. The crisis also provided space for advocating more sharp boundaries, thought to have been compromised by the diaspora's alien setting. Thus, leaders emphasized the importance of Sikh baptism and strict religious observances; as a reaction to the crisis, several hundred undertook baptism, among them many leaders who were mostly clean-shaven. Far from being an unmitigated disaster, the crisis provided an opportunity to re-examine the faith:

> After the brutal eruption of this holocaust, there seems to be a jolting effect on the Sikh mind, who woke up from a long slumber. Sikhs who had deviated from basic Sikh principles started learning them again, they took on the Sikh attire, the *Gurbani*, and an understanding of history. They started teaching Punjabi to their children. The *Amrit* [baptism] became popular. Many stopped using intoxicants.[34]

A call for revival of ethnic consciousness and greater public awareness was emphasized. The Sikh Welfare Foundation of North America appealed to fellow Sikhs:

> With all that is happening with Sikhs, it is time to organize to improve our image, welfare and self-dignity. We should work to shatter the myth India has created that Sikhs are terrorists; become an ambassador; study Sikhism and history; create an understanding among ourselves, and among our communities and citizens of the country we live in. . . . Ensure Sikh children receive the best education and achieve scholastic merits; mothers should teach children about our religion . . . celebrate the following holidays in addition to our national holidays: April 13th is our New Year Day – the birthday of the Khalsa. Ensure our gurdwaras provide baptism [Amrit] on that day. Observe June 6th as the Martyrdom Day: to honour our martyrs of the massacre in the Golden Temple.[35]

Thus, an initial mobilization was easy and spontaneous. However, the creation of an effective movement required foresight and planning; in this the role of new leaders was crucial.

*Shifting loyalties*

The crucial event has contributed to a perceptible shift in Sikhs' collective loyalty. While many Sikhs have acquired citizenship, perhaps a majority in Britain and America, they have shared an ethnic identity of being an Asian, an Indian, a Punjabi or a Sikh in various situations. With the 1984 events there has been a shift towards a firm sense of the hyphenated Sikh, the British Sikh, the Canadian Sikh or the American Sikh. Moreover, new leaders have offered a radical solution to the community's collective dilemma, a sovereign homeland that offers an easy answer to nagging doubts of individuals and at the same time resolves multifaceted issues of the community in an alien setting. The assertion of a Sikh nation's right for self-determination provides an impeccable and honourable resolution to the question, Where do we belong? Overseas situations have thrown up many cases of "tradition in question". Cases of discrimination for wearing the turban or carrying a kirpan have required many mobilizations; these issues have arisen, in many Sikh leaders' perception, because Sikhs have no "national status". While support has been sought from the religious centre, the Akal Takhat in Amritsar, on several issues it would be much easier to resolve many cases if Sikhs had a sovereign country. In Britain the Census Office has received many representations for separate Sikh enumeration, and in Canada the Akali Dal asked the federal government to recognize Sikhs as a distinct ethnic group:

> We do hope that this brief would better state our position as *Canadian Sikhs* [emphasis in original] and the government will not fall into error in dealing with questions whenever the question of so-called "East-Indians" or "origins in India", comes up. Even our "origins" go further than "India", since our people are composed of the Indo-Scythian stock that had settled in northern India since the first century AD.[36]

Issues of collective identity have been prompted by overseas situations, where state administration routinely requires categories and boundaries. In 1982 a British Columbian gurdwara hoisted the Indian flag alongside the Sikh flag on Indian independence day, 15 August. This was the subject of considerable controversy among Canadian Sikhs, leading to the intervention of Amritsar: the Akal Takhat *jathedar* and other head priests from Punjab had to clarify the situation. Kirpal Singh, the Akal Takhat *jathedar*, Amritsar, sent an instruction not to fly the Indian flag alongside the Sikh flag.[37]

Shifts in group loyalty are immensely difficult to measure, but some illustrations can be cited. A good illustration comes from the annual reports of the Khalsa Diwan Society, Vancouver. In 1981 its report depicted the Gadrites and Indian freedom fighters. In 1982 it carried a photo of the Sikh volunteers who joined the *Dharam Yudh Morcha* in the Punjab.[38] The 1984 report displayed the damaged building of the Akal Takhat; inside it carried the tenth guru's stanza under the title "Sikh National Anthem" – an innovation. The report paid tribute to the new Sikh martyrs:

> The *sant* [Bhindranwale] was neither a 'secessionist' nor a 'terrorist' as the official and other agencies would have us believe. He has been more sinned against than sinning.[39]

The last phrase evoked a Californian Sikh's struggle for citizenship in America. At the Surrey gurdwara, its report for 1987 juxtaposed the Canadian national anthem with the Sikh national anthem.[40] The subtle shift in group loyalty can be seen through a long struggle over the name of a market, "Punjabi" or "Indian Market" in Vancouver, indicating a perceptible shift from an "Indianness" towards "Punjabiness". This can also be seen over a contest between the Sikh delegation and an Indian delegation at the unfurling of a Sikh flag at the UN Congress of Ethnic Groups. While Sikh delegates "proudly" joined in the world's ethnic group parade, the Indian delegates walked out in protest against the inclusion of the Sikh flag.

The international arena has provided some space for the symbolic inclusion of the Sikhs in the world community. For Sikh leaders, the act of lobbying the host states has contributed to their self-worth (Weiner 1989). At the Dag Hammarskjold Plaza across the street from the UN building, Sikhs have joined the theatre for ethnic diaspora protests. Similarly, attempts to gain non-governmental organization (NGO) status at the United Nations or the keen contest for membership of the Unrepresented Nations and Peoples Organization (UNPO) should be seen in this context of seeking respectability. The membership of UNPO, for a brief period, was interpreted as a "major milestone for Sikh independence" as the Sikh flag was hoisted at the Hague.[41]

The quest for homeland has then become a part of the Sikh diaspora's imagining, providing a sense of pride and recognition. Before the 1980s, Punjab and India were mere geographical spaces; the "critical event" has differentiated the two regions into contesting issues, Punjab emerging as a homeland and Punjabi nationalism replacing the Indian nationalistic feelings. However, these loyalties have shifting and indefinite answers. Although Punjab had a feeble connotation of sacred territory due to its association with the Sikh gurus, and from its rivers as part of Punjabi myths and romances, only a tragic event could bring such recessed sensibilities into the public sphere. The diaspora claim on the Punjab as a homeland is a new innovation and symbolic identification of an insecure diaspora.

## A collective fate?

The "critical event" has brought home a new feeling of endangered and collective fate of the community scattered in many countries. A sharp sense has arisen of the Sikh community's vulnerability, and the need for control over its institutions and resources. The communications revolution has helped to link various overseas communities; cases of discrimination against its members in Southall, Stockton, Vancouver and Singapore often attract the attention of the worldwide Sikh diaspora. This interlinking has contributed to a sharpened sense of common causes and the endangered fate of the community. Thus, the wso asked:

> The issues facing the Sikhs in India are too serious to be left to the emotional outbursts of a few individuals. Sikhs must develop approaches on a sophisticated level, beyond individual whims and work TOGETHER, to develop strong organizations. It thus becomes the utmost responsibility of

the politically conscious Sikh wherever he or she may be –
in order to foster full commitment and discipline for its
effective workings.[42] (Emphasis in the original)

As a result of the traumatic event, there is a much closer connection not only with Punjab itself, but also with various constituents
of the diaspora in Europe, North America and the Far East. This
is partly helped by the communications revolution.[43] There is
much concern about the collective image of the community. Thus,
in 1991 the Sikh Missionary Center, Detroit, undertook the task
of Sikh definition in various encyclopedias.[44] They asked the
publishers to define Sikhs as an adherent of a monotheistic
religion of India founded about 1500 by Guru Nanak and marked
by rejection of idolatry and caste, instead of the usual description
of the Sikh as member of a Hindu sect, or Sikhism as an offshoot
of Hinduism. A case of Punjabi versus Hindi books in libraries,
cases of discrimination against Sikhs, news of control over a particular gurdwara, the role of the Indian media and "its agents"
within the community, all are frequent subjects of the Punjabi
media.[45]

Events affecting the diaspora find much discussion through
various columns, events such as the arrest of Sikh visitors in the
Punjab, the conditions of jailed Sikhs[46] and the welfare of Sikhs in
the Middle East.[47] Reports of other countries' involvement in the
movement, such as the Khalsa Naujawan Sabha of Hong Kong,[48]
plus reports of protest marches and resolutions are carried by the
Punjabi media of the Far East,[49] Australia[50] and New Zealand.[51]
Such an international network draws an easy comparison with the
Gadr movement, which also shared a common theme of undoing
the "humiliation" and the Indian government's neglect of overseas citizens. A scholar's comment regarding the Gadr movement
seems highly applicable to the contemporary struggle:

> Abandoned by British in their fight against Canadian
> immigration legislation, for the first time a section of Jat
> Sikhs broke from their quiescent loyalism to adopt the
> revolutionary nationalism of the Ghadar movement – with
> all its consequences for the community's political develop-
> ment. The fate of a small but highly significant group of

Indian exiles helped focus attention on the complex racial, political and constitutional issues arising in the rapid evolution of a complex multi-racial empire. (Fraser 1978: 51–52)

Further parallels exist in terms of the leaders' tactics, their personal rivalries, the fiery songs, the rhetoric and style of mobilization, and the emphasis on sacrifices. Thus, the "Gadr syndrome", as defined by Juergensmeyer, should find some qualified support in the present movement:

> A militant nationalist movement . . . created abroad by expatriates, for whom the movement is also an outlet for their economic and social frustrations, and a vehicle for their ethnic identities. It is the fusion and the mutual interaction of ethnic anger and nationalist pride. (Juergensmeyer 1969: 173)

Discriminatory immigration policies, however, have played no role in the present movement. Nor is the diaspora's cry for a homeland born out of economic frustrations; by all accounts, in all three countries Sikhs have done generally well in their new homes. However, there are other close parallels. The present movement's impact in differentiating Sikhs among Indian loyalists and fiery Punjabi nationalists parallels the Gadr movement, which split the Sikh leadership into Indian nationalists and loyalists. Another characteristic shared by both movements is the divergence between the diaspora's perception and the home situation. To their shock, the Gadr activists found a loyalist community in the Punjab with few signs of discontent. In the contemporary movement, as Punjab is returning to the realpolitik of elections, power sharing by the Akalis, and with most militants killed, the diaspora's commitment to the Sikh homeland might seem a deviation.

An essentially secular political movement for Punjab's autonomy, is tied up with the dynamics of Sikhs' religious identity, both in the Punjab and in the diaspora. In overseas countries the movement is essentially organized around and within the gurdwaras. Attempts to explain the Sikh diaspora's involvement in the homeland issue will engage social scientists in the future. Some current hypotheses can be examined here rather briefly. In a study of British Sikhs, Goulbourne (1991) deplored Sikhs' "communal option" but blamed the home government and the host state's policies for making such an option attractive to migrant groups. Helweg (1989: 331) and especially Mahmood (1996) have pleaded to situate Sikhs' reaction in their "psychological and cultural" framework. Dusenbery (1995) has offered a more credible proposition, arguing that in Western countries "state ideologies and public policy have [been] predicated on a common assumption of place of origin and in particular on national origins". In such multicultural societies, bargaining for resources among ethnic groups almost "requires" a recognized homeland for migrant groups. So, it is not surprising that diaspora Sikhs have taken up such a project, in order to gain respect and recognition as a separate entity with a claim on the new country of Khalistan.

As seen above, this hypothesis is supported by many Sikh leaders' perception of their situation in the diaspora. Thus, many leaders point out that, year after year, issues of religious authority have arisen in almost every country: justification for the turban and kirpan; provision for Punjabi in schools, on radio and on television. They have led to campaigns that deploy the same basic arguments across the global Sikh diaspora. In many turban and kirpan cases, community leaders sought the Indian High Commission's help but felt let down by its "unsympathetic" attitude. This contributed in small ways towards a Sikh state. Disputes regarding certain gurdwara rituals and practices, the role of *sants*, tension between orthodox and modern Sikhs, representation on state and voluntary bodies, have led to frustrations over "authority". A large number of leaders believe that many such issues would not have arisen, or would have been more easily soluble, if the community had had an independent state.

Such social and religious frustrations felt by community leaders have probably played a major part in rallying Sikhs behind the homeland issue. Somehow they feel differences between Sikh norms and those of the host societies; the gulf between the private world of an ethnic community and the public space would be more easily negotiated if leaders could "authenticate" their voices as of a nation recognized by the world. There is a widespread realization, sometimes bordering on paranoia, that without a state, the community's language, culture and religious traditions, both in the Punjab and in the diaspora, face certain oblivion. A state offers a way out of the painful transition of the Sikh diaspora facing a crisis of legitimacy for its religious, linguistic and cultural traditions. It seems that the Sikh diaspora has been transformed since the events of 1984; from a confident community able to look after its own house, it has become an introspective "victim diaspora".[52]

The cry for state has therefore become a necessity in terms of the community's self-respect and dignity. Accordingly, the theme of the present struggle may lie in the phrase "not to be dictated by others". Seen in this light, Khalistan may be less of a statement of political sovereignty than of "personal dignity", "religious integrity" and "ethnic identity". As a sympathetic scholar has suggested, it may help to interpret the homeland issue as "the utterance of the Sikh soul which yearns for fullness of expression".[53]

Consequently, the diaspora involvement is also supplying an ideological framework, widening Sikhs' consciousness of their place in the world, bringing a considerable shift in collective loyalty, redefining Sikh ethnicity in terms of an ethnonational bond. With the exception of psychologists, social scientists tend to be uncomfortable in confronting the nonrational. The ethnic bond is perhaps irrational and emotional. It can be described, even analyzed, but not explained rationally. Theories lag behind the conceptual tools necessary to deal with group passions, the symbols that move them and the intensity of attachments which cut across borders and nations. Said & Simmons put it (1976: 14) like this:

> As emerging actors in the international system, they [the ethnic groups and the emerging new ethnic groups] are indications that our perceptions of international relations and the causes of war and peace lag behind the consciousness of the men and nations we study. The ethnic nation cannot compete with the state in nuclear warheads and warships but it continues to exercise formidable influence over the primary authority patterns of men. It is from this exercise of power that revolutions are born.

Thus, the cry for a homeland can be interpreted as a demand for "honour" and "respect" or a wish to be seen as equals among the world of nations. A comprehensive explanation should include the community's memories, myths and values, and how they have been interpreted and mobilized by its elite. The Sikh self-perception, as it unfolds in the diaspora literature for homeland, points towards the complexity of culture and the place of the human experience in its constitution. Diaspora Sikh politics and its role in Punjabi affairs might be understandable as symbolic solidarity between co-ethnics separated by distance, but sharing many common assumptions, meanings and the semantics of language.

# Conclusion


Sikhs in the diaspora, especially the Sikh communities of Canada, the United States and Britain, have played a considerable role in the political, economic and social life of Punjab, as well as being affected by events in the Punjab and India. Through remittances, exchange of ideas and ideology, visits and pilgrimages to ancestral homes and kin, the Sikh diaspora communities have kept a lively cultural exchange. They have also nurtured political associations. Their richer sections have invested in a range of projects from economic assistance to considerable donation for religious, educational and charitable works. While the overseas Sikh communities do not meet *sufficient* conditions to be described as a diaspora, they do seem to have acquired certain *necessary* elements of a psychological and sociological nature which are essential to its consciousness. First-generation overseas migrants are obviously related to the homeland in many ways, but the events of June 1984 had a "traumatic" effect and generated considerable response and solidarity among the second and third generations.

In the aftermath of the army action in the Golden Temple, the role of British and North American Sikh communities has been significant in popularizing the idea of a Sikh homeland. Support for organizations campaigning for the Sikh state has been substantial, both material and moral. It has internationalized the issue of a Sikh homeland. Reaction to the Punjabi crisis has led to a sustained campaign for Khalistan among a section of the Sikh leadership abroad. The mode of mobilization and the formation of new organizations have been informed by cultural, moral and religious traditions of the Sikh society. This study highlights the complex nature of identity formation and the developmental process of an ethnic community. While a broader loyalty towards India probably still exists, the events of the past decade have caused perceptible changes in their loyalties, and they have also affected their relationship with the host societies. The Punjabi crisis has probably generated a realignment of Sikh identity towards Punjabi in small yet perceptible ways, though such shifts are inherently difficult to quantify.

The impact of the Punjabi crisis has enabled them to redraw a strict definition of Sikh identity, highlighting the religious tradition and collective symbols of the community instead of the geography, language and cultural traits. These developments within the community serve to underline the "situational" nature of ethnic consciousness, while the articulation of the demand for a "homeland" is seen to be anchored in the primordial givens. The reaction also shows how the events of 1984 have been seen and interpreted as a threat to the collective entity of the Sikh community, a humiliation for the community's pride. A somewhat ambiguous and complex set of attachments towards an imaginary homeland has been reinforced by the "crucial" event, which posed a challenge to the deeply held beliefs and feelings.

The characteristic call for mobilization has been to avenge this humiliation and to achieve a secure homeland where such a threat could not arise in the future. Thus, in its reaction there appears to be an interplay of culture, group consciousness and the uncertainty of migrant status in the host society. With the settler countries providing a limited expression of their cultural and religious traditions, conditions have perhaps existed for such frustrations to be channelled into the cause of yearning for a homeland. The "Khalistan movement" abroad may also indicate Sikh migrants' alienation from the host societies. Neither equal citizens, nor having enough power to express their cultural ambitions, the aspiring community leaders have looked back on their "land of origins" for prestige and honour. Such a reaction ought not be brushed aside as the brainchild of a few misguided zealots.

In terms of geography and mobilization characteristics there are clear parallels with the Gadr movement. The formation of the

Gadr movement was attributed to the exclusionary policies of the Canadian and American governments, coupled with an uncaring attitude of the Indian colonial state towards the plight of its overseas peoples. The Khalistan movement may also be located within those parameters. The home government's unsympathetic attitude towards a minority's aspirations, seen through an unparalleled attack on its religious centre and the host states' policies, coupled with a sense of alienation from those societies, may have provided all the ingredients necessary for the mobilization towards a secure and independent homeland.

A sovereign "homeland" offers the possibility of becoming a substitute for an alienated diaspora elite. Contemporary evidence suggests this is the case for a small section of the Sikh diaspora of Britain and North America. However, the strength of an alienated elite could grow in the future. An independent Punjab was an "imagined homeland" for few Sikhs until the 1984 army action in Amritsar. But the subsequent crisis and its handling by the Indian state, and its pressure on host states to contain the Sikh diaspora's expressions of sympathy, might have converted the dream of homeland into a serious and attractive scenario for many Sikhs. A distinct minority of Sikhs are now committed to the achievement of an independent country. Whether the silent majority would be convinced of the minority's arguments depends upon two factors: the sense of security they feel in their new homes in Britain and North America, and the future developments in their homeland, the Punjab. That both of these factors are beyond the diaspora's control points towards the dilemma of a diaspora's ambivalent attitudes and loyalties. The Sikh diaspora's reaction to the events in Punjab and its characteristic pattern of mobilization provide a clear example of how, through one "crucial event", a confident and "secure" diaspora can become conscious of a "threatened homeland" and mobilize in its defence.

# Appendices

APPENDIX 1

# Letter from Sant Harchand Singh Longowal, president of the Shiromani Akali Dal, to overseas Sikh leaders; *Indo-Canadian Times*, 15 October 1982

I am sending this special letter to all of you because you should know what is happening to the Panth. It is now 144 days into the Dharam Yudh Morcha. Some 17,557 Sikhs have courted arrest. Of these 44 have been tortured to death in jails. Another 34 were crushed under a train. Jails have become black holes, over-crowded, no water, no roof and nothing whatsoever to eat.

You should take a deputation to the Indian High Commission office on 17 October, with a letter stating how Sikhs are being repressed in India. You should make the world aware how India is treating the Sikh Panth and to show that all Sikhs, wherever they are, share the anguish of Panth.

I am stating with firm conviction that the *Dharam Yudh* will continue until the cruel Indian government agrees to our just demands. The Punjab is almost boiling while the Congress leaders are dithering and enjoying themselves. Of peace, justice and rule of law, which the Congress leaders are never tired of evocation, there is nothing like, but the Khalsa has kept itself within the limits. The government is being provocative with extreme measures. Our youth is willing to do some daring. Many innocents have been killed and are being killed.

I hope you have already received the report of the appointed

214

commission. Please send a copy of the memorandum that you would give to the Indian High Commission on 17 October to the Akali Dal Office in Amritsar.

I remain,
Servant of the Panth,

Sant Harchand Singh Longowal
President, Shiromani Akali Dal
Amritsar.

# Excerpts from extradition treaties

## Between India and Canada

The treaty was signed by Charles J. Clark for the government of Canada and Narayan Tiwari for the government of India and it came into effect on 10 February 1987

### Article 1: duty to extradite

1. Each contracting state agrees to extradite to the other, subject to the conditions of this Treaty, any person who, being accused or convicted of an offence of an extradition offence as described in Article 3, committed within the territory of one State, is found in the territory of the other State, whether or not such offence was committed before or after the coming into force of this treaty.

### Article 3: extradition offence

1. An extradition offence is committed when the conduct of the person whose extradition is sought constitutes an offence punishable by the laws of both contracting States by a term of imprisonment for a period of more than one year.

## Between India and the United Kingdom

The treaty was signed in London by Kenneth Clarke and S. B. Chavan on 22 September 1992

## *Article 1: duty to extradite*

1. Each Contracting State undertakes to extradite to the other, in the circumstances and subject to the conditions specified in the Treaty, any person who, being accused or convicted of an extradition offence as described in Article 2, committed within the territory of the one state, is found within the territory of the other state, whether such offence was committed before or after the entry into force of this Treaty.

## *Article 2: extradition offences*

1. An extradition offence for the purposes of this Treaty is constituted which under the laws of each Contracting State is punishable by a term of imprisonment for a period of at least one year.

# Letter from the *jathedar* of the Akal Takhat, Amritsar, to the gurdwara management committee, Surrey, British Columbia, Canada

Office Sri Akal Takhat Sahib
Sri Amritsar

Letter No. 75/5/82
Sri Amritsar.

21 September 1982

Tara Singh Hayer
Editor
Indo-Canadian Times
Vancouver, BC.

Sardar Tara Singh ji,

*Wahiguru ji ka Khalsa, wahiguru ji ki fateh.*

Your letter of 18 August 1982 reached us here on 20/9/1982 and also received a copy of the *Indo-Canadian Times*. You have written that on 15 August, to celebrate the Indian independence day, an Indian and Canadian government's flags were unfurled in the Surrey Gurdwara premises.

May I make it clear that within the boundary of a gurdwara, no other flag be it of the government or another denomination, except that of the Khalsa ji's own *Nishan Sahib* is to be allowed.

Yours faithfully,

(Kirpal Singh)
Head Granthi
Sri Durbar Sahib

and Jathedar
Sri Akal Takhat Sahib
Sri Amritsar ji

# Excerpts from a letter to the secretary-general of the United Nations by Dr Manohar Singh Grewal, president of the World Sikh Organization, USA; *World Sikh News*, 17 June 1988

His excellency, Javier Perez de Cuellar
Secretary General of the United Nations
United Nations,
New York, 10017.

Re: The Genocide of the Sikhs in India

Your excellency,

The situation in the Punjab is becoming more alarming. The bleeding Sikh nation is in agony. Once again Indian paramilitary forces are holding innocent people in the Golden Temple as hostages. As per news reports, "they can't drink water or even go to the toilet without being shot at" (*The New York Times*, 13 May 1988). By what law is everybody in the Golden Temple complex is being presumed guilty and shot at on sight? For too long, the Indian government has been engineering incidents to justify a new wave of oppression. Since Punjab is closed to the foreign press (except for the guided official tours), the world does not know the truth about Punjab. As recorded in the human rights report:

an undeclared, unilateral ruthless war – against hundreds of innocent defenceless men and women in far-away tiny villages of Punjab from where their voices do not reach the rest of India" (Oppression in Punjab, page 9)

All attempts by the International Committee for Red Cross and Amnesty International to go to Punjab have been rebuffed. Similar requests by US congressmen and Members of British Parliament for visiting Punjab on a fact-finding mission were not granted. Recent reports indicate that the government has hired hard-core criminals known as "Red Brigade" to kill the Sikhs. Besides every Sikh who is killed in "fake encounters" is declared a "separatist", or "extremist" and the paramilitary forces are acting prosecutors, jurors and judges without any accountability. The Sikhs' struggle for retrieving their distinct national status, lost during the partition fiasco of 1947 is almost four decades old. They have been struggling for the kind of environment where the Sikh heritage could pick up the "bits of a shattered rainbow" to borrow Tennessee Williams' words. In this quest for justice they are subjected to tyranny and oppression. . . . More than four decades ago the UN Charter enshrined "the faith in fundamental human rights, in the dignity and worth of human person, in equal rights of men and women and nations large and small . . ."

Your excellency, as Secretary General of the World Organisation, you represent the conscience of humanity and the UN inspires hope for freedom and justice. . . . Thousands of innocent Sikh orphans, widows and older parents whose loved ones have been lynched, for them freedom of religion and expression have been reduced to the "right to cry in the wilderness". Their voices, though inaudible amidst the media blitz of misinformation and deception, are appealing to the world community and the UN to urge the ruling regime of India to stop the genocide of the Sikhs. . . . In the meantime, the 1948 Convention on the Prevention and Punishment of the Crime of Genocide should be invoked. India should be asked to lift the occupation of the Sikh homeland.

. . . when the normal conditions are restored the people of Punjab should be given the opportunity to determine their own destiny through an independent and impartial referendum . . .

With best wishes and regards,

Yours sincerely,
Manohar Singh Grewal, Ph.D
President, World Sikh Organization, USA

# Appeal from Sant Harchand Singh Longowal, president of the Shiromani Akali Dal and coordinator of the Punjab Dharam Yudh Morcha, to Members of the Khalsa Diwan Society, 8000 Ross Street, Vancouver, British Columbia; *Indo-Canadian Times*, 25 November 1983

*Dear Sikhs,*

*Waheguru ji ka Khalsa, waheguru ji ki fateh*

The Khalsa Diwan Society has been sending regularly a generous amount of help towards the "Martyrs Fund" opened for the benefit of Sikh families, by Shiromani Gurdwara Parbandhik Committee and Shiromani Akali Dal. I am very grateful to the Khalsa Diwan Society for their enthusiasm shown towards Dharam Yudh Morcha.

The Shiromani Akali Dal has pursued the constitutional rights of the Panth and the Punjab with determination. Although the central government has used all means of repression and oppression to subdue the Sikh nation's rights, hundreds of Sikhs have been martyred, about 200,000 have courted arrest and thousands of Sikhs are in jails. This tradition continues . . .

I have come to know that the election for KDS for 1984 are due on

3 December 1983. The KDS is a famous organisation of patriots. Its importance and role is attested by the number of its members. At the critical times when we are engaged in the Panthic struggle, the control of Ross Street Gurdwara must be in the hands of those sympathetic to the Sikh Panth. The Khalsa Diwan Society has already contributed very significantly to the cause of Sikhs in the Punjab, those elected in the past year have proved worthy of their offices. I was very impressed by their dedicated work when I was on tour of Canada.

I appeal to voters to elect only those persons who are clearly committed to the cause of the Panth and disown those whose activities will weaken religious and other progressive tasks undertaken by the Society.

With thanks and respect,

Servant of the Panth,

Harchand Singh Longowal
President
Shiromani Akali Dal

# Excerpts from the Anandpur Sahib Resolution

*The Working Committee of the Shiromani Akali Dal adopted a draft of the new policy and programme at Sri Anandpur Sahib on 16–17 October 1973. Later it was passed in the form of 12 resolutions at the "Open Session" of the 18th All-India Akali Conference at Ludhiana on 28–29 October 1978. On the basis of these resolutions, the Akali Dal started a campaign for Punjab's autonomy. The text of these resolutions, as authenticated by Sant Harchand Singh Longowal, is reproduced below.*

## Postulates

(i) The Shiromani Akali Dal is the very embodiment of the hopes and aspirations of the Sikh Nation and as such is fully entitled to its representation. The basic postulates of this organisation are human co-existence, human progress and ultimate unity of all human beings with the spiritual soul.

(ii) These postulates are based on the great principles of Sri Guru Nanak Dev ji namely; a meditation on God's name, dignity of labour and sharing of fruits of this labour. (*Nam japo, kirat karo, vand chhako*)

## Purposes

The Shiromani Akali Dal shall ever strive to achieve the following aims:

(i) Propagation of Sikhism and its code of conduct; denunciation of atheism.

(ii) To preserve and keep alive the concept of distinct and independent identity of the Panth and to create an environment in which national sentiments and aspirations of the Sikh Panth will find full expression, satisfaction and growth.

## Political goal

The political goal of the Panth, without doubt, is enshrined in the commandment of the Tenth Lord, in the pages of Sikh history and in the very heart of the Khalsa Panth, the ultimate objective of which is the pre-eminence of the Khalsa through creation of a congenial environment and a political set-up.

## Weaker section and backward classes

The Shiromani Akali Dal aims at grooming the Sikhs in a strong sturdy nation highly educated, fully aware of its fundamental rights, very well versed in various arts and ever ready to honour the more outstanding of its sons. . . .

# Notes

## Introduction

1. Government of India, *White Paper on the Punjab problem* (1984: 4).
2. White Paper, 1984, Annexure XI, lists the number of casualties as civilians/terrorists, making no distinction between the two. Of the total 554 persons, 493 were killed in the Golden Temple, 23 in other gurdwaras, and 38 in curfew violations in the Punjab. Of the 121 injured, 86 were in the Golden Temple, 14 in other gurdwaras and 21 due to curfew violations. Of the 92 army casualties, 83 were killed in the Golden Temple, one in another gurdwara, 8 in curfew violations. Among the 287 injured, 249 were in the Golden Temple, 24 at other gurdwaras, 14 through curfew violations. Of the total 4,712 persons arrested, again categorized as civilian/terrorists, 1,592 were arrested from the Golden Temple, 796 from other gurdwaras and 2,324 in curfew violations. The government figures have been disputed by unofficial sources, the latter estimates have put pilgrims killed in the Golden Temple between 1,000 and 1,500. No official inquiry was launched into the largest tragedy in the Punjab's history. Thus the number of dead have found no independent confirmation, nor indeed was a list of "officially dead" ever published. Unofficial enquiries proposed by the SGPC and other eminent citizens were strongly "discouraged".
3. India, White Paper (1984: 1–2). Also see Indian Parliament Debates (Lok Sabha, vol. XLIX, no. 3) on the White Paper, 25 July 1984, pp. 212–328.
4. The word comes from the Greek language; it means dispersion and originated in the Greek translation of the book of Deuteronomy in the Bible (Deut. 28.25): "thou shalt be a diaspora in all kingdoms of the earth" (Oxford English Dictionary).

5. See Tarzi (1991), Zolberg et al. (1989), Mills (1996), Weiner (1996). The scale of the problem can be gauged by the numbers affected. Globally, over 20 million people are officially designated as refugees living in countries other than their own. In ten European countries, some 2,065,900 people had applied for asylum during 1988 and 1992, few were granted asylum.
6. Ethnic groups in international politics include the classical diaspora, Jews, to the modern diasporas such as Armenians, Ethiopians, Hispanics, Irish, Lithuanians, Latvians, Indians and Blacks in America, Chinese in the Far East and the Americas, and Europeans in America. Other cases of migrant groups in international politics include Bangladeshis, Muslims and Afro-Caribbeans in Britain; Kurds, Moroccans, Algerians and Tunisians in France; Cubans and Mexicans in America; Croats, Kurds and Turks in Germany; Koreans in Japan; Palestinians in America and the Middle East; Tibetans in India; Vietnamese in the Far East and America. Diasporas involved with their homeland campaigns in the recent past include Armenians, Jews, Kashmiris, Kurds, Latvians, Nagas, Palestinians, Sikhs, Tamils, Tibetans and Ukrainians (Esman 1986, 1992; Sheffer 1986; Safran 1991; Neville n.d.; Said 1977).

## Chapter 1

1. A song by Firozdin Sharf in the pre-1947 period.
2. As part of the Sikh prayer, a Punjabi passage reads evocatively thus, "*Sikhān nū sikhī dān, Srī Amritsar jī de darsn ishnān*" (McLeod 1984b: 105).
3. The Sikh kingdom was far from united, many Sikh rulers east of Sutlej kept alliances with the British power. Nor was his rule as impartial to all his subjects as Sikh historians suggest. See Duggal (1989) Singh, K. (1962) and Kapur Singh (1959).
4. Punjabi armies faced English regiments supported by Hindustani sepoys, known as "Purabias". The first battle was fought at Mudki in December 1846 and the final at Chillianwala in January 1849. See Hasrat (1968) and Gough & Innes (1887).
5. Leitner (1883: 31). "Gurmukhi language and literature is not the contemptible and barbarous which educational reports and the interested students of Hindu and Mohammedan underlings make it out to be."
6. The Chief Khalsa Diwan was established in 1902 in Amritsar, from a chain of about 20 Diwans and Sabhas, the first Diwan was established in Amritsar in 1893. The Central Sikh League was established in 1919. See Chaliland (1993).
7. See Grewal (1996). Thus the Akalis withdrew support for the Working

Committee under Motilal Nehru, which recommended universal franchise with no weightage minorities except for Muslims. Another contest concerned the "national flag". Kharak Singh sought the Sikh colour as India's third community. The flag committee chaired by Jawaharlal Nehru clarified that the flag was "national" and did not represent any community. The issue was resurrected by Jarnail Singh Bhindranwale in 1983 when he cited the Sikh colour's absence in the Indian flag as another example of "Hindu domination and discrimination against the Sikhs".

8. Quoted in Nayar (1966: 89). The memorandum by Akali Dal, 22 March 1946. Also see *Some Documents on the Demand for the Sikh Homeland*, 1969.

9. *The Punjab Boundary Commission Report*, 1947.

10. Its Minorities Subcommittee rejected separate electorates by 26 to 3 votes. Hukam Singh and four Muslims demanded that the Council of States and House of People should be elected by proportional representation. For the House of People this was rejected.

11. In the 1941 census, Hindus and Sikhs were 26 per cent and 13 per cent respectively. In 1951, after the partition, Hindus were 61 per cent, Sikhs 35 per cent and Muslims just 1 per cent.

12. *Spokesman*, 29 August 1951.

13. Report of States Reorganization Commission, Government of India, 1955. Commenting upon the Commission's ruling that Hindi and Punjabi are similar, Hukam Singh wryly observed, "While others got States for their languages, we lost even our language". See *The Punjab Problem*.

14. See Sarhadi (1971), Nayar (1966, 1968) and Mann (1969). For arguments about a Punjabi-speaking state, see Bawa (1948), Virk & Harbans Singh (1948), Prem Singh (1966) and Gurnam Singh (1960).

15. Akali Dal Conference Resolution, Ludhiana, 4 July 1965. Cited in Harbans Singh (1983: 369–70). It was drawn up by Kapur Singh, a member of parliament, and moved by Gurnam Singh, the leader of the Akali Dal in Punjab's legislative assembly.

16. In the 1971 census, the population of Sikhs was 54 per cent, Hindus 44 per cent; by 1991 the Sikh population was 61 per cent.

17. In 1967, 1969 and 1980 the Akali coalition ministries were dismissed. On Akali politics and the formation of Punjab ministries, see Wallace & Chopra (1981), Grewal (1996), Narang (1983) and Oren (1974).

18. *Raj karega Khalsa* (Khalsa shall rule) has been part of Sikh vocabulary since the eighteenth century. In contemporary Punjabi, *qaum* is commonly used for nation or community, along with *des* for the country. While *des* may convey an idea of Punjab or refer to India, the word *qaum* always referred to the Sikh community. Also see McLeod (1978).

19. Shiromani Akali Dal, *Anandpur Sahib Resolution*, 1978, p. 1.

20. S. Cohen (1988). The "marital races" idea was scrapped in 1949. In 1974

NOTES

the Sikh army ratio was set at 2.5 per cent, still above their population of just 2 per cent.

21. See Joshi (1984, 1992) Surjeet Jalandhry (1985) and Swamy (1984). Sant Bhindranwale's rise and prominence into Akali politics remains an enigma. Called a saint, he was subsequently painted as a demonic figure by Indian official pronouncements. His presence in the Golden Temple was used as an excuse for army action. From 1982 onwards, he preached, through fiery language, religious orthodoxy and blamed the Akali leaders for compromises. Official versions have branded him a terrorist who sent "hit squads" from the Golden Temple to murder his opponents; while alive, he was not charged with such heinous crimes attributed to him posthumously. For the Sikh youth who took up arms, he became a martyr.

22. Accounts of the army action in the Golden Temple and subsequent developments include Nayar & Singh (1984) Amrik Singh (1985), Tully & Jacob (1985), Joshi (1984), Singh & Malik (1985), Akbar (1985), Bhullar (1987), Chopra et al. (1984), Iqbal Singh (1986), Harminder Kaur (1990), Madhok (1985), Brar (1993) and Kumar & Sieberer (1991). Among academic studies, see Kapur (1986) and Jeffrey (1987). Some scholarly articles are Leaf (1985), Koehn (1991), Mahmood (1989), Pettigrew (1987, 1991, 1992b, 1995), Gurharpal Singh (1987, 1992) and Hapke (1984). Many documents relating to the movement are collected in Deora (1991/2). Brass provides comprehensive analysis of Sikh politics in two major studies (Brass 1974, 1991).

23. *Text of the Memorandum of Settlement.* Also see *Indian Express,* New Delhi, 25 July 1985. The accord was implemented only slightly as below. (1) The Anandpur resolution was referred to the Sarkaria Commission, who rejected it as a basis for centre–state relations. (2) Chandigarh was to be transferred to Punjab by 26 January 1986 after compensation for its transfer either by money or territorial adjustment to be settled by a commission. Three commissions (Matthew, Venkataramiah and Deasi) failed to provide agreement; the centre suspended its transfer for an indefinite time. (3) River waters: a tribunal headed by a supreme court was to adjudicate on July 1985 consumption as a baseline for its consideration. In May 1987 the Eradi Commission instead reduced Punjab's share while doubling Haryana's share. (4) The November 1984 Anti-Sikh Delhi riots were referred to the Mishra Commission, who absolved Congress (I) of responsibility and placed guilt on the Delhi police. (5) Army deserters were to be rehabilitated and given gainful employment. By August 1985, of 2,606 deserters, 900 had been rehabilitated. (6) A small number of political detainees were released, and instead of withdrawal of special powers, in May 1988, the government passed the 59th amendment to the Constitution, providing for emergency powers in Punjab. (7) Religious demands were to be considered by an enactment of the All-Indian Gurdwara Act; this was not implemented. In May 1988 a

NOTES

Religious Institutions (Prevention of Misuse) Ordinance was issued; see
Indian Parliament Debates, 10 August 1988, pp. 279–418.
24. Sethi (1992) and Pettigrew (1995). In the absence of official enquiries into
major massacres and violent incidents, estimates of the number of persons killed during 1984–1995 vary enormously. Jaijee (1995) provides a
range of estimates from different sources: 21,119 (Punjabi police) and
20,000 "disappeared". The Punjab Congress estimates 39,387, while the
Akali Dal estimates 145,000 killed. The Punjab Human Rights organizations estimate 80,000 with 50,000 disappearances. Estimates of those
killed in the Golden Temple vary from 1,000 to 10,000; for Operation
Woodrose 8,000 and for the November 1984 riots in Delhi and other
northern cities 20,000. The latter figures are obviously exaggerated.
25. During 1989–91 some areas were liberated by militants who imposed
many rules, ordered a stoppage to Hindi broadcasts and Punjabi to be
adopted for official work.
26. Justice R. N. Mishra, former chief justice of India, who headed a report
on the anti-Sikh riots was appointed head of the commission with four
members. Also see Saini (1994: 192). A different perspective on human
rights is provided in Welch & Leary (1990), arguing that, in many Asian
states, ethnic allegiance of the state personnel makes it difficult to control
such violations.
27. The Akali Dal and the SGPC presented a memorandum to the UN secretary in New Delhi on 22 April 1994, "demilitarisation and decolonisation
of Punjab is crucial and indispensable to the Sikh people to enjoy full
freedom and exercise their economic social and cultural rights in accordance with the UN Declaration on the Granting of Independence to Colonial Countries and Peoples".
28. *Indian Express*, 28 April 1995. The Supreme Court has also used a constitutional provision to payments consequential upon the derivation of a
fundamental right.
29. Leaders of the Babbar Khalsa, the Khalistan Commando Force, the
Khalistan Liberation Force, the Bhindranwale Tiger Force and other
groups were killed. Jaijee (1995) quoting from the Punjab Legislative
Assembly Proceedings: a reply by the chief minister to a starred question
lists a total of 41,684 rewards given to policemen between January 1991
and December 1992. According to Vaughan (1993), "elite Indian intelligence force had received intelligence training in Israel and returned to
apply its skills in Punjab".
30. *Spokesman*, 17 August 1981.
31. See Chaddah (1982), G. Singh and G. L. Singh (1946), Harbans Singh
(1983), Gopal (1994) and Bomball (1983). Brass (1974: 277) has noted, "of
all the ethnic groups and peoples of the north, the Sikhs come closest to
satisfying the definition of a nationality or a nation. The Punjabi-
speaking Sikhs are a people objectively distinct in religion, though not in

231

language, from other ethnic groups in the north, who have succeeded in acquiring a high degree of internal social and political cohesion and subjective awareness, and who have achieved political significance as a group within the Indian union."

32. For Singh Sabhas' role in the formation of Sikh identity, see Oberoi (1987, 1988, 1993, 1994), Fox (1985), McLeod (1978, 1989), Mann & Kharak Singh (1990), Kapur Singh (1959), Brass (1985) and Gopal (1994).

33. Pettigrew (1991: 40): "Possessing territorial sovereignty became especially important not only because of the events of 1947 and 1984 and the feeling of humiliation that developed during and after 1984. For a nation whose primary reference had been a book rather than a land, . . . no sense of boundary was provided by their very tolerant religious scripture".

34. Since the 1960s, whether to draw on Hindi and Sanskritic origins or Urdu and Persian loan words for Punjabi technical words has been a central issue among Punjabi creative writers and linguists.

35. State functions are generally preceded by recitation of India's national anthem, followed by a Sikh hymn. A Punjabi governor, Surendra Nath, is reported to have banned the Sikh anthem, but it was revived. At such ceremonies, speeches are concluded with *Jai Hind* (Victorious India); on several occasions, Sikh ministers, almost by habit, conclude by community greeting.

36. See Jeffrey (1994) for an alternative view; also see Hubel (1996).

37. Harbhajan Singh in *Nik suk* (1990). Among many popular songs celebrating the beauty and lands of the Punjab is the following passage:

> My country is awashed with boastful sirdars
> In my country reside benevolent saints and fakirs
> fair women, more beautiful than the legendary Hīr
> God looks upon it with kindness
> Nanak and Gobind – our national heroes, bless its rivers and the land.

Another poet Puran Singh wrote:

> Those carefree young men of this land
> play poker with death
> through love, they be slaves
> Under tyranny, their fists will resist

38. *Facts about the Punjab Situation*, Chandigarh, 1986.

39. *India Today*, 15 April 1988. In Bombay, Bal Thackeray issued a month's ultimatum to Sikhs, "They should send a delegation to Amritsar instructing the high priests to issue a *hukamnama* (written order) against the extremists otherwise they will be boycotted economically". He accused Bombay Sikhs of providing funds for militants and for supporting the demand for Khalistan.

NOTES

40. See Grewal (1991) and Khushwant Singh (1966) for concluding remarks in his two-volume history of the Sikhs. In this, Sikh nationalists, like others from the developing world, believe "it is the state which constructs the nation". Also see Geertz (1968).

41. See Talbot (1995), Das (1995) and Nandy (1990). In recent Sikh militant discourse, Hindus are seen as "others". Among Hindu perceptions of Sikhs, one is of *kesdhari* Hindus (sword arm of Hindus), staunch Indian nationalists. The other, more recent, is the disloyal and prosperous community: "There is a growing feeling that the Sikhs have always been very influential and have occupied positions of privilege . . . so that the only way of dealing with them is to firmly and violently put them down" (Kothari 1989: 83).

42. A reading of Nehru and Gandhi's lives could illustrate this process through its geography, by rejecting its religious heritage and through a hegemonic liberal Hinduism; both approaches attempt to include the "outsiders" in an "Indian community".

43. Loknath Misra. Constituent Assembly Debates, official report, 1949, vii, no. 20, 1948, p. 283.

44. See Brown (1994) for the definition of such a state in Southeast Asia.

45. See Simeon (1994), who has argued that Brahmins with 5 per cent of the Indian population, held 72 per cent of Indian administrative posts. All scheduled castes together accounted for 10 per cent of class 1 posts in the Indian state, despite 40 years of reservations.

46. For a further discussion of hegemonic and other measures of control over minorities, see O'Leary and Paul (1990), Gurharpal Singh (1995), Smooha (1990), Lustick (1979) and Talbot (1996).

47. With this process, according to Enloe (1977: 143), "supposedly 'integrative' policies in, say, language or administration are likely to be perceived by those not members of the ruling group as not so much as ethnically neutral as simply favouring the regime's own constituents over members of other communal groups".

48. For centre–state relations, among numerous studies, see Kohli (1988), Sathyamurthy (1984, 1985), Dua (1981), Verney (1986) and Gupta (1988).

49. Popular vocabulary to dearticulate regional nationalism includes frequent use of terms such as "communalism", "tribalism" or "subnationalism"; see Connor (1994: 89–117). India passed an antisecession law as a constitutional amendment in 1963 after Tamil agitation.

50. Geertz (1983: 124) has argued, "at the political centre of any complexly organised society . . . there is both a governing elite and a set of symbolic forms expressing the fact that it is in truth governing. . . . They justify their existence and order their actions in terms of a collection of stories, ceremonies, insignia, formalities, and appurtenances that they have either inherited or invented".

51. Jaffrelot (1993). Between 1989 and 1991 its share of votes increased from 11.4 per cent to 20 per cent and its seats in parliament from 86 to 120 with popular support in the Hindi belt.
52. Frykenberg (1993: 249). The Bhartiya Jana Sangh (BJS) established in 1951, and the Vishva Hindu Parishad (VHP) was established by Golwalker in 1964. For elaboration of Hindutva, as a political expression, see Nandy & Trivedi (1995), Anderson & Damle (1987). On Indian secularism, see Smith (1963), Upadhyaya (1992) and Nandy (1988). On Ayodhya, see Gopal (1993).
53. See Kothari (1989). Also see International Commission of Jurists: *State of emergency: their impact on human rights* (1983): "regimes which do not provide any lawful means for the transfer of political power and which in consequence are inclined to regard any criticism of the government as an act subversive of public order".
54. See Verney & Frankel (1986) among others for such a model.

# Chapter 2

1. One of many phrases in the Punjabi language relating to migration.
2. Among major studies for different countries, noteworthy are Sandhu (1969) for Malaya, La Brack (1988b) and Tatla (1991) for the United States, Buchignani et al. (1985) and Chadney (1984) for Canada, McLeod (1984a) for New Zealand and Helweg (1987) and Tatla & Nesbitt (1994) for Britain.
3. This short passage is from a poem by Mohan Singh, recorded by a British popsinger.
4. After the Law Commission Report presented by Macaulay, the government enacted reforms in 1837 which included strict enforcing of passage regulations, a written contract, five years' service renewable for a further five-year term, the return of the emigrant to the port of his or her departure and the women's quota at 25 per cent. The indentured system was abandoned in 1920.
5. Of India's population of 318.9 million in 1921, the overseas Indians numbered 2.5 million. Their distribution was Burma 887,077, Jamaica 18,610, Ceylon 635,761, Zanzibar 13,500, Malaya 470,180, Tanganyika 10,000, Mauritius 265,524, Uganda 3,518, South Africa 161,329, Hong Kong, 2,000, British Guiana 124,938, South Rhodesia 1,184, Trinidad 122,117, Canada 1,016, Fiji 60,634, Australia 300, Kenya 22,822, UK 5,000. See Indian communities in the British Commonwealth, 1921, and *Report of the Committee on Emigration from India* 1910, Comm 5193.
6. *Annual Report for Trinidad 1902–3*, cited in Tinker (1974: 58).
7. In a letter to the deputy commissioner of Jullundur signed by 46 Punjabis from this district. Fiji's Sikh migrants are indicated in brackets among

the Indians: 1878–9, 498 (3); 1882–3, 922 (105); 1883–4, 1,514 (101); 1884–5, 2,316 (37); 1885, 540 (8); 1886, 1,012 (5); 1887 (0); 1888, 537 (2); 1889, 675 (1); 1890, 1,155 (3); 1891, 1,055 (8); 1892, 1,529 (8); 1893, 781 (6); 1894, 1,082 (2); 1895, 1,432 (1); 1896, 1,179 (8); 1897, 1,339 (2); 1898, 567 (0); 1899, 931 (6); 1900, 2,304 (63).

8. A. Marsden, 4 September 1913. *Report of the Committee on Emigration from India*, 1910, Minutes and Evidence.

9. Government of Hong Kong, *Blue Books*, various years. Also see Vaid (1972: 37). In 1871, 182 Sikhs and 126 Muslims from the Punjab worked in the Colony's police force; and in line with contemporary colonial thinking, Sikhs, Punjabi Muslims and Chinese were trained and raised in separate regiments under European officers with their own establishment staffs from the same nationality.

10. Gurdwaras are another way of accounting for Sikh population in each state; Perak has 32 gurdwaras, Selangor 15; Wilayah Perekutuan 10; Pahang 7; Juhore 6; Penang 5, Kelentan and Kedah, 3 each; Perlis and Malacca 1 each.

11. C. W. Harrison (1920: 131–2) wryly commented on Sikhs' expectation of jobs: "Had the police rejected him as a recruit he would have had to descend to the profession of a watchman to some large firm, or some wealthy Chinese. This is not so desirable as the police. . . . Perhaps our Sikh policeman might have been reduced to the purely unofficial occupation of herding cows".

12. Hill (1949: 189,240). Of 16,312 men who were repatriated at the end of their contracts, 6,484 were invalided and 2,493 died. Only 6,724 opted to remain in Kenya at the end of their contract in 1904; by then the railway line had reached Kisumu.

13. See Barnard (1975) and Bhachu (1985). Among prominent Kenyan Sikhs, Makhan Singh became well known in the trade union movement. He had arrived in Uganda with the Sikh regiment in 1914, set up a transport business, and became a game hunter and president of the Mbarara Indian Association, supporting East Africans' struggle for independence; see Makhan Singh (1969). Kirpal Sigh Sihra financed the Kenya Airways in 1965 as a private company taken over by the government.

14. Kenya's Asian population in 1962 declined from 176,600 to 78,600 in 1979. *Kenya Population Census*, 1962, vol. IV, pp. 69, 85.

15. Johnson's account of Sikh emigration is contained in *Report of the Committee on Emigration from India*, 1910, Comm. 5193, Minutes of Evidence.

16. W. Laurier to Lord Grey, 6 September 1907, Provincial Archives of Canada, Grey Papers.

17. *Forum* (1910: 617) commented, "for miles their turbaned figures may be seen wielding crow-bar or shovel along the tracks . . . they live in camps and colonies, and their usual expenses a month to little more than 3

dollars a month, a sum that would scarcely support a white man for three days".

18. The yearly Indian migration to the UK between 1955 and 1966 was 5,800, 5,600, 6,600, 6,200, 2,950, 5,900, 23,750, 22,100, 17,498, 15,513, 18,815 and 18,402 in 1966. See Commonwealth Immigration Act 1962, Control of Immigration: Statistics 1966, Comm. 3258, p. 4.

19. As Sikhs are not enumerated as a separate category, estimates are derived from Indian figures which differ considerably. The Christian Research Association in its UK handbook has listed Sikhs at 500,000 as against 400,000 Hindus. The Central Statistical Office's *Social Trends* for 1990, listed active adult membership with Sikhs at 390,000, Hindus, 140,000 and Muslims 990,000. *Religions in UK* (1997) has a figure of 400,000 for Sikhs. Problems in calculating Hindu, Muslim and Sikh populations are discussed by Knott & Toon (1982).

20. Official figures list Asian Indians as 1900–6, 870; 1907–14, 5,943; 1915–29, 1,646; 1930–44, 183; 1945–65, 6,371; 1966–81, 215,640.

21. The numbers of Indian labourers working in the Middle Eastern countries were 1976, 4,200; 1977, 22,900; 1978, 69,000; 1979, 171,000; 1980, 236,200; 1981, 276,000; 1982, 239,545.

22. House of Commons, 23 October 1992. Charles Wardle's answer to a written question.

23. The numbers of Indian citizens applying for asylum during 1987–96 were 1987, 126; 1988, 293; 1989, 630; 1990, 1,530; 1991, 2,075; 1992, 1,450; 1993, 1,275; 1994, 2,030; 1995, 3,255; 1996, 2,250. These figures are from annual reports of the Immigration and Nationality Department.

24. *Lancet* (1995: 345, 225–6) reported between November 1991 and May 1994, 45 Sikh men from the Punjab who alleged detention and torture were referred to the Medical Foundation. Although examinations were done long after the last detention (two to eight years), the medical report confirmed, all subjects had physical symptoms and signs attributable to ill-treatment. Thirty had one or more scars that were consistent with abuse. The most common complaint was of pain on walking, principally in those who had abduction of the hips and/or application of the roller (*ghotna*). Psychological disturbance was obvious in all; post-traumatic stress disorder included loss of concentration and of memory, intrusive thoughts, flashbacks, panic attacks, and especially recurrent nightmares reproducing events during the detention.

25. See *Globe and Mail*, 25 July 1987; *Winnipeg Free Press*, 26 July 1987; *Toronto Star*, 6–7 August 1987.

26. Rolf Nygren, a Swedish mariner, and Jasbir Singh Rana, from Halifax, were arrested for illegal smuggling of immigrants. A few weeks later another Dutch trawler was searched for suspicion of carrying Sikhs. The parliament was called to amend refugee laws.

27. This assumes that the majority of Indian applicants were Sikhs; thus in

1994, 1,171 Indian citizens applied for asylum, increasing to 1,370 in 1996.

28. The *Daily News* in Los Angeles, 15 and 18 January 1985, reported police allegation of Sikhs being smuggled into America. It noted, however, that the case could have political overtones. After a year's surveillance, through a Sikh temple on Vermont Avenue, Los Angeles, five people were arrested. Afrik Singh was alleged to be the ringleader of Iqbal Singh Samra, Jugraj Singh Kahlon, Kulwinder Singh Kahlon, Opinder Jit Singh and Juswant Singh Dhillon, seeking payment of $3,000 each from six Sikhs through Mexico. They were charged for forging passports and documents.

29. While Daya Singh Lahoria and his wife were extradited to India, another Sikh, Kulbir Singh, is awaiting trial in Nevada jail. A long-drawn-out case, contested between Indian and Sikh organizations, concerns Ranjit Singh Gill and S. S. Sandhu, alleged by Indian authorities to have been involved in murder cases. Two Sikhs have pleaded they fled as they were wrongly implicated by the police and could not expect a fair trial in the Punjab. Khem Singh Gill, father of Ranjit Singh Gill, distinguished scientist and a former vice-chancellor of Punjab Agricultural University, Ludhiana, appealed to US authorities not to accept India's request for extradition. See PHRO, *Set free Gill and Sandhu*, 1990.

30. *Indian Express*, 1 June 1994. Kuldeep Singh on return from Germany was detained at New Delhi airport and the police escorted him to his parents, demanding Rs10,000 for his release. When his parents could not raise the money within the time, they were phoned to pick up their son's dead body from the jail.

31. Quoted in *Sikh Review*, December 1992, p. 56. At that time, 2,600 Sikhs had applied for refugee status. In December 1996 a prominent Sikh militant, Wassan Singh Zaffarwal, who led the underground movement from Pakistan, also sought asylum.

## Chapter 3

1. These songs form part of Punjabi folklore.
2. Sikhs are a large proportion of air traffic flying into New Delhi from Britain and North America, perhaps 3,000 visitors a month. Reflecting this, some airlines employ Punjabi-speaking air hostesses. For a few years, a Birmingham–Amritsar flight was operating. A company financed by Canadian Sikh businessmen operates coaches from Delhi airport to Punjabi cities.
3. Overseas residents of Khatkar Kalan, Jalandhar, and Morawali, Hoshiarpur, have funded improvement schemes for their villages.

NOTES

4. Dhudike Village Society, with many Sikh migrants in the Far East and the Pacific states, bought a booklet to commemorate the old veterans. In Chitti, Jalandhr, a memorial to Santa Singh (d. 14 June 1925), a martyr of Jaito Morcha, was erected by a trust fund from Britain.

5. Nairobi Singh Sabha formed in 1900 was affiliated to the Chief Khalsa Diwan, Amritsar. Besides listing many fundraising activities, it mentions Arya Samaj's conversion of a Sikh, which led to a protests. See *Khalsa Advocate*, 1910.

6. Sant Domeliwale built schools and repaired historic buildings in the Punjab, including Mata Gujri Sarai, Sirhind; Gurdwara Chounka Sahib; Amarjit Secondary School, Domeli; Gurdwara Chak Preman; Babbar School Babeli; School Rohan Jattan.

7. The career of Budh Singh of Dhahan, Jalandahr, provides an interesting insight into individual motivation and linkages with the Punjab. After living in Canada for 20 years, he returned to his village to set up a trust which has established a hospital and a school and has organized mobile eye camps. The trust is registered as the Canada–India Guru Nanak Mission Medical and Educational Society in Canada. Budh Singh has made regular rounds of Britain and Canada to seek funds. Lists of donors and the trust's activities are published in *Jivan Sewa*; see the Baisakhi issue, 1993.

8. Kartar Singh returned from California as Gadr leader and was hanged in 1916. The Kartar Singh Sarabha Trust was initiated by Sukhdev Singh Grewal and Harnek Singh Grewal, who have collected funds from Britain and North America.

9. *Punjabi Tribune*, 21 May 1993.

10. Gurcharan Singh Shergill, a travel agent in the Midlands, established Amardeep Singh Shergill Memorial College in 1993 in the memory of his only son, who died young as a student at the London School of Economics.

11. The project was launched in 1985 by Iqbal Singh Khera, a Walsall businessman. It has involved the Shiromani Gurdwara Parbandhak Committee and aims "to give this ancient town a proud place on the map of the world, as befits the founder of our faith, Guru Nanak".

12. *Des Pardes*, 10 March 1968. Letter from Dr Jagjit Singh Chohan, finance minister, Punjabi government.

13. Difficulties arise due to the nature of transactions; a substantial proportion have been sent via agents, so they are not reflected in the bank portfolios. This is especially true for the period 1960–70, when the rupee's official dollar and sterling exchange rates varied more significantly than the black market.

14. *Des Pardes*, 26 January 1992. It reported a marriage arranged between a Canadian and British Sikh family, with wedding guests from the Punjab and North America.

NOTES

15. Gurdwara managers and ıwa leaders have often met to stop the "dowry menace". In the 1990s the Sikh Women's Forum in Britain highlighted this issue; for an early discussion see *Des Pardes*, 16 December 1973, when a Punjabi comrade's son was scandalized due to "heavy dowry".

16. In the 1990s there is some evidence of sponsorship misuse, where a bridegroom or bride has been chosen on the understanding that the other family sponsors a relative on a reciprocal basis. Abortion of a female child, by determining the sex of the embryo, has seen sharp criticism, especially in Canada. A number of doctors have been accused of playing upon community prejudices; see Fair (1996).

17. Of a dozen bhangra pop groups, better known are Komal, Nachdey Hasdey, Suraj, Amar, Sangam, DCS, Chirag Pehchan, Bally Sagoo, Alaap, Holle, Hira, Ajuba, Nishanna, Culture Shock, Indian Apache, Golden Star.

18. One cassette with sales of over 100,000 copies had a nostalgic theme on a rural idyll, *Tūtak tūtak tūtīān, hi yamālo, ājā tūtān vāle khūh te.*

19. *Des Pardes*, 24 April 1992. Letter from Gurdev Singh Johal, the Sports Committee of the Khalsa Diwan Society, Vancouver, 15 March 1992, to the secretary of the Indian Kabaddi Association in Britain. A similar letter from Didar Singh Bains, chairman of the American Kabaddi Federation, invited players to Yuba City.

20. *Des Pardes*, 15 May 1992.

21. The numbers of students for Punjabi GCSE examinations were 1995, 1,732; 1994, 1,479; 1993, 1,509; 1992, 1,440; 1991, 1,281; 1990, 1,220. For A levels, numbers steadily increased from 88 in 1990 to 259 in 1997.

22. S. S. Kalra, Dr Jagat Singh Nagra, Darshan Singh Bhogal, Gurbachan Singh Sidhu, Shivcharan Gill, R. S. Bedi and others have published relevant teaching materials. New publishers Magi and Mantra have published dual-language series.

23. *Des Pardes*, 23 May 1980.

24. See Khalsa School Report and *Calgary Herald*, 17 January 1987, p. G9.

25. BBC Radio's Asian network was criticized by Sikh listeners for its lack of Punjabi coverage, alleging that Urdu and Hindi were given undue prominence. For an early protest, see *Des Pardes*, 27 September 1970. In 1991 the broadcasting of *Mahabharat* by the BBC was also objected to; see *Sikh Reformer* 1992. Another protest was lodged against the BBC's language programme, Hindi–Urdu *bol chal*, pointing out that among the Muslim and Hindu populations of Britain, a majority spoke Punjabi, hence a Punjabi language programme was needed!

26. Awards include the Giani Gurmukh Singh Musafir Award, the Languages Department Award and the Sahit Academy Award; the latter is by Darshan Singh Dhaliwal, an American Sikh. Diaspora Punjabi literature is taught at Punjab's universities. A Manjit Memorial Literary

Award, Vancouver, is offered to Punjabi writers: Sant Singh Sekhon, Santokh Singh Dhir and Kulwant Singh Virk are past recipients.

27. The Punjab dailies *Ajit, Jag Bani* and *Punjabi Tribune* carry regular news of diaspora events.

28. The first issue proclaimed, "Today, there begins in foreign lands, but in our country's language, a war against the British raj. What is our name? Gadr, What is our work? Gadr. Where will Gadr break out? In India"; see Puri (1994).

29. Mukhtiar Singh, *Punjab Times*, 1000th special issue, 1984.

30. Among the contemporary media receiving diaspora funds are *Dastkar*, a journal from Ludhiana, *Desh Sewak*, a CPI(M) daily, *CPI(M)* and *Aj di awaz*.

31. Thus, Samabula Gurdwara in Fiji, provided free kitchen, shelter and surety money to satisfy immigration regulations for the incoming Sikhs. In the late 1950s, complaints against a Southall gurdwara as a dumping place for "illegal immigrants" obviously missed the "natural" role of a gurdwara.

32. Annual Report, 1991–2. It donated small sums to Tarn Taran, the Institute of Sikh Studies, Save the Children Fund, and the relief fund for Sikh victims in Delhi.

33. *Des Pardes*, 24 April 1992. During his visit to Britain in 1992, he organized a special session for young children; also see Dusenbery (1988).

34. According to Paramjit Singh Chandan, of the Nishkam Sewak Jatha, Birmingham.

35. Plaques in the Golden Temple testify to this attachment. Thus money was donated by Bradford Sikhs Harbans Singh (Golatian Kalan, Sialkot), Bawa Singh (Dhesian), Mohan Singh (Kot Awa Khana, Jalandhar) and Liverpool Sikh Godi Singh (Bhatra Kot Bhagat Singh, Amritsar).

36. Among numerous such connections, Nander, a major historic shrine in south India, advertises especially for overseas Sikhs for its religious services. For an Akhand Path, devotees are asked to send £ 31, preferably by money order.

37. Josh (1978: 230). North American Punjabis sent between $40,000 and $50,000 to help Gadr families.

38. In April 1974 Yogi Harbhajan Singh confronted the bareheaded Sikhs coming into the gurdwara, which erupted into a fight. In this campaign the orthodox Sikhs were helped by a Maoist group. Throughout 1975 the trouble kept brewing, leading to many scuffles.

39. During 1993–4 a proposal for an Ontario Management Board for Gurdwaras was circulated with endorsement from Punjab's religious leaders.

40. For the Surrey gurdwara controversy, see *Indo-Canadian Times*, June / July 1996. For Southall, see *Punjab Times* or *Des Pardes*, October 1997.

41. *Indo-Canadian Times*, November 1983; see letter to attorney-general and appeal to Sikh societies.

42. Ganga Singh Dhillon, an American Sikh, established the Sri Nankana Sahib Foundation in 1976 as a non-profit organization to "secure full freedom of worship and facilities for the Sikh shrines in Pakistan, and to acquire the right of management so that proper services in the gurdwaras are performed in accordance with the true Sikh traditions".

43. A typical notice of the pilgrimage in the Punjabi media (*Punjab Times*, 25 October 1985) runs as follows: "The *Jatha* departs to Pakistan for a historic tour of Guru Nanak's birth place and other sacred shrines . . . Dera Sahib, Panja Sahib, and finally to Nankana Sahib where we shall celebrate Guru Nanak's birthday. From here we will depart to Punjab crossing Atari border on 30 November reaching Amritsar the same evening".

44. In 1993 a large rally at Thetford marked the centenary of Dalip Singh's death. His grave at Elveden, near Cambridge, has become a place for pilgrimage. A Sikh family acquired Dalip Singh's painting in the possession of Lord Dalhousie at a Sotheby auction for £ 58,000 in May 1990. On the 150th anniversary of Maharajah Ranjit Singh, Punjabi government officials borrowed historical relics from Britain. Some arms associated with Guru Gobind Singh returned from Britain were reverentially paraded throughout Punjab. The remains of Udham Singh, hanged in 1939 for murdering General Dwyer in London, were received by Punjabi government officials.

45. Following a violent clash between some Sikhs and Nirankaris in Amritsar in April 1978, a *hukamnama* (a religious indictment) was issued from the Akal Takhat, Amritsar. The bitterness that followed claimed the life of the Nirankari chief in 1979. During his wife's visit to Britain, she was provided with a police guard. *Express and Star*, August 1989.

46. *Des Pardes*, June/July 1971, letters column. The debate continued off and on; see this paper for 1973, 1976 and 1978.

47. Dr Ambedkar, a leader of the untouchables from Gujarat, had considerable influence throughout India, though Punjab's Chamars were least affected. However, in Britain the Ambedkar groups had considerable resources to preach to the Punjabi Chamars.

48. In a survey of 100 Ravidasis, Leivesley (1985) asked them to identify their religion; 5 of them said they were Hindus, 70 identified themselves as Ad-dharmis, 21 as Ravidasis, with one saying Radhasoami; none identified themselves as Sikh.

49. A small number of publications illustrate this process. Books on Ramgarhia Sikhs have been sponsored from abroad; see Rehal (1979) and Hamrahi (1994). Similarly, a history of Mazhabi Sikhs also received patronage; see Ashok (1987).

50. See Friends of Punjab (1978).

51. Lote completed this project on 14 September 1977, when he was honoured by a local gurdwara. Jarnail Singh, a Canadian Sikh, has translated a classic pamphlet, "Hum Hindu Nahin", besides working on a French translation of the Guru Granth. Another Canadian, Pritam Singh Chahil, has published a new English translation of the Guru Granth.

52. Kesar Singh, from Vancouver, has published accounts of Gadr heroes besides writing many creative works.

53. The first such reunion was held in December 1986. Veterans of Sikh regiments and the Punjab Frontier Force met old comrades and British officers in Southall; among the other guests were Sidney Bidwell, the local MP, and the mayor of Ealing.

54. Established in 1967, the foundation has supported 13 Sikh orphans of the Delhi riots, assisted two Sikh students at US universities, and funded the Sikh studies programme at Columbia University, funded San Jose Khalsa School and sponsored the Sikh art conference at the Asian Art Museum in San Francisco in 1992. It sponsored lecture tours of Dr Ganda Singh, G. S. Mansukhani, Gopal Singh and Hardit Singh Malik. In the early 1970s it published a directory of Sikhs in North America and *Sikh Sansar*, a journal.

55. In 1991 the society approached the publishers of Merriam Webster's Dictionary, the American Heritage Dictionary, the Oxford American Dictionary and others, requesting changes in their Sikh coverage. As a result, Webster's Dictionary changed its entry for *Sikh* to "an adherent of a monotheistic religion of India founded about 1,500 by Guru Nanak and marked by rejection of idolatry and caste", from a previous entry which defined Sikhs as a member of a Hindu sect, or an offshoot of Hinduism.

56. Dr Pashaura Singh was appointed at the University of Michigan in 1992, Dr Harjot Oberoi took up the Sikh studies chair at the University of British Columbia and Dr Gurinder Singh Mann lectures at Columbia University.

57. This chair, the Kartar Singh Dhaliwal Professorship of Punjab/Indian Studies, to be filled in September 1998 and is based at the university's Milwaukee campus.

58. This was sponsored by the European Institute for Sikh Studies set up in London.

59. See O'Connell in Singh & Barrier (1996). For the Chandigarh group's criticism, see Mann & Singh (1990), Mann & Saraon (1988) and *Abstract of Sikh Studies*, published by the Institute of Sikh Studies, Chandigarh. The debate highlights some aspects of the Sikh elite in the diaspora and in the Punjab. Many participants seemed unfamiliar with the questioning environment of the Western academy. Moreover, arguments, many couched in abusive language, especially in *World Sikh News* and the Punjabi media of Vancouver, were hardly conducive to any fruitful dialogue. See especially writings by Dilgeer and Sekhon (1992); they

branded many scholars as "anti-Sikh"; their list reads like a roll-call of eminent scholars. Also see *Sikhs Past and Present*, 4(1), 26 and also 5(1), 21. In a rhetorical analysis of the community's past history, they have routinely used the term *Hindu* pejoratively, nor have they spared many Sikh statesmen, writing their names as Sinh instead of Singh!

60. As some Sikh groups campaigned for Dr Harjot Oberoi's removal, the university authorities stood by the "Sikh professor's right to publish"; see *Vancouver Sun*, 20 and 23 June 1994. Dr Oberoi resigned from the Sikh studies position in 1996 and the chair is now vacant. For Punjabi teaching, the university has employed Sadhu Binning on a tenured post. The second Sikh scholar, Dr Pashaura Singh at the University of Michigan, was summoned by the Akal Takhat *jathedar* to Amritsar, where he tendered an "apology"; see "Punishing of heretical scholar", *Vancouver Sun*, 8 July 1994.

61. According to Singh (1993: 255), "Sikh intellectuals have displayed a predominantly Hindu intellectual disposition", while the Sikh intellectual tradition has always relied on Udasis and Nirmalas, whose world view was defined far more by the Sanatan Hindu than the Sikh tradition. However, "by continuing to categorise it under the rubric of Hinduism (or Islam or a syncretism of Hinduism and Islam) readers, hearers and scholars unconsciously transfer the role and image of women in those societies over the Sikh world".

62. Software experts have contributed to a number of Punjabi language programs, including the Anandpur, Lippi, Dhuni and Akal system. Other projects on aspects of Sikh history, scriptures, Punjabi language and encyclopedias are in progress.

# Chapter 4

1. Part of a popular Gadr song, it is available in many pamphlets.
2. KDS, Vancouver. *Memorandum to Canadian Government*, 1913. The second delegation went to London in March 1913. Its members, Balwant Singh, Nand Singh and Narain Singh, also visited Punjab and had a meeting with the Punjabi governor.
3. The Khalsa Diwan Society and the United India League's representation to the government of Canada, Ottawa, 15 December 1911. IOR L/P &J/ 6/1310 (414/14).
4. Hindu Friends Society of Vancouver, BC Rev. L. B. Hall to Colonial Office, 28 April 1911. Imperial Conference 1911. Papers laid before the conference, Commd. 5746–1, 279–81.
5. *Vancouver Province*, 12 December 1908, section 2, p. 1.
6. IO memo on Indian immigration to Canada, 26 August 1915 in Chamber-

lain to Hardinge, 10 September 1915, House of Commons, vol. 121, no. 52.

7. As in previous footnote. Chamberlain to Hardinge, 10 September 1915, 10 memo on Indian immigration to Canada, vol. 121, no. 52. ". . . specifically affects the Sikhs from whom many of our best soldiers are drawn and on whom, from the mutiny onwards we have been accustomed to rely with confidence for whole-hearted support of the British raj. For the first time in their history there has now been serious discontent among them and this has been largely due to, at least made possible by, the exploitation of their grievances in this matter".

8. Many poems appearing in the *Gadr Weekly* were collected into pamphlets; see Barrier (1971).

9. *Lahore Conspiracy Case*. Of the 175 revolutionaries, 18 were hanged, 58 transported for life and the remainder were given less severe sentences. But the episode showed according to O'Dwyer (1925: 194.), "the defiant and highly explosive temper of the returning Sikhs. It was distorted by unscrupulous agitators in the Punjab and the Gadr agents abroad into a gratuitous attack by an oppressive government on unoffending Sikhs".

10. The American government held its own conspiracy trial in 1918. Eight Germans, seven Americans and fourteen Indians received sentences ranging from four months to two years; see *US v. Bopp Franz et al*. A more modest and non-violent organization was established in 1917 by Lajpat Rai, who was exiled to New York. The Home Rule League also issued a paper, "Young India". Rai returned to India in 1920 and for a year another organization, Friends for the Freedom of India, was also formed; both groups dissolved soon after Rai's departure.

11. Lord Hunter's Committee blamed tactless handling of overseas Sikhs' grievances as a factor leading to the 1919 tragedy.

12. D. Naoroji was elected MP for Finsbury in 1886, M. M. Bhownagree for Lambeth North in 1895 then for Lambeth North in 1906; and Shahpuri Saklatvala for Battersea North from 1922 to 1931; see Kosmin (1989).

13. The Indian National Army (INA) was raised in Malaya in December 1941 from the British Indian Army deserters and prisoners taken by the Japanese forces. Among prominent Sikhs who joined the INA were Colonel Niranjan Singh Gill, Major Mahabir Singh Dhillon, Major Nripendra Singh Bhagat, Captain Gurbakhsh Singh Dhillon and Captain Thakur Singh, along with Mohan Singh, who rose from the sepoy rank to lead this army. The Japanese Army was defeated in Imphal in 1944 by the Allied Defence Forces; see Mohan Singh (n.d.).

14. *Punjabi Darpan*, 11 July 1986. The Indian Workers Association was set up on 3 March 1957 in Southall, its name derived from a similar organization of 1938. Ratan Singh, Amar Singh Takhar, Ajit Singh Rai, Harbans

Singh Ruprah, Jaswant Singh Dhami were founder members, with an office at 16–18 Featherstone Road, Southall. It acquired a cinema in 1966.

15. Harkishan Singh Surjeet presided over the reorganized IWA, when Prem Singh retained the presidency, Avtar Johal became general-secretary, Avtar Sadiq became deputy general-secretary and Makhan Johal became vice-president.

16. *Des Pardes*, 5 and 12 December 1975.

17. *Des Pardes*, 20 July 1977.

18. *Des Pardes*, December 1978. The Akalis and IWA protestors burned the Indian flag in front of the cinema.

19. *Des Pardes*, April 1974 and 8 December 1974.

20. *Des Pardes*, 18 July 1975. The CPI (R) leaders, Darshan Singh Canadian and Jagjit Singh Anand faced stiff opposition at the Dominion Cinema, Southall, in 1975; the cinema was the main platform for Indian leaders to address the Punjabi community.

21. *Des Pardes*, 16, 23 and 30 September 1973. See exchange of letters between Karam Singh Kirti and Vishnu Dutt Sharma. Also a bitter duel of words between Avtar Johal and Vishnu Sharma on the latter's acceptance of official patronage.

22. Dusenbery (1981: 110). The NACOI, the East Indian Canadian Citizens Welfare Association, the Fraser Valley East Indians Canadian Welfare Association, the East Indian Defence Committee, the IPANA or the East Indian Workers Association compete for funds and recognition in the wider Canadian society by suggesting themselves as "pan East Indian ethno-political organisations".

23. The procession was led by Congress ex-minister Buta Singh and by Mangu Ram, the founder of Ad Dharma in the Punjab. The Guru Ravidas Sabha headed by Shankar Lal Darbhang, leader of Ravidasis and Adi Dharmis, met the Indian prime minister, Morarji Desai, in London. He asked the Indian premier to tell the BBC and ITV television companies to stop calling Jagjivan Ram a leader of "untouchables". The Republican Party arranged a protest on 4 September 1977, led by Charan Dass, senior vice-president of the Punjab Republican Party, during his visit to Britain. Another protest march took place on 2 October 1977.

24. At a meeting in Ealing town hall on 8 September 1968, three British MPs witnessed its proceedings: David Ennals, Sir Edward Boyle and Stephen Jacob.

25. *Conference Proceedings of the Sikh Council of North America*, 1976.

26. *Manchester Evening News*, 22 June 1959.

27. A protest march was organized in Wolverhampton on 4 February 1968, followed by two more on 24 April and 12 May.

28. *Des Pardes*, 28 September 1969, has an interview with Sohan Singh Jolly.

NOTES

29. *Express and Star*, 16 January 1969.
30. *Times*, 7 April 1969.
31. House of Commons, Debates, written answer, 20 November 1992, p. 400.
32. See *Globe and Mail*, 14 and 23 December 1989; also see *Toronto Star*, 12 July 1989 and 7 July 1990.
33. See *Vancouver Sun* and *Globe and Mail*, 19 July 1986.
34. *Halifax Chronicle Herald*, 13 May 1991.
35. Three Calgary sisters, Dawn Miles, G. Kantelberg and Kay Mansbridge, started a crusade in the western provinces. They sold coins and calendars depicting Sikhs as imposters and outsiders with badges saying "Keep the RCMP Canadian". The Liberal leader, Sharon Carstairs, expressed concern in the Manitoba legislative assembly; Dr Gulzar Cheema, a Liberal MLA from Kildonan, also urged people not to buy such calendars. One cartoon asked, Who is the minority in Canada?
36. *Halifax Chronicle Herald*, 15 August 1991.
37. *Globe and Mail*, 12 November 1993. "Snubbing was unacceptable", wrote the *Vancouver Sun*, 13 November 1993; also see a letter by Indian High Commissioner P. K. Budhwar, *Montreal Gazette*, 3 December 1993.
38. *Vancouver Sun*, 20 November 1993. The Jewish Congress also urged an end to antiturban rule. *Vancouver Sun*, 25 November 1993. *Vancouver Sun*, 3 January 1994. "Turbans and legions"; see editorial in *Globe and Mail*, 10 January 1994.
39. *Calgary Herald*, 10 June 1994; also see *Canadian Jewish News*, **35** (8), 16 June 1994, p. 15.
40. House of Commons, June 1994; see also, Debates, 15 February and 29 November 1995, when a private member's bill on the Royal Canadian Legion was debated.
41. See *Toronto Star* and *Globe and Mail*, 10 August 1994.
42. See *Toronto Star*, 9 July 1994; *Macleans* **107** (29), 18 July 1994, p. 17. Also see *Equinox* **13** (4), July/August 1994, pp. 28–41; *Vancouver Sun*, 12 October 1994.
43. Lal (1996); also see *The Modesto Bee*, reported in *World Sikh News*, 25 February 1994.
44. *New York Times*, 12 October 1971; quoted in Jeffrey (1987).
45. *Des Pardes*, 30 July 1972.
46. *Des Pardes*, 12 December 1971.
47. *Des Pardes*, June, 1972.
48. *Des Pardes*, 3 December 1972. Amar Singh Ambalvi, a legal adviser to the Akali Dal from Amritsar, witnessed the event.
49. *Des Pardes*, November 1979.
50. The corporation was led by a Sikh businessman, Gurbachan Singh Sidhu.
51. The resolution was passed, then the Sikh Educational Conference clarified its stand.

52. Khushwant Singh (1992: 41–2), a noted journalist and historian from Delhi, debated the issue of Sikh homeland with Ganga Singh Dhillon. He wrote, "In your articles you make a large number of assertions which are totally at variance with my reading of Sikh history . . . the demand for Khalistan is based on erroneous interpretation of the word 'nation' which has an entirely different connotation when used by historians you quoted and acquired a sinister innuendo after the Muslim League demand for Pakistan. The demand is manifestly mischievous and goes against the interests of the Sikhs. It is wrong of you to dismiss the strong opposition to this demand among the Sikhs themselves as being born out of fear of the government or the Hindu majority. Nor do for that matter, people like me oppose it to seek any favour from the government. . . . We have the interests of the Khalsa at heart as much as you and your supporters in the States and Canada. Only we happen to be, as it were, on the scene, and you, despite your emotional attachment to your ancestral faith, live in comfort in a foreign country. For you this may be an academic exercise; for us it is hard reality".

53. The National Council of Khalistan also issued the monthly *Babbar Khalsa* in September 1981, edited by Hardial Singh Thiara. In the first issue, on 4 September 1981, it announced, "No power on earth can stop the formation of Khalistan".

54. *Indo-Canadian Times*, 4 September 1981; letter from Surjan Singh.

55. *Indo-Canadian Times*, 2 February 1979; the Convention was held at the main gurdwara on 25 December 1978.

56. *Des Pardes*, 14 January 1983. While praising Dr Chohan's services to the Panth in publicizing its cause in the international community, Sant Bhindranwale took exception to Dr Chohan's lax faith.

57. See Appendix 1 for the full text of this letter.

58. Surjit Singh Gill, secretary of the Khalsa Diwan Society, Vancouver.

59. The resolution was passed on 30 September 1981.

60. *Indo-Canadian Times*, 8 October 1982. The resolution was passed on 19 September 1982. Kewal Singh Chohan, president of the Singh Sabha, Winnipeg, also asked for the relaxation of immigration rules, "due to great difficulties and delays experienced by the Canadian citizens of Punjabi Origin, an office of Canadian immigration be established in the Punjab so that pending cases could be expedited. In view of the present volatile condition of the Punjab, Sikh community of Manitoba requests that the people who have applied for refugee status be granted immigration on humanitarian ground. We further request that open work permits should be issued while the hearing of cases is pending".

61. Sikh demo in Metro to seek freedom; *Toronto Star*, 5 March 1984, p. A6.

62. *Indo-Canadian Times*, 12 August 1983. Of the 17 committee members:

Jagjit Singh Sidhu, president, Abstford; Gian Singh Sandhu, senior vice-president, Williams Lake; Daljit Singh Sandhu, secretary, Vancouver; Surinder Singh Jabbal, recording secretary, Vancouver; Avtar Singh Baghri, treasurer, Kunail; Charan Jit Singh Sandhu, member, Prince Charles; Raghbir Singh Grewal, member, New Westminster.

63. *Indo-Canadian Times*, 9 September 1983; letter from Gurcharan Singh, secretary, Shiromani Akali Dal, Amritsar, to Mota Singh Jheeta and Charanjit Singh Randhawa.

64. *Indo-Canadian Times*, 15 October 1982.

65. *Indo-Canadian Times*, 22 October 1982; this march was held on 16 October.

66. *Indo-Canadian Times*, 12 November 1982. At a meeting at the Ross Street Gurdwara, Vancouver, on 4 November, amid jubilant and rather noisy scenes, the *Jatha* was given the equivalent of Rs107,000 for the *Dharam Yudh Morcha*. The *Jatha* members paid for their own fares. However, three of them, Canadian citizens, were deported immediately; the other two were allowed to proceed to Amritsar, where they were warmly received by Akali leader Sant Harchand Singh Longowal.

67. Also see *Indo-Canadian Times*, 5 November 1982.

68. *Indo-Canadian Times*, 22 October 1982. Letter from Dr J. S. Chohan to Sant Harchand Singh Longowal and other Akali leaders, dated 2 October 1982.

69. Bachitter Singh, an Akali leader from Southall, joined the campaign and spent most of 1983 in a Punjabi jail.

70. *Globe and Mail*, 19 April 1984, p. 14.

# Chapter 5

1. A popular Punjabi song from Canada by Madan Maddi.

2. *New York Times*, 7 June 1984. Tejinder Singh Kahlon, president of the Sikh Cultural Society, New York, called the army attack "outrageous immoral" and by doing so, "Mrs Gandhi was laying the foundation of a separate Sikh state" and a letter from Ujagar Singh of New York–New Jersey described them as "highly painful events". Its editorial said, "Sikhs in the United States are angered over Golden Temple assault". Next day's editorial was headlined "The gamble in the Golden Temple". It informed its readers by asking them, "Who are the Sikhs and why are they angry?" A week later (14 June) it carried the editorial "A Falkland factor for Mrs Gandhi".

3. Major newspapers, both national and provincial, reported on these protests. See especially the *Vancouver Sun*, the *Globe and Mail*, the *New York Times*, the *Los Angeles Times* and the *Washington Post*. The community

media carried detailed reports; see, for example, Promod Puri's account of Vancouver Sikhs march to the Indian consulate in *Link*.

4. See *Montreal Gazette*, 19 July 1984. On 7 June it had reported the Indian Consulate Office closed under Sikh protest. Also see *Indo-Canadian Times*, 27 July 1984. Four Sikhs were tried for attacking the Indian high commissioner in June 1984. Also see *World Sikh News*, 19 September 1986.

5. *Indo-Canadian Times*, 7 September 1984; letter from Harbhajan Singh Chera.

6. *The Sikh News*, 2 September 1984; editorial, "If the shoe fits".

7. *Calgary Herald*, 14 August 1984.

8. It was alleged that the Indian government had blocked aid to the victims of the Delhi riots. Raghbir Singh, "Obstacles to render aid to Sikhs" in *Sikh Symposium*, 1985.

9. The wso's first National Executive Committee included President Ganga Singh Dhillon, Senior Vice-President Lakhbir Singh Cheema, Administrative Director Dr Manohar Singh Grewal and Treasurer Bir Ishwar Grewal.

10. *World Sikh News*, 3 July 1987. In 1987 Manohar Singh Grewal became President with Dr Naunihal Singh as a director of administration and Dr Harbans Singh Saraon as director of finance. On 25 February 1993 the wso announced its new executive committee for the United States: Dr Gurcharan Singh Dhillon (president), Surinder Pal Singh Kalra, (director of administration), Dr Harbans Singh Saraon (senior vice-president), Lakhbir Singh Chima (vice-president, West), Balwant S. Hansra (vice-president, Midwest), Harbhajan Singh Gill (vice-president, East), Amolak Singh (vice-president, South), Gurmej Singh Gill, (director of finance).

11. *World Sikh News*, 4 February 1994. See a letter by Ajit S. Sahota, who said, "other groups and their leaders have put up 'stupid' conditions before they even talk with the wso leaders".

12. *Indo-Canadian Times*, 6 December 1985. It quoted a Sikh leader's view regarding Bhullar, who "disappeared in September 1986, after blackmailing us all and even without arousing slightest suspicion".

13. Members of the National Council noted, "Ganga Singh Dhillon has lost credibility . . . due to his anti-Panthic activities". Among various charges cited against Mr Dhillon was a meeting with Tirlochan Singh Riyasti, a senior congressman of the Punjab and the appointment of J. S. Bhullar as wso's secretary-general. These charges were based on reports in the *Hindustan Times*, 28 January 1985, which carried Mr Dhillon's letter on its front page. However, Mr Dhillon pleaded that Delhi newspapers had deliberately distorted his speech to discredit him. See a report in the *Delhi Record* and also the *Khalsa* (Switzerland) August 1987.

14. *Indo-Canadian Times*, November 1985. The first National Panel of the ISYF

consisted of Satinderpal Singh, president, with other officers Gurdial Singh (Toronto); Barjinder Singh Bhullar (Calgary); Amarjit Singh Saran (Edmonton); Hardial Singh Garcha (Vancouver); Manjit Singh Dhami (Vancouver); Jasjit Singh Aujla, Harminder Singh (Montreal); Gurdev Singh Sangha (Kitchner, Ontario); Surinder Kaur, Jagtar Singh Sandhu and Pushpinder Singh.

15. This constitution is virtually the same as the one issued for ISYF, United Kingdom, in September 1984.
16. Babbar Khalsa International, "constitution", Birmingham n.d. This says that the Babbar Khalsa was set up in 1976 as a *chlda vahīr* (moving column).
17. Apart from Talwinder Singh Parmar, other prominent members included Darshan Singh Saini, Tejinder Singh Raipur, Ajaib Singh Bagri, Kashmir Singh and Santokh Singh. The American branch is managed by Ajit Singh Bainipal with Swaran Singh on the West Coast and Harinder Singh in New Jersey.
18. *India Today*, 15 September 1985. It reported, "Babbar Khalsa has launched an all-out effort to recruit Sikhs abroad for the creation of Khalistan through a Khalistan Liberation Army . . . in February 1982, the organisation hired Johann Vanderhorst, a veteran mercenary who had fought in Rhodesia to train Sikh recruits in British Columbia. Vanderhorst hired fellow mercenaries by putting advertisements in Canadian papers offering salaries of US$ 1,250 a month to train people in the use of weapons and combat techniques. . . . The Indian government obtained clandestine pictures of the training camp in BC which have been handed over to the Canadian government".
19. Kashmeri & McAndrew (1989) working for the *Globe and Mail*, and the *Toronto Star*, have speculated that Talwinder Singh Parmar was supported by the Indian intelligence agencies to destabilize the Canadian Sikhs' campaign.
20. While Parmar was acquitted, five other Sikhs were arrested for plotting to sabotage an Air India plane; see *Globe and Mail*, 25 March 1986. On 2 June 1986 Gurcharan Singh Banwait, Chatar Singh Saini, Kashmir Singh Dhillon, Santokh Singh Khaila and Ravider Singh Anand, all members of Babbar Khalsa, were charged under section 423 (1) of the Canadian Criminal Code and with murder. See *Globe and Mail*, 2–6 June 1986.
21. A request by Parmar's family for his body and autopsy, although supported by a local MP, was spurned by Canadian authorities; see *Vancouver Sun*, 16 and 19 October 1992.
22. Sukhdev Singh worked as a contractor under the false name Jasmer Singh. He was reported to be living with Jawahar Kaur in a modern residence in Patiala, enjoying a luxurious lifestyle unbecoming for a militant leader.

23. Gursharan Singh from Michigan, and Ajit Singh Pannu in California. An American Sikh, Ras Amrit Singh, acts as its press secretary.

24. According to KDS annual reports, its budget rose from $40,000 in 1972 to $630,248 in 1984 to $751,145 in 1987. The budget of Delta Surrey Gurdwara was $489,908 in 1987.

25. It is known that a follower demanded the refund of his large donations to the Nanaksar gurdwara built in the 1970s on the outskirts of Vancouver.

26. A resolution was passed unanimously by the gurdwara in New York on 16 March 1986 to bar such incidents in the future.

27. *World Sikh News*, 18 February 1994; see the editorial "On changing US perception of India".

28. *The Sikh Herald*, a monthly, was launched from Edmonton. Later the *Khalsa*, a flysheet, was published for a few months.

29. *World Sikh News*, 2 September 1988. A letter from Vikram Singh informed readers that, as a result of demonstration against the *San Francisco Chronicle*, a meeting was arranged with its editors who agreed to review the coverage of Sikhs and Punjab events.

30. Among the voluminous correspondence, see his letter to Professor Robert Hardgraves at the University of Texas, who argued that Khalistan will be a tragedy for the Sikhs. *Washington Times*, 20 September 1993; *New York Times*, November 22, 1993; *Christian Science Monitor*, 26 April 1994.

31. Council of Khalistan, press statement, 6 August 1993. In another letter (Council of Khalistan, news sheet, 2 March 1995) to Punjab's police chief, K. P. S. Gill, Aulakh reminded him: "The gurus taught us to oppose tyranny not to serve it. Stop shedding the blood of your brothers. When your masters are through with you, you are just another Sikh. . . . How do you sleep in the oceans of your countrymen's blood that you have shed for the Indian oppressors?"

32. ISYF (1994) with Dal Khalsa.

33. *World Sikh News*, 2 September 1988. He was shot at his office on 29 August 1988. The WSO-Canada chairman, Gian Singh Sandhu, and other Sikh leaders condemned the attempted murder immediately. He survived, although paralyzed in the lower half of his body, and is actively involved in the paper.

34. For a sample of this literature, see Mann (1985), Sadhu & Sukhpal (1986) and *Canadian Punjabi literature and culture* (1991).

35. *World Sikh News*, 2 August 1991.

36. *Indo-Canadian Times*, 20 November 1987.

37. *World Sikh News*, 2 September 1988. It added: "Religious ceremony in the memory of Avtar Singh Brahma and the President of Pakistan Zia-ul-Huq by Sikh-Muslim Friendship Society, the WSO, Babbar Khalsa International, Sikh Youth of California, for the peace of the great martyrs who

became victim of their enemy's conspiracies. This will take place at Lee Marathon School, San Jose on 4 September 1988".

38. *World Sikh News*, 5 August 1988.

39. *World Sikh News*, 15 April 1988; appeal by the wso president, Dr Manohar Singh Grewal, and Naunihal Singh.

40. *World Sikh News*, 19 February 1988. At a conference on 24–25 October 1987 on "Crisis in Punjab" at the University of California, Los Angeles, chaired by Professor Stanley Wolpert, the wso delegates clashed with Jagjit Singh Arora, Inder K. Gujral and M. K. Rasgotra, who defended the Indian position. The wso was supported by some students on its stand for a Sikh state.

41. See the *Khalsa*, no. 6, December 1991.

42. The NACOI officials had a meeting with the wso regarding the latter's membership of the Canadian Ethnocultural Council. *World Sikh News*, 10 April 1991.

43. On 12 October 1987 over 3,000 Sikhs participated; and again on 20 October 1987 the protest against Rajiv Gandhi took place, when a part of Lafayette Park in Washington DC became full of saffron turbans and *dupattas*.

44. *World Sikh News*, 17 June 1988.

45. *India Times*, 3 June 1994; *India Today*, 15 June 1994. The demonstration was held on 19 May 1994.

46. *World Sikh News*, 4 October 1991. Gurtej Singh, a leader of Sikh Youth of America, led the demonstration against Stephen Solarz on 29 September 1991 in front of the Hyatt Regency Hotel. According to Election Commission records, Solarz received substantial funds for his election campaign from American Hindus. Solarz was chairman of the Subcommittee of Foreign Affairs.

47. *Washington Times*, 15 August 1994. The Indian independence day was marred by protest, and again on 26 January 1995, the Council of Khalistan protested, calling the Indian ambassador, S. Ray, a "butcher" of the Punjab. Inside the ambassador read the Indian prime minister's national address, and then played patriotic Hindi songs; outside the protestors called for the entry of Amnesty International into India to examine its black record of human rights and the true face of Indian democracy. In the evening more than 600 people attended the celebrations. In Chicago Dr Aulakh questioned Professor Rudolph, guest speaker at the Indian celebrations, over his optimism about India's future. *India Abroad*, 3 February 1995.

48. *Hindustan Times*, 13 June 1986. The Indian diplomats involved were Ravi Mathur and the first secretary, N. Nayar, on 12 June 1986. Six Canadian Sikhs were charged, including Satinderpal Singh, the ISYF leader.

49. *Indian Express*, 8 October 1987. Panthic Committee members Gurbachan Singh Manochahal, Wassan Singh Jaffarwal, Gurdev Singh, Dalbir Singh

and Dalvinder Singh announced a Council of Khalistan in Amritsar in October 1987, consisting of Gurmeet Singh Aulakh, Council of Khalistan; Arjinder Singh Sekhwan, United States; Tejinder Singh Babbar, Canada; Tejpal Singh Dhami, Canada; Harinder Singh, Norway; Shamsher Singh, Akal Federation; Satnam Singh Paonta, Dal Khalsa; Gurnam Singh Bundala; Wadhawa Singh Babbar; Resham Singh Malohan; and Sanktar Singh, AISSF.

50. Council of Khalistan news sheet, June 1995.

51. *World Sikh News*, 22 March 1991. Bimal Kaur, widow of Beant Singh, was enthusiastically welcomed in Stockton gurdwara. She called upon Western Sikhs to fight against the Indian government which is "enslaving us".

52. In Freemont, Darshan Singh, ex-*jathedar* of Akal Takhat, was barred entry into a gurdwara as he was alleged to have compromised with the Indian state. Gurtej Singh, president of the Sikh Youth of California, along with Jaswinder Singh were arrested for the incident. A similar incident happened again at *Kirtan*, organized by the Sikh Foundation of Virginia, where his programme was disrupted.

53. They travelled to Punjab via Pakistan and joined their favourite militant groups. Harjinder Singh, a Toronto Sikh died in October 1988. Mohinder Singh, born in Malaysia in 1956 but a Canadian citizen, died in July 1989. Balbir Singh and Surinder Singh died in 1989, Bhupinder Singh in 1990, while Surinder Singh Ravi died in 1988. An ISYF member, Sukhmander Singh Cheema of West Newton, Canada, was implicated in a Punjabi bombing. See *World Sikh News*, 9 April 1993.

54. Talwinder Singh had a small but dedicated group of followers in Europe. This Belgium-based group brought out the monthly *Jado-Jahid* (The Struggle); see the June 1993 issue and *Des Pardes*, 29 August 1986. Also see the *Indo-Canadian Times*. Gurmej Singh, a Babbar Khalsa leader from Britain, has exchanged many visits, although his passage got progressively more difficult. He was arrested while crossing to Vancouver and deported in August 1986 to Britain.

55. *World Sikh News*, 21 November 1986. R. S. Bajwa, Dr Hamdam, S. Azad, Rajwant Singh and Sen Barbara Mikulski participated in this meeting in November 1986.

56. *San Francisco Chronicle*, 3 July 1985. They were arrested from Dolomite, Alabama, at a "Mercenary School" run by Frank Camper. Also see *Hindustan Times*, 30 June 1985; *Indian Express*, 1 July 1985; *Times of India*, 1 July 1985. The FBI case was concluded in June 1987, when Birk was jailed for ten years, Sukhwinder Singh seven years, Gurinder Singh and Jasvir Singh Sandhu five years each.

57. Mr Code felt, "It certainly seemed to me as a matter of fundamental human decency that a country should not be sending vast amounts of money and signing extradition treaties with a country where the police

appear to be executing the brothers of Canadian Sikhs after receiving police intelligence from Canadians and misusing it.... You can only contrast this with what would have happened if there was information that the Soviet police were executing the brothers of Canadian citizens. It just seemed to me be a blatant double standard". See Kashmeri & McAndrew (1989).

58. House of Commons, Debates, 15 September 1987. Also see *Globe and Mail*, 10 and 15 September 1987.
59. See *Globe and Mail*, 12 November 1987.
60. House of Commons, Debates, 24 November 1987. p. 11127; also see debate on 22 January 1988. "RCMP raid Balkar Singh's house"; see *Calgary Herald*, 24 April 1992.
61. *Des Pardes*, February 1995. Released after three days, he alleged that the interrogating officers warned overseas Sikh leaders would be sorted out soon.
62. *India West*, 20 May 1988; Mr Bajwa was arrested in February 1985.
63. *India West*, 11 September 1987. The Punjab Human Rights Organization, in a letter of 7 February 1990 appealed to the US government not to extradite the two Sikhs, arguing that the crimes alleged by the Indian government were "forged". Mr Ronald Kuby and Ms Mary Pike, the defence counsels, visited India but were refused entry into Punjab. The Punjab Human Rights Organization sent out a petition.
64. See *World Sikh News*, 27 September 1991 and 20 December 1991. It reported asylum for Ashok Singh, Harpal Singh, Charanjeet Singh and Davinder Singh.
65. House of Commons, Debates, 27 November 1992, 11 December 1992 and 10 February 1993.
66. Many leftist meetings were organized to pay homage to comrades killed allegedly by Sikh militants. Pash, a Punjabi writer killed while on a visit to Punjab from America, was also remembered through writings and meetings.
67. *Indo-Canadian Times*, 21 September 1984.
68. *Vancouver Sun*, 22 August 1984; *Indo-Canadian Times*, 31 August 1984; this letter was published in several papers.
69. *Indo-Canadian Times*, 31 August 1984; letter from Ajit Singh Nanar.
70. *Indo-Canadian Times*, 21 September 1984; see Dr Gurpartap Singh Birk's letter.
71. *Indo-Canadian Times*, 26 April 1985.
72. He wrote, "Justice Bains has been arrested because of his views . . . to call for 'Khalistan' cannot be called seditious. Indians have many different and competing visions for the country, and in this respect, the call for 'Khalistan' has as much validity as the call for the 'unity and integrity' of India, and this will remain the case until such time that the sovereign people of India succeed in the struggle to renew the country on the basis

of a free and a voluntary union. . . . To persecute someone for exercising their right to conscience or freedom of speech can never be justified" (*Punjabi Guardian* n.d.)

73. *San Francisco Chronicle*, 12 January 1987. Harsharan Singh Gill, a raisin grower from Bakersfield, along with six Sikh arms workers pleaded not guilty in Freemont municipal court to charges of assault with a deadly weapon and felony possession of a billy stick. One of the group fired rifle shots into the crowd. A spokesman of the temple branded them as stooges of the Indian government, who were attempting to smear the reputation of Bay Area Sikhs.

74. Air India flight 182, a Boeing 747 from Toronto to Bombay via Montreal and London, went down in the Irish Sea on 23 June 1985, killing all 329 people aboard. Simultaneously, another bomb blast at Narita Airport, outside Tokyo, claimed the lives of two workers who were unloading baggage from CP Air flight 003 from Vancouver to Tokyo. The luggage was being carted from Air Canada flight 301 to Bangkok. India charged that some Canadian Sikhs were involved; see Mulgrew (1988) and for a more passionate charge against Sikhs see Blaise & Mukherjee (1988). However, Kashmeri & McAndrew (1989) argued that Indian intelligence was involved. The controversy has raged without conclusion. In 1992 the Security Intelligence Review Committee cleared the Indian intelligence services of causing the crash as it had no "evidence to support this theory"; see *India Mail*, 1 December 1992.

75. Reyat's extradition demanded by Canada; see *Globe and Mail*, 6 and 8 February 1988.

76. House of Commons, Debates, "Sikh Organisations", March 1988.

77. The institute was given $75,000 for a feasibility study. Many ex-ISYF members joined this alliance. Balwinder Singh Sandhu became president at a meeting on 21 June held at the Surrey gurdwara.

78. *World Sikh News*, 5 April 1991. Gian Singh Sandhu wrote, "We have the WSO working for Sikhs. We have also other small organisations and associations. We do not need the Tory government to start a new organisation, telling Sikhs how they should behave. It is our opinion that this is unwarranted meddling in our affairs. It is a ploy to divide and conquer. . . . The latest we have heard from the 'Sikh Congress' is a 65 page report on completion of phase one. . . . You can be sure that nothing will ever be said against India, for that may embarrass our ally and sister commonwealth country".

79. Mrs Shirley Maheou St Laurel, MP for Cartierville constituency, accused the government of sponsoring the new Sikh organization, even paying for air fares to bring certain Sikh leaders together.

80. See the *Vancouver Sun* for 9, 10, 12, 13 and 14 September 1988, under the title "Canada and the Sikhs: a state under siege". In two articles in March 1986 from Canada, the London *Times* correspondent caught the mood of

the Canadian media. Thus, the *Victoria Times* columnist reacting to Canadian Sikh demonstrations against the Rajiv–Longowal Accord of July 1985, instructed the Sikhs bluntly, "If they wish to make it their business, they should return to India to do so". The *Globe and Mail* commented, "Canadian Sikhs . . . have by their offensive behaviour hurt the reputation of their community in Canada". The *Winnipeg Free Press* lauded cooperation between the Canadian and Indian intelligence services aimed at Sikh militants as "proper and appropriate".

81. *Vancouver Sun*, 6, 8 and 10 June 1995; Satendarpal Singh was branded a "separatist terrorist".
82. *World Sikh News*, 15 April 1988.

# Chapter 6

1. A popular record by Derby-based group Bāz.
2. Reports of protests appeared in all national dailies; see *Times* 6, 11 and 18 June 1984; *Sunday Times*, 10 June 1984.
3. A Hindu temple in Southall was damaged slightly in June 1984; this was the only outward sign of the Hindu–Sikh discord. In October, as news came of the Indian prime minister's death, the media reported many Hindus praying in various temples.
4. A North London gurdwara through an advertisement in a national newspaper called for an enquiry into the anti-Sikh riots in Delhi. While Indarjit Singh, editor of the *Sikh Messenger*, wrote an article for the *Guardian*, many letters in the English press showed stark differences between Sikhs' views and other Indians' views. The English media took a critical attitude to Sikhs' noisy demonstrations. Only in *New Statesman* (16 November 1984 and 12 April 1985) Amrit Wilson wrote, "As for anti-Sikh feelings the word Sikh and terrorist became synonymous in the government controlled media and the speeches of politicians. The storming of the Golden temple at Amritsar was repeated by most national papers and radio and television in a shamelessly biased fashion" (16 November). For a review of the English press from an Indian perspective, see issues of *India Weekly*.
5. *Times*, 1 November 1984, and other dailies.
6. *Evening Mail*, 6 November 1984; a Birmingham gurdwara donated £2,000 to Delhi's distressed Sikhs.
7. *Sikh Messenger*, Summer 1987. Indarjit Singh sought clarification of an Indian army news sheet, *Baatcheet* 153, July 1984, from the Indian High Commission, who replied that the newsletter referred to those Sikhs only who were baptized by late "Shri" Jarnail Singh Bhindranwale. Indarjit Singh wrote back saying, "[You] seek to distort the Sikh religion

by suggesting that there are different types of *amritdharis*. To suggest . . . vows are taken to commit murder and terrorism, is quite absurd and adds further insult to existing injury".

8. Visa regulations for British and Canadian citizens were introduced on 14 June 1984. Prior to this, India had not required visas from citizens of both these countries, and they were admitted indefinitely, regardless of their purpose.

9. In some Midland cities, games were renamed in the memory of new Sikh "martyrs". The police authorities were thought to be apprehensive due to the Indian authorities' objections.

10. *Des Pardes*, 29 June 1984.

11. It led to a protest against the BBC, and the Indian prime minister wrote to Britain to express concern about British Sikhs' reaction; *Times*, 18 June 1984.

12. For a few months, Radio Caroline, a pirate station outside British territorial waters, broadcast a programme of Sikh religious and cultural affairs for half an hour.

13. *Observer*, 5 May 1985, the report was filed by Shyam Bhatia.

14. ISYF *Draft Policy Programme and the Constitution*, September 1984.

15. See Gill Manjit Singh, "When the British judiciary does what India pleases", *Guardian*, 7 January 1985. Jasbir Singh was detained on return from Dubai on 14 December. He was refused entry to Britain due to India's pressure. The High Court rejected his appeal and he was flown to Dubai, to Thailand and then to Manila, where his passport was confiscated and a special Indian plane took him to a Delhi jail. He was implicated in the plot to kill Indira Gandhi. Also see *Tribune*, 17 April 1985, and *Times*, 11 February 1986, for a "Prisoner of Conscience" column.

16. Jasbir Singh was released from jail on 4 March 1988 and appointed head priest of the Akal Takhat on 9 March. After his interview with the BBC on 9 March 1988, he was accused of betrayal and suspected of complicity in the "Black Thunder Operation", when the police raided the Golden Temple on 9 May.

17. Parminder Singh Bal, Amar Yadwinder Singh Samrai and Narinderjit Singh Rai are office-bearers of this group.

18. Based in the Midlands and led by Balwinder Singh Chaherhu, this group controls one gurdwara; its members are dissidents from the main organization.

19. Thirteen Sikhs belonging to the *Akhand Kirtani Jatha* were killed during the clash with a dissenting sect of Nirankaris.

20. *Times*, 11 December 1985; *Guardian*, 7 June 1986. Rajiv Gandhi expressed his displeasure with the British government over "the granting of British citizenship to an exiled Sikh extremist".

21. *Des Pardes*, 7 December 1984. The statement issued by Sukhdev Singh,

NOTES

the Babbar Khalsa chief of Punjab, reported a secret meeting held in Tarn Taran, where several decisions were taken. These included thanking Beant Singh and Satwant Singh for killing the Indian prime minister; asking Sikhs to support Sikh families arriving in the Punjab from other areas; condemnation of Akali leaders over their silence about the Delhi riots and warning them to prepare themselves for appropriate sentences if they failed to side with the Sikhs; a call to boycott those Hindus who celebrated over the army control of the Golden Temple and who perpetuated crimes on innocent Sikhs after the Indian prime minister's assassination; asking Sikhs to offer themselves for guerilla warfare. Its strong language was echoed by a concluding Punjabi proverb, *gurh dī bhājī ladduan vich morhī jāvegī.*

22. See *Wangar* for 1991. Its headlines such as *Panth tere dīān gūnjān dino din paingīān* (Everyday the Panth will rise further) and indiscriminate printing of the responsibilities for murders suggested an approval of violence. Many such press releases were reprinted from the Punjabi press.

23. *Wangar*, October 1991. Madan Singh, for example, argued that the killing of innocents was incompatible with Sikh ethics. However, his seemed a lonely voice and even he was unsure how the militants could declare somone guilty without recourse to a justice system.

24. Gurdeep Singh, *Wangar*, February 1992, pp. 27–8.

25. Gurdeep Singh's much publicized surrender on 12 August 1992 coincided with the killing of Sukhdev Singh, the chief of Babbar Khalsa. His confessional statement was widely discussed in the Punjabi media. He was given police protection on his return to Britain after spending two years in a Punjabi jail.

26. See Jaswant Singh's *Nanakvad.*

27. Besides publishing Gajinder Singh's poetry books, some Punjabi writers were honoured, including Harinder Singh Mehboob with the Bhai Kahan Singh Nabha Award in 1990. Mehboob was given the Indian Sahit Academy Award in 1991 for a poetry book, *Jhanā dī rāt*; its two poems on Beant Singh, the assassin of the Indian prime minister, led to ferocious controversy.

28. Manmohan Singh and Jaswant Singh Thekedar were expelled from the organization and Ranjit Singh Rana took over the leadership. Jaswant Singh Thekedar was granted asylum in July 1993. His family was granted a flat in 1984, which drew strong objections from Vishnu Dutt Sharma, a Punjabi Hindu leader, leading to an enquiry by the Housing Department.

29. *Sikh Messenger*, Autumn 1985. The Leeds Sikh Council held a seminar in April 1985, seeking an independent inquiry into the 1984 riots in Delhi. Lord Hatch, who had seen some riot victims in Delhi, compared the Sikhs' tragedy to South Africa's Sharpeville. The conference strongly

NOTES

condemned some Sikh celebrations of the Indian prime minister's death, as they contravened Sikh ethics. A priest who had lost his family in the Delhi riots also spoke at the conference.

30. *Coventry Evening Telegraph*, 2 August 1984; *Des Pardes*, April 1993. The Charity Commission has often intervened in its elections.

31. *Sunday Times*, 17 May 1987; *Erith and Crayford Times*, 13 August 1987. The Belvedere Gurdwara, Kent, was the scene of contention among two rival groups.

32. *Des Pardes* and *Punjab Times*, October 1985. On a cold and rain-drenched night of 18 October 1985, over 300 Sikhs kept an all-night vigil outside the gurdwara until the early hours of the morning, when the police intervened to reopen the building.

33. *Des Pardes*, 23 September 1988. In the main Southall gurdwara, the ISYF after two years control had to fight again in 1986. A *sant*, who mediated between the two factions and opened another building as a gurdwara, fled as the quarrel escalated and one person was stabbed.

34. *Khalistan News*, 10 April 1987. "A clarion call to Ramgarhia and Ravidasi Sikhs" asked them to join the Sikh struggle based on equality, irrespective of caste and creed.

35. The meeting on 22 July 1984 was attended by Prem Singh, Baldev Ubhi, H. S. Gahir and Mohan Singh, among others. A resolution was moved by Sardul Marwaha. Dr J. S. Chohan sought apology for past misunderstanding between Ramgarhias and Jats, and praised the Ramgarhias as the community's "cream". He asked amid laughter and applause, "Can Khalistan be governed without the Ramgarhias' expertise?"

36. From 1983 onwards, Congress leaders and ministers from India were not welcomed at mainstream gurdwaras. They had to address the Sikhs through Ravidasi or some Ramgarhia gurdwaras.

37. In January 1985 a Ramgarhia gurdwara in Birmingham sent £3,500 for orphans and widows of the Delhi riots.

38. *Solihull Daily Times*, 29 January 1986. A Ravidasi and member of the Indian Overseas Congress, Mr Badhan, stated that "extremist Sikhs have threatened him".

39. He cautioned Sikh voters during the February 1992 elections, arguing that elections deflect from the Sikh nation's clear objective of independence.

40. ISYF, *Annual Report*, Walsall, September 1986.

41. *Guardian*, 31 March 1995; *Express and Star*, 30 May 1995. Raghbir Singh, editor of *Awaz-e-Quam*, was arrested on 29 March 1995 in connection with the murder of Tarsem Singh Purewal, editor of Punjabi weekly *Des Pardes*. He was detained under the National Security Act and served with a notice of intention to deport on "national security" grounds. The ISYF, many MPs, human rights activists, and the National Union of Journalists protested. He was released on 6 December 1996.

42. *Des Pardes*, 28 June 1991. The appeal was issued jointly by the Khalistan Council, Babbar Khalsa International, the International Sikh Youth Federation, Shiromani Akali Dal, the Republic of Khalistan, Dal Khalsa International, the Khalistan Liberation Movement and the Akhand Kirtani Jatha.
43. *Khalistan News*, January 1988; see "charter of Khalistan".
44. *Independent*, 5 September 1992. Davinder Singh Parmar died on 27 August 1992.
45. On important occasions in the Sikh calendar, he has placed an advertisement in Punjabi weeklies setting down a case for a Sikh homeland.
46. See Balhar Singh Randhawa (1985) Lote (1985) and Baldev Bawa (1994). Gurcharan Singh Lote wrote several poems on the tragedy, but believing in the inevitable victory for Sikh independence:

> Our times command, the Panth will be free one day
> Those who felt dishonoured, from Europe to North America
> Have aligned for its protection, to save our wounded nation
> and resolved, says the poet, to uphold nation's honour
> (Khūnī churasī, p. 31)

Another poet, Baldev Bawa, wrote a long poem evoking much affection for the Punjab:

> Punjab, oh my country, is forlorn among nations
> Write thy name, on the vast canvas of the sky
> Let the beautiful moon encircle you
> let it shine among the studded stars.

47. Donations by Babbar Khalsa members and sympathizers have gone to the Bhai Fauja Singh Public Charitable Trust, Amritsar; see the list in various issues of *Wangar*.
48. Khalistan Council, Press Release, Slough, 30 April 1990.
49. An attempt was made on the life of Sangtar Singh Sandhu, the only Sikh leader to welcome the Indian prime minister in September 1985.
50. *Times*, 18 October 1985; *Sunday Observer*, 13 October 1985. The case was decided at Birmingham High Court on 28 December 1986. Of the three Sikhs, Sukhwindar Singh Gill and Jarnail Singh were found guilty and jailed for 14 and 20 years respectively, and Parmatma Singh was freed.
51. Punjab's police chief, K. P. S. Gill, was met by a large demonstration on 23 June 1994; his press conference was cancelled.
52. She toured Britain in April 1991 after a visit to North America.
53. *India Abroad*, 26 August 1994. Manjit Singh was invited by Manubhai Madhvani, a Hindu businessman and organizer of the 1994 Spiritual Unity in London Festival. Manjit Singh was questioned by Khalistani leaders while Dr Chohan observed, "It was degrading for us to see him sitting . . . at a lower level than Morari Bapu during the *katha*".

54. Jasbir Singh Ghuman and Jagroop Singh Batth, two Babbar Khalsa activists, were arrested in London, accused of conspiracy to murder Sumedh Saini, deputy inspector general of Punjab's police, on a visit to London in August 1997. Another British Sikh, Gurnam Singh, was arrested in Punjab after a tip by the British police; see *Asian Age*, 11 November 1997.

55. Michael Foot, along with other Labour leaders, paid warm tributes to Indira Gandhi's rule; see the British media for November 1984.

56. The Green Party, *Policy statement: Punjab*, September 1988. The Green Party, *Background Papers on Punjab*, 1988.

57. Letter to Jagdish Singh, 21 February 1990. Similarly, Plaid Cymru leader Gwynor Evans wrote, "We are in full support of Sikh national freedom . . . India is an empire just as the USSR was". Letter, 7 June 1994.

58. *Guardian*, 20 August 1986.

59. *Times*, *Guardian*, 2 and 18 September 1995. Karamjit Singh Chahal was arrested on 16 August 1990 and threatened with deportation to India "for reasons of national security and reasons of political nature". After the Appeal Court rejected Chahal's plea for asylum, the case was taken to the European Human Rights Commission. The Home Office argued that Chahal was a terrorist. Max Madden called for Chahal's bail supported by 83 cross-party MPs. The *Independent*, 4 August 1992, reported, "The Indian government has put intense pressure on Britain to send Chahal to India". Chahal was released on 15 November 1996.

60. Khalsa Human Rights, Report 1994. His brother Jagvinder Singh in Leicester was informed that Tejinder had died. However, the Khalsa Human Rights is campaigning that Tejinder is still alive, like many other "disappeared" persons.

61. Khalsa Human Rights, Annual Reports, 1994–5. Khalra was arrested or abducted in Amritsar on 6 September 1995 from his residence and has "disappeared". His "crime" seemed to expose the alleged secret cremation of hundreds of bodies in Amritsar. Another case of a "disappeared" Sikh, Harjit Singh, was brought to public attention by Amnesty International through a full-page advertisement in a national daily. The Khalsa Human Rights also printed the names of lawyers considered to be at risk because of their defence of Sikh activists; among them were Jagdev Singh, Jagvinder Singh, Kulwant Singh, Sukhvinder Singh Bhatti, Ranjan Lakhanpal and Ranjit Singh.

62. House of Commons, 19 December 1986, pp. 1504–16. *Sikh Messenger*, Summer 1987; also see *Times*, 10 December 1986 and 22 April 1987. Mrs Kuldip Kaur was arrested in December 1986 during a visit to India and released on 11 April 1987. She was held in prison without charge and harassed. Her local councillor, Michael Craxton, wrote to the Indian High Commission on 22 April 1987. The *Observer*, 12 May 1991, ran a

story linking Tory MP Terry Dicks with Mohinder Pal Singh Bedi (Mrs Kaur's husband) in some dubious business deals.

63. This meeting was arranged by the Sikh Human Rights and Keith Vaz MP on 25 July 1989. D. S. Gill read out summaries of many cases of human rights abuse in the Punjab.

64. Thus on 1 July 1992, the ISYF, the Dal Khalsa, the Akali Dal, the Khalistan Liberation Front, the Sikh Information Centre and the Sikh Refugee Association joined to present their case to MPs. Buta Singh Rai led the delegation.

65. It has published two booklets on Sikh issues.

66. Although the visit led to some minor scuffles, the new ambassador attended to Sikhs' complaints by making staff changes at the embassy; see *Des Pardes*, December 1990.

67. The ISYF sent about £7,500 to Thakur Singh, who distributed it among widows and distressed families.

68. *Des Pardes*, February 1989; also *Wangar*, no. 20, 1989.

69. In Germany the Babbar Khalsa is led by Resham Singh; in other European countries there are many active members. In France a Khalistan House was opened on 9 November 1990. In Switzerland a factional fight among Babbar Khalsa members led to Balwinder Singh's killing in 1990.

70. Activist Harvinder Bhuderhi confronted Punjab's police chief, K. P. S. Gill, on his visit to Belgium in 1994.

71. Its three members, Manjit Bagi, Mohinder Singh and Gurdeep Singh Pardesi (Pardesi, a Sikh, has hijacked an Indian Airlines plane to Lahore), were given asylum in Germany in 1995. Another Sikh hijacker, Jasbir Singh, sought asylum in Switzerland in 1995.

72. House of Commons, Debates, 11 November 1988.

73. Harjinder Singh Dilgeer, member of Dal Khalsa, writer and columnist, was deported to Sweden in September 1986.

74. *Khalistan News*, March 1993. Letter from Parshotam Singh and Satnam Singh who protested on behalf of "the Sikh community of Australia" against India's attack on "Sikhs on international level".

75. The Babbar Khalsa issued a pamphlet on three Sikhs involved in the incident, Jugraj Singh, Jagwinder Singh and Sadhu Singh, comparing their deeds with Udham Singh; see *aj de Udham Singh*. The military court sentenced the two Sikhs for ten and eight years of imprisonment; Jugraj Singh was killed during the abduction incident.

76. *Guardian*, 6 February 1986; Mr Rai was jailed for life at the Old Bailey.

77. A journal, *Unity*, was launched to promote unity among overseas Indians. Its office-bearers for 1988–9 were President Daljit Singh Shergill, Senior President R. Singh, Vice-Presidents A. K. Singh and A. S. Grover, General Secretaries B. S. Sood and Harbans Singh, with Founder President Jaswant Singh.

78. *Sandesh International*, a Punjabi weekly from Southall, launched a vigorous campaign against Sikh separatists. Its subeditor, Kartar Singh, was killed in an arson attack on Sandesh's office in July 1984. Its proprietor, Ajit Sat Bhamra, was jailed for heroin smuggling amid controversy over Indian High Commission patronage.

79. *Des Pardes*, 31 August 1984; also see *Sandesh International*, August/September, 1984.

80. *Independent*, 13 November, 1987; *Des Pardes*, 20 November 1987. Darshan Das was shot dead on 11 November 1987 and his two close followers, Joga Singh and Satwant Singh Panesar, died later in hospital. Rajinder Singh Batth and Manjit Singh Sandher, both belonging to the ISYF, were given life sentences for the murder.

81. *Lokta*, July 1987. It called for the implementation of the Rajiv–Longowal accord, separation of religion and politics, an inquiry into the Delhi riots, release of Jodhpur detainees, publication of Indira Gandhi's murder report and elections in the Punjab. Also see Maksoodpuri (1989), Makhan Singh (1994).

82. *Express and Star*, 8 July 1986. At the IWA(ML) meeting at Summerfield School, several people were hurt as the ISYF activists disturbed the meeting. Another similar incident happened in July 1987.

83. Meetings were held to pay homage to Chanan Singh Dhoot, Deepak Dhavan, Darshan Singh Canadian and other communists who were allegedly murdered by militants.

84. Pargat Singh escaped with minor injuries during a violent attack on 7 November 1985; the house of his successor, Dr Jasdev Singh, was attacked by an unknown gang.

85. Swaraj (1984); see, for example, some evidence from Bristol in Barot (1995).

86. Tatla & Singh (1989) provide a general overview of the Punjabi press. The Punjabi media has been under much pressure to toe India's official line. Tarsem Singh Purewal, editor of major Punjabi weekly *Des Pardes*, was denied entry to India, complaints against him were filed with Ealing Council and the Press Advisory Council. He was murdered on 25 January 1995 as he stepped out of his office. The police have made no arrests; speculation is rife about "underworld agents", "India's hit men" or "Khalistanis". *Independent*, 26 and 27 January 1995. Amit Roy's report on his murder in the *Sunday Telegraph*, 29 January 1995, "Madness under the Turban" led to a furore as many Sikh readers demanded an apology for implicating the entire community.

87. *Birmingham Post*, 23 February 1989; see Geoffrey Dear's statement to the press. The paper quoted Gurmej Singh Gill, "Mr. Dear is telling lies and we are very annoyed". The *Coventry Evening Telegraph*, 6 February 1989, reported the arrest of Inderjit Singh Reyat, a local car worker, who was later extradited to Canada.

88. A memorandum presented by Gurmej Singh Gill, Balwinder Singh and Tarsem Singh stated, "Your visit and hobnobbing with the Indian authorities has aroused suspicion and fears among the Sikh community ... who are naturally concerned about their kith and kin in the Punjab".

## Chapter 7

1. A passage from the Gadr songs.
2. This was issued in July 1984 after the army action in the Golden Temple.
3. In a written reply to the upper house of the Indian parliament, Rajiv Gandhi, the prime minister, listed these organizations: National Council of Khalistan, World Sikh Organization, Dal Khalsa, Nankana Sahib Foundation, Babbar Khalsa, Akhand Kirtani Jatha, All India Sikh Federation, Dashmesh Regiment, Sikh Youth Movement, International Sikh Youth Federation, Sikh Youth Federation, Sikh Student Association of North America, Sikh Council of North America, Sikh Association of North America, Sikh Students Federation, Federation of Sikh Societies, North American Akali Dal, International Akali Dal, Guru Nanak Foundation of America, Guru Gobind Singh Foundation, International Sikh Solidarity Organization, Sikh Defence Council, Sikh Cultural Centre and Khalsa Diwan Society. This indiscriminate list made no distinction between purely religious organizations and others, even the discredited Akali Dal was included.
4. *India Today*, July 1985. It reported additional intelligence operatives from the Research and Analysis Wing and the Intelligence Bureau posted at several embassies abroad.
5. Lok Sabha, Debates, 18 April 1985, pp. 343–400. Saifullah Chowdhury.
6. Lok Sabha, Debates, 18 April 1985. K. K. Tewary quoted from Nixon's book, "It was no more in the order of all India to be one country than it was for all Europe to be one country: linguistically, ethnically and culturally India is more diverse than Europe". Tewary also cited Hardgrave's book as another proof of America's sinister designs.
7. Lok Sabha, Debates, 18 April 1985. Regarding Dr J. S. Chohan's role, he noted: "That extremist, fiendish, secessionist leader who has been operating in connivance with the British and America authorities, went on BBC and announced prizes for the assassination of Madam Gandhi. Then after that when Madam Gandhi was assassinated when the terrible tragedy overtook the nation, again the same person was allowed to go on BBC and gloat over the success of his murder squad". He questioned how the Sikh Council of North America could put an appeal in the *New*

*York Times,* which called for "the determination of the destiny of Sikhs by themselves".

8. Lok Sabha, Debates, 18 April 1985. Khursheed Alam Khan, the minister of state in the Ministry of External Affairs.

9. Manjinder Singhh Grewal, an Akhand Kirtani Jatha member from Britain, and two Babar Khalsa members, Harjit Singh from America and Resham Singh from Germany were charged with a plot to murder Beant Singh.

10. Malik & Robb (1994) contains articles from the conference "India and Britain – recent and contemporary challenges", University of London, 21–23 September 1992. It has many references to the Sikh and Kashmiri lobby in Britain.

11. *Hindustan Times,* 3 August 1984; *Times of India,* 21 and 25 September 1984. Chohan's speech was interpreted by Indian authorities as incitement to violence, and drew strong reaction from the Indian papers. Bowing to Indian pressure, air time for Sikh leaders was phased out by the BBC.

12. *Guardian,* 7 June 1986.

13. The *Observer* called the arrest of Sikhs a "fishing expedition". See the more popular papers' coverage of the Indian premier's visit. The *Daily Mail* headlined a story "My enemies in your midst".

14. *Sunday Times,* 23 December 1984.

15. *Times,* 15 April 1985.

16. As part of the talks, it was agreed that Jaswant Singh Thekedar, wanted by the Indian police for alleged murder of two police officers in 1982, would not be offered asylum in the UK.

17. House of Commons, Debates, 11 November 1988.

18. See Mani (1995). Home Secretary Kenneth Baker was followed by Foreign Secretary Douglas Hurd. House of Commons, Hansard no. 1577, 13 January 1992, pp. 463–4. Mr John Major, the British prime minister during his visit to India in January 1993 assured the Indian government, "to continue to work closely . . . to defeat the evil of terrorism". See K. Subrahmanyam (pp. 112–29) in Malik & Robb (1994), who alleged drug traffic in Europe carried out by Kashmiri and Sikh militants, and noted that "the visit of the Home secretary and the British Prime Minister, coincided when the London branch of the Jammu and Kashmir Liberation Front was dissolved and significant successes in the Punjab in tracking down hard core terrorists took place simultaneously".

19. House of Commons, Debates, vol. 229, no. 222, 22 July 1993.

20. *India Today,* 15 October 1992; also see Siddharth (1992) for a dissenting note.

21. After signing the treaty in London, Indian Home Minister S. B. Chavan granted Ian Martin, a former secretary-general of Amnesty International, a restricted visit to New Delhi. Speaking at a conference organ-

ized by the Univeristy of London, he said the "threat . . . come from terrorism combined with religious fundamentalism, planned and financed from across our borders". See Malik & Robb (1994: xiii).

22. House of Commons, Debates, India (Sikh Community), 11 November 1988, pp. 718–26.
23. House of Commons, Debates, India (Sikh Community), 11 November 1988.
24. Richard Balfe, Max Madden and John Taylor went to Punjab on a fact-finding mission in 1990.
25. House of Commons, Debates, 22 March 1990.
26. House of Commons, Debates, no. 1575, 12 December 1991, p. 510 and issue no. 1577, 13 January 1992, pp. 463–4. He asked the Home Secretary to seek information from the government of India on "how many police officers and other ranks from the Punjab police force have been prosecuted for crimes up to 31 March 1991; the list of crimes committed and punishments made". Mark Lennonx-Boyd, another minister of state for the Commonwealth said, "In response to our expression of concern the Indian government have told us that up to March 31 1991, a total of 157 police officers and other ranks have been punished for human rights violations in Punjab".
27. House of Commons, Debates, Written Answers, 13 January 1992, p. 461.
28. To the questions (a) what complaints have been received in the last three years? and (b) what investigations have been undertaken by the Metropolitan Police into the irregular expenditure of funds by organizations which promote the political, social and economic interests of the British community, Peter Lloyd replied that this information could only be obtained at disproportionate cost.
29. House of Commons, Debates, vol. 199, no. 22, 29 November 1991, p. 1241.
30. House of Commons, Debates, 29 November 1991, pp. 1244–8.
31. For a discussion of this point, see Pritam Singh (1992).
32. As a member of the House of Commons Public Accounts Committee, he had learned that in the past six years no aid project was granted in these two provinces, observing "this is very surprising. Many hundreds of thousands of residents in the uk have their families in these two states and pay British taxes, none of which appears to go in the form of overseas aid to these states". British aid to India in the past six years was 1989–90, £75.85 (million); 1990–91, £88.26; 1991–2, £128.14; 1992–3, £94.72; 1993–4, £79.23; 1994–5, £82.65.
33. House of Commons, Debates, 17 March 1994, p. 1054. He cited the case of Harjit Singh, who had "disappeared" in April 1992, and censorship of the Punjabi newspaper *aj di awaj*. He quoted from the Amnesty International report, "However provocative, the grave abuses committed by armed separatist groups can never justify the security forces

resorting to arbitrary detention, torture, extrajudicial executions or "disappearances".

34. House of Commons, Debates, vol. 259, no. 101, 9 May 1995.
35. *Observer*, 5 October 1997.
36. See *Awaz-e-Quam*, October 1997.
37. *Observer*, 19 October 1997; Gerald Kaufman, "Our mess is now their obscenity". Also see the *Sunday Times*, 19 October 1997, "Misplaced Moralising" and the *Times* editorial on 16 October 1997, "A guest in India". It argued that "by abruptly announcing that the Queen is debarred by protocol from speaking at a state banquet in Madras given by Governor of Tamil Nadu, Indian government has shown considerably less maturity". In a letter to the *Times*, Cook defended his remarks over Kashmir with Pakistani Premier Nawaj Sharif.
38. See Kashmir Singh's letter in the *Asian Times*, October 1997.
39. *World Sikh News*, 31 October 1986. Wally Herger was given $10,000 for a fundraising dinner. Guests included Dr N. S. Kapani, Didar Singh Bains and Dr Gurinder Singh Grewal, who spoke of their concern about the Punjab. *World Sikh News*, 5 August 1988. Dan Burton was presented with a Sikh Heritage Award. *World Sikh News*, 26 February 1993. The senator was presented with a plaque "in recognition of your solidarity and support to the Sikhs nation": wso, usa, 1993. Vic Fazio was honoured at the National Press Club in February 1993, while Pete Geren was honoured in a gurdwara; see *Dallas Morning News*, 10 January 1994.
40. Less than 1.5 per cent of American trade is with India, while the United States is the largest trading partner of India, and a major source of technology and investment. In 1992 India's total bilateral trade with the United States was $5.7 billion, with a $1.5 billion surplus. Moreover, us support for economic assistance to India from international institutions is crucial.
41. Letter to president, 14 October 1987. It said: "The us supplied over 500 million dollars in economic aid to India over the last three years. We are concerned ... to know that India offered a 10.4 million dollar aid package to communist Sandinistas in Nicaragua. India has no mission in Israel, but maintains warm relations with plo".
42. 103rd Congress, vol. 139, no. 52, 22 April 1993. Among cases highlighted in the Congress are Gurdev Singh Kaonke, arrested on 20 October 1992, tortured and killed while the police claimed he had "escaped during custody"; Kulwant Singh Saini, a Sikh lawyer, killed along with his wife and two children. Names of 28 Punjabi lawyers vulnerable to Punjab's police were also printed on 2 August 1994; the issue of mail censorship in Punjab during July 1994 was also taken up, and cases of "unidentified bodies" cremated by the police. Also see *Washington Post*, 6 December 1994.
43. 100th Congress, 2 August 1988.

44. US Congressional Records, Special Order Debate, 2 June 1987. These and some earlier congressional proceedings relating to Punjab are also collected in the International Sikh Organization (1988).
45. US Congressional Special Order Debate, 2 June 1987.
46. He was refused permission to visit Punjab but met the Indian prime minister.
47. *India West*, 7 July 1989.
48. Congress Records, 19 February 1991; it had 29 cosponsors.
49. Congressional Record, 25 June 1992, HR 5241 was approved by 219 members with 200 against. As a result, about $27 million was cut from the Indian aid programme. See Shrivastava (1993), who noted that "certain organisations of the Sikhs and Kashmiris have successfully lobbied members of the US congress. Some congressmen and Senators are genuinely interested in the issue of human rights, but quite a few only find it useful in their favourite game of India-bashing. The state department has taken a fairly balanced view.... US economic assistance to India amounts to no more than $40 million. If India should opt out of this aid too, it would send the right signal to the United States. After all one has to draw a line somewhere. The US must put an end to this annual India-bashing exercise".
50. 103rd Congress, HR 1519, 30 March 1993. Laws mentioned were TADA Act of 1987, National Security Act of 1980, Jammu and Kashmir Public Safety Act of 1978, and Armed Forces (Punjab and Chandigarh) Special Powers Act of 1990.
51. Proceedings and Debates of the 103rd Congress, vol. 139, no. 85, 16 June 1993. Mr Pallone thought the amendment would greatly reduce "America's ability to influence the Indian government", not only in terms of human rights but on a wide range of economic and security concerns. Mr Herger argued the Indian government must be told that "torture and murder of its citizens" cannot be tolerated. Stearns cautioned against "singling out India for symbolic punishment" as it was not in the American national interest. Richardson argued the amendment would reduce America's ability to influence New Delhi on human rights.
52. *Tribune*, 17/18 June 1993.
53. *World Sikh News*, 14 May 1993.
54. Congress Proceedings, HR 1561. The American Overseas Interests Act stipulated the cut of $70.4 million in US development aid to any country which did not vote with the US at the UN at least 25 per cent of the time.
55. *Washington Times*, 25 May 1995.
56. *Tribune*, 1 July 1995.
57. *Washington Times*, 16 May 1994; *India Abroad*, 26 August 1994.
58. 103rd Congress, House Concurrent Resolution 134, 5 August 1993. The resolution was supported by Dan Burton (Rep. Ind.), Gary Condit (Dem.

Calif.), Dana Rohrabacher (Rep. Calif.), Floyd Flake (Dem. NY), Duncan Hunter (Rep. Calif.), Christopher Cox (Rep. Calif.), Walter Tucker (Dem. Calif.), Philip Crane (Rep. Ill), Robert Underwood (Dem. Guam.), William Jefferson (Dem. La.), William Lipinski (Dem. Ill.), Charles Wilson (Dem. Tex.). In a letter of 30 July 1993 to fellow Congress members, Pete Geren wrote: "Sikh homeland is the birthplace of the Sikh nation. Sikhs ruled the Punjab from 1765 until it was annexed by the British in 1849. They are a formidable people with a clear desire for freedom, the universal right of all nations. It is time that we cease turning a blind eye to India's brutal denial of freedom and human rights. We must support the Sikh nation in its just struggle for freedom".

59. Letter, 17 November 1993; *India Abroad*, 10 December 1993.

60. Letter to Gary Condit, 27 December 1993.

61. *India Abroad*, 10 December 1993; *India Today*, 15 December 1993. The latter described Congress members supporting the resolution as "India bashers". *Tribune*, 5 June 1994, headlined "12 US congressmen support Khalistan".

62. *Tribune*, 30 January 1994; 6 and 22 February 1994. Lt. Col. Pratap Singh presented a memorandum saying, "being dispossessed and stateless, the Sikhs have no means of voicing their anguish to the international organisations". He expressed thanks for the president's statement and recorded appreciation of the American Sikhs, in particular Gurmeet Singh Aulakh. Maninder Singh Bitta, president of the Punjab Youth Congress, led a protest march in Delhi.

63. Embassy of India, Washington. Its official spokesman's statement on 24 January 1994 said: "The situation in the Punjab today is indeed peaceful. We reject any statement that speaks of a "solution that protects Sikh rights". A solution has indeed been attained in Punjab by the people of Punjab by democratic means, where the rights of all Indians including Sikhs are protected under the law, regardless of their religion".

64. *Times of India*, 21 January 1993; *Hindustan Times*, 29 April 1993. The State Department report for 1992 said that the paramilitary forces and the police had committed excesses on civilians, particularly in Assam, Kashmir and Punjab. It also cited numerous cases of political killings along with abduction and extortion by militants.

65. Letter, 14 February 1994, citing the Amnesty International 1993 report, which chronicled 80 cases of "disappearances". The letter pointed out that "the Indian government continues a policy of brutal repression against the Sikh nation". It sought a cut in "developmental aid to India" of just $41 million to "communicate" America's concern for protection of "human rights in the Sikh homeland". It went on to assert that the Indian government, which spent $6.8 billion in conventional arms purchases from 1989 to 1992, had no "pressing need for American developmental assistance". As human rights are high on the American foreign policy

agenda, America should also "champion these principles" in the Sikh homeland.

66. Letter to President Clinton, 7 October 1995.

67. Forty-three Congress members wrote to Secretary of State Warren Christopher on 10 February 1995, expressing grave concern about the pending extradition treaty. The letter was sponsored by Peter King, with signatories from both sides.

68. *India West*, 7 July 1989. Raj Dutt, president of the Indian-American Political Committee, who lobbied hard against the Herger amendment, commented: "Dr Aulakh and the Khalistanis have been very organised, and did a fabulous job of lobbying for this amendment. The apathy of the Indian community has really shown on this one".

69. *World Sikh News*, 16 August 1993. Letter by Parmjit Singh Ajrawat, a member of the Council of Khalistan, to Gary Ackerman: "We write to you this letter with great remorse and concern regarding your stand against the Sikhs along with pro-India lobbying in the US Congress with special reference to the Burton Amendment. . . . You are a Jew and come from a minority background like us. We are shocked and dismayed to know that a person of Jewish descent will stand on the House floor openly condemning an aggrieved minority and join hands with a tyrant government of India who in recent years has come to be recognized as one of the worst offenders for human rights of its own citizens".

70. *Hindustan Times*, 6 February 1993.

71. *World Sikh News*, 4 March 1994. Senator Cathie Wright introduced SJR28 concerning human rights violations in the two states.

72. *Tribune*, 31 August 1992.

73. House of Commons, Debates, 25 June 1985, p. 6150. Mr Lee Benjamin (Regina West) cautioned against jumping to the conclusion "about the possible involvement of one or more members of East Indian or other communities".

74. According to Gurcharan Singh, secretary of the Federation of Sikh Societies. *Shamshir-e-Dast*, September 1985, Jaswinder Singh of ISYF Vancouver noted the press's role in the incident and clarified how the ISYF had clearly condemned it.

75. *Toronto Star*, 18 June 1984.

76. See several articles in Rubinoff (1988, 1992) for a discussion of Indo-Canadian relations.

77. *Times*, 24 March 1986. It noted, "compassion for Sikhs and for their justifiable concern about the plight of brethren in India is in short supply".

78. The Indo-Canadian treaty was signed by Charles J. Clark for the government of Canada and Narayan Tiwari for the government of India and came into effect on 10 February 1987.

NOTES

79. *India West*, 22 July 1988. At this time, he also put in a request for the extradition of three Sikhs from India.
80. House of Commons, Debates, 1987.
81. This letter was issued on 11 December 1987. Also see *Globe and Mail*, 25 February and 24 May 1988. Another MP, Mr Kaplan, sent a letter seeking an apology from Clark. See *Toronto Star*, 14 March 1988.
82. House of Commons, "Sikh Organisations: the Government Position", 10 March 1988; Hansard, vol. 129, no. 269.
83. Quoting from the *Globe and Mail* for 13 December 1986, E. G. Drake, an assistant deputy minister in external affairs, wrote to a secretary of state official: "Documents obtained under the Access to Information Act reveal that an External Affairs official believe a federal grant for a chair in Punjabi literature and Sikh studies at the University of British Columbia would be misunderstood by the Government of India. . . . While I fully understand that Canada's multiculturalism policies will be guided by Canadian domestic considerations, the implications in terms of foreign policy must also be considered."
84. House of Commons, Debates, "Sikh Organisations: the Government Position", 1988.
85. *India West*, 22 July 1988.
86. *Toronto Star*, 18 April 1988.
87. According to Kashmeri & McAndrew, Indian intelligence pressure was such that "the CSIS officers were convinced that the Indian government 'will use both legitimate and illegitimate means'". The two journalists concluded, "the Indian disinformation operation was a success" (1989: 94). An opinion poll was conducted for the Macauliffe Institute of Sikh Studies at the University of Toronto, interviewing 500 English-speakers and francophones. The results were summarized thus, "the turban had become synonymous with violence".
88. See Hyder (1991). A reader compared Sikhs' treatment with those from Europe; in *World Sikh News*, 25 February 1994: "Shortly after the Sikhs, 1,300 'refugees' from east Europe mostly from Bulgaria and Rumania arrived in Gander, Newfoundland, they costed us a $1,000 a month while waiting (in hotel rooms) to be processed. On the other hand when East Indians had arrived they were herded into a military camp. The Sikh community was asked to post bonds for each and every refugee claimant, totalling nearly $500,000. Only then were they released from military confinement. No other ethnic group has been asked to post security bonds, before or since. Why are there different rules for Sikhs?"
89. House of Commons, Debates, 3 September 1989, p. 8730. *Maclean's Magazine* published this information, leaked by some official, which proved to be false.
90. *World Sikh News*, July 1987; *Des Pardes*, July 1987. In Britain, Jasbir Singh

and Niranjan Singh Mann were questioned by police. The Khalsa Diwan Society provided $70,000 to cover the legal and other costs.

91. *Indo-Canadian Times*, 7 August 1987.
92. House of Commons, Debates, 11 August 1987, pp. 7905–8807. Although the legislation was under consideration from May, it was expedited in the house's special session. Mr Benoit Bouchard, minister of employment and immigration, outlined measures to control abuses in the refugee system.
93. Santokh Singh's case generated a lengthy debate. See House of Commons, Debates, 17 May 1988, p. 15542; 24 May, p. 15715; 2 June, p. 16099.
94. Maheshinder Singh, whose father was killed in 1992 in Punjab, while his brother "disappeared" in 1993, had sought asylum. He was arrested on 5 December 1994 by the Canadian police for alleged crimes in India; his extradition under the Indo-Canadian treaty is awaiting decision by the supreme court.
95. House of Commons, Debates, Mr Heap, 3 October 1989, p. 42241.
96. Mr Derek Lee (Scarborough), House of Commons, Debates, 21 February 1992, p. 7478. See also the adjournment motion debate on 17 March 1992, pp. 8394–5.
97. House of Commons, 4 June 1996. Earlier on 31 October 1994, Malhi had called attention to the exhibition on the riots and human rights violation in the Punjab; the exhibition was held in the Commonwealth Room after the question period. He had reminded the house to remember those innocent people who died during the Blue Star operation. House of Commons, 5 June 1995.
98. House of Commons, 27 May 1996.
99. *Khalistan Times*, no. 6, 1987. The UN committee of Cyprus, Sri Lanka, France, Bulgaria, Cuba, Soviet Union, the United States and Malawi considered the application on 25 February 1987 for Category 1 Consultative Status and rejected it as the Sikh commonwealth aimed to undermine the "sovereignty of a member state".
100. *World Sikh News*, 17 June 1988.
101. Held at Vienna on 14–25 June 1993. The Sikh deputation consisted of a large delegation carrying placards and documents on India's abuses of human rights in the Punjab. The Indian delegation was led by a Sikh, Finance Minister Manmohan Singh, along with Atal Bihari Vajpayee and a Punjabi newspaper editor, Jagjit Singh Anand, and Gurcharan Singh Galib, a Sikh MP. Among the Indian delegates, a Sikh was seeking censure of Pakistan for abetting terrorism.
102. Sikh activists took part in the UN human rights day on 10 December 1991 in San Francisco. *World Sikh News*, 13 December 1991. A presentation was made to the United Nations on the violation of human rights in India at the Centre of Human Rights, Geneva, in 1990.

103. *Council of Khalistan Newsletter*, 28 October 1993.
104. *World Sikh News*, 23 April 1993. The Panthic Committee addressed the United Nations followed by a letter to American President George Bush. Also see *World Sikh News*, 20 December 1991. In another letter they asked the International Monetary Fund to sanction India's economic aid for its poor human rights record.
105. *World Sikh News*, 10 September 1993. See the statement by Michael Van Wanj Van Praag, UNPO chairman.
106. *Khalsa*, December 1991. The Norwegian Institute of International Affairs held the seminar in cooperation with the International Peace Research Institute, Amnesty International and Sikh representatives Dr G. S. Aulakh, Col. Partap Singh, Dr D. P. Singh, editor of the *Voice of Khalistan*, Thomas Eriksen of PRIO, Dr Neumann and Dr Skar, the NUPI director.
107. Gunnar Skaug's letter concerned Col. Partap Singh, who attended the seminar at the invitation of the International Institute of International Affairs (NUPI). After his return he formed the Khalsa Raj Party "for a free and independent Khalistan". Its means were clearly stated as "peaceful, democratic and non-violent. . . . According to rules of free, democratic societies, Col. Partap Singh broke no law. Rather, he exercised his democratic right to free speech. Furthermore as Norway and India are trading partners and India is one of our major aid-receiving countries, we strongly feel it to be our moral duty to act on these issues. . . . In view of these facts, your excellency, I am compelled to admonish the Indian government for its violation of human rights".

# Chapter 8

1. These passages are from the Gadr song collections.
2. A song among many by *dhadi-jatha* of Mohan Singh Khiali, from the Midlands.
3. See Thandi (1996) for a brief discussion of a Coventry gurdwara's disputes to illustrate this point.
4. *Des Pardes*, 15 August 1987. An International Defence Committee was set up to fight their case. However, according to Gajinder Singh, the leader of the hijackers, they "were more in the mood to make capital out of our case rather than actually helping us". Virtually all the representatives who went to meet them in Lahore jail branded other organizations as "traitors" to the Sikh cause. Gajinder Singh wrote regularly from Lahore jail to *Sikh Pariwar*, the Dal Khalsa monthly. Gajinder's companions are now refugees in Europe.
5. Popular quotations which invariably form part of such literature are *Koī kisī ko rāj na de hai, jo lai nij bal se le hai* (Nobody is offered sovereignty, it

is gained by force); or *Je jinde pat lathī jāye, tetā harām jetā mūh khāye* (If life is full of humiliation, more dastardly to accept such conditions of living); or *Rāj binā nā dharam chale hai, dharam binā sabh dale male hai* (Without a state, religion cannot be protected, nor a state can be administered without religious guidance).

6. B. S. Mahal in *World Sikh News*, 16 April 1993.
7. Government of India (1984), White Paper, pp. 35–42.
8. See *Sikhs in their homeland* (1984), a government-sponsored pamphlet, widely circulated among overseas Sikhs.
9. Letter from the Indian High Commission, London, to Clare Short MP (Birmingham, Ladywood), 2 July 1984.
10. Kuldip Nayar (1985: 391–2): "Most of the Sikhs have not come round; . . . cut off from India and getting their information through sketchy reports in newspapers and rumours, the Sikhs abroad have only a one-sided story of what has happened in Punjab. I have never heard from anyone such exaggerated accounts of Operation Bluestar and the killings in Delhi and elsewhere in the wake of Mrs Gandhi's assassination as in the United States and Canada. . . . They are not at all in touch with reality and live in a make-believe world of their own. The divide between the Sikhs and the Hindus visible in the Punjab is visible abroad as well. The Hindus do not visit the Sikh gurdwaras and the old Punjabi spirit is lacking".
11. Chopra (1985: 337) in Amrik Singh (1985): "The majority of Sikhs living abroad . . . have suffered great anguish and have held fast to their sense of responsibility and reality and have continued to realise that it is within India that the Sikhs have to work out their new destiny, and however difficult the task or imperfect the results, no other destiny holds better promise for them. But some of those who are abroad, have seized the opportunity to dance upon the agony of the Sikhs living in India. Their numbers are small, but they can be divided into three categories: fools, knaves and buffoons".
12. Kshitish (1984: 139–43): "The army was investigating reports that a few days before the army action, there had been a meeting at the Golden Temple between Jarnail Singh Bhindranwale, the self-appointed president of Khalistan, Jagjit Singh Chauhan, Ganga Singh Dhillon and a Pakistan General. The documents recovered from the basement of the Akal Takhat indicate . . . three had briefed Bhindranwale in detail about how the last phase of the Khalistan conspiracy was to be accomplished".
13. The *Times of India*, 9 October 1991, termed the Khalistani media as "subversive", citing both Punjabi and English language publications which were "trying to undermine India's image as a democracy". It also reported on the Associated Press report of 27 June 1991 about ten new would-be nations: Lithuania, Estonia, Latvia, Croatia, Georgia, Khalistan, Kurdistan, Eritrea, Slovenia and Tamil.

NOTES

14. *India Abroad*, 7 December 1990. It describes Dr Aulakh's work as a lobbyist, "Obsession: creating Khalistan: indefatigable lobbyist is nemesis of Indian officials". According to the paper, Dr Aulakh left his job as a medical researcher at Harvard University to espouse the call for a separate Sikh state.

15. *World Sikh News*, 16 April 1993. B. S. Mahal from Quebec wrote: "The leitmotif running through the five pamphlets of the proxy war paints a totally one sided picture of the insurgency in Punjab. Punjab's problems, complex and pregnant with nuances, have been reduced to one issue only, namely, law and order. Even given that, all the killings, brutality, human rights violations, extortion, bombings etc., are laid at the feet of the Sikh separatists aka Sikh terrorists. . . . A distinction, however, needs to be made between the ruler and the ward. The former ought never to sin, the latter may err and will be forgiven. Such distinction exists not in the Indian governance".

16. D. S. Gill, preface to *Indo-us shadow over Punjab*, 1992, viii.

17. Recent fiction has added, in its small ways, towards a portrayal of Sikhs as terrorists. In her novel *Jasmine*, Mukherjee (1991), a distinguished professor of literature at Berkeley, describes the heroic struggle of a Punjabi girl's settlement into America. She posits a Sikh terrorist at strategic breaks in her narrative. Her heroine's "progressive and anti-feudal" husband is murdered by Sikh "hit men", and when she is about to fall in love with a learned man in New York, her love is thwarted by a Sikh terrorist's appearance. Salman Rushdie's (1988) controversial novel *The Satanic Verses* narrates cryptically a Sikh terrorist's fantasy in an aeroplane. Sharma (1986) in *Days of the Turban* sends a Sikh, the central character of his novel, to Europe to join the gun running and drug trafficking carried out by Sikh terrorists.

18. *World Sikh News*, August 1986.

19. Ishtiaq Ahmed (1996: vii) obtained a grant from the Swedish Agency for Research Cooperation (SAREC) with developing countries for a research project on Sikh politics in 1986. The Indian ambassador lodged an oral complaint to the Foreign Office, alleging that such research was deterimental to Indian interests, and SAREC's decision to support conflicted with its aims of promoting cooperation between Sweden and a developing country.

20. Dharam's son was jailed for the Vancouver shooting of Tara Singh Hayer, editor of a Punjabi weekly. Dharam became a controversial figure and was alleged to be the leader of a cult at his large study centre.

21. Text of a resolution passed at Sacramento on 28 July 1991.

22. Chuhan (1984). "As a British citizen", Chuhan argued, "while he has no right to pass any judgements on the suitability of the Anandpur resolution; however, its clause no. 10 takes away the inheritance from the female sex. It is wrong, sexually discriminatory and above all against the

distinctive feature of Sikhism under which both members of both sexes are treated equally". He went on: "I realise practical difficulties experienced by farmers in the provision of Hindu Succession Act of 1956. The only alternative is to seek a better legislation and not to take away the right of inheritance of the female section of the society". Chuhan conjectured (correctly) that the "drafting committee was all male".

23. London School of Economics, *The Khalistan Society*, 1995.
24. *Des Pardes*, June–July 1984. Dr Tejpal Singh, Dr Amrit Singh, Dr Rajinder Pal Singh, Dr Piara Singh and Dr Amarjit Singh, three medical experts and two engineers, applied for American citizenship in protest against the Indian army action at the Golden Temple. In a statement they said, "India is now like a foreign land to us. American Sikhs have no relation with India".
25. *Times*, 6 July 1984.
26. *Indo-Canadian Times*, 31 August 1984. This is a poem by Anant Kanpuri from New York. Another poet, Ajit Rahi from Australia, wrote:

> . . . by a canal bridge, after deliberate killing
> an encounter is announced
> how far is the day
> when your horrible deeds will rebound . . .
> O, murderer, how poor you are,
> how pitiful the hope
> to link state's survival
> by eliminating us all. (*Des Pardes*, 7 February 1986)

Sher Singh Kanwal, an American Sikh, expressed his anguish at the destruction of the Akal Takhat:

> It's not the Akal Takhat – an immortal throne that you destroyed
> It's my heart you have wounded
> The demolished house of my god will ensure
> India will perish in the dust (*Des Pardes*, April 1985, Vaisākhī edition)

27. *Des Pardes*, 18 January 1985.
28. See Pettigrew (1992a: 87). The following song recorded by a Derby-based group is typical of many in circulation:

> Till we breathe our last
> we promise to fight
> our aim is independence
> our destiny and honour

29. An example of outrage felt by individuals is the case of Dr G. S. Birk. With a doctorate in computer technology from Manchester University, he quit his lucrative New York job. During the visit of Indian Prime

NOTES

Minster Rajiv Gandhi to America, Dr Birk and four associates were arrested under "threat to US national security" and jailed. See *Indo-Canadian Times*, 19 June 1987.

30. Darling (1934: 50): "The pride or izzat is one of the Punjabi's deepest feelings and as such must be treated with great respect. Dearer to him than life, it helps to make him the good soldier that he is. But it binds him to the vendetta". The calls for "revenge" point towards social and cultural norms; such expressions need comparative analysis with other groups.
31. *Indo-Canadian Times*, 17 November 1985. The ISYF appeal for its annual convention on 10 November 1985.
32. *Indo-Canadian Times*, 25 October 1985.
33. *Awaz-e-Quam*, 25 April 1991. It says, "Acting upon the commands of the Sikh Nation's War Cabinet – the Panthic Committee, chosen by the *Sarbat Khalsa* at Sri Akal Takhat on 26 January and 29 April 1986, the Council of Khalistan – the political wing of the Panthic Committee is holding a Khalistan Day Rally and International Conference on 27–28 April 1991. To carry the Sikh struggle forward, it will review the struggle so far and plan for the future".
34. Dr Harbans Singh Saraon, "Impact of operation Bluestar on Sikh psyche", *World Sikh News*, 19 February 1988.
35. *World Sikh News*, 19 February 1988.
36. Text of a letter by Molla Singh, president of the Shiromani Akali Dal Association of Canada, to Rt. Hon. John Roberts, secretary of state, government of Canada, 23 August 1977; quoted in Cambell (1977).
37. *Indo-Canadian Times*, 8 October 1982; *Indo-Canadian Times*, 21 September 1982. Letter from Kirpal Singh, *jathedar* of the Akal Takhat, Amritsar.
38. Khalsa Diwan Society, Vancouver, *Annual Report* 1982. It carried a photo of *Shahidi Jatha* (Delegation of Martyrs) for the Punjab. Singh Randhawa, Amar Singh Thind, Kehar Singh Bains, Buta Singh Panesar, Mehar Singh Gill, Thaman Singh Brar went to take part in the Punjab autonomy campaign. Each person is carrying a kirpan.
39. Khalsa Diwan Society, Vancouver, *Annual Report* 1984. The report has photos of General Shahbheg Singh and Amrik Singh. It proclaimed that the Indian government has "decided to annihilate the Sikh nation, and Sikhs are determined to fight". It notifies that 198 persons took *Amrit* during the year. The back page carries a photo of Mewa Singh with the caption "A Sikh martyr of Canada, born in Lopoke, Amritsar, hanged in New Westminster BC, Canada in October 1914".
40. *Annual Report* for Surrey gurdwara 1987, p. 2. The national anthem of Sikhs, "Grant me this boon, O'lord" is paralleled with the Canadian national anthem, "O Canada, our home and native land, true patriot love in all thy sons command".
41. *World Sikh News*, 29 January 1991. It describes the ceremony in Hague on

277

24 June 1993 in the presence of Lord Ennals, HSF Prince Hans-Adam II of Liechtenstein, Ireland's Nobel peace prizewinner, M. Corrigan Maguire, and many other dignitaries. The UNPO was set up in 1989 and has seen four of its members become independent: Estonia, Armenia, Georgia and Latvia. The UNPO is funded by American and European foundations and the $1,000 fees it charges from its members. Its 39 members represent 130 million people, "the oppressed, the colonised, the neglected and rebellious flag-bearing delegates from five continents" who are "diplomatic outcasts, unwelcome in the international bodies where their fate is discussed". *Time*, 1 February 1993, quotes the UNPO secretary-general, Michael van Walt, saying "there are some 5,000 distinct peoples in the world, but fewer than 200 states . . . many groups want only basic human rights . . . but other, fifty, have the historical and political legitimacy to form new separate states". It further quotes a Sanjak Muslim at the UNPO, "I realised we are not the only ones to go through hard moments. I was touched by the Indians from America, by the men from Khalistan, and I had never before heard of Scania".

42. *World Sikh News*, 19 February 1988.

43. The almost random selection of news relating to European Sikhs which appeared in *Des Pardes* in 1986 illustrates this exchange: 70 Belgium Sikhs burned the Indian flag in front of the Indian Embassy on 21 February 1986 (7 March 1986); the German Sikhs protested in Frankfurt on India's independence day (12 September 1986). In Stockholm, Jasbir Singh, editor of *Khalistan News*, a weekly newspaper, sent telegrams to Amnesty International against his deportation (January to March 1986). In the Paris gurdwara, Sant Bhindranwale's photo was removed by Nirankaris and communists on the eve of Indian Prime Minister Rajiv Gandhi's visit to Paris, leading to scuffles. From Oslo, a reader complained about the dearth of Punjabi books in the public library, contrasting with many Hindi books (19 December 1986).

44. They approached Merriam Webster's Dictionary, the American Heritage Dictionary and the Oxford American Dictionary among others.

45. *World Sikh News*, 10 September 1993. Balwinder Singh and Hardeep Singh were deported from Hong Kong after negotiations between India and the Hong Kong government. A special team of Punjab's police brought them back; they struggled with the police, hurting themselves by breaking a glass panel at Bangkok airport. They were forcibly put on a Calcutta-bound aeroplane on 7 September 1993.

46. *Des Pardes*, 30 May 1986. See a letter from Jasbir Singh Sandhu and others in an American jail to British Sikh.

47. *World Sikh News*, 11 February 1994.

48. *Indo-Canadian Times*, 26 April 1985.

49. The *Indo-Canadian Times*, 25 October 1985, reported a communication from Hong Kong concerning the government of India's decision to im-

pound three Sikhs' passports. With a photocopy of the Indian High Commission's letter, it highlighted cases of Gurmukh Singh Dhillon, Daljeet Singh Gill, Balwinder Singh Sahrai. Charan Singh, vice-president of the Khalsa Diwan of Hong Kong, narrated how they were being harassed by the Indian government's action and asked Sikh leaders what to do "if our appeal to Ministry of Foreign Affairs is to be scrapped and put into rubbish bin, then?"

50. *Indo-Canadian Times*, 22 June and 7 July 1984. According to the news report, a resolution for a Sikh state was passed in Sydney and a protest march was held in Melbourne by 300 Sikhs led by Ajit Singh Rahi, Dr Manjit Singh Sekhon, Dr Joginder Singh Sekhon, Shahbeg Singh, Dr J. S. Sidhu and Charan Singh Kooner.

51. *Wangar*, 1993. It reported a Sikh Youth Federation meeting on 24 February 1993, where tributes were paid to martyrs.

52. See Cohen (1997) for an elaboration of characteristics of the "victim diaspora".

53. *Saturday Windsor Star*, 26 September 1987, "Strife stalks the Punjab".

# Glossary and abbreviations

| | |
|---|---|
| Ākāl Takhat | The sacred building opposite the Harimandir. This was severely damaged during the Indian army invasion in June 1984. Rebuilt in haste by the government of India, it was handed back to Sikh priests in October 1984. This "government-built" shrine was demolished again by the Sikh priests and community leaders in April 1986 and is now being rebuilt |
| Akālī Dal | A major political party of the Sikhs formed in the 1920s. Its full name is Shiromani Akali Dal. Factions usually take the name of leader, e.g. Akali Dal (Mann) |
| akhand pāth | Continuous reading of the Guru Granth from beginning to end in about 48 hours |
| amrit | Sikh form of initiation rites |
| amrit-dhāri | A baptized Sikh wearing five Ks |
| anand | Sikh marriage ritual |
| Baisākhī | An important day in the Sikh calendar; in April 1699 the Khalsa was raised by the last guru, Gobind Singh |
| bhaī | Brother, title of respect |
| bhangrā | A folk dance of the Punjab |
| bhog | Concluding ceremony in a gurdwara |
| CPI | Communist party of India |
| CPI(R) | Communist party of India (Right) |

| | |
|---|---|
| CPI(L) | Communist party of India (Left) |
| chamār | A traditional low caste among the Sikhs; also called Chūhrhā |
| Congress | Indian National Congress; a major political party since the 1920s, it split in the 1970s. Factions take the name of the leader e.g. Congress (I), Indira (Gandhi) faction |
| DBYH | Desh Bhagat Yadgar Hall, Jalandhar – a Gadr party memorial |
| dhādī | Traditional bards |
| dharam | Religion |
| Gadr/Ghadar | A political movement among Indian migrants in the Pacific states during 1913–7; also spelled *Gadr* or *Ghadhar* |
| ghallūghārā | Two major massacres of Sikhs in 1742 and 1762 |
| giddhā | A folk dance of Punjabi women |
| granthī | An employee at the gurdwara rendering essential services |
| gurbanī | Sacred scriptures also called *banī* |
| Gurdwārā | Sikh temple |
| gurū | The divine guide |
| Gurū Granth | The Sikh scriptures compiled by Guru Arjan in 1603–4; also called the *Ādī Granth* |
| gurmatā | A resolution by a representative body of Sikhs |
| Harimandir | The central shrine enclosed by the pool, part of the Golden Temple buildings complex, Amritsar; also called *Darbār* or *Durbār* Sahib |
| Hīr Rānjhā | A popular romantic folktale of Punjab; others are Mirzā Sahiban, Pūran Bhagat, Sassī and Sohnī |
| hukumnāmā | A religious order, issued from the Akal Takhat, Amritsar |
| ISYF | International Sikh Youth Federation |
| izzat | Honour, self-respect, dignity |
| Jalandhar | A district in central Punjab, also spelled Jullundur |
| Jathedār | Head or head priest, e.g. the *jathedar* of the Akal Takhat, Amritsar |

| | |
|---|---|
| jujhārū | Hero, militant; another recently popularized word is *khārhkū* |
| Kakkas | Five items of Khalsa dress: *Kachā, Kes, Kanghā, Kirpān, Karā* |
| Kabaddī | A popular game of Punjab |
| kes-dhārī | A Sikh who keeps his or her hair |
| Khālsā | Collective name given to Sikh society; also called *Khālsā-Panth* or *Gurū Panth* |
| KDS | Khalsa Diwan Society; first established in 1907 in Vancouver |
| Khalistān | Land of the Khalsa; the name of the Sikh homeland comprising perhaps the present Punjab and some surrounding areas |
| kirpān | Sword or dagger worn as part of the five Ks |
| kīrtan | Singing of hymns |
| langar | Free kitchen attached to every gurdwara from which food is served to all |
| mazhabī | The Sikh caste of the sweeper class |
| mīrī-pīrī | Doctrine of temporal and spiritual authority |
| monā | A Sikh who cuts his or her hair |
| morchā | Campaign |
| nām | The divine name |
| Nāmdhārī | A Sikh sect |
| Nirankārī | Another Sikh sect |
| panj piāre | The cherished five; five Sikhs of good standing chosen to represent a *sangat* |
| Panth | Literally path, a collective name for the Sikhs; also used as *Khālsā-Panth, Gurū-Panth* or *Sikh Panth* |
| pardes | Foreign country |
| Pingalwārā | A well-known home for the destitute in Amritsar |
| qaum | Nation, a community or people, sometimes spelled *quam* |
| rāgī | Traditional hymn singers in a gurdwara |
| Rāmgharīā | A social group among the Sikhs whose traditional occupation was of carpenters and artisans |

283

| | |
|---|---|
| Rahit Maryādā | The Sikh code of conduct approved in the 1950s |
| SGPC | Shiromanī Gurdwārā Parbandhak Committee, an elected body of Sikhs which has managed historic gurdwaras in Punjab, Haryana and Himachal Pradesh since 1925 |
| sabhā | An association or society |
| sahaj-dhārī | A nonbaptized Sikh |
| sangat | Sikh congregation; also called *sādh-sangat* or *gurū-sangat* |
| sant | A holy man |
| Sat srī akāl | A common form of Sikh greeting. Another greeting is used when addressing the *sangat* or the Sikh congregation: *Wahegurū jī kā, Khalsa, wahegurū jī kī fateh* |
| shahīd | A martyr; also shahīdī, martyrdom |
| shudhī | A characteristic form of Hindu rites to convert untouchables |
| Singh Sabhā | Sikh reform movement initiated in 1873 |
| Udasī | A sect tracing their lineage from Nanak's son, Sri Chand |
| watan | Homeland; a similar word is *des*, meaning a country |

# Bibliography

## Official and semiofficial publications

### Canada

House of Commons, Parliamentary Select Committee. *Proceedings relating to Visible Minorities*, 1986.

*House of Commons, Official Reports*, 1984–1996.

*Extradition Treaty between Canada and India*. Ottawa: Queen's Printer for Canada, 1989. (Treaty Series 1987, no. 14).

Canada: Immigration and Refugee Board Documentation and Research Branch.

*India: Sikhs outside Punjab. 1992.*

——— *Information on the treatment on return by Indian authorities of unsuccessful Sikh refugee claimants*. 25 March 1994.

——— *India: Sikhs in Punjab: 1994–95*, 1996.

——— Annual reports, 1985–95.

### India

Government of India. *Army in India Committee*, 1912, vol. III.

——— *White Paper on the Punjab agitation*. New Delhi: Government of India Press, 1984.

——— *The Sikhs in their Homeland: India*. New Delhi, 1984.

——— *Memorandum of settlement on Punjab, July 25, 1985*. New Delhi: Government of India Publications, 1985.

——— *Lok Sabha proceedings and debates*, 1984–1995.

——— *Selected speeches and writings of Rajiv Gandhi, 1984–95*. New Delhi, Government of India, Publications Division, 1987.

National Human Rights Commission of India, *Report on visit to Punjab*, 25 July 1994.

Committee for Information and initiative on Punjab, New Delhi. *State terorism in Punjab; a report*. 1989. 61p.

People's Union for Democratic Rights (PUDR) and People's Union for Civil Liberties (PUCL). New Delhi. *Who are the guilty? Report of a Joint Inquiry into the causes and impact of the riots in Delhi from 31 October to 10 November*. Delhi: 1984.

———*1984 Carnage in Delhi: a report on the aftermath*. November 1992.

## Punjab

All-India Sikh Students Federation. *Some documents on the demand for the Sikh homeland, basic speeches, writings and press interviews* by Sirdar Kapur Singh, and some other documents. Chandigarh: 1969.

Desh Bhagat Yadgar Committee, Jalandhar *Ghadar party da ithas* (P). Jalandhar: Sahinsra, Gurcharan Singh. et al. 1961.

———*Ghagar dian goojan series* 1–4. n.d.

Government of Punjab. *Facts about the Punjab situation*. Chandigarh: 1986.

———*Gurdeep Singh: statement*. Chandigarh: August 1992.

Gurdwara Parbandhik Committee, Delhi. *The Sikhs: portrait of courage*. Karnail Singh. Gurdwara Parbandhik Committee, Delhi and Sikh Defence Council, 1966.

Northern India Saini Cultural Society. *Directory of Saini Sikhs in UK, USA and Canada*. Chandigarh: 1988.

Punjab, Communist Party of India (Right). *Save Punjab, save India*. n.d.

———*The Punjab crisis and the way out*. 1984.

Punjab Human Rights Organization (PHRO) (from 1992 International Human Rights Organisation, IHRO). *Representation to the president of India on death sentences of Satwant Singh and Kehar Singh, judicial murder?* 1988.

———*Darshan S. Dalla: a case study of how India disregards its courts*. 1990.

———*Sikh villages ransacked: a report on torture by India's security forces*. 1991.

———*I swear: a collection of 20 affidavits on violations of human rights in Punjab*. March 1990.

———*The rape of Punjab: Indian state's indignities on Sikh women and children*. 1989.

———*The fascist offensive in Punjab: reports on human rights violations*. 1989.

———*India dishonours Sikh womanhood*. August 1991.

———*Set free: Ranjit Singh Gill and Sukhminder S. Sandhu, a PHRO appeal to US government*. n.d. (1989).

———*Text of Representation by PHRO to the US Government regarding extradition proceedings against AISSF leaders, Ranjit Singh Gill and Sukhmandir Singh Sidhu*. Ludhiana and London: 1990.

———*Darshan Singh Dalla: a case study of how India disregards its courts*. Ludhiana: 1990.

———*Punjab bulldozed*.

———*Sikhism and human rights*. 1989.

——*I swear . . . : a collection of 20 affidavits on violation of human rights in Punjab*. 1989.

——*The rape of Punjab: Indian indignities on Sikh women and children*. 1989.

——*The fascist offensive in Punjab: reports of human rights violations*. (2 February 1986 to 21 May 1989)

——*The torture chamber in Ladha Kothi*: a report by Justice C. S. Tiwana under Commission of Enquiries Act.

——*They remained disappeared*. n.d.

——*Plebiscite in Punjab: the Sikh case*. 1994.

——*Indo-us Shadow over Punjab*. London, 1992.

Punjab, Jamhurī Adhikār Sabhā, Ludhiana. *Punjab: people fight back: a report to the nation*. 1987.

——*Punjab dā santāp jārī hai* (P). 1991.

——*Punjab: doshī kaun, kaun pahredār* (P). n.d.

——*Kāle kanūn te jamhurī haq* (P). n.d.

Punjab, Nari Manch. *Etī mār pai kurlāne: Punjab vich aurtān te ho rhe sarkārī jbr dā ripot* (P). n.d. 20p. Reproduced by Babbar Khalsa, Birmingham.

Shiromani Gurdwara Parbandhik Committee (SGPC). *Sikh rhit maryādā* (P). 1950.

——*Rehat Maryada: A guide to the Sikh way of life*. Amritsar, 1970.

——*Sikh ate Bhārtī rājnītī* (P). Amritsar: 1974.

——*Desh bhar de vakh vakh shairan vich sikhān te hoye hamlian sbandhī sub kmetī dī ripot* (P). n.d. 22p.

——*Truth about Punjab: SGPC White Paper* (written by Gurdarshan Singh Dhillon). Amritsar, 1996.

Shiromani Akali Dal, Amritsar. *Facts about Punjabi Suba agitation: a collection of memorandums presented before the Das Commission*. Amritsar: SGPC 1965.

——*The Punjab problem: an elucidation*. Hukam Singh. n.d.

——*A plea for Punjab speaking state: a memorandum* by Hukam Singh. Amritsar: Shiromani Akali Dal, n.d.

——*Anandpur Sahib Resolution*. Amritsar: 1978.

## Kenya
Population Census. *Non-African Populations*, vol. IV, 1962.

## United Kingdom
Great Britain: Secretary of State. *Report of the Committee on Emigration from India to the Crown colonies and protectorates*, 1909. Report with Evidence. London: HMSO, 1910. (Cd. 5192–4)

India Committee. *To enquire into the condition of Indian immigrants into the four British colonies; Trinidad, British Guiana or Demerara, Jamaica and Fiji, and in the Dutch colony of Surinam, 1912*. Report. Delhi: MPGOI, 1912. (Cd. 7744–7745)

*Extradition Treaty between the government of the United Kingdom of Great Britain and Northern Ireland and the government of the republic of India.* London: HMSO, 1992. (Cd. 2095)

House of Commons. Debates, 1984–1996

Home Office: Immigration and Nationality Department, Reports, 1984–1997.

## Amnesty International: London

*India: Review of human rights violations.* 1988.
*India: Some recent reports of disappearances.* 1989.
*India: Human rights violations in Punjab, use and abuse of the law.* 1991.
*India: Torture, rape and deaths in custody.* 1992.
*India: An unnatural fate: disappearances and impunity in the Indian states of Jammu and Kashmir and Punjab.* 1993.
India: Punjab police: beyond the bounds of law, May 1995.
*Annual Reports.* 1985–1995.

## Medical Foundation: London

*Lives under threat: a study of Sikhs coming to the UK from the Punjab.* London: Medical Foundation for the Care of Victims of Torture, 1996.

## Minority Rights Group: London

*The Sikhs* (Christopher Shackle) 1985. London: Minority Rights Group, Report no. 65.

## United Nations

UN Commission on Human Rights. *Report on religious discrimination–India.* Geneva: UN Commission on Human rights, E/CN.4/1993/62, 1993.

Secretariat of the Intergovernmental Consultations on Asylum, Refugee and Migration: Luxembourg: *Statistics in Focus.*

Secretariat. *Hearings on Non-Governmental Organisations. Human Rights and the United Kingdom: the challenge to government.* A forum of non-governmental organizations held in advance of the UN World Conference on Human Rights, Vienna, 14–25 June 1993. Bristol: Crantock Communications, 1993.

## United States

US *Congressional Records,* 1985–1996
*United States versus Bopp Franz defendant et al.* London, 1968.
United States: Department of Justice. *India: Sikhs and human rights in India/ Punjab, 1993–94.* Washington: INS Resource Information Center, 1994.
———Country reports on human rights practices for 1994, India. 1995.
———Immigration and Naturalization Service, Annual Reports, 1985–95.

United States: Department of State, Office of Asylum Affairs, Bureau of Democracy, Human Rights and Labor, *India: comments on country conditions asylum claims.* Washington DC, February 1995.

*Asia Watch*
*The Punjab Crisis: Human rights in India.* University Press of America, 1991.

*Human Rights Watch*
*Dead Silence: the legacy of abuses in Punjab.* Washington DC. Physicians for Human rights, 1994.


## Pamphlets, books, manifestos, etc., by diaspora Sikh organizations and individuals

Adil, Bakhshi Singh. *Shiromanī Sūrbīr Sukha Singh* (P). Published by Swaran Singh Saggu, Birmingham. n.d.

Ashok, Shamsher Singh 1987. *Mazbī Sikhān dā itihās* (P). Published by Kartar Singh Nayar, Southall.

Babbar Khalsa International. *Khalsa shall rule.* Birmingham. n.d.

——*Case for Khalistan*, by Surjan Singh. Vancouver: Babbar Khalsa, 1982.

——*Zālam nū Wangār* (P), by Nirmal Singh Narur (a collection of poems). Germany: Babbar Khalsa International. n.d. (1991?).

——*Aj de Ūdham Singh* (P). n.d. (1992).

Bains, Ajit Singh. 1988. *Siege of the Sikhs: violation of human rights in Punjab.* Toronto: New Magazine Publishing.

Bains, Hardial 1985. *The call of the martyrs: on the crisis in India and the present situation in the Punjab.* London: Workers' Publishing House.

Bawa, Baldev 1994. *Punjabnāmā* (P). Published by the author, Southall.

British Sikh Punjabi Literary Society 1985. *Punjab dā maslā: chār drishtīkon.* Birmingham.

*Canadian Punjabi sāhit te sabhiachār* (P). London, Ontario: Third Eye Publications. 1990.

Chauhan, M. S. 1984. *The genocide of Sikhs in Punjab: where do you stand?* Southall: Sikh Missionary Society.

Chowdhary, Hardip Singh & Anup Singh Choudry 1985. *Sikh pilgrimage to Pakistan: illustrated guide.* London: Gurbani Cassette Centre.

Chuhan, M. S. 1984. *The Sikhs at the crossroads: Kesrī Paper on Sikh demands for right of self-determination.* Gurdwara, North London.

Dalit Sahitya Akademy. *The birth pangs of Khalistan.* Middlesex: International Sikh Youth Federation. n.d.

Dal Khalsa. *Vidhān.* Birmingham. n.d.

————1988. *Jang jarī hai* (P) Gajinder Singh. Birmingham: Sikh sāhit ate sabhiarchārik kendar.

————1990. *Sūraj te Khalistan* (P) Gajinder Singh. Birmingham: Sikh sahit ate sabhiarchārik kendar.

————1990. *Vasīatnāmā* (P) Gajinder Singh. Birmingham: Sikh sahit ate sabhiarchārik kendar.

————*Panj tīr hor* (P). Gajinder Singh. Published by Manmohan Singh, Middlesex. n.d.

Dharam, S. S. 1986. *Internal and external threats to Sikhism*. Arlington, Illinois: Gurmat Publishers.

Dhillon, Ganga Singh 1981. *Presidential address to 54th All India Sikh Educational Conference*, 13–15 March 1981. Published by Ganga Singh Dhillon, Chandigarh.

Dhillon, Ganga Singh 1985. Give us Khalistan and leave us in peace. *Illustrated Weekly of India*, 21 July.

Dilgeer, H. S. 1988. *Khalistan dī twarīkh* (P). Published by the author, Oslo.

Dilgeer, H. S. 1989. *Sikh hijacker* (P). Oslo: Guru Nanak Institute of Sikh Studies.

Dilgeer, H. S. & A. S. Sekhon 1992. *The Sikhs struggle for sovereignty: an historical perspective*. Published by the authors, Edmonton and Oslo. n.d.

*Directory of Saini Sikhs in UK, USA and Canada*. Published by Northern India Saini Cultural Society, Chandigarh. 1988.

Federation of Sikh Societies of Canada. *Proposal for Chair of Sikh Studies*. Vancouver: Federation of Sikh Societies of Canada. 1986.

Friends of Punjab 1978. *Report of preliminary study tour of Punjabi folk art, crafts and architecture*, Spring 1978.

Gurdwara, Handsworth, Birmingham 1984. *A reply to the White Paper*, S. S. Sangha (ed.). Birmingham.

Gurdwara, Leamington Spa 1984. *An eye witness account of the invasion of the Golden Temple, 1984* (Punjabi/English).

Gurdwara, Smethwick 1985. *Why Khalistan*. Smethwick.

Gurutej Singh Khalsa 1985. The Khalsa: its universality. In *Sikh Symposium 1985*, Jarnail Singh (ed.). Willowdale, Ontario: Sikh Educational and Welfare Society.

Hamrahi, Atamjit 1994. *Bartanvī sajan suhelrhe* (P). Ludhiana: Punjabi sahit sabhiyachar kendar.

Hans, Surjit 1986. *Sikh kī karn* (P). Coventry: Punjabi Parkashan.

Indo-Canadian Times 1985. *Sant Jarnail Singh Bhindranwale* (P). Vancouver: Indo-Canadian Publishers.

International Sikh Organization 1988. *US Congress on Sikh struggle for freedom in India*, Raghbir Singh Samagh (ed.). Toronto.

International Sikh Youth Federation 1985. *The betrayal of Sikhs* (written by J. S. Bhullar, G. S. Brar, M. S. Sidhu). Birmingham.

———1985. *Ik sir hor chahīdā* (P). Mohan Singh Kukerpindia. Southall.

———1993. *Akal Takhat dī vār* (P). Gurdev Singh Matharu. Birmingham.

———1994. *Bharat dī akhauti ektā torn wich hī Sikh qaum ate mnukhtā dā bhlā hai.* (P). Toronto and London. (Issued jointly with Dal Khalsa) International Sikh Youth Federation (Damdami Taksal) 1988. *Video of Gurbachan Singh Manochahal.*

———1991? *Ragmālā vivran* (P).

Jaswant Singh (Thekedar). *Nānakvād* (P). Southall. n.d. (1984?)

Kanwal, Sher Singh 1996. *Rāj karegā Khalsa* (P). Published by the author.

Kapoor, S. S. 1984. *The invasion of the Golden Temple.* Middlesex: World Sikh Organisation.

Khalistan Affairs Centre. *Lest we forget.* Washington: Khalistan Affairs Centre. n.d. (1995?)

Khalistan Council, London 1990. *Panthak kmetī valon jārī kite hoye nītī patr* (P). London: Sikh International Centre.

———1985. *Oppression in Punjab* (reproduction of a Citizens for Democracy report to the nation). London.

Khalistan Government-in-exile 1991. *An SOS to world conscience.* Gravesend.

Khalsa Diwan Society, Vancouver. *Annual reports,* 1981–8.

———1945. *Petition of Khalsa Diwan Society for voting franchise.* Vancouver, 25 January 1945, 9p.

Khalsa Human Rights, Leicester. *Annual reports,* 1993–7.

Letters

Harchand Singh Longowal to Khalsa Diwan Society, 1983

Sant Harchand Singh Longowal to Bawa Singh

Sant Bhindranwale to Dr Jagjit Singh, 1984

Gurjit Singh to overseas Sikhs, an open letter

Kirpal Singh, Jathedar Akal Takhat, Amritsar, to Management Committee, Guru Nanak Gurdwara, Surrey BC

Manjit Singh, Jathedar Anandpur Sahib, to Editor *Indo-Canadian Times*

Jathedar Talwandi Sabo to *Indo-Canadian Times*

Parmjit Singh Panjwarh to overseas Sikhs, January 1988

Dr Pashaura Singh to G. S. Tohra, President SGPC, Amritsar, August 1993

Panthic Committee to overseas Sikhs, July 1993

Lote, G. S. 1985. *Khuni churasi.* Birmingham: published by the author.

Makhan Singh, 1969. *History of Kenya's trade union movement to 1952.* Nairobi: East Africa Publishing House.

Makhan Singh 1994. *Khalistan nahin banega.* Published by the author, Derby.

Maksoodpuri, Harbaksh 1989. *Krāntīkārī Sikh lahir ate prti-krāntī.* Chandigarh: Punjab Book Centre.

Mann, Gurdev Singh 1985. *Akāl takhat dī var* (P). Vancouver: Indo-Canadian Publishers.

Narang, Sarup Singh 1990. *Khalistan dī lorh kion* (P). Hitchin: Sikh Educational Council and Southall: Gurdwara Singh Sabha.

National Sikh Society of Ottawa 1983. *Proceedings of the 1980 Sikh Conference*, B. S. Samagh & Gurcharan Singh (eds). Ottawa.

Panchi, Charan Singh. *Sikh Homeland*. Published by the author, Birmingham. n.d. (1977?)

Prashar, Ishar Singh. *Vīhvīn sadī da Rāmgarhīā* . (P). Privately published. n.d. (1991?)

Randhawa, Balhar Singh 1985. *Sādā masīhā* (P). Birmingham.

Randhawa, Balhar Singh. *Sajrīan pairhan* (P). Published by the author, Leicester.

Rehal, Gurdial Singh 1979. *Ramgarhīā itihās* (P). Apra: Ithāsik Tract Society.

Rehal, H. S. *Kis udham te rāj mile* (P). Wolverhampton. n.d.

Sadhu and Sukhpal (eds) 1986. *Jangal de virudh* (P). Amritsar: Pals Parkashan.

Sanathan, S. M. & S. R. Iyengar 1983. *Hindu Sikh conflict in Punjab: causes and cure*. London: Transatlantic India Times.

Shergill, N. S. 1986. *Sikh gurdwaras and Sikh organisations abroad*. Published by the author, Southall.

Sihra, K. S. 1985a *The Sikh Commonwealth*. London.

Sihra, K. S. 1985b *Sikhdom*. South Harrow: Sikh Commonwealth.

Sikh Council of Kenya 1982. Sikhs in sports. *The Sikh*, vol. 10.

Sikh Council of North America 1984. *Sikh dharm te siāsat*. Pritam Singh. Los Angeles.

———1983. *Directory of Sikh Societies and Gurdwaras*. New York.

———1976. *Proceedings of the Sikh Council of North America*.

Sikh Cultural and Educational Society 1985. *Sikh Women's Seminar*. Ontario: Sikh Social and Educational Society.

Sikh Educational Council 1991. *Conference brochure, 1991*. Issued by Dr B. S. Bagga and Dr Pargat Singh, Hitchin.

Sikh Foundation (USA). *Annual Reports.*

Sikh Human Rights Group. *File of Karamjit Singh Chahal*. Southall.

———1985. *Seminar on human rights in India*. London.

Sikh Human Rights Internet 1990. *Disappearances in Punjab*. Reading.

Sikh Missionary Society, Southall. *Annual Reports.*

———1987. *The Turban Victory*, 2nd edn. Sidney Bidwell MP.

Sikh Social and Educational Society 1979. *Proceedings of the Sikh Conference, 1979*. J. Singh, John Spellman, Hardev Singh (eds). Willowdale, Ontario.

———1981. *Proceedings of the Sikh Heritage Conference*. Willowdale, Ontario.

———1984. *Sikh Conference, 1984*. Willowdale, Ontario.

Sikh Society of Cambridge University 1986. *Sikhs, arms and terrorism*. Devinderjit Singh. (Cambridge Research Papers on Sikhism)

Sikh Students Federation 1977. *Afro-Sikhs in Kenya*. Nairobi: Nanak Parkash, Surinder Kaur.

Sikh Study Forum. 1988. London. *Sikh jagat vich fut te is de kārn* (P). Niranjan Singh.

Sikh Union, Nairobi. *Silver jubilee, 1934–1959: souvenir brochure.* Prepared by Narain Singh et al.

Teja Singh 1989. *Jīvan kahānī rāj yogī sant Atar Singh jā māhārāj de varosāe sant Tejā Singh jī dī apnī kalm ton likhī hoi, bhāg dūjā* (P). Kalghī dhar Trust.

Uday Singh, 1987. *The waxing and waning of the Khalistan movement abroad.* Published by the author, Birmingham and Toronto.

Ujjal, Dosanjh. *The East Indian community of Vancouver: a look from within.* Vancouver. n.d.

Unna, Warren 1985. *Sikhs abroad, attitudes and activities of Sikhs settled in USA and Canada.* Calcutta: The Statesman.

University of Toronto, Macauliffe Institute of Sikh Studies 1988. *A survey on racial minorities in Montreal.* Toronto.

World Sikh Organization 1984. *The Constitution.* New York: WSO.

## Newspapers and periodicals

### Canada

*Awaz-e-Qaum* (weekly, Punjabi), Toronto, 1985–

*Canadian Darpan* (weekly, Punjabi), Vancouver, 1984–1988

*Charhdi Kala* (weekly, Punjabi), Vancouver, 1985–

*Indo-Canadian Times* (weekly, Punjabi), Vancouver, 1977–

*Link* (weekly, English), Vancouver. 1984–

*The Sikh Times* (monthly, English), Vancouver, 1985–1988

*The Spokesman* (weekly, English), Toronto, 1984–1985

*The Shashmir-e-Dast* (monthly, English/Punjabi), Vancouver 1985

*The Sikhs: past and present* (Biannual 1991– ). Edmonton. (Eds. Dr. H. S. Dilgeer & Dr. A. S. Sekhon)

*The Truth* (Occasional, English), Quebec, 1985–86.

*Vancouver Sun*, Vancouver.

*The Globe and Mail*, Toronto.

### Great Britain

*Awaz-e-Qaum* (Punjabi weekly) Birmingham, 1986–

*Charcha* (Punjabi monthly) 1984–6

*Des Pardes* (Punjabi weekly) London, 1965–

*Khalistan* (English/Punjabi) London, 1986

*Khalistan News* (English/Punjabi) London, Newsletter of the Khalistan Council, 1984–

*Khalistan Times*, (English) 1983–7, D. S. Parmar (ed.)

*Khalistan Bulletin* (English) 1984–5

*Lalkar* (Punjabi/English quarterly) London, 1968–
*Lokta* (Punjabi/English quarterly) Leicester, 1985–7
*Punjab Times* (Punjabi weekly) London/Derby, 1965–
*Sikh Courier* (biannual) London, 1966–
*Sikh Messenger* (biannual) London, 1983–
*Sikh Pariwar* (Punjabi monthly) Birmingham, 1987–92
*Unity*, London 1985–
*Wangar* (Punjabi monthly) Birmingham, 1987–94.

*The Times*
*The Observer*
*The Guardian*

## Europe
*The Khalsa*, Switzerland, 1985–6
*Shahadat*, Mannheim, Germany, 1987
*Jado-Jahid*, Belgium, 1993–4

## United States
*India Abroad* (weekly) New York, 1985–8
*India Times* (weekly) New York, 1984–5.
*India West* (weekly) Los Angeles
*Sikh Thought*, Missouri, 1985
*World Sikh News* (English/Punjabi weekly) Stockton, 1985–96
*The New York Times*
*The Washington Post*

## Secondary sources

Ahmed, I. 1996. *State, nation and ethnicity in contemporary South Asia*. London: Pinter.
Akbar, M. J. 1985. *India: the siege within: challenges to a nation's unity*. Harmondsworth: Penguin.
Alexander, M. & S. Anand 1979. *Queen Victoria's Maharajah Duleep Singh, 1838–1893*. London: Weidenfeld and Nicolson.
Ali, I. 1988. *Punjab under imperialism*. Princeton, New Jersey: Princeton University Press.
Anderson, B. 1983. *Imagined communities: reflections on the origin and spread of nationalism*. London: Verso.
Anderson, W. K. & Sridhar D. Damle 1987. *The brotherhood in saffron: the Rashtriya Swamyamsevak sangh and Hindu revivalism*. London: Sage.

Appadurai, A. 1990. Disjuncture and difference in the global economy. *Public Culture* **2**(2), 1–20.

Arendt, H. 1973. *The origins of totalitarianism*, 5th edn. New York: Harcourt.

Armstrong, J. A. 1976. Mobilized and proletarian diaspora, *American Political Science Review* **70**(2), 393–408.

Austin, G. 1966. The Indian constitution: cornerstone of a nation. Oxford: Clarendon Press.

Banga, I. 1978. *Agrarian system of the Sikhs: late eighteenth and early nineteenth century*. New Delhi: Manohar.

Barnard, R. 1975. *The Flying Sikh*. Transafrica Publishers.

Barot, R. 1995. The Punjab crisis and Bristol Indians. *International Journal of Punjab Studies* **2**(2), 195–215.

Barrier, N. G. 1971. *Banned: controversial literature and political control in British India*. Columbia, Missouri: University of Missouri Press.

Barrier, N. G. 1989. Sikh emigrants and their homeland. See Barrier & Dusenbery (1989), 49–89.

Barrier, N. G. & V. A. Dusenbery (eds.) 1989. *The Sikh diaspora: migration and the experience beyond Punjab*. Delhi: Chanakya Publications.

Bawa, H. S. 1948. *A plea for a Punjabi speaking province*. New Delhi: the author.

Beetham, D. 1970. *Transport and Turbans: a comparative study of a migrant community*. London: Oxford University Press.

Bhachu, P. 1985. *Twice migrants*. London: Tavistock.

Bharti, J. 1978. Conflict in East Indian community in Toronto, historical overview. *Asiandian* **3**(1), 10–14.

Bhullar, P. 1987. *The Sikh mutiny*. Delhi: Siddarth.

Blaise, C. & B. Mukherjee 1988. *The sorrow and the terror: the haunting legacy of the Air India tragedy*. New York: Penguin.

Bombwall, K. R. 1983. The nation state and ethno-nationalism: a note on the Akali demand for a self-determined political status for Sikhs. *Punjab Journal of Politics* **9**, 166–83.

Brar, Lt. Gen. K. S. 1993. *Operation Bluestar: the true story*. New Delhi: UBS Publications.

Brass, P. 1974. *Language, religion and politics in North India*. Cambridge: Cambridge University Press.

Brass, P. (ed.) 1985. *Ethnic groups and the State*. London: Croom Helm.

Brass, P. 1990. *The politics of India since independence*. Cambridge: Cambridge University Press.

Brass, P. 1991. *Ethnicity and nationalism: theory and experience*. New Delhi: Sage.

Brett, R. 1995. The role and limits of human rights: NGOs at the United Nations. *Political Studies* **XLIII**, 96–110.

Brief, D. 1984. *The Punjab and recruitment to the Indian army, 1846–1918*. MLitt thesis, University of Oxford.

Brown, D. 1994. *The state and ethnic politics in Southeast Asia*. London: Routledge.

Buchignani, N. I. Doreen, R. Srivastava 1985. *Continuous journey: a social history of South Asians in Canada*. Toronto: McClelland and Stewart.

Burlet, S. & H. Reid 1995. Cooperation and conflict: the South Asian diaspora after Ayodhya. *New Community* **21**(4), 587–97.

Calvert, H. 1936. *The wealth and welfare of the Punjab*, 2nd edn. Lahore: Civil and Military Gazette.

Cambell, M. G. 1977. *The Sikhs of Vancouver: a case study in minority–host relations*. MA thesis, University of British Columbia.

Chaddah, M. S. 1982. *Are Sikhs a nation?* Delhi: Delhi Sikh Gurdwara Management Committee.

Chadney, J. G. 1984. *The Sikhs of Vancouver*. New York: AMS Press.

Chaliand, G. (ed.) 1989. *Minority peoples in the age of nation-states*. London: Pluto Press.

Chaliand, G. 1993. *The Kurdish tragedy*. London: Zed Books.

Chary, M. S. 1995. *The eagle and the peacock: US foreign policy towards India*. Westport, Connecticut: Greenwood Press.

Chopra, G. 1928. *The Punjab as a sovereign state*. Lahore.

Chopra, P. 1985. A turning point for Sikhs. In *Punjab in Indian politics*, Amrik Singh (ed.), 331–52. Delhi: Ajanta.

Chopra, V. D., R. K. Mishra, N. Singh 1984. *Agony of the Punjab*. New Delhi: Patriot.

Cohen, R. 1996. Diasporas and the nation-state: from victims to challengers. *International Affairs* **72**(3), 507–20.

Cohen, R. 1997. *Global diasporas: an introduction*. London: UCL Press.

Cohen, S. 1988. The military and Indian democracy. In *India's democracy: an analysis of changing state–society relations*, Atul Kohli (ed.), 125–145. Princeton, New Jersey: Princeton University Press.

Connor, W. 1993. Beyond reason: the nature of the ethnonational bond. *Ethnic and Racial Studies* **16**(3), 373–88.

Connor, W. 1994. *Ethno-nationalism: the quest for understanding*. Princeton, New Jersey: Princeton University Press.

Cunningham, J. D. 1849. *A history of the Sikhs from the origin of the nation to the battle of the Sutlej*. London: John Murray.

Darling, M. 1934. *Wisdom and waste in the Punjab village*. London: Oxford University Press.

Das, V. 1995. *Critical events: an anthropological perspective on contemporary India*. Delhi: Oxford University Press.

Deora, M. S. 1991/2. Akali agitation to Operation Bluestar and aftermath (4 vols). New Delhi: Anmol Publications.

Dewitt, J. Jr 1969. *Indian Workers Associations in Britain*. London: Oxford University Press.

Dhami, M. S. 1977. Political parties and state autonomy issue – a case study of Akali Party. In *National power and state autonomy*, K. R. Bombwall (ed.), 157–78. Meerut.

Dhami, M. S. 1985. Communalism in Punjab: a socio-historical analysis. *Punjab Journal of Politics* **XI**(1), 26–37.

Doreen, I. 1979. South Asian stereotypes in the Vancouver press. *Ethnic and Racial Studies* **2**, 166–89.

Dua, B. 1981. India: a study in the pathology of a federal system. *Journal of Commonwealth and Comparative Politics* **19**(3), 257–73.

Duggal, K. S. 1989. *Ranjit Singh – a secular sovereign.* New Delhi: Abhinav Publications.

Dusenbery, V. A. 1981. Canadian ideology and public policy: the impact of Vancouver Sikh ethnic and religious adaptation. *Canadian Ethnic Studies* **13**(3), 101–19.

Dusenbery, V. A. 1988. Punjabi Sikhs and Gora Sikhs: conflicting assertions of Sikh identity in North America. See O'Connell et al. (eds), 334–55.

Dusenbery, V. A. 1995. A Sikh diaspora? Contested identities and constructed realities. In *Nation and migration: the politics of space in the South Asian diaspora,* Peter van der Veer (ed.), 17–42. Philadelphia: University of Pennsylvania Press.

Embree, A. T. 1972. *India's search for national identity.* New York: Knopf.

Embree, A. T. 1990. *Utopias in conflict.* Berkeley, University of California Press.

Enloe, C. H. 1973. *Ethnic conflict and political development.* Boston: Little, Brown.

Enloe, C. 1977. Ethnic diversity and potential for conflict. In *Diversity and development in Southeast Asia,* G. L. Pauker, Frank H. Golay and Cynthia H. Enloe (eds). New York: McGraw-Hill.

Esman, M. J. 1986. *Diasporas and international relations.* See Sheffer (1986), 333–49.

Esman, M. J. 1992. The political fallout of international migration. *Diaspora* **2**(1), 3–41.

Fair, C. C. 1996. Female foeticide among Vancouver Sikhs: recontextualising sex selection in the north American diaspora. *International Journal of Punjab Studies* **3**(1), 1–44.

Ferguson, C. A. 1975. *A white man's country.* Toronto: Doubleday.

Fox, R. G. 1985. *Lions of the Punjab: culture in the making.* Berkeley: University of California Press.

Fraser, T. G. 1978. The Sikh problem in Canada and its political consequences, 1905–1921. *Journal of Imperial and Commonwealth History* **7**, 35–55.

Frykenberg, R. E. 1993. Hindu fundamentalism and the structural stability of India. In *Fundamentalisms and the state,* Martin Marty & R. Scott Appleby (eds). Chicago: Chicago University Press.

Geertz, C. 1968. The integration revolution: primordial sentiments and civil politics in new states. In *Old societies and new states,* C. Geertz (ed.), Glencoe, Illinois: Free State.

Geertz, C. 1983. *Local knowledge in interpretive anthropology.* New York: Basic Books.

Gill, C. 1983. The birth of the Farmworkers Organising Committee. Unpublished paper, Vancouver.

Gillis, J. R. 1994. *Commemorations: the politics of national identity.* Princeton, New Jersey: Princeton University Press.

Gopal, S. 1993. *The autonomy of confrontation: the rise of communal politics in India.* London: Zed Press.

Gopal, S. 1994. *Politics of Sikh homeland, 1940–1990.* Delhi: Ajanta.

Gough, C. J. S. & A. D. Innes 1887. *The Sikhs and the Sikh wars: the rise, conquest and annexation of the Punjab state.* London: A. D. Innes & Co.

Goulbourne, H. 1991. *Ethnicity and nationalism in post-imperial Britain.* Cambridge: Cambridge University Press.

Gould, H. A. & Sumit Ganguly (eds) 1992. *The hope and the reality: US-Indian relations from Roosevelt to Reagan.* Boulder, Colorado: Westview Press.

Gregory, R. G. 1972. *India and East Africa: a history of race relations within the British Empire, 1890–1939.* London: Oxford University Press for IRR.

Grewal, J. S. 1991. *The Sikhs of the Punjab.* Cambridge: Cambridge University Press.

Grewal, J. S. 1996. *The Akalis – a short history.* Chandigarh: Punjab Studies Publications.

Grewal, J. S. & H. K. Puri (eds) 1974. *Letters of Udham Singh.* Amritsar: Guru Nanak Dev University Press.

Gupta, U. N. (ed.) 1988. *Indian federalism and unity of nation: a review of Indian constitutional experience.* Allahabad: Vohra.

Gurr, T. R. 1993. *Minorities at risk: a global view of ethno-political conflicts.* Washington DC: United States Institute of Peace Studies.

Gurr, T. R. 1994. *Ethnic conflict in world politics.* Oxford: Westview Press.

Hamdard, S. S. 1943. *Azad Punjab.* Amritsar: the author.

Hapke, H. M. 1984. The political economy of Sikh nationalism. *Journal für Entwicklunspolitik* **4**, 13–26.

Harrison, C. W. 1920. *Illustrated Guide to the Federated Malay States.* London.

Hasrat, B. J. 1968. *Anglo-Sikh relations: a reappraisal of the rise and fall of the Sikhs.* Hoshiapur: V. V. Research Institute.

Hawley, J. S. & G. S. Mann (eds) 1993. *Studying the Sikhs: issue for North America.* Albany: State University of New York Press.

Helweg, A. W. 1983. Emigrant remittances: their nature and impact on a Punjab village. *New Community* **10**, 435–43.

Helweg, A. W. 1987. *Sikhs in England: the development of a migrant community,* 2nd edn. Delhi: Oxford University Press.

Helweg, A. W. 1989. Sikh politics in India: the emigrant factor. See Barrier & Dusenbery (1989), 305–36.

Hess, G. R. 1969. The Hindu in America: immigration and naturalization policies and India, 1917–1946. *Pacific Historical Review* **38**, 59–79.

Hill, M. F. 1949. *Permanent way: the story of Kenya and Uganda railway.* Nairobi: East African Literatures Bureau. (Vol. 1, reprinted in 1976)

Hubel, T. 1996. *Whose India? The independence struggle in British and Indian fiction and history*. London: Leicester University Press.

Hyder, S. G. 1991. *The dialectic of crisis*. MA thesis, University of Calgary.

Isemonger, F. C. & J. Slattery 1919. *An account of the Ghadar Conspiracy, 1913– 15*. Lahore: Superintendent, Government Printing.

Jaffrelot, C. 1993. *The Hindu nationalist movement 1925–1990s*. London: Hurst.

Jaijee, I. S. 1995. *Politics of genocide*. Chandigarh: Baba Publishers.

Jalal, A. 1985. *The sole spokesman: Jinnah, the Muslim League and the demand for Pakistan*. Cambridge: Cambridge University Press.

Jalal, A. 1995. *Democracy and authoritarianism in South Asia: a comparative and historical perspective*. Cambridge: Cambridge University Press.

Jeffrey, R. 1987. Grappling with history: Sikh politicians and the past. *Pacific Affairs* **60**, 59–72.

Jeffrey, R. 1994. *What's happening to India: Punjab, ethnic conflict, Mrs Gandhi's death and test for federalism*, 2nd edn. London: Macmillan.

Johnston, H. 1979. *The Voyage of the Komagata Maru: the Sikh challenge to Canada's colour bar*. Delhi: Oxford University Press.

Johnston, H. 1988a. The surveillance of Indian revolutionaries. *BC Studies* **78**, 3–27.

Johnston, H. 1988b. The development of Punjabi community in Vancouver since 1961. *Canadian Ethnic Studies* **XX**(2), 1–19.

Johnston, H. 1988c. Patterns of Sikh migration to Canada: 1900–1960. See O'Connell, et al. (eds), 296–313.

Jones, K. W. 1976. *Arya Dharm: Hindu consciousness in 19th century Punjab*. Berkeley: University of California Press.

Josephides, S. 1991. *Towards a history of Indian Workers Association*. Coventry: Centre for Research in Ethnic Relations, University of Warwick.

Josh, S. S. 1978. *The Hindustan Ghadar Party: a short history* (2 vols). New Delhi: People's Publishing House.

Joshi, B. R. 1985. Washington, Delhi and Sikhs: adventures in wonderland, *Economic and Political Weekly*, 1 June, 954–55.

Joshi, C. 1984. *Bhindranwale: myth and reality*. New Delhi: Vikas.

Joshi, M. 1992. *Combatting terrorism in Punjab: Indian democracy in crisis*. Conflict studies 261. Research Institute for the Study of Conflict and Terrorism, London.

Juergensmeyer, M. 1969. The Ghadar syndrome: immigrant Sikhs and nationalist pride. See Juergensmeyer & Barrier (1969), 173–90.

Juergensmeyer, M. 1982. *Religion as a social vision: the movement against untouchability in 20th century Punjab*. Berkeley: University of California Press.

Juergensmeyer, M. & N. G. Barrier (eds) 1969. *Sikh studies: comparative perspectives on a changing tradition*. Berkeley: Graduate Theological Union, University of California Press.

Kapur, R. 1986. *Sikh Separatism: the politics of the faith*. London: Allen & Unwin.

Kapur S. 1959. *Parasharprasna*. Jullundur: Hind Publishers.

Kapur S. 1966. *Betrayal of the Sikhs*. Delhi: Akali Dal.

Kapur S. 1982. *Sachi Sakhi*. Vancouver: Modern Printing House.

Kashmeri, Z. & B. McAndrew 1989. *The soft target: how the Indian intelligence penetrated Canada*. Toronto: James Lorimer.

Kaur, M. 1983. The Golden Temple: past and present. Amritsar: Guru Nanak Dev University Press.

Kaur, H. 1990. *Bluestar over Amritsar*. Delhi: Ajanta.

Kaur, S. 1977. *Afro-Sikhs in Kenya: Nanak Parkash*. Nairobi: Sikh Students Federation.

Kedourie, E. (ed.) 1970. *Nationalism in Asia and Africa*. London: Frank Cass.

Knott, K. & R. Toon 1982. *Muslims, Sikhs and Hindus in the UK: problems in the estimation of religious statistics*. Religious Research Paper 6. University of Leeds.

Koehn, S. D. 1991. Ethnic emergence and modernisation: the Sikh case. *Canadian Ethnic Studies* **33,** 95–116.

Kohli, A. (ed.) 1988. *India's democracy: an analysis of changing state-society relations*. Princeton, New Jersey: Princeton University Press.

Kohli, A. 1990. *Democracy and discontent: India's growing crisis of governability*. Cambridge: Cambridge University Press.

Kosmin, B. A. 1989. London's Asian MPs: the contrasting career of three Parsee politicians. *Indo-British Review* **16**(2), 27–38.

Kothari, R. 1989. Cultural context of communalism. *Economic and Political Weekly*, 14 November, 83–5.

Kshitish 1984. *Storm in Punjab*. Delhi: World Publications.

Kumar, R. N. & G. Sieberer 1991. *The Sikh struggle: origin, evolution and the present phase*. New Delhi: Chanakya.

Kundu, A. 1994. The Ayodhya aftermath: Hindu versus Muslim violence in Britain. *Immigrants and Minorities* **13**(1), 26–7.

Kux, D. 1992. *India and the United States: estranged democracies, 1941–1991*. Washington DC: National Defense University Press.

La Brack, B. 1988a. *Sants* and the *sant* tradition in the context of overseas Sikh communities. In *The sant: a devotional tradition of India*, K. Schomer & H. McLeod (eds) Berkeley: University of California Press.

La Brack, B. 1988b. *The Sikhs of Northern California: 1904–1986*. New York: AMS Press.

La Brack, B. 1989. The new patrons. See Barrier & Dusenbery (1989), 261–304.

Lal, V. 1996. Sikh kirpans in California schools: the social construction of symbols. *Amerasia* **22**, 57–89.

Leaf, M. 1985. The Punjab crisis. *Asian Survey* **25**, 475–98

Leitner, G. W. 1883. *History of indigenous education in Punjab since annexation and in 1882*. Patiala: Languages Department. Reprinted in 1971.

Leivesley, A. D. W. 1985. *Ravidas community problem in the West Midlands and Northern India*. MPhil thesis, University of Aston in Birmingham.

Leonard, K. 1992. *Making ethnic choices: California's Punjabi Mexican Americans*. Philadelphia: Temple University Press.

Lepervanche, M. M.de 1984. *Indians in a white Australia: an account of race, class and Indian immigration to Eastern Australia*. Sydney: George Allen & Unwin.

Lipton, M. & J. Firn 1975. *The erosion of a relationship: India and Britain since 1960*. London: Royal Institute of International Affairs and Oxford University Press.

Littlejohn, C. Scott 1964. Some aspects of social stratification among the immigrant Punjabi communities of California. In *Culture, change and stability*, R. Beals (ed.), 105–16. Los Angeles: University of California Press.

Lustick, I. 1979. Stability in deeply divided societies: consociationalism versus control. *World Politics* **31**(3), 325–44.

McGarry, J. & B. O'Leary 1993. *The politics of ethnic conflict regulation: case studies of post-colonial conflicts*. London: Routledge.

McLeod, W. H. 1978. On the word Panth: a problem of terminology and definition. *Contributions to Indian Sociology* **12**(2), 287–95.

McLeod, W. H. 1984a. *Punjabi community in New Zealand*. Amritsar: Guru Nanak Dev University Press.

McLeod, W. H. (ed.) 1984b. *Textual sources for the study of Sikhism*. Manchester: Manchester University Press.

McLeod, W. H. 1989. *Who is a Sikh? The problem of Sikh identity*. Delhi: Oxford University Press.

McMahon, R. J. 1994. *The cold war on the periphery: the United States, India and Pakistan*. New York: Columbia University Press.

Madhok, B. 1985. *Punjab problem: the Muslim connection*. New Delhi: Hindu World Publications.

Mahboob, H. S. 1990. *Jhanā dī rāt*. Gardhivala: Harinder Singh Mahboob.

Mahmood, C. K. 1989. Sikh rebellion and the Hindu concept of order. *Asian Survey* **29**, 326–340.

Mahmood, C. K. 1996. *Fighting for faith and nation: dialogues with Sikh militants*. Philadelphia: University of Pennsylvania Press.

Malik K. N. & P. Robb (eds) 1994. *India and Britain: recent past and present challenges*. New Delhi: Allied Publishers.

Mangat, J. S. 1969. *A history of the Asians in East Africa 1886 to 1945*. Oxford: Oxford University Press.

Mani, V. S. 1995. Indo-British treaty. *International Studies* **32**(2), 139–50.

Mann, J. S. & H. S. Saraon 1988. *Advanced studies in Sikhism*. Irvine, Calif.: Sikh Community of North America.

Mann, J. S. & Kharak Singh 1990. *Recent researches in Sikhism*. Patiala: Punjabi University.

Mann, J. S. (ed.) 1969. *Some documents on the demand for the Sikh Homeland*. Chandigarh: Jaswant Singh Mann.

Manor, J. 1993. The BJP in South India: the 1991 election. *Economic and Political Weekly*, 22 May, 1019–20.

Marienstras, R. 1989. On the notion of diaspora. In *Minority peoples in the age of nation-states,* Gerrard Chaliand (ed.), 119–25. London: Pluto Press.

Mills, K. 1996. Permeable borders: human migration and sovereignty. *Global Society* **10**(2), 77–106.

Mukherjee, B. 1991. *Jasmine.* London: Virago.

Mulgrew, I. 1988. *Unholy terror: the Sikhs and international terrorism.* Toronto: Key Porter Books.

Nandy, A. 1988. The politics of secularism and the recovery of religious tolerance. *Alternatives* **13**(3), 177–94.

Nandy, A. 1990. The discreet charm of Indian terrorism, *Journal of Commonwealth and Comparative Politics* **XXVIII**(1), 25–43.

Nandy A. & Shikha Trivedi 1995. *Creating a nationality: the Ramjanambhumi movement and the fear of the self.* New Delhi.

Narang, A. S. 1983. *Storm over the Sutlej: the Akali politics.* New Delhi: Gitanjali.

Nayar, B. R. 1966. *Minority politics in the Punjab.* Princeton, New Jersey: Princeton University Press.

Nayar, B. R. 1968. Punjab. In *State politics in India,* Marion Weiner (ed.), 433–502. Princeton, New Jersey: Princeton University Press.

Nayar, K. 1985. After the accord in Patwant Singh (ed.), 390–402.

Nayar, K. 1991. *India House.* New Delhi: Penguin.

Nayar, K. & Khushwant Singh 1984. *Tragedy of Punjab: Operation Bluestar and After.* New Delhi: Vision Books.

Neville, M. *India and the Nagas.* Report 17. Minority Rights Group, London. n.d.

Noorani, A. G. 1984. Civil liberties: the terrorist ordinance, *Economic and Political Weekly,* August, 1188–9.

Oberoi, H. S. 1987. From Punjab to Khalistan: territoriality and metacommentary. *Pacific Affairs* **60**(1), 26–41.

Oberoi, H. 1988. From ritual to counter ritual: rethinking the Hindu-Sikh question 1884–1915. See O'Connell et al. (eds), 136–58.

Oberoi, H. 1993. Sikh fundamentalism: translating history into theory. In *Fundamentalisms and the State.* Martin E. Marty & R. Scott Appleby (eds), 256–85. Chicago: Chicago University Press.

Oberoi, H. 1994. *The construction of boundaries: culture, identity, and religious diversity in the Sikh tradition.* Delhi: Oxford University Press.

O'Connell, J. T. 1988. Postscript: comments from Toronto. See O'Connell, et al. (eds), 442–6.

O'Connell, J. T. 1996. The fate of Sikh studies in North America. In *The transmission of Sikh heritage in the Diaspora,* P. Singh and N. G. Barrier (eds), 269–88. New Delhi: Manohar.

O'Connell, J. T., M. Israel, Willard G. Oxtoby (eds) 1988. *Sikh history and religion in the twentieth century.* Toronto: Centre for South Asian Studies, University of Toronto.

O'Dwyer, M. 1925. *India as I knew it*. London: Constable.

O'Leary, B. & A. Paul 1990. Introduction; Northern Ireland as the site of state and nation-building failures. In *The future of Northern Ireland*, John McGarry & Brendan O'Leary (eds). Oxford: Clarendon Press.

Oren, S. 1974. The Sikhs, Congress and the Unionists in British Punjab, 1937–1945. *Modern Asian Studies* **8**(3), 397–418.

Pettigrew, J. 1987. In search of a new kingdom of Lahore. *Pacific Affairs* **60**(1), 1–25.

Pettigrew, J. 1991. Betrayal and nation-building among the Sikhs. *Journal of Commonwealth and comparative politics* **XXIX**(1), 25–43.

Pettigrew, J. 1992a. Songs of the Sikh resistance movement. *Asian Music*, Fall/Winter, 85–118

Pettigrew, J. 1992b. Martyrdom and guerilla organisation in Punjab. *Journal of Commonwealth and Comparative Politics* **30**(3), 387–406.

Pettigrew, J. 1995. *The Sikhs of the Punjab: unheard voices of state and guerrilla violence*. London: Zed Books.

Pollock, S. 1993. Ramayana and political imagination in India. *Journal of Asian Studies* **52**(1) 260–75.

Popplewell, R. 1988. The surveillance of Indian revolutionaries in Great Britain and on the Continent, 1905–1914. *Intelligence and National Security* **3**(1), 56–76.

Puri, H. K. 1994. *Ghadar movement: ideology, organisation and strategy*, 2nd edn. Amritsar: Guru Nanak Dev University Press.

Randhawa, M. S. 1954. *Out of ashes: an account of the rehabilitation of refugees from West Pakistan in rural areas of East Punjab*. Chandigarh: Public Relations Department, Government of Punjab.

Reeves, F. 1989. *Race and local borough politics*. Aldershot: Avebury.

Rubinoff, A. G. (ed.) 1988. *Canada and South Asia: issues and opportunities*. Toronto: Centre for South Asian Studies, University of Toronto.

Rubinoff, A. G. (ed.) 1992. *Canada and South Asia: political and strategic relations*. Toronto: Centre for South Asian studies, University of Toronto.

Rudolph, L. I. & S. H. Rudolph 1988. Confessional politics, secularism and centrism in India. In *Fundamentalism, revivalism and violence in South Asia*, James K. Bjorkman (ed.), 75–87. Riverdale Co.

Rushdie, S. 1988. *The Satanic Verses*. London: Viking.

Safran, W. 1991. Diaspora in modern societies: myths of homeland and return. *Diaspora* **1**(1), 83–99.

Said, A. A. (ed.) 1977. *Ethnicity and us foreign policy*. New York: Praeger.

Said, A. A. & L. R. Simmons 1976. *Ethnicity in an international context: the politics of dissociation*. New Brunswick, New Jersey: Transaction Books.

Saini, R. S. 1994. Custodial torture in law and practice with reference to India. *Journal of the Indian Law Institute* **36**(2), 166–92.

Sandhu, K. S. 1969. *Indians in Malaya: some aspects of their immigration and settlement, 1786–1957*. Cambridge: Cambridge University Press.

Sandhu, K. S. 1970. Sikh immigration into Malaysia during British rule. In *Studies in the social history of China and South-East Asia*, J. Chen & N. Tarling (eds), 335–54. Cambridge: Cambridge University Press.

Sarhadi, A. S. 1971. *Punjabi Suba: the story of the struggle*. Delhi: Uttar Chand Kapur.

Sathyamurthy, T. V. 1984. *Centre–state relations with special reference to India: the case of Punjab*. Derap Working Papers, Bergen.

Sathyamurthy, T. V. 1985. Indian nationalism and the "national question". *Millennium: A Journal of International Studies* **14**(2), 172–94.

Sethi, R. M. 1992. The perception of popular justice through state power and the counter legal systems. *Social and Legal Studies* **1**, 307–20.

Shain, Y. 1994. Marketing the democratic creed abroad; US diasporic politics in the era of multiculturalism. *Diaspora* **3**(1), 85–111.

Sharma, P. 1986. *Days of the turban*. London: Bodley.

Sheffer, G. (ed.) 1986. *Modern diasporas in international politics*. London: Croom Helm.

Shrivastava, B. K. 1993. Indo-American relations: search for a new equation. *International Studies* **30**(2), 215–34.

Siddharth, V. 1992. New Indo-British extradition treaty: what is the purpose? *Economic and Political Weekly*, 21 November, 2531–2.

Sidhu, M. S. 1983. Sikhs in Peninsular Malaysia: their distribution and occupations. *Asian Profile* **11**, 293–307.

Sidhu, M. S. *The Sikhs in Kenya*. Chandigarh: Punjab University Press. n.d.

Silverman, J. 1989. The India League in the freedom movement. *Indo-British Review* **16**(2), 47–56.

Simeon, D. 1994. Tremors of intent: perceptions of the nation and community in contemporary India. *Oxford Literary Review* **16**(1–2), 225–45.

Singh, A. (ed.) 1985. *Punjab in Indian politics: issues and trends*. New Delhi: Ajanta.

Singh, G. *The Sikhs of Fiji*. Suva: South Pacific Social Science Association. n.d.

Singh, G. (ed.) 1980. *Maharaja Duleep Singh's Correspondence*. Patiala: Panjabi University Press.

Singh, G. 1984. *Communism in Punjab: a study of the movement up to 1967*. Delhi: Ajanta.

Singh, G. 1987. Understanding the Punjab problem. *Asian Survey* **27**, 1268–77.

Singh, G. 1992. The Punjab elections, 1992: breakthrough or breakdown. *Asian Survey* **32**, 988–99.

Singh, G. 1995. The Punjab crisis since 1984: a reassessment. *Ethnic and Racial Studies* **18**, 476–93.

Singh, G. 1997. The Punjab legislative assembly elections of February 1997: the BJP's regional road to power? *Contemporary South Asia* **6**(3), 273–83.

Singh, G. & G. L. Singh 1946. *The idea of the Sikh state*. Lahore: Lahore Book Shop.

Singh, G. & I. Talbot (eds) 1996. *Punjabi identity: continuity and change.* New Delhi: Manohar.

Singh, G. 1960. *A unilingual Punjabi state and the Sikh unrest.* New Delhi: Super Press.

Singh, H. 1983. *The heritage of Sikhs* (revised edition). Bombay: Asia Publishing House.

Singh, I. 1986. *Punjab under siege: a critical analysis.* New York: Allen McMillan and Enderson.

Singh K. & G. S. Dhillon 1992. See Singh, K. (1992), 187–92.

Singh, K. 1962. *Ranjit Singh: Maharajah of the Punjab, 1780–1839.* London: George Allen & Unwin.

Singh, K. 1966. *A History of the Sikhs* (2 vols). Delhi: Oxford University Press.

Singh, K. 1992. *My bleeding Punjab.* Delhi: UBS Publishers.

Singh, M. *Soldiers contribution to Indian independence: the epic of the Indian National Army.* New Delhi: Army Educational Stores. n.d.

Singh, N. (ed.) 1987–9. *Malve de lok gīt* (4 vols). Patiala: Punjabi University Press.

Singh, N. G. K. 1993. *The feminine principle in the Sikh vision of the transcendent.* London: Cambridge University Press.

Singh, P. & N. G. Barrier (eds) 1996. *The transmission of Sikh heritage in the diaspora.* New Delhi: Manohar.

Singh, P. & Malik H. 1985. *Punjab: the fatal miscalculation.* Delhi: Patwant Singh.

Singh, P. 1966. *A need for a Sikh Homeland.* Patiala: Prem Singh.

Singh, P. 1992. Economic interests and human rights in Indo-British relations: House of Commons debate on Punjab. *Economic and Political Weekly,* 28 March, 631–6.

Singh, S. 1946. *The Sikhs demand their Homeland.* Lahore: Lahore Book Shop.

Singh, T. M. 1945. *Meri yaad* (P). Amritsar: Sikh Religious Book Society.

Smith, A. D. 1981a. War and ethnicity: the role of warfare in the formation of self-images and cohesion of ethnic communities. *Ethnic and Racial Studies* **4**, 375–97.

Smith, A. D. 1981b. States and homelands: the social and geopolitical implications of national territory. *Millennium: A Journal of International Studies* **10**, 187–202.

Smith, A. D. 1983. *State and nation in the third world.* London: Wheatsheaf Books.

Smith, A. D. 1986. *The ethnic origin of nations.* Oxford: Blackwell.

Smith, D. E. 1963. *Secularism in India.* Princeton, New Jersey: Princeton University Press.

Smooha, S. 1990. Minority status in an ethnic democracy: the status of the Arab minority in Israel. *Ethnic and Racial Studies* **13**(3), 389–414.

Stohl, M. & G. A. Lopez (eds) 1986. *Government violence and repression: an agenda for research.* Westport, Connecticut: Greenwood Press.

Surjeet, J. 1985. *Bhindranwale sant*. Jalandhar: Punjab Pocket Books.

Swamy, S. 1984. Three days in the Darbar Sahib: an incisive report by a Member of Parliament. *Spokesman*, 2 September.

Swaraj, P. 1984. *Indira Gandhi*. London: Heron Press.

Tabori, P. 1972. *The anatomy of exile: a semantic and historical study*. London: Harrap.

Talbot, C. 1995. Inscribing the other, inscribing the self; Hindu-Muslim identities in the pre-colonial India. *Comparative Studies in History and Society*, 692–722.

Talbot, I. 1988. *Provincial politics and the Pakistan movement: the growth of the Muslim League in North-West and North-East India 1937–47*. Karachi: Oxford University Press.

Talbot, I. 1996. Back to the future? The Punjab Unionist model of consociational democracy for contemporary India and Pakistan. *International Journal of Punjab Studies* 3(1), 65–74.

Talwar, K. S. 1968. The Anand Marriage Act. *Panjab past and present* 2, 400–10.

Tarzi, S. M. 1991. The nation-state, victim groups and refugees. *Ethnic and Racial Studies* 14, 441–52.

Tatla, D. S. 1991. *Sikhs in North America: an annotated bibliography*. Westport, Connecticut: Greenwood Press.

Tatla, D. S. 1992. Nurturing the faithful: the role of sant among Britain's Sikhs. *Religion* 22, 349–74.

Tatla, D. S. 1993. This is our home now: reminiscences of a Punjabi in Coventry. *Oral History* 21, 68–74.

Tatla, D. S. 1994a. Minor voices: the Punjabi press of North America, 1907–1988. *International Journal of Punjab Studies* 1(1), 71–99.

Tatla, D. S. 1994b. *The politics of homeland: a study of ethnic linkages and political mobilisation amongst Sikhs in Britain and North America*. PhD thesis, University of Warwick.

Tatla, D. S. 1996. *Theses on Punjab: a bibliography of dissertaton*, vol. 2. *North America 1900–1995*. Association for Punjab Studies, Coventry.

Tatla, D. S. & E. Nesbitt 1994. *Sikhs in Britain: an annotated bibliography*, 2nd edn. Coventry: University of Warwick.

Tatla, D. S. & G. Singh 1989. The Punjabi press. *New Community* 15(2), 171–184.

Thandi, S. 1996. The Punjabi diaspora in the UK and the Punjab crisis. In *The transmission of Sikh heritage in the Diaspora*, Pashaura Singh and N. G. Barrier (eds), 227–52. New Delhi: Manohar.

Thapar, R. 1989. Imagined religious communities: ancient history and the modern search for a Hindu identity. *Modern Asian Studies* 23(2), 209–31.

Thompson, M. 1974. The second generation: Punjabi or English? *New Community* 3, 242–8.

Tinker, H. 1974. *A new system of slavery: the export of Indian labour Overseas, 1830–1920*. London: Oxford University Press for IRR.

Tinker, H. 1976. *Separate and unequal: India and the Indians in the British Commonwealth 1920–1950*. London: Hurst.

Tinker, H. 1977. *The banyan tree*. London: Oxford University Press.

Tully, M. & S. Jacob 1985. *Amritsar: Mrs Gandhi's last battle*. London: Pan Books.

Upadhyaya, P. C. 1992. The politics of Indian secularism. *Modern Asian Studies* **26**(4), 815–53.

Vaid, K. N. 1972. *The overseas Indian community in Hong Kong*. Hong Kong: Centre for Asian Studies, University of Hong Kong.

Vaughan, B. 1993. The use and abuse of intelligence services in India. *Intelligence and National Security* **8**(1), 1–22.

Verney, D. V. 1986. The limits of political manipulation: the role of the governors in India's "administrative federalism" 1950–1984. *Journal of Commonwealth and Comparative Politics* **XXIV**(2), 169–96.

Verney D. V. & F. R. Frankel 1986. India: has the trend towards federalism implications for the management of foreign policy? A comparative perspective. *International Journal* **XII**, 572–99.

Virk, K. S. & H. Singh 1948. *Greater East Punjab: a plea for a linguistic regrouping*. Ludhiana: Lahore Book Shop.

Wallace, P. & S. Chopra (eds) 1981. *Political Dynamics of Punjab*. Amritsar: Guru Nanak Dev University Press.

Weiner, M. 1987. Political change: Asia, Africa and the Middle East. In *Understanding political development*, M. Weiner & S. P. Huntington (eds). Boston: Little, Brown.

Weiner, M. 1989. Asian-Americans and American foreign policy. *Revue Européene des Migrations Internationales* **5**(1), 10–22.

Weiner, M. 1996. Bad neighbors, bad neighborhoods: an inquiry into the causes of refugee flows. *International Security* **21**(1), 5–42.

Welch, C. E. & V. A. Leary 1990. *Asian perspectives on human rights*. Boulder, Colorado: Westview Press.

Weller, P. (ed.) 1997. *Religions in the UK: a multi-faith directory*. Derby: University of Derby and the Inter-faith Network for the UK.

Wilson, G. K. 1990. *Interest groups*. Oxford: Blackwell.

Zolberg, A., A. Suhrke, A. Sergio 1989. *Escape from violence: conflict and the refugee crisis in the developing world*. Oxford: Oxford University Press.

# Index

Abdali, Ahmad Shah  15
Abercrombie, Neil  168
Ackerman, Gary  168, 270 n. 69
Ad-dharam  79, 241 n. 47–8
Adi Granth  1, 14–15, 28, 31, 69, 76–7,
  80–3, 100, 114, 152, 187, 198
Afghans  15
Africa  3, 6, 8, 36, 50, 56, 61, 65, 85, 89,
  178
Air India tragedy  121, 133, 175, 179,
  189, 192, 255 n. 74
*Aj di awaz*  128
Akal Takhat
  critical event  77
  destruction by the Indian army  1
  disregard by the state  126
  Hargobind, guru  14
  Indian official reaction  1, 152
  *jathedar* and scholars  82, 128, 148
  poetry  126, 146
  sacred site  28
  Sikhs' reaction to destruction  1, 77,
    113, 137
  in traditional discourse  32
Akali Dal
  Akali Janata government  148
  Akali leaders  25, 138, 140–2
  campaign for Punjabi-speaking
    state  22–3
  charter of demands  1, 27
  coalition governents  24, 26, 29–30,
    148
  and Congress  18
  Memorandum to Cabinet Mission
    [1946]  19
  mobilization  12–13
  Muslim League's demand  19
  Nankana incident  18
  nation-building  30
  origin  18
  pragmatism  34
  and SGPC  31
  towards Punjab nationalism  34
Akali Singh Sikh Society  99, 107
*Akali te pardesi*  73
Akalis  12
  *see also* Anandpur Sahib Resolution;
    Dharam Yudh Morcha; Sant
    Harchand Singh Longowal
  alliances  26–7
  demand India as a multinational
    state  34
  other orthodox groups  26
Akhand Kirtani Jatha  26, 120, 140,
  142, 156
Albania  95
Alexander, M.  90
Ali, I.  16
aliens  183
Amar Singh  78

309

*Amardeep* 153
Amardeep Singh Shergill Memorial
   College 238 n. 10
Amarjit Singh 125, 185
Ambedkar, Dr. 80, 98
*Amelie* 60
American Hindus 168, 171, 252 n. 46
Amnesty International 29, 126, 149,
   160, 168
Amrik Singh 1
Amrik Singh [ISYF] 138, 164
*amrit* 200
*amritdhari* 138
Amritsar 1, 5, 11, 14–15, 17–18, 26–7,
   32, 44, 49, 64, 73, 75, 77–8, 82, 85, 98,
   105–7, 110, 116, 125, 129, 130, 138,
   156, 164, 196, 201–2, 211
Anand
   Jagjit Singh 95
   Sushila 90
Anandpur 14
Anandpur Sahib Resolution 27, 34,
   107, 109, 194, 196, 225–6
Anderson, B. 7, 32
Anglo-Asian Conservative Association
   148
Anglo-Saxons 52
Anglo-Sikh relations 16, 18, 68, 81,
   90, 151, 161
Anglo-Sikh wars, Chillianwala,
   Mudki 228 n. 4
Anokh Singh 146
Anti-Asian League 51
anti-Sikh riots 33, 58, 138
Appadurai, A. 34
Arab countries 50, 57
Arendt, H. 7
Arjan, Guru 14
Armenians 3
Armstrong, J. A. 188
Arnold, Jacques 164
artisans 50, 55, 58
Arya Samaj 17
   *see also shudhi*
*asa di var* 76
Asian Americans 61
Asian Exclusion League 53

Asians 7, 51–2, 54–7, 61, 68, 70, 97–9,
   148, 177–8, 201
asylum 58–60, 120, 131, 177, 178
Aujala
   Dr A. K. S. 104
   Gian Singh 101, 104
Aulakh, G. S. 121, 124, 127–9, 150,
   171, 185–7
Aurangzeb, mogul emperor 14
Austin, G. 22
Australia 42, 49, 87, 151, 204
*Awaz-e-Quam* 124, 145
Axworthy, Lloyd 107
Ayodhya 37, 189
Azad, Prithvi Singh 80

Babbar Akalis 90
Babbar Khalsa 118, 120–2, 128–9, 133,
   140, 142, 144–6, 148, 150–1, 155–6,
   171–2, 175–6, 185, 187–8, 250 n. 17
Babylonian 5
Bachittar Singh 164
Badal, Parkash Singh 30
Badhan, Mohinder 80
Bagri, Ajaib Singh 121
Bahadur Shah, mogul emperor 14
Bahrain 58
Bahujan Samaj Party 98
Bains
   Ajit Singh 131, 133, 149, 254 n. 72
   Didar Singh 116
   Hardial 133
*Baisakhi* 79, 105, 123
Bajwa, Jasbir Singh 122, 130
Bakhshish Singh Giani 104
Balbir Singh 129, 143
Balkar Singh 130
Balwant Singh 87, 89
Banga, I. 16
Barnala, Surjit Singh 29
Barrier, N. G. 63
*Basera* 73
Basques 196
Batala 65
Batth, Rajinder singh 263 n. 80
Bawa, Baldev 146
Bay Area, California 103, 133

BBC 140, 158
Beant Singh 30, 148, 171
Beaumeir, Colleen 179
Beetham, D. 101
Belgium 58, 151
Bellingham 51
Bengal 35
Bengali 52
Berkeley 53, 70, 79, 81–2, 99, 127
Besant, Annie 91
Bhag Singh 87
Bhagat Singh 32, 90
Bhai Ditt Singh 65
Bhakra Dam Project 24
Bhamra, Ajit Sat 153, 263 n. 78
Bhangra 68, 239 n. 17–18
Bharti, J. 97
Bhatra Sikhs 55, 66
Bhindranwale, Jarnail Singh 1, 27, 34,
   105–6, 119, 128, 138, 141–2, 150, 191,
   202, 227 n. 7, 230 n. 21
Bhullar, J. S. 116, 121
bilateral trade 160, 165, 267 n. 40
Birk, Gurpartap Singh 127, 129, 276
   n. 29
Birmingham 104, 137, 140–2, 145, 148,
   152–3, 163
blasphemy 82
Bluestar Operation 1, 178
Bonn 157
Bosnia 178
Brahma, Avtar Singh 146
Brass, P. 13, 38
Brett, R. 7
Bristol 137
British Aerospace 159
British African colonies 44
British aid 163
British Columbia 51–3, 57, 70, 78, 81–
   2, 85–6, 96, 100, 106, 175, 178, 193,
   199
British empire 46, 86, 88
   travel within 87
British India 16, 88
Bucharest 151
Buchignani, N. I. 89
Buddhism 79, 80

Budh Singh 238 n. 7
Bukhalter, Holly 169
Burlet, S. 189
Burton, Dan 166–7, 169, 171
Buta Singh 28, 123

Cabinet Mission 19
Calcutta 44, 47, 51, 73, 88
Calgary 102, 114–15
California 51–4, 56–7, 67, 69, 81–2,
   85–6, 90, 102–3, 116, 118–19, 128, 165,
   171
California Aliens Land Act 54
California Senate 103
Californian Sikh Youth 116
Calvert, H. 43
camps for Sikh pupils 54, 69–70, 74–5
Canada
   see also RCMP, CSIS, Babbar Khalsa
   Air India disaster 188–90
   boycott of Sikh organizations 133,
   173
   Canada-Sikh relations 177
   Canadian Farmworkers Union 96
   Department of Multiculturalism
   97–100
   foreign aid to India 178
   House of Commons debates 173–6
   India blames Canada for "helping
   Sikhs" 157, 181
   Indian Overseas Congress 98
   Indian parliament discusses 157
   Indira Gandhi's appeal 172
   Indo-Canadian extradition treaty
   172
   MPs on Punjab issue 178
   pan-East Indian Organisations 98
   parliament mission to Punjab 178
   prejudice and justice 134
   Team Canada Mission to India 179
Canadian Security and Intelligence
   Service 133, 135, 177, 178
Canadian Sikhs 57, 66, 81, 86, 101,
   108, 122, 130–1, 171–3, 179, 192, 194,
   201
   100th anniversary of Sikh settlers
   179

Akali Dal 99
Akali leaders' appreciation of
  Canada Sikhs 108
Akalis' plea for separate
  representation 201
appeal by Dosanjh and rebuttals
  132–3
Babbar Khalsa 120–1
*Canada darpan* 126
conferences 82
delegation 109
election at Ross Street gurdwara:
  Nanar versus Sandhu group 109
extradition of British Sikhs 133
families 66
female abortions 68
Gadr rebellion 89
gurdwaras 74, 109
immigration 41, 48, 52–5, 57–60
International Sikh Youth Federation
  119–21
Kabaddi 68
Khalistan flag 176
leaders' credibility 185–6
leftist groups 92, 97
literary societies 71
marriage alliances 68
Members of Parliament 100
memorandum on "Sikhs as a
  nation" 107, 109
Naxalite migrants 95
Nirankaris 79
population 60
Punjab village connections 64
Punjabi TV programmes 70
reaction to army attack on the
  Golden Temple 115
refugees 60, 177
Sandhu group 109
separatism 103
societies 75
support for *Dharam Yudh Morcha*
  108
Teja Singh's petition to Ottawa 87
veterans 102
White Paper on Canadian Sikh
  organisations 156

WSO-Canada 116–18
Canal Colonies 16, 44–6
Carter, Lily 99
Cassidy, Mike 177
Catholics 174
CBS 115
Central Sikh League 228 n. 6
Chadney, J. G. 67
Chahal, Karamjit Singh 140, 149, 261
  n. 59
Chahil, Pritam Singh 242 n. 51
Chaliand, G. 3, 7
Chamars 79, 80
  *see also* Mazhabi Sikhs
Chan, Raymond 178
Chandigarh 27, 64, 82, 105, 131
*Charcha* 153
*Chardhi kala* 120, 124–5
Charlesville 60
Chary, M. S. 165
Chatar Singh 121
Chicago 127
Chief Khalsa Diwan 18, 26, 48, 85, 98
Chima, Jaspreet Singh 102
Chima, Rajinder Singh 102
Chima, Sukhjinder Kaur 102
Chinese people 3, 49, 80, 86, 95, 181
Chohan, Gurdev Singh 132
Chohan, Jagjit Singh 65, 103–6, 109,
  132, 140, 141, 145, 150, 154, 156, 186,
  187, 247 n. 56, 248 n. 66
Chohan, Kewal Singh 247 n. 60
Chopra, G. 16
Chopra, P. 158
Christians 17, 35
Christopher, Warren 169
Chuhan, Maluk Singh 196
CIA 96, 157
Clark, Joe 172, 174, 176
coalition 18, 24, 26, 30, 34, 122
Code, Michael 130
Cohen, R. 5
Cologne 150
Colonial Office 47
Colonial rule 16, 18, 20, 30, 35
Commonwealth meeting 127, 164,
  176

Communist Party of Punjab 92
  Communists 13, 131, 144, 153, 186
  Lal Group 92
Condit, Gary 170
Connor, W. 7, 13
"continuous journey" 52
coolies 46
Copps, S. 133, 174
Coventry 91, 123, 137, 144
Creagh, C. V. 48
critical event 197
Croatians 173
Cubans 181
Cunningham, J. D. 16

Daily Akali 73
Dal Khalsa 26, 122, 125, 143, 145, 151, 156
Dalip Singh, prince 55, 79, 90, 100
  see also Elveden
Damdami Taksal 26, 142, 150
Darbara Singh 96
Darshan Singh 71, 82, 148
Das, Tarknath 52, 88
Dayanand, Swamy 17
democratic centralism 22
demography 18–19
Des pardes 71, 104, 146
Desh Bhagat Parvarik Shayta Kmeti 76
Desh Sewak 73
Dewitt, J. 95
dhadis 68, 76, 123, 146
Dhaliwal, Harbance Singh 100, 178–9
Dhaliwal Darshan Singh 71, 82, 242 n. 57
Dhami, M. S. 31
Dharam S. S. 194
Dharam Yudh Morcha 9, 26–7, 29, 31, 33, 99, 106, 108–10, 121, 125, 138, 140, 166, 202, 205
  Chohan's appeal to Akali Dal 109–10
  Dharam Yudh Morcha Action Committee (Canada) 108
  Longowal's appeal 106
  Sikh diaspora's support 99–100, 113

White Paper 190
Dhawan, S. S. 101
Dhillon
  Baltej Singh 102
  Ganga Singh 118–19, 157, 165, 186, 193
Dhingra, Madan Lal 91
Dhinsa, Amrik 177
Dhudike Village Society 238 n. 4
diaspora
  classification 4
  criteria 5–7
  definition 2–3, 5
  Hindus 189
  Indian diaspora 3
  Jewish diaspora 3
  Punjabi diaspora 6, 8
Dicks, Terry 160–2, 164
Dilgeer, H. S. 151, 242 n. 59
discrimination 6, 23, 61, 153, 201, 203–4
disinformation 156, 192
Ditt Singh 65
divide and rule policy 16
Doaba 55, 64, 92
Domeliwale, sant Harbans Singh 65, 238 n. 6
Dominicans 181
Dominion Cinema, Southall 96
Doreen, I. 86, 89
Dosanjh, Ujjal 100, 131–2, 178
Dubai 58
Dulla 68
Duncan, B. C. 174
Duplessis, Suzanne 178
Dusenbery, V. A. 6, 206
Dutt, Raj 171

East Africa 50, 56, 61, 65, 85
  East African Rifles 50
East India Company 46
East Indian Canadian Citizens Welfare Association 96
East Indian Defence Committee 95, 131
East Indian Welfare Association 95
East Indian Workers Association 116

Ecuador 140
Edmonton 95, 102, 114, 175
elections 18–19, 22, 26, 29–30, 76–7,
 96, 100, 108, 118, 122–3, 144, 150, 171,
 179, 192, 205
Elveden 79, 90, 241 n. 44
Embree, A. T. 36
emigration 5–6, 41–2, 44, 46–7, 55, 58
Enloe, C. 7
Esman, M. J. 4
Estonians 174
ethnic boundaries 17
ethnic cleansing 20
ethnic conflict 12, 13, 30
ethnocide 3
Europeans 3, 16–17, 48, 60, 74, 90,
 129, 151, 161, 191, 194
exile 2–3, 142
extradition cases 237 n. 29, 265 n. 21
extradition treaty 159–60, 170, 172,
 189
 India-Canada 216, 270 n. 78
 India-UK 216–17

Far East 5–6, 8, 42, 44, 46, 48, 51–3,
 55–6, 58, 61, 74, 85–6, 91, 116, 204
Fascel, Dante 171
Fateh Singh 23, 99
Fazio, Vic 165, 166
FBI 253 n. 56
federalism 13, 38
Federation of Indian Organizations
 97
Federation of Sikh Societies 115
female workers 96
Ferguson, C. A. 52
Ferozepore 64–5
Festival of India 109
Fiji 46–7, 49
Filipinos 181
films 67, 68
folklore 16, 33, 45
foreign aid 159, 167, 168, 178, 181
Forum 235 n. 17
France 151
Frankfurt 68, 151
Fraser, T. G. 205

Fraser Valley 96
free labour 50
French Revolution 7
Fresno 89, 119, 129
Friends of Punjab 241 n. 50

Gadr 18, 53, 71, 76, 79, 86, 89–90, 92,
 98, 132, 184, 204–5, 210–11, 244 n. 7–
 10
Gajinder Singh 127, 143, 273 n. 4
Ganda Singh 90
Gandhi, Indira 12, 26–7, 32–3, 58, 96,
 101, 109–10, 115–16, 138, 140, 153,
 158, 172, 198
Gandhi, M. 20
Gandhi, Rajiv 29, 127, 147, 159, 161,
 165, 176
Ganguly, S. 165
Garel-Jones, Tristan 163
GCSE Punjabi students 239 n. 21
genocide 3, 8, 28, 113, 180, 199
Geren, Pete 169
Germany 58, 61, 121, 151, 156
ghallugharas 15, 28
giddha 68
Gill, C. 96
Gill, D. S. 149
Gill, Harsharan Singh 255 n. 73
Gill, K. P. S. 147
Gill, Ranjit Singh 130
Gill, Sukhwinder Singh 260 n. 50
Gill, Surjit Singh 247 n. 58
Gillis, J. R. 32
globalization 4
Gobind, Guru 14–15, 65, 192
Godsiff, R. 160
Golden Temple 1, 9, 11, 14, 16–17, 34,
 58, 105, 111, 113, 115, 131, 137–8, 140,
 145, 150, 152, 154, 158, 164, 166, 172,
 178, 183–4, 191, 198, 200, 209, 227 n.
 2, 272–9
Golden Temple Corporation 105
Gorakh 15
Goulbourne, H. 206
Gould, H. A. 165
granthis 64
Greeks 2

Green Party 148
green revolution 12, 25, 41, 65
Gregory, R. G. 50
Grewal, Dr Manohar Singh 127, 180, 220–2
Grewal, J. S. 91
Grey, Lord 51
Gujarat 17, 35, 47
Gujral, Inder Kumar 164–5
Gujratis 41, 97
Gurbachan Singh 79
*gurbani* 200
Gurdaspur 44
Gurdeep Singh 142–3, 258 n. 24–5
Gurdev Singh 78, 121, 125, 132, 146
Gurdit Singh 53, 88
gurdwaras 18–19, 50, 52–3, 67, 70, 74, 76–8, 80, 82, 86–8, 90, 96, 99, 101, 104–8, 110, 113–14, 118–19, 122–3, 129, 138, 141, 143–6, 148–50, 152–3, 162, 185, 201–2, 204, 206
  Ross Street Gurdwara, Vancouver 77, 108, 114, 119, 122
Gurharpal Singh 20, 30, 71, 92
Gurinder Singh 83, 129
Gurmej Singh [Gill] 140, 142, 151
Gurmel Singh 142
Gurmukh Nihal Singh 72
Gurnam Singh 101
Gurr, T. R. 8
Gurtej Singh 253 n. 52
Guru Amar Das Mission 74
Guru Gobind Singh College, Jandiala 65
Guru Ravidas Foundation 80
Gurutej Singh Khalsa 195

Hague, the 203
Hamdard, S. S. 19
Handsworth 152
Harbhajan Singh 33, 75, 115
Harbhajan Singh Yogi 75, 240 n. 38
Hardayal, Lala 53, 88–9
Hargobind, Guru 14
Hargobindpur 14
Harimandir *see* Golden Temple

Harjit Singh 261 n. 61
Harmander Singh 140, 150
Harpal Singh 119, 141, 186
Harrier jets 159
Haryana 129
Hawaii 51
Hawley, J. S. 83
Hayer, Tara Singh 251 n. 33
Helweg, A. W. 66, 206
Hemkunt 79
Herger, Wally 165, 167
heritage 3, 33, 35, 68, 70, 79, 81
heroes 32, 76, 146
Heseltine, M. 159
Hess, G. R. 52
hijackers 143, 185
Hill, M. F. 50
Hind Mazdoor Lahir 109
Hindi 17, 22–3, 32, 37–8, 70, 89, 153, 204
Hindi Sabha 89
Hindoos 52
Hindu Code Bill 32
Hindu Marriage Act 32
Hinduism 17, 36, 79–80, 82, 204
Hinduized identity 38
  *see also* Punjabi Hindus
Hindus 12, 14, 16–20, 21–3, 26–7, 29, 31–8, 49–53, 57, 66, 80, 82–3, 97, 100, 104, 125, 128, 133, 142, 146, 152–4, 163, 168, 170–1, 187, 189, 193, 198, 204
  backlash 29
  diaspora 189
  India domination 19
  leaders' vision of independent India 18
  nationalism 21, 35–6
  nationalism versus Indian nationalism 21
  Sikh discord 256 n. 3
Hindustani Association 52
*Hir* 68
hockey 69
Holy Land 2, 19, 22
Home Rule League 91, 244 n. 10
Honduras 52, 71

Hong Kong  44, 48–9, 51, 53, 56, 71, 204
Hopkinson, J.  189
Hoshiarpur  44, 64–5
House of Commons  100, 102, 134, 149, 160–1, 163, 173, 176, 191, 266 n. 22–34
House of Lords  101
Howe, G.  159
Huddersfield  144
*hukamnama*  16
Human Rights Commission  102
Hyde Park, London  103, 137

illegal migrants  54, 61, 167, 178
Immigration and Naturalization Service  60
Imperial Valley  54, 67, 99, 100
imperialism  21, 35, 87, 148
Indarjit Singh  256 n. 4, 7
indentured labour  46, 50
India
  anti-Indian activities  104
  anti-Sikh riots  29
  Armed Forces [Punjab and Chandigarh] Special Powers Act 1983  29
  Armed Forces Special Powers Act 1990  29
  centre-state relations  12, 27, 34, 233 n. 48
  colonial and post-colonial state contrast  20–1
  Congress Party  12–13, 18–22, 24, 26–7, 29–31, 36, 38, 53, 77, 126, 148–9, 163
  constitution  110, 160
  as ethnocracy  36
  extradition demands  61
  forging an Indian identity  32
  governability crisis  38
  independence day  106, 128
  liberation  88
  minority nationalisms  35
  as a multi-nation state  27
  nation-building process  13

National Human Rights Commission  30
National Security Act 29, 1980
northeastern states  21, 37
official language  22, 37
parliament  264 n. 5–8
state nationalism  12–13
States Reorganization Commission 229 n. 13
student revolutionaries  91
Supreme Court  30, 54, 131
Terrorist Affected Areas [Special Courts] Act 1984  29
Terrorist and Disruptive Activities [prevention] Act [TADA], [1985] 29, 130, 163, 169
wars with Pakistan  110
India House  91, 149
India League  89, 91
India Office  87, 90
India Society  99
Indian
  army  1, 9, 16, 28, 38, 44–6, 48–51, 58, 81, 86–8, 113, 115, 131, 137, 138, 145, 156, 160, 168, 172, 178, 183, 191, 193–4, 198, 209, 211, 230 n. 22
  asylum seekers in Germany  58
  community of Britain  90
  diaspora  3
  emigration  46–7
  high commission's role in turban cases  103
  intelligence  119–20, 143, 167, 191
  justification for army action  1
  national anthem  37, 202
  officials in Lahore  128
  overseas population  234 n. 5
  policies towards Kashmir and northeastern states  35–6
  provincial politics and central government  27
  regional nationalities  21
  secularism  13, 21–2, 31, 36, 90, 125, 141, 196, 205
  Sikhs' dual loyalty  11
Indian Consulate offices  103, 105–7,

109, 114, 128–9, 137, 154, 158, 163, 187, 199
Indian Emergency 96
Indian National Army 91, 244 n. 13
Indian Ocean 3, 166
Indian Overseas Congress 91, 96, 98, 109, 116, 119, 128, 144, 151–2, 186
Indian Peoples' Association of North America [IPANA] 98
*Indian Sociologist* 91
Indian Workers Association 91–2, 95, 109, 116, 153, 244 n. 14
Indians 3, 46, 48–52, 54, 56, 61, 88–9, 91, 95–8, 128, 132, 152–3, 184, 201
Indo-British relations 140, 147, 158–9, 189
Indo-Canadian relations 71, 124–5, 171–2, 179, 193
*Indo-Canadian Times* 71, 124–5
Indo-Chinese 95
Indus Valley 41
Institute of Sikh Studies, Chandigarh 242 n. 59
International Commission of Jurists 234 n. 53
International Ethnic Parade 127
International Military Education and Training 168
International Sikh Youth Federation 118–20, 122–6, 128, 130–1, 133, 138, 141–2, 144–5, 147, 149–50, 152–3, 155, 164, 171–2, 175–6, 185–8, 199, 249 n. 14
Internet 83
Iraq 58
Ireland 121, 170, 197
Isemonger, F. C. 73
Islam 19, 83
Israel 2, 115, 132, 173–4

Jagjit Singh 79
Jahangir, mogul emperor 14
Jaijee, I. S. 29
Jaito 86
Jalal, A. 22
Jalandhar 44, 47, 55, 64–5, 76, 128

Jallianwala 18, 90, 164
Jan Quin 57
*janamsakhi* 14
Janata Party 30, 37, 98, 149
Japanese 53, 86, 91
Jarnail Singh [Canada] 242 n. 51
Jarnail Singh [UK] 260 n. 50
Jasbir Singh *see* Rode Jasbir Singh
*jathedar* 77–8, 202
Jats 15, 44, 66, 79, 145, 186, 204
Jawala Singh 53
Jerusalem 2, 5
Jews 2–4, 102, 114–15, 173–4, 189, 196
Jhang 44
Jharkhandis 125
Johal, Avtar 92
Johal, Bikar Singh 122
Johnson, Sir Harry 51
Johnston, H. 88
Jolly, Sohan Singh 101
Jones K. W. 17, 163
Josephides, S. 95
Josh, S. S. 89
Joshi, Jagmohan 92
Juergensmeyer, M. 79, 205
Jullundur *see* Jalandhar

*Kabaddi* 68–9, 239 n. 19
Kabir 15
Kahlon, Tejinder Singh 248 n. 2
Kahn Singh 17
Kanpur 106
Kanwal, Sher Singh 125, 276 n. 26
Kanya Mahavidiala College, Ferozepore 64
Kapany, N. S. 82
Karnana 47
Kartar Singh Sarabha Trust 238 n. 8
Kashmir 8, 21, 35, 160, 162–4, 167–71, 194
Kashmiris 7, 35, 125, 128, 147, 165
Kaur, Basant 148
Kaur, Kuldip 149, 261 n. 62
Kaur, Madanjit 16, 28
Kaur, S. 50
Kaushal, Ram 153

Kedourie, E. 8
Kent 144
Kenya 50, 56
Khabra, Piara Singh 95, 160
Khalistan 11, 29, 114–15, 120–1, 123–
9, 132, 137–8, 140–7, 149–50, 156, 161,
164–5, 170, 174–6, 180, 185, 187–8,
191, 193–6, 206–7, 209–11
Khalistan Commando Force 126
Khalistan Council 138, 140–2, 144–5,
147, 149–50, 161, 185, 187
Khalistanis 128–9, 153, 198
Khalra, Jaswant Singh 149, 178–9, 261
n. 61
*Khalsa Advocate* 86
Khalsa College, Amritsar 64
Khalsa Diwan, Hong Kong 278 n. 49
Khalsa Diwan Society, Vancouver
52–3, 64, 68, 76, 85, 87, 89, 95,
98–100, 104, 106–7, 108, 132, 177,
199, 202, 243 n. 2–3, 277
n. 38–9
Khalsa Human Rights 149, 261 n. 60–
1
Khalsa Naujawan Sabha 204
*Khalsa samachar* 86
Kharak Singh 131
Khatkar Kalan 237 n. 3
Khera, Iqbal Singh 238 n. 11
Khushwant Singh 16, 247 n. 52
Kilgour, D. 131
Kilindini 50
King, Peter 169
Kirpal Singh, *jathedar*, Akal Takhat
218–19
*kirpan* issue 100, 102–3, 118, 131, 201,
206
*kirtan* 76, 126
*kirtan sohila* 76
Kirti 73, 92
Kirti Party 92
Knopf, D. 35
*Komagata Maru* 53, 88
Krishnavarma, Shyamji 91
Kuldeep Singh 237 n. 30
Kuldip Singh 74, 102
Kundu, A. 189

Kurds 7, 196
Kux, D. 165

La Brack, B. 57, 65, 67
Labh Singh 127, 146
Lahore 14, 17, 44, 73, 79, 128, 143, 185
Lahore Conspiracy Case 244 n. 7
Lakhbir Singh 119–20, 186
Lal, Bhajan 129
Lal Singh 179, 192
Lalkar 154
Land Alienation Act [1900] 16
*langar* 14, 77, 108
Latvians 173, 174
Leary, B. 8
Lee, Derek 131
leftist associations 91–2, 96–7, 100,
104, 106, 110, 131, 184
Leicester 144, 147–9, 153
Leonard, K. 54, 67
Lepervanche, M. M. de 49
Liberal Party 102, 173
Libya 141
Lidder, Sohan Singh 152
Lipinski, William 166
Lithuanians 173
Littlejohn, C. S. 54
Livingston 102–3
Liviu Radu 151
*Lokta* 154
London 51, 65, 71, 74–5, 82, 87, 89–91,
96, 109–10, 140, 144, 147–8, 157, 191,
196
Longowal, Harchand Singh 29, 106,
108, 214–15, 223–4.
Longowal-Rajiv agreement 230 n. 23
Lopez, G. A. 7
Los Angeles 68, 75, 82, 114–15
Lote, Gurcharan Singh 81
LuceCellar Bill 56
Ludhiana 44, 64
lumber industries 51, 53
Luton 144, 149, 152
Lyallpur 44

Macauliffe Institute of Sikh Studies,
Toronto 133

McDougall, Barbara 176
McGarry, J. 8
McLeod, W. H. 49
McMahon, R. J. 165
Madan Singh 258 n. 23
Madden, Max 160–2
*mahants* 17–18
Maharashtra 35
Mahboob, Harinder Singh 32, 258 n. 27
Mahmood, C. K. 36, 206
Makhan Singh 235 n. 13
Malay States Guides 49
Malaya 44, 46, 49, 64
Malayasia 42
Malhi, Gurbax Singh 100, 102, 178–9
Malik, K. N. 158, 189
Malkit Singh 68, 129
Malott, J. 168–9
Malwa 55
Manchester 100–1
Maninder Singh 130
Manjit Singh, *jathedar* 129, 143, 148, 179, 192, 260 n. 53
Manly, J. 174
Manmohan Singh 143
Mann, Gurinder Singh 83
Mann, Simranjit Singh 127
Manor, J. 38
Maoists 95
Marchi, Sergio 173
Marienstras, R. 3
Martial races 16, 44, 229 n. 20
martyrs 15, 32, 89, 107–8, 126, 146, 150, 197, 199–200, 202
Marysville 53
Massa Singh 121
Matharu, G. S. 146
Mazhabi Sikhs 81
media 9, 17, 32, 63, 65, 69, 71, 86, 104–5, 114, 122–5, 134–5, 137, 143–6, 150, 157, 163, 168, 171, 179–80, 187–92, 197, 199, 204
Menon, Krishna 91
Meredith, Val 134
Mewa Singh 277 n. 39
Mexican Sikhs 54

Mexico 54
Michigan 81–2
Michigan Sikh Society 81
Middle East 41, 57, 204
Midlands 55, 65, 78, 98, 143, 153, 154
Mihan Singh, sant 78, 123
Mihar 80
Militant groups 29–30, 58, 61, 121, 126, 128, 142–3, 149–51, 158–9, 162, 168, 170, 187–8, 205, 231 n. 29, 233 n. 41
Milwaukee 71
minorities
 hegemonic control 233 n. 46
 politics 18
 violent control 35
Mir Mannu 187
Mirpuris 41
*Mirza* 68
Mishra, R. 169
*Misls* 15–16
missionaries 17–18, 64
Mizos 125
Moguls 14–15, 33, 41, 68, 187
Molla Singh 277 n. 36
Mombasa 50–1
*Monteagle* 52
Montgomery 44
Moon, Penderel 20
Moranwali 237 n. 3
Morley, John 52
Multan 44
Multiculturalism 97, 132–3
multinational 7, 126, 160, 196
museums 32, 65
Muslim League 19–20
Muslims 16, 19–20, 129, 161, 189

Nagas 125, 137, 147, 189
Nairobi 50
Namdharis 79, 109, 145, 186, 195
Nanak, Guru 14–15, 18, 79, 152, 204
Nanaksar 78
Nankana 18, 79, 118
Narain Singh 89
Narita airport 133

nation 4, 7–8, 11–13, 19, 21, 26, 30–6, 38, 105, 107, 124, 127, 137, 141, 175, 180, 193, 195–6, 198–9, 206–7, 145–147
National Alliance of Canadian Sikhs 133
National Association of Canadians of Origins in India [NACOI] 97, 127
National Sikh Centre 192
nationalism 3, 7, 11–13, 19, 21, 24–5, 31, 33–6, 118, 126, 157, 193, 196, 203–4
nationality 12–13, 19, 23, 30, 126, 195
Naxalite movement 6, 95–6, 110, 184
Nayar, K. 149
Nehru, J. 20, 24
Nepalis 48
Netherlands 58
New Delhi 12, 27, 58, 73, 98, 100–1, 104, 159
New Jersey 122, 126, 130, 171
New York 77, 99, 103, 114, 116, 118, 122–3, 127, 157, 171, 175
*New York Times* 103
New Zealand 42, 49, 204
Nikki, Gunninder Kaur Singh 83
Nirankaris 26, 79, 105–7, 120
Nishkam Sewak Jatha 76
non-governmental organizations [NGOs] 180, 203
Noorani, A. G. 29
Norway 151, 181
Nottingham 144
Nova Scotia 60, 177
Nunziata, John 172, 179

Oberoi, Harjot 17, 26, 34, 82
O'Connell, J. T. 134
Oman 58
Ontario 57, 75
Oregon 53
Ottawa 52, 78, 87, 118, 179
*Ottawa Citizen* 179
overseas patronage 73
Oxford 74

Pacific states 6, 44, 53, 86, 89, 184
Pakistan 6, 19–21, 23, 65, 68, 79, 81, 120–1, 128, 141, 143, 165–6, 184

Palestinians 3, 7, 114–15, 173, 196
Panchi, C. S. 101, 103–5
Panjab 10
Panjabi 10, 70
Panthic Committee 121, 128, 142, 147, 150, 176, 252 n. 49, 273 n. 104
Pargat Singh 141, 153, 263 n. 84
Paris 90–1, 157
Parliament 100, 131
debates on Sikhs and the Punjab
Canada 102, 133, 135, 172–4, 176–9
India 37, 157
UK 91, 95, 148–9, 151, 160–2
Parliament of World Religions 127
Parmar, Devinder Singh 103, 260 n. 44
Parmar, Talwinder Singh 120, 151, 156, 250 n. 17, 19–21
Parmatma Singh 260 n. 50
Parmvir Singh 102
Parsis 41
Partap Singh Lt. Col. 269 n. 62, 273 n. 107
partition 6, 19–22, 55, 62, 103
Pash 254 n. 66
Patiala, maharajah of 74, 90
Patten, John 162
peasants 12, 15–16, 18, 26, 32, 44, 64, 90, 188
Peel School 102
Penang 48, 49
Perak 49
Persia 41
Philip, Duke of Edinburgh 88
Philippines 51, 58, 71
pilgrimage 6, 11, 28, 78–9, 81
*pingalwara* 64
Plaid Cymru 261 n. 57
Poles 177
Pollock, S. 37
Popplewell, R. 91
population 11, 18–20, 29, 49–50, 53, 56–8, 61, 69, 71, 74, 92, 99–100, 163, 167, 192
princely states 20–1
print revolution 17

Pritpal Singh 122
Progressive Writers Association 71
Punajb autonomy campaign *see*
*Dharam Yudh Morcha*
Punjab
  annexation 16
  anti-Punjabi policies 24
  army connections 49
  army recruitment 16, 44
  azad Punjab 19
  British policy 18
  British rule 43
  campaign for Punjabi speaking state
    22–3
  Canadian liaison office 100
  central Punjab 15
  Chandigarh issue 27
  chief minister 26, 96
  common language 17
  Communist Party 92, 95
  conversion by missionaries 17
  crisis 12, 29
  death toll 169
  diaspora's relationship with 6, 8
  elections [1946] 19
  elections [1985] 29
  electoral politics 26
  elite 17
  emigration from central areas 41
  factors in emigration 42, 46
  fairs 45
  flow of information 63
  governor 14
  heroes 32
  Hindi versus Punjabi 32
  Hindus' out-migration 33
  an imagined homeland 3
  lion of Punjab 16
  memories of sovereignty 16
  nationalism 18–19, 24–5, 34, 203
  Naxalite moverment 95
  partition 6, 20, 55
  peasantry 16, 44, 89
  periodicals from Punjab 73
  pilgrimage 79
  police excesses 130–1
  population 18, 22

post-1966 Punjab 24
  refugees fleeing from 58
  remittances 64–5
  reorganization 24
  sants 78
  as Sikh homeland 13, 22
  Sikh rule 12
  Sikhs' claim on Punjab 19
  Sikhs' loyalty 28
  social classes 15
  social exchange 66
  socio-economic changes 25
  state-sanctioned abuse 169
  students in UK 55
  terror of security forces and
    militants 29
  unclaimed bodies 164
  village republics 16
  war-like situation 61
  yearning for independence 33
Punjab Accord 29, 150, 230 n. 23
  *see also* Longowal-Rajiv agreement
Punjab and East Punjab States Union
  [PEPSU] 22
Punjab Human Rights Organization
  29, 126, 149
Punjab Legislative Assembly 231 n.
  29
Punjab Studies 71, 82
Punjab Times 71
Punjab Unity Forum 152
Punjabi
  Hindus 34, 49, 152
  identity 68, 80
  Muslims 17
  Muslims in the UK 55
  nationalism 34
  press 71
  Punjabi-Mexican families 67
  region 27
  versus Indian heroes 32
  women 45
*Punjabi darpan* 153, 154
Punjabi language 14, 17–18, 20, 22–4,
  27, 32, 34, 44–6, 48–9, 51, 53–6, 63, 65,
  69–70, 83
  in Britain 69

literary awards 239 n. 26
literature 228 n. 5
media 9–10
poetry 68, 70–1, 125, 146, 197
pupils 69, 74–5, 118
in schools 203–4, 206
software 83
teachers 239 n. 22
teaching
at university level 70
in Vancouver 74
television programmes
*Ankhila Punjab* 70
*Rangila Punjab* 70
*Sanjha Punjab* 32, 70, 199
versus Hindi 204, 231 n. 25, 232
n. 34, 239 n. 25
weeklies 114
Puran Singh Karichowale 110
Purbias 16
Purewal, Tarsem Singh 259 n. 41, 263
n. 86
Puri, H. 89, 91

Queen, the British sovereign 102, 164,
267 n. 37

racial discrimination 153
Radhasoamis 79
Raghbir Singh 102, 145, 149, 259 n. 41
*ragis* 76
Rahi, Ajit 276 n. 26
Rai, Jasdev Singh 263 n. 84
Rai, Lajpat 244, n. 10
Rai, Sulakhan Singh 152
Rai, Zorawar Singh 104
Raipur, Tejinder Singh 129
Rajasathan 72
Ram, Jagjivan Ram 80
Ram, Mangu 245 n. 23
Ram Raghbir Singh 102
Ramanand 15
Ramgarhia Sikhs 50, 66, 81, 109, 144–
5, 186, 195, 259 n. 34–7
Rampal Singh 121
Rampuri, Gurcharan 131
Rana, Ranjit Singh 143, 145

Randhawa, B. S. 146
Randhawa, M. S. 20
Ranjit Singh 102
Ranjit Singh; maharajah of Punjab 16,
28, 31–3, 79, 123, 130, 193
Rao, V. K. R. V. 127
Raphael, Robin 170
Rasgotra, M. K. 189
Rathore, Mohinder Singh 143
Ravi, Ravinder 197
Ravidasis 80, 98, 145, 186
Ray, S. S. 170, 252 n. 47
Reagan, Ronald 165–6
Reeves, F. 101
Reform Party 100
refugees 3, 6–7, 33, 42, 55, 58–61,
130, 133, 143, 149, 151, 177, 198, 236
n. 26
Canada 271 n. 88
torture 236 n. 24.
*rehras* 76
Reid, H. 189
remittances 238 n. 13
Republic of Khalistan 116
revolutionaries 18, 53, 68, 70, 89–91,
95–6, 154, 204
*see also* Gadr, Babbar Akalis
Reyat, Inderjit Singh 255 n. 75, 263 n.
87
Ribeiro, J. 151
Rils, Nelson 173
Robb, P. 148, 189
Robinson, S. J. 174
Rode, Jasbir Singh 119–20, 122, 128–
30, 141–2, 150, 257 n. 15–16
Romania 151
Rooker, J. 163
Rotterdam 60
Royal Albert Hall 75
Royal Canadian Legion [RCL] 102,
246 n. 37–40
Royal Canadian Mounted Police
[RCMP] 102, 133, 177, 246 n. 35
Royal Festival Hall 109
Rudolph, L. I. 38
Rudolph, S. H. 38
Russia 90

Sagar, G. S. 100
Said, A. A. 207
Saini Sikhs 81
*salwar kameej* 67
San Diego 124
San Francisco 51, 71, 79, 86, 89–90,
    114, 128, 132
San Francisco Conspiracy Case 90
*Sandesh international* 152–3
Sandher, Manjit Singh 263 n. 80
Sandhu, Gian Singh 134, 176, 186, 255
    n. 78
Sandhu, Harmander Singh 150
Sandhu, Jasbir Singh 129
Sandhu, Joginder Singh 105
Sandhu, K. S. 49
Sandhu, Sukhminder Singh 130
Sandhu, Sukhvinder Singh 127
Sandhu, T. S. 101
Sang Dhesian 65
Sanskrit 17
*sant* 27, 29, 34, 64–5, 78, 99, 105–6,
    108, 119, 123, 125, 138, 141, 202
Santa Barbara, California 82
Sarabha, Kartar Singh 32, 90
Saraon, Harbans Singh 277 n. 34
Satinderpal Singh 249 n. 14, 252 n. 48
Saudi Arabia 58
Saund, Dalip Singh 100
Scottish National Party 148
Sea Eagle 159
Sekhon, Daljit Singh 130
Selangor 49
self-determination 3, 22, 118, 124, 148,
    163–5, 169–70, 195–6, 201
Sewa Singh 140
Shahbeg Singh 1, 138, 146
Shahpur 44
Shain, Y. 155
*Shamsheer Dast* 124
Shanghai 49, 53
Sharma, Vishnu Dutt 92, 96, 146, 153
Sheffer, G. 4
*Shere Punjab* 105, 154
Shiromani Gurdwara Parbandhak
    Committee [SGPC] 18, 26, 82, 107
Short, Major Billy 20

*shudhi* 17
Shumway, Norman 165–7, 171
Sialkot 55
Siam 71
Sidhu, Malkit Singh 129
Sihota, Moe 100, 178
Sihra, K. S. 193–4, 235 n. 13
Sihra, Nand Singh 89
Sikh Council 99
*Sikh Courier* 73
Sikh Cultural Society 99, 123, 248 n. 2
Sikh Diaspora 3, 5
    academic studies 81
    assassination of ex-governor 91
    bilingual learners 67–72
    bond with the Punjab 33
    characteristics of mobilization 184
    communist solution 95, 126, 133
    comparison with Jews and
        Palestinians 114–15
    conspiracy 153
    controversies 152
    creative site 80–4
    cry for homeland 104, 183–5, 203–5
    cultural norms 67
    *Dharam Yudh Morcha* 106–7
    dilemma 211
    discourse on homeland 193–7
    discovery of rural arts 81
    early links 86
    early organizations 91
    economic links 64–7
    funds for Punjab 128
    and green revolution 65
    gurdwara funds for militants 162
    gurdwaras 98
    human rights issues 130–1, 162, 192
    identity 68
    Indian agent provocateurs 141
    Indian Emergency, the 96
    Indian government's views 156–7
    investment in educational
        institutions 65–6
    language and culture 68–71
    leadership 185, 199
    links with militants 121, 150–1, 187
    literature and arts 68, 70–1

lobbying 149, 155
memorandum to Indian High
  Commissions 109–10
pilgrimage 789
plea for self-determination 118
pop, Punjabi singers 68
post-1947 links 91
proletarians 188
Punjabi press 71–2
Punjabi software 83
re-alignment of loyalties 210
refugees 61
relations with other diasporas 129
relatives 149
religious tradition 76–8
remittances 65
settlement 41–2
shared sentiments 206
social links 67–8
social milieu 188
support for autonomy campaign
  106–9
support for Jaito 86
surveillance 190
traditional preachers 77
turban cases 103
victim diaspora 207
Sikh Educational Conference 105
Sikh Educational and Cultural
  Society 75
Sikh Forum 152
Sikh Foundation 81, 242 n. 54
Sikh Herald 124
Sikh Heritage Award 81–2
Sikh Homeland Front 103–5
Sikh Human Rights, UK 149, 162,
  167, 178, 188
Sikh Messenger 73
Sikh Missionary Center 81, 204
Sikh Missionary Society, Southall 64,
  74
Sikh News 114
Sikh Reference Library 1, 198
Sikh Review 73
Sikh Sabha 238 n. 5
Sikh Society of Calgary 115

Sikh Welfare Foundation of North
  America 81
Sikh-Nirankari clash 120
Sikhism 17, 75, 79–80, 82, 200, 204
Sikhs 1–6, 8–9, 11–34, 35, 38–9, 41–2,
  44–5, 47–67, 69–71, 73–92, 95, 97–111,
  113–16, 118–35, 137–43, 145–81, 183–
  211
  diplomacy 155, 165
  flag 202–3
  folklore 16
  homeland 8, 9, 11, 13, 20, 103–6,
    113, 118, 135, 140, 147–8, 153, 162,
    169–70, 181, 183, 187, 194–5, 205,
    209
  identity 13–14, 31, 69, 82, 100, 127,
    210, 232 n. 32
  marriages 32, 66
  migrants 2, 48–9, 56–7, 64–5, 67, 91
  militants 29, 30, 58, 61, 126, 149,
    151, 162, 170, 205
  "terrorists" 1, 115, 157, 161, 200
  as a nation 26, 231 n. 31
  rule 12, 68, 241 n. 44
  separatism 103–4, 125, 131, 133,
    151–2, 156
  shrines 1, 26, 65
  soldiers 16, 18, 44, 47–8, 50–1, 81
Sikhs studies 70, 74, 81–3, 175, 242 n.
  60–1, 271 n. 83
Silverman, J. 91
Simmons, L. R. 207
Singapore 48, 58, 68, 71, 78, 203
Singh, V. P. 149
Singh Sabha 17, 77, 82, 144
  Nairobi 238 n. 5
  Singapore 48
Singhvi, L. M. 160
Sino-Indian clashes 184
Skaug, Gunnar 273 n. 107
Slattery, J. 73
Slough 152
Smethwick 144
Sohan Singh 101, 150, 152
Solarz, Stephen 128, 171, 252 n. 46
Somaliland 50

South Africa 3, 89, 178
South Asians 70, 97–9
Southall 64, 67–71, 74, 76–7, 95–6, 140–1, 143, 148–50, 152–3, 203
Soviet Union 125, 166, 173
Sparrow, Barbara 102
Speedy, Captain 49
Spellar, John 163
Sri Nankana Sahib Foundation 241 n. 42, 249 n. 13
Stewart, Christine 178
Stockton 53, 74, 76, 118, 124, 203
Stohl, M. 7
Sudan 50
Suffolk 55, 79, 90
Sukhdev Singh 121, 257 n. 21
Surendra Nath 232 n. 35
Surjan Singh 105, 116, 247 n. 53–4
Surjeet, Gian Singh 146
Surjeet, Harkishan Singh 95
Surrey, B. C. 69, 77, 119–20, 122, 202
Swaran Singh 146, 152
Switzerland 61, 151

Taiping 48
Takhat Singh Girls' High School, Ferozepore 65
Tamils 125, 189
Tara Singh, Master 19, 23, 31
Teja Singh 52, 74, 78, 87, 90
Tejinder Singh 149
Telgu 22
Thailand 42, 49, 58
Thapar, R. 35
Thatcher, M. 157, 159
Thekedar, Jaswant Singh 143, 156, 258 n. 26, 28
Thind case 54
Thompson, M. 67
Thurn, Sir Everad 47
Tinker, H. 47
Toor, T. S. 152, 161
Toronto 57, 78, 82, 95, 97, 107, 114, 119, 121–3, 130, 133, 157, 176
Torricelli, Robert 168
Trinidad 47, 71

Tripathi, M. L. 176
Truth 124
Tuli, Suneel Singh 102
turban cases 76–80, 86, 99–102, 118, 130, 195, 197, 201, 206
Turks 4

Udasis 16–17
Udham Singh 91, 241 n. 44, 262 n. 75
Uganda 50, 56
Uganda Railway Line 50
Uganda Rifles 50
Unionist Party 18
United Akali Dal 128, 142
United India League 89
United Kingdom
    British aid projects in Punjab and Kashmir 163
    British aid to India 163
    Commonwealth 158
    diplomatic row with India 142, 157
    export of tractors 65
    Extradition treaty 160–1
    government advice to United Kingdom Sikhs 159
    Indo-British relations 159, 190
    MPs' visit to Punjab 161
    Parliament debates 148, 151, 160–2, 172
    Rajiv Gandhi's visit 159
    Thatcher's clarification 157, 159
United Kingdom Sikhs
    Akalis 106
    artist 81
    Asian music 68–70
    BBC's Asian language programme 70
    Census Office plea 201
    communists 92, 94–6
    conferences 82
    the death of Indira Gandhi and the celebrations 138
    diplomacy 155
    early Sikhs and Indians 90–2
    East African Sikhs 56
    entry denied 151

gurdwaras  74, 78, 144
homeland issue  103–5
human rights  185
Indian MPs  91, 244 n. 12
Indian Overseas Congress  98
Indian security services  161
Jasbir Singh Rode  119
Kabaddi  68
Khalistan Council  185
loyalties  201
Member of Parliament  100
migration from Far East  49, 51
migration from Punjab  55–7
Namdharis  79
National Security Act  149
networks  63
Niraknaris  79
Nishkam Sewak Jatha  76
police vigilance of "Sikh
    terrorists"  154
political groups  85
population  236 n. 19
Punjab Human Rights Chapter  151
Punjabi press  73–4
reaction to attack on the Golden
    Temple  138
refugees  59
remittances  76
Sikh Homeland Front  104
turban cases  100–2
veterans  81
visa restrictions  149
visit of Punjab police chief  147
White Paper  156
United Nations  7, 11, 23, 105, 107,
    127, 165, 169–70, 180, 194–5, 202–3
United States  2, 8, 41–2, 51, 54–6, 60–
    1, 63, 65–71, 74–6, 79, 81, 85, 91, 95,
    98–9, 101, 110, 113, 118, 121–4, 128–
    30, 132, 137, 147, 150–1, 157, 165, 168,
    170–1, 188, 191, 195, 200–1, 204, 209,
    211
    Congress proceedings  51, 53, 103,
        121, 125, 127, 151, 155, 157, 165–71,
        173–4, 178, 181, 185, 188
    ethnic diplomacy  189
    foreign aid to India  167

Hindus  168, 170–1
Immigration and Naturalization
    Service  60
immigration policies  54–5
impact of Punjab crisis on
    America  167
India's reaction  157
Indo-American relations  165–6
President of the  170
State Department  168, 170
United States Sikhs
    Akali Dal  99
    American converts to Sikhism  75
    appeal  200
    contacts with European Sikhs  129
    contribution to the Golden Temple
        buildings  76
    Council of Khalistan  185–6
    Dal Khalsa  122
    Gadr activists  76
    Gadr memorials  79
    gurdwaras  121
    identity  201, 204, 211
    Kabaddi matches  68
    leadership  188
    marriages  54
    migration  42, 51–5
    murder plots  129
    networks  63
    population  56
    refugee cases  130
    remittances  65–6
    summer camps  70
    support for Dharam Yudh Morcha
        110
    support for self-determination  181
    support for statehood  113
    television  70
    turban and kirpan cases  101
    visa restrictions  151
    visits of communist leaders  95
University of British Columbia  70,
    81–2, 193
University of California, Santa
    Barbara  82
University of Columbia  52, 82
University of Michigan  81

University of Toronto 82
University of Wisconsin 71, 82
Unrepresented Nations and Peoples
   Organization [UNPO] 7, 180, 203,
   277 n. 41
Urdu 17, 70

Vancouver 44, 51, 53, 57, 64, 67–8,
   70–1, 75–8, 88, 95–6, 98–9, 104–9, 113–
   14, 119–23, 126–7, 129, 132–3, 156–7,
   176–7, 179, 199, 202–3
*Vancouver Sun* 132
Vanderhorst, Johan "affair" 156
Vasdev, Darshan Das 152, 161, 263 n.
   80
Victoria 53, 57, 86
Victoria, Queen 51
videos 68, 145, 191
Vienna 180, 272 n. 101
*Voice of Sikhs* 118

Waldegrave, William 151, 159, 161
Walsall 141
Wangar 142, 145, 146
Washington D. C. 51, 53, 121, 125,
   127, 151, 157, 165, 170, 173–4, 178,
   185, 188
Weiner, G. 134
Weiner, M. 36, 202
Weller, P. 74
West Indies 3, 46

West Mount 129
West Punjab 16, 65
Westland helicopters 159
White, Ted 179
White dominions 48
White Paper, Government of India 1,
   35, 156, 190, 227 n. 1–3
White workers 51, 54
Wilson, G. K. 155
Winnipeg 102, 107
Wolverhampton 101–4, 138
World Punjabi Writers conferences 71
World Sikh Convention 78
World Sikh Council 78
*World Sikh News* 118, 123–4
World Sikh Organization 116, 118,
   121–4, 126–8, 130, 133–4, 171–2, 175–
   7, 180, 185, 187–8, 195, 203, 249 n. 9–
   11
   and Akali Dal 122
   and ISYF 123
World Wars 16, 18, 44, 48–9, 91, 177
Wyllie, Sir William Curzon 91

Yatron, Gus 171
Yiddish-Speaking Communities 3
Yuba City 53, 56, 68, 116, 126

Zaffarwal, Wasan Singh 237 n. 31
Zail Singh 26, 28, 145
Zakria Khan 15